Tragedy in Transition

Tragedy in Transition

Edited by
**Sarah Annes Brown and
Catherine Silverstone**

Blackwell
Publishing

BLACKWELL PUBLISHING
350 Main Street, Malden, MA 02148-5020, USA
9600 Garsington Road, Oxford OX4 2DQ, UK
550 Swanston Street, Carlton, Victoria 3053, Australia

First published 2007 by Blackwell Publishing Ltd

1   2007

Library of Congress Cataloging-in-Publication Data

Tragedy in transition / edited by Sarah Annes Brown and Catherine Silverstone.
    p. cm.
    Includes bibliographical references and index.
    ISBN 978-1-4051-3546-7 (hardcover : alk. paper) — ISBN 978-1-4051-3547-4 (pbk. : alk. paper)
1. Tragedy—History and criticism. I. Brown, Sarah Annes. II. Silverstone, Catherine.

    PN1892.T66 2007
    809′.9162—dc22

                                                2007010739

PN 1892
, T66
2007
086172870

A catalogue record for this title is available from the British Library.

Set in 11.5/13.5pt Bembo
by SPi Publisher Services, Pondicherry, India.
Printed and bound in Singapore
by Markono Print Media Pte Ltd

The publisher's policy is to use permanent paper from mills that operate a sustainable forestry policy, and which has been manufactured from pulp processed using acid-free and elementary chlorine-free practices. Furthermore, the publisher ensures that the text paper and cover board used have met acceptable environmental accreditation standards.

For further information on
Blackwell Publishing, visit our website at
www.blackwellpublishing.com

Contents

Notes on Contributors

Sarah Annes Brown is Chair of the Department of English, Communication, Film, and Media at Anglia Ruskin University. In addition to numerous short pieces on various aspects of classical reception, her publications include *The Metamorphosis of Ovid: From Chaucer to Ted Hughes* (1999), *Ovid: Myth and Metamorphosis* (2005), and an edition of Nicholas Rowe's translation of *Lucan's Pharsalia* (1997, with Charles Martindale). She is currently writing a book about transhistoricism.

Robert Douglas-Fairhurst is Fellow and Tutor in English at Magdalen College, University of Oxford. He is the author of *Victorian Afterlives: the Shaping of Influence in Nineteenth-Century Literature* (2002), general editor of the *Nineteenth-Century Studies* series, and editor of the *Tennyson Research Bulletin*. Recent publications include a new edition of Dickens's *Christmas Books* (2006) and articles on I. A. Richards, Samuel Beckett, and A. E. Housman. He is currently editing *Great Expectations* (forthcoming in 2007) and researching a book on Victorian magic.

Ewan Fernie is Senior Lecturer in English at Royal Holloway, University of London. He is author of *Shame in Shakespeare* (2002), editor of *Spiritual Shakespeares* (2005), and coordinating editor of *Reconceiving the Renaissance* (2005). He is also general editor (with Simon Palfrey) of the *Shakespeare Now!* series of "minigraphs." He is writing two books with Palfrey that seek to release and shape new intellectual energies by breaking with conventional critical forms: a false life of Shakespeare called *Shakespeare Agonistes* and a story which begins the day after *Macbeth*.

Edith Hall was appointed joint Chair in Classics and in Drama at Royal Holloway, University of London, in 2006. She has held posts in Classics at the universities of Cambridge, Reading, Oxford, and Durham. Her books include *Inventing the Barbarian* (1989), an edition with translation and commentary of Aeschylus' *Persians* (1996), *Greek and Roman Actors* (2002, with Pat Easterling), *Greek Tragedy and the British Theatre* (2005, with Fiona Macintosh), and *The Theatrical Cast of Athens* (2006). She is currently completing a study of the cultural impact of the Homeric Odyssey.

John Henderson is Professor of Classics at the University of Cambridge and a Fellow of King's College. His books on Latin authors include monographs on Plautus, Phaedrus, Seneca, Statius, Pliny, and Juvenal, besides general studies of epic, comedy, satire, history, art, culture, and the history of classics. *Plautus Asinaria: The One About the Asses*, *"Oxford Reds": Classic Commentaries on Latin Classics*, and *The Medieval World of Isidore of Seville: Truth from Words* were published in 2006, and work in hand includes *Terence Hautontimorumenus: Getting Your Own Back On Yourself*, *Brothers Keepers: Cicero's Letters to Cicero*, and *Sculpture with People: The Vigeland Sculpture Park at Frogner: Oslo's Mønster*.

Alison Hennegan is a Fellow Commoner in English at Trinity Hall, Cambridge where, amongst other things, she teaches the compulsory Tragedy Paper to third-year undergraduates. For many years she combined freelance teaching for Cambridge colleges and the English Faculty with work in journalism (Literary Editor of *Gay News*, 1977–83, diarist and reviewer for the *New Statesman*), publishing (The Women's Press), and arts broadcasting. A classicist *manquée* (terrible linguist), she works primarily on literature of the nineteenth and twentieth centuries. Her numerous literary passions include the English Decadence, the Great War, very early detective fiction, children's literature, gay and lesbian writing, and a host of lesser known nineteenth- and twentieth-century women authors. *The Lesbian Pillow Book*, an informal historical reader of works devoted to love between women, was published in 2000. She has published widely and variously on literary subjects: her piece in this volume brings together two very long-standing loves – Oscar Wilde, and Greek tragedy.

Anne C. Henry is a Fellow and Director of Studies in English at Trinity College, Cambridge. Her recent publications include 'Quid ais omnium? The emergence of suspension marks in Early Modern Drama', *Renaissance Drama*, 35 (2005) and '"Explorations in Dot- and Dashland": George Meredith's Aphasia', *Nineteenth-Century Literature*, 61:3 (2006).

Peter Hollindale was Reader in English and Educational Studies at the University of York, where he taught one of the earliest undergraduate courses on children's literature, and also specialized in Elizabethan and Jacobean drama. Among his publications are two editions of *Peter Pan*, one of the prose texts and the other of *Peter Pan and Other Plays* (1995), and a study of critical terminology for children's literature, *Signs of Childness in Children's Books* (1997). He is currently retired.

Mark Houlahan is Senior Lecturer in English at the University of Waikato in Hamilton, New Zealand. He has published widely on issues of adaptation and appropriation in Shakespeare and other Renaissance playwrights. He is the author of *The Shakespeare Survival Kit* (2003) and coeditor of *Telling Lives: Essays in Biography and History* (2006).

Raphael Lyne is Senior Lecturer in English at the University of Cambridge, and a Fellow of New Hall. He is the author of *Ovid's Changing Worlds: English Metamorphoses, 1567–1632* (2001) and *Shakespeare's Late Work* (2007).

Fiona Macintosh is Senior Research Fellow at the Archive of Performances of Greek and Roman Drama and a member of St. Cross College, University of Oxford. Her publications include *Dying Acts: Death in Ancient Greek and Modern Irish Tragic Drama* (1994) and *Greek Tragedy and the British Theatre 1660–1914* (2005, with Edith Hall). She has coedited numerous volumes, including *Medea in Performance 1500–2000* (2000), *Dionysus Since 69: Greek Tragedy at the Dawn of the Third Millennium* (2004), and *Agamemnon in Performance 458BC to AD2004* (2005). She is currently completing *Sophocles' Oedipus Tyrannus: A Production History.*

Neil Rhodes is Professor of English Literature and Cultural History at the University of St. Andrews. His publications include *Shakespeare and the Origins of English* (2004) and *The Renaissance Computer: Knowledge Technology in the First Age of Print* (2000, with Jonathan Sawday).

Catherine Silverstone is Lecturer in Drama, Theatre, and Performance Studies at Queen Mary, University of London. She has written several articles on Shakespeare and performance. She is currently writing a book entitled *Shakespeare and Trauma: Contemporary Performances on Stage and Screen*.

Jennifer Wallace is Lecturer in English at Peterhouse, University of Cambridge. She is the author of several books including, most recently, *Digging the Dirt: The Archaeological Imagination* (2004) and *The Cambridge Introduction to Tragedy* (2007).

Rowland Wymer is Chair and Head of English, Communication, Film, and Media at Anglia Ruskin University, Cambridge. His publications include *Suicide and Despair in the Jacobean Drama* (1986), *Webster and Ford* (1995), and *Derek Jarman* (2005), as well as a number of coedited collections of essays, including *Neo-Historicism* (2000) and *The Accession of James I: Historical and Cultural Consequences* (2006). He is currently working on a book titled *Science, Religion, and Science Fiction*.

Vanda Zajko is Senior Lecturer in Classics at Bristol University. She has wide-ranging interests in the reception of classical literature. Recent publications include 'Hector and Andromache: Identification and Appropriation' in C. A. Martindale and R. F. Thomas (eds.), *Classics and the Uses of Reception* (2006) and *Laughing with Medusa: Classical Myth and Feminist Thought* (2006). Her coedited volume *Translation and "the Classic"* will be published in 2008.

Preface

This volume was inspired by the experience of teaching and examining the compulsory Tragedy paper at the University of Cambridge. Over the space of three hours students are required to show substantial knowledge of Greek and Shakespearean tragedy, but are also encouraged to explore tragedies from any other period, as well as to investigate the possibilities for tragedy in nonliterary mediums such as music, film, and sculpture.

Preparing students for this paper made me reflect on what I think is a growing gulf between the ways in which academics and students experience the study of English literature. Over the course of their degree, students at Cambridge and elsewhere have to demonstrate a good understanding of all periods of English literature. However, if they progress to graduate study they are swiftly required to specialize, almost always focusing on a topic which is confined to a particular historical period. Indeed, this periodization is reflected in nearly every aspect of the subject's organization: undergraduate modules, MA programmes, conferences, and job vacancies. Although historically grounded research of this nature has a clear value, it is, I think, a pity that institutional structures and related cultural pressures have discouraged transhistorical work in English studies. In fact, transhistorical research is encouraged far less than interdisciplinary research. Although literary scholars are encouraged to (try to) come to terms with science, art, theology, and philosophy we are made to feel anxious about attempting to engage with the literature of different centuries simultaneously.

Thus the prospect of teaching Cambridge's Tragedy paper fills some academics with alarm, as its brief is explicitly transhistorical. However, for others it represents a liberation from the confines of period boundaries and a chance to extend one's own knowledge. When giving lectures on the Tragedy paper I would encourage the students not to compartmentalize different periods, answering one question on Euripides, one on Shakespeare, and one on Ibsen, say. Instead, I suggested, they would probably produce better work if they explored parallels and contrasts between different eras within each individual question: for example, compare Euripides' *Hippolytus* not with the *Bacchae* or *Medea* but with Seneca's *Phaedra* and Sarah Kane's *Phaedra's Love*.

The same rule can be applied to the work of established academics, and this wish to encourage transhistorical research (and support transhistorical teaching) influenced the way this volume's essays were commissioned. As well as approaching scholars with an established reputation in the field of classical reception, such as Edith Hall and Fiona Macintosh, we targeted writers with a strong association with a particular literary period, but encouraged them to leave their comfort zone and incorporate their reading and teaching interests into their chapters. Thus Robert Douglas-Fairhurst, whose previous published work has focused on Victorian literature, here writes on the theme of tragedy and disgust in Aeschylus and Shakespeare as well as in Dickens and Hardy. And Ewan Fernie, who is strongly associated with Shakespeare, extends his reach back to Sophocles and forwards to Cormac McCarthy.

It would have been easier to commission a collection of essays which covered ostensibly similar ground but within a simpler, chronological progression, offering discrete pieces on Greek, Roman, Medieval, and Renaissance tragedy, and so on. But that approach would almost certainly not have pushed the boundaries of our understanding of tragedy in the same way *Tragedy in Transition* does. As well as foregrounding the transhistorical, the organization of this volume has been designed to open up new territory as well as to shed new light on established debates within tragedy. We are prepared to read about exile (Wallace) and the gods (Hall) when we open a book about tragedy but probably won't expect chapters on childhood (Hollindale), homosexuality (Hennegan) and, particularly, science fiction (Wymer).

In her Afterword Catherine Silverstone draws attention to the similarities between tragedy itself and the criticism it elicits. Just as tragedy tests and expands its own and society's boundaries, so we hope that this volume extends the ways literary criticism and cultural theory can illuminate this most powerful and pervasive form.

S. B.
April 2007

Introduction: Tragedy in Transition

Sarah Annes Brown

The persistence of tragedy may in part be ascribed to its capacity to be adapted and transformed across periods and cultures, indeed to be enriched by such displacement. This robustness perhaps signals a particular bond between the workings of tragedy and the dynamic of transition. Tragedy seems to have been most potent at moments of cultural or political up-heaval, reflecting and anticipating change. As Robert Douglas-Fairhurst puts it, "tragedy and transition are natural soulmates" (76). One of the most famous Greek tragedies, *The Eumenides*, for example, explicitly dramatizes a paradigm shift from a pre-Hellenic world of savage instinct to an apparently more civilized world whose tutelary deity is Apollo. Seen through a Hegel-ian lens, tragedy represents a process of cultural evolution through dialectic and, ultimately, synthesis.

In other ways, too, tragedy may be associated with a dynamic of transi-tion. As well as being mimetic of cultural change, tragedy presses and probes less tangible boundaries within a culture. Some of these are explored in depth in this volume – the boundary separating human and non-human, for example, or the uneasily shifting line which demarcates disgust from desire. One of Greek tragedy's most potent emblems is the *pharmakon*, ambigu-ously pivoting between poison and cure.[1] And at its Greek inception trage-dy's form instantiated this engagement with transition through the use of the Chorus, a group which (at least some of the time) seems to inhabit a liminal space between stage and real worlds. This sense of metatheater is still present in modern tragedy but is more usually produced by other means – particularly, as we shall see, through obtrusive intertextual interventions.

It is ironic or at least reflexive that tragedy, a genre so concerned with testing, threatening, and proving different kinds of boundaries, has itself been subjected to so much analysis in an attempt to define its own parameters. How many boxes – fatal flaw, noble hero, serious tone, unhappy ending – need to be ticked in order for us to reach a diagnosis of tragedy? Some indication of the problematic nature of this process is given if we remember that the *Oresteia* actually has a happy ending, and my own preference is for a liberally inclusive definition of tragedy – if we are asking the question of a text "is this a tragedy?" then my view is that the answer is probably "yes."

Perhaps because of its preoccupation with the transitional in various manifestations, tragedy operates with special charge when it is dislocated or changed – in other words, when it is actually in transition. Peter Burian well describes the effect created by works inhabiting a genre which is so embedded in its own traditions, which is "forever repeating but never the same":

> The particular shape and emphases of a tragic plot, as the product of variation in the shape and emphases both of known legendary material and of familiar formal constituents, can forcefully direct or dislocate spectators' attention, confirm, modify, or even overturn their expectations. . . . Seen in this light, a tragic plot inheres not simply in a poetic text, but also in the dialectic between that text in performance and the responses of an informed audience to the performance as repetition and innovation.[2]

Because so many later tragedies are adaptations or responses to earlier examples, a kind of palimpsest effect may be created whereby the audience – and in some cases the *dramatis personae* – is aware of the precursor text and imports it into the new drama. Thus in Herbert Weir Smyth's translation of Aeschylus' *Agamemnon* (published in 1926 by the Loeb Classical Library) a Shakespearean contamination occurs. Anticipating the murder of Agamemnon, the Chorus says: "Why ever thus persistently doth this terror hover at the portals of my prophetic soul?" (Aeschylus 1963: 83). The phrase "prophetic soul" is memorably used by Hamlet when he learns that his father, like Agamemnon, has been treacherously slain: "O my prophetic soul" (1.5.41), he exclaims to the ghost, apparently because he had already suspected the truth. Smyth's echo is reinforced by the description of terror hovering at the soul's portals, personifying the emotion as a malignant presence. In Act 3 of *Hamlet* the prince sees his father's ghost when he is closeted with Gertrude and calls: "Look where he goes, even now out at the portal" (3.4.127). As well as flagging an affinity between the Greek and the English revenge plays, Smyth creates a moment of uncanny charge because the echo occurs at a moment of prophecy, and (through the phrase "thus persistently") suggests a repeated cycle. Within the terms of the *Oresteia* the Chorus, when it asks "Why doth my song, unbidden and unfed, chant strains of augury" (83), is foretelling the imminent death of Agamemnon. But for the reader of Smyth's translation the Chorus's foresight reaches a full two thousand years into the future. Their lines enact as well as describe the act of prophecy, foretelling the tragic repetition of the pattern established by Aeschylus in another tale of a wronged father and a vengeful son.

Thus we can observe that one effect of tragedy in a state of transition, when its narrative traditions attract a patina through repeated receptions, or an "aura," to use Walter Benjamin's term, is to invite any sense of tragic determinism to become disassociated from the gods or fate, and become instead a function of intertextual or metatheatrical self-consciousness. This is particularly evident in Seneca's *Medea*, a play which then (and now) was overshadowed by its more famous Euripidean source. A sense of belatedness is created by the Romanized atmosphere which pervades the play, as when the Chorus (Seneca 2002: 113) alludes to *Fescennina carmina*, a specifically Italian reference to a kind of fleering verse named after Fescennia, a small city on the Tiber. The metatheatricality is heightened by a persistent ambiguity in the play's many references to the past. These might either evoke Medea's personal past, her earlier life and particularly her horrific murder of her brother, or else her literary life as a tragic antiheroine.[3] For example, when she thus exhorts herself: "scelera te hortentur tua / et cuncta redeant", "Your own crimes must urge you on, every one of them must return" (129) we may think of her former deeds in Colchis or her earlier manifestation in Euripides. Similarly her exit line "coniugem agnoscis tuam? / sic fugere soleo," "Do you recognize your wife? This is how I always escape?" (1021–2) reads like a knowing nod to Euripides. Increasingly the heroine herself seems weighed down by a sense of *déjà lu*, of acting a part written down for her and which she cannot escape. "Medea nunc sum," "now I am Medea" (910), she exclaims at the crisis, as though conscious of the role she must inhabit and aware of her own notoriety, almost as though for her, as for us, Medea was already a legend. We can identify a very similar moment in another text derived from Euripides, Ted Hughes's translation of Racine's *Phèdre*. Hippolytus, when he articulates his fastidious virtue and recoils from Phaedra's desire, asserts not simply that

"C'est par là [his aversion to sinful lust] qu'Hippolyte est connu dans la Grèce" (1109) but that "my aversion to it *is a legend*" (Hughes 1998: 54, my emphasis).

Most of today's readers of Seneca's *Medea* will already have read Euripides' earlier play. But we will probably be less alert to the similarly secondary qualities of *Hamlet*. However, it too was based on a well-known story which had been adapted into a successful tragedy (now lost) shortly before Shakespeare wrote his own version. Like Medea, Hamlet at times seems haunted by a sense of his own fictionality. Wilamowitz-Moellendorff (1919: 162) observes that Seneca's Medea seems to have read Euripides' *Medea*, and we might equally say that Shakespeare's playgoing prince seems to have watched the Ur–*Hamlet*. Hamlet at times seems on the verge of puncturing the membrane between the stage world and reality, most obtrusively when he links personal with literary memory by apparently alluding to the Globe Theatre (although the world and his head are the more immediately obvious referents):

> Remember thee?
> Ay thou poor ghost, whiles memory holds a seat
> In this distracted globe.
>
> (1.5.95–7)

His frustrations, his feelings of being overlooked, of being "th'observed of all observers" (3.1.148), almost implicate the audience as well as Elsinore's courtiers and, like the protagonist of *The Truman Show*,[4] we sense him grasping toward consciousness of his own constructedness. Ophelia tells him that he is "as good as a chorus" (3.2.222) and he does indeed seem to share the choric quality of liminality, of being in transit between stage and audience, a quality most hauntingly apparent in his dying words:

> You that look pale, and tremble at this chance,
> That are but mutes or audience to this act,
> Had I but time, as this fell sergeant death
> Is strict in his arrest, oh I could tell you –
> But let it be.
>
> (5.2.313–17)

Here Hamlet appears to address the "real" as well as the inset audience. Whereas most dramatic characters know less than their audiences Hamlet actually gives the impression of knowing more, of being privy to secrets which must remain tantalizingly hidden not just from Horatio but from us as well. His apparent transformation at the end of the play, his passive acceptance of his fate, might be attributed to a knowledge that Act 5 has been reached as much as to any special change of heart. In his melodramatic assertion, "This is I, Hamlet the Dane" (5.1.224–5), we hear an echo of Medea's similar articulation of a role fulfilled.

Whereas Seneca's Medea and Shakespeare's Hamlet seem weighed down by an unexplained intuition of their own textuality, the transition from fate to literary tradition is suggested still more forcibly when the author is inserted into the text as a surrogate divinity. A particularly striking example of this process can be seen in Akira Kurosawa's 1957 film adaptation of *Macbeth*, *Throne of Blood*. Here the three witches are replaced by a single numinous figure who is encountered spinning in the forest by Washizu (Macbeth). Although she can be seen as a traditional "minister of fate," her wheel uncannily suggests a film projector and reminds us that the real arbiter of Washizu's destiny is the filmmaker and the literary tradition he inherited. Fortuitously, the physical characteristics shared by the spinning wheel and projector pick up on a rather similar but more established (and crosscultural) pattern of linguistic connection between spinning and writing. Thus in a very different production, Catullus' *Carmen 64*, we can see a parallel connection between the gods, or fate, on the one hand and the creating artist on the other. (In Latin, as in Greek and indeed English, there are striking links between the vocabulary of weaving or spinning and of literary composition. *Textum*, for example, can mean woven but, more metaphorically, can also be used of literary style.) This long poem presents an ostensibly happy occasion, the marriage of Peleus and Thetis, but it is attended by the spinning Fates and overshadowed by the Trojan War in which the couple's unborn son Achilles, will play a pivotal role. The long central section of the poem consists of an elaborate *ecphrasis*, a compelling account of a coverlet on which Ariadne, deserted on Naxos by Theseus, is depicted. She is paradoxically more lifelike and more vocal than the "real" guests at the wedding, and the plaint of this woven heroine is suffused by a discourse of weaving and spinning in various contexts, encouraging us to make links with the Fates spinning their threads of destiny. We are reminded that the lives of Peleus and Thetis are as woven and determined as that of the more "fictional" Ariadne, and also that the ultimate controlling artist here is really Catullus, who has woven the two strands of this complex poem together so memorably, creating a subtle (from the Latin *subtilis*, meaning finely woven) web through the implicit thematic links between the frame and inset narratives. In a sense these hints at authorial presence in both Kurosawa and Catullus replace the essentially theatrical role of the Chorus, fulfilling a similar function through their edgy, ludic manipulation of the boundary between art and reality.

But recycling tragedy is more than a matter of spinning an ever more reflexive vortex "about it and about it." It could be argued that the obtrusive textuality of the examples discussed above dilutes their tragic impact. Johnson said of tragedy: "If we thought murders and treasons real, they would please no more" (Johnson 1960: 9). But insistent reminders of a tragedy's fictionality are at least as likely to compromise tragedy. Yet the textual layers within the tragic tradition need not necessarily weaken or distract from a text's tragic impact. Indeed, in various ways the repetition or adaptation of a tragic narrative can allow a still more intense engagement with the conflicts and predicaments which characterize the genre to emerge. If we think, for example, about Hegel's conception of tragedy (a powerful if not a totalizing model), whereby tragedy represents the collision of different perspectives and irreconcilable pressures, we can see how this intratextual dynamic can be replayed and intensified at an intertextual level. Not all tragedies can be mapped equally neatly onto a Hegelian binary. But if we think about two which do conform broadly to such a model, *Prometheus Bound* and the *Bacchae*, we can see how their central conflicts are enriched through the processes of reception.

Prometheus Bound stages a conflict between the Titan Prometheus, who might be said to represent subversion and the quest for knowledge, and Zeus, upholder of law, order, and the status quo. But any such account inevitably flattens the drama, for the two protagonists (like Antigone and Creon) have more in common then they might want to acknowledge. The play has proved conducive to sharply contrasting readings, both critical and creative, and the battle between the forces of rebellion and divine authority, in particular, elicits very varied responses.[5] Thus Marlowe's Prometheus figure, Dr. Faustus, is the product of a Christian culture which privileges divinity in a way which is alien to Greek tragedy – whose gods are far from perfect and who, in any case, do not always agree with one another. Aeschylus' equivocal presentation of Prometheus has apparently given way to outright condemnation, for Faustus's parallel search for knowledge leads to his damnation. But just as Zeus and Prometheus in Aeschylus are not simple opposites, so Marlowe's work can be seen less as a palinode to Aeschylus than as a reformulation of the same problems. Although on the surface Faustus seems condemned by the play, many audiences and readers have found him as deserving of sympathy as Prometheus and have seen the harshness of his fate as a reflection of the rigidity of this version of God rather than of Faustus's unforgivable evil.

The same pattern can be seen in a work which, by contrast, on the face of things reacts against the supposed conservatism of Aeschylus. Shelley's palinode *Prometheus Unbound* (1820) allows the rebel to emerge triumphant. At the end of the play, because Prometheus (contrary to myth) fails to reveal that Thetis' son will be greater than his father, Zeus is destroyed by his son Demogorgon. This championing of Prometheus implies a link between Shelley's powerful precursors, the Greek tragedians, and the Olympian gods. Shelley, like Prometheus, wants to throw off the shackles of the tyrannous past. Yet various factors complicate this apparent identification. As a Titan, Prometheus belonged to the race which had predated the Olympians and been dethroned by them, and it is thus Jove, in a sense, who represents rebellious youth. Also, as Shelley himself acknowledged in his Preface to the play, in altering Aeschylus so radically he was only following the example of Greek writers themselves, who freely adapted their own sources (Shelley 1959: 119). And in any case, Aeschylus' treatment of Prometheus is already enmeshed in a dialectic too complex to be simply reversed. Even if the Titan does seem obstinate and vengeful by the end of the original play, Aeschylus was surely, to some degree, himself of Prometheus' party. Although he gives the impression of being antagonistic to Aeschylus, Shelley engages very directly with his source, clearly maintaining the structure and conventions of Greek tragedy. In this he resembles Prometheus who, in articulating resistance to Jupiter, adopts Jupiter's language in order to express his hostility.[6] To sum up, the complex patterns of the relationship between Aeschylus and his two followers, Marlowe and Shelley, illuminate suggestively the similarly uncertain relationship between Zeus and Prometheus.

A dynamic of reversal overlaying and in a sense compromising the play's central *agon* is even stronger in the *Bacchae*. Here the figure of the outsider is particularly prominent. However, over the course of the play this role, first filled by the exotic Dionysus, is taken over by the hapless Pentheus, who refuses to join in the new god's worship and is killed by his own mother. This is an extraordinarily unsettling and powerful drama which manipulates and confuses its audience's judgment and sympathies. It is so shifting, so tricky, as to defeat attempts to react against or reverse it by later writers. In *Christus Patiens*, a twelfth-century Byzantine drama about the Passion, we find an apparently bizarre, even perverse, reconfiguration of Euripides whereby Christ (through near-quotation from the *Bacchae*) emerges as a hybrid of god and sacrificial victim, two roles originally split between Dionysus and Pentheus. But because the oppositions of the *Bacchae* are so fluid, its boundaries seeming to invite transgression, any such reconfiguration of its core elements seems rather to fulfill than disrupt the original play.

If the movement between texts can tellingly reinforce the complex *loci* of conflict dramatized by so many individual tragedies, such movement is even more effective at communicating and commenting on a still more central quality of tragedy, the genre's near universal enactment of loss, decline, and destruction. The process of transition between texts can itself produce a tragic dynamic, reinforcing or even contradicting the resonances of either text read in isolation.

Although *King Lear* is (even by tragic standards) a remarkably bleak play, its afterlife outdoes it, as though rising to the challenge implicit in Edgar's words: "The worst is not/so long as we can say 'this is the worst'" (4.1.27–8). Dr. Johnson found the death of Cordelia unbearable, but the intertextual, moral decline from Shakespeare's heroine to Edward Bond's tyrant (in the 1971 play *Lear*) is arguably more unsettling. By the end of the play the main representative of something like sanity or virtue is the ghost of a murdered boy. Eventually, and inexplicably, the ghost himself is "killed." The effect is similar to that generated by Lucan's bleakly apocalyptic description of Troy: "etiam periere ruinae," "the very ruins have been destroyed" (*Pharsalia* 9.969). In another response to *King Lear*, *Endgame* (1958), Beckett seems to identify in Shakespeare's play a kind of aesthetic pleasure or comfort which is refused us in his own work:

> If he could have his child with him ... [*Pause.*] It was the moment I was waiting for. [*Pause.*] You don't want to abandon him? You want him to bloom while you are withering? Be there to solace your last million last moments? [*Pause.*] He doesn't realize, all he knows is hunger, and cold, and death to crown it all. But you! You ought to know what the earth is like, nowadays.
>
> (Beckett 1964: 52)

Beckett uses the play's many allusive moments to heighten the sense of repetition within the drama, drawing attention to an overall sense of doom which is both cyclical and entropic.

This kind of intensification of bleakness and horror is most conspicuous within the revenge tradition. Revenge is characterized by its capacity for disproportionate escalation, and this dynamic can operate over a sequence of related texts as well as within individual ones. A particularly explicit example of intertextual revenge is played out in Shakespeare's *Titus Andronicus*. Here the mutilation of Lavinia is unambiguously modeled on Ovid's account of Tereus' similarly horrific treatment of Philomela.[7] The act of imitation is not only Shakespeare's but the rapists' themselves who (for Gothic thugs) are remarkably well up on their Latin, and even learn from Tereus' mistakes by cutting off their victim's hands as well as her tongue, thus ensuring that she cannot copy Philomela's stratagem and reveal her rapists' identity in a tapestry. This process of upping the ante is taken still further by Sarah Kane in *Cleansed* (1998). Like a furious Jacobean avenger, or perhaps *Kill Bill's* Beatrix Kiddo,[8] she overtops both Ovid and *Titus* when Carl's feet as well as his hands and tongue are amputated. This process of continuing, escalating dismemberment is reflected in the texture of the play, pared down and brutalized as it is.

A rather different kind of tragic intensification is dramatized in the gap between the classical and neoclassical versions of Phaedra's fall and Sarah Kane's *Phaedra's Love* (1996). Although, as might be expected from the author of *Blasted* and *Cleansed*, she exaggerates the violence of the earlier versions in horrific fashion, in some ways the most striking characteristic of the play is the way Hippolytus' death is transformed. Rather than being a tragic fall it becomes a curiously positive move, offering the opportunity for a strange kind of personal growth. In working up to tragedy rather than down Kane underlines the worse-than-tragic emptiness of Hippolytus' banal existence. The virtuous prince has been reinvented as a kind of Athenian Psycho, sated by commodity culture, relentless TV violence, and compulsive but joyless sex.

This curious transformation of a poignant tragedy into a happy solution points to another characteristic of tragedy in transition. For if an intensification of tragedy's horror and violence can be seen to produce a kind of intertextual tragic fall, the loss of tragedy can also become, more paradoxically, a source of tragedy. Generally we think of tragedy as a movement down, a fall or loss. But is there such a thing as "upward tragedy"? Can rising, in other words, be tragic? In *The Waste Land* the faceless mass of the apathetic from the first circle of the Inferno are reincarnated as the living Londoners who swarm over London Bridge:

> Unreal City,
> Under the brown fog of a winter dawn,
> A crowd flowed over London Bridge, so many,
> I had not thought death had undone so many.
> Sighs, short and infrequent, were exhaled...
> (Eliot 1971: ll.60–4)

Although in one sense this vision is manifestly less hopeless than that offered at the beginning of the *Inferno*, in another sense it represents a diminution. A vision of infinite, divinely planned bathos acquires a kind of perverse sublimity. The same *peri bathous* problematizes and enriches Pope's own tribute to mediocrity, the *Dunciad*:

> She comes! the Cloud-compelling Pow'r, behold!
> With Night Primaeval, and with Chaos old!
> Lo! the great Anarch's ancient reign restor'd
> Light dies before her uncreating word:
> As one by one, at dread Medaea's strain,
> The sick'ning stars fade off th'aethereal plain;
> As Argus' eyes by Hermes' wand opprest,
> Clos'd one by one to everlasting rest:
> Thus at her felt approach, and secret might,
> Art after Art goes out, and all is Night.
> (Pope 1963: *The Dunciad Variorum* 3.337–46)

But, by contrast with these lines or with Dante's own stately description of the Futile,

> and there the folk forlorn
>
> Rushed after it, in such an endless train,
> It never would have entered in my head
> There were so many men whom death had slain.
> (Dante 1971: *Inferno* 3.54–7)

the random movements of suburban traffic described by Eliot, although they may be allowed some glimmerings of pleasure or variety absent from Dante, remain more intransigently banal.

A different kind of tragic decline can be located in Dante's *Commedia* itself. Many different texts and writers make their presence felt in Dante's poem and, despite the work's title, and the positive trajectory from the Inferno to Paradise traced by the narrative, there are unsettling moments of tragic affect for the narrator, most memorably when he is forbidden from expressing sympathy for the engaging adulteress Francesca. Here we can perhaps locate tragedy in the shift, or "rise," from a Classical to a Christian paradigm. Although we can identify Francesca's sad story as in some way "tragic," perhaps the real tragedy here lies in knowing that we are not allowed to sympathize with her and that to do so is in a sense heretical because she has been damned by God. As Virgil (Dante's guide through the Inferno) epigrammatically observes later in the poem: "Qui vive la pietà quand' è ben morta" (*Inferno* 20.28). One aspect of *pietà* (piety) must destroy the other (pity).[9]

> Here pity or here piety must die
> If the other lives; who's wickeder than one
> That's agonized by God's high equity.
>   (20.28–30)

Here it is implied that those who sympathize with the agonies of the damned are implicated in their own wickedness. But Virgil almost seems to undermine himself when he prefaces this declaration with the irritated: "Why!/And art thou too like all the other fools?" (20.26–7), thus implying the very normality of Dante's softheartedness. For there is something inhuman about such perfection as Virgil seems to require. We shrink from it or, in the case of "Dante," faint. Dante's pity is only human after all and his poem's readers may find the wrenching of *pietà* from itself as unnatural and painful as Marsyas' flaying, as described by Ovid. "Quid me mihi detrahis," "why do you tear me from myself" (Ovid 1984: *Metamorphoses* 6.385), he cries. It is hard to recognize or like a version of humanity, no matter how divinely approved, which has sloughed off pity. We sense a decline from human to bestial as having an obvious and unproblematic tragic potential. But the prospect or reality of the reverse movement, toward perfection, can create a surprisingly similar sense of tragic loss. Two very different examples of such a humanly perverse response can be found in Tennyson's *In Memoriam* (1850) and Arthur C. Clarke's *Childhood's End* (1953).

In poem 47 of *In Memoriam* Tennyson betrays his equivocal attitude toward unindividuated bliss, an attitude which is never completely canceled out by the more piously optimistic but less compelling poems which conclude the volume. He views his projected elevation to Heaven with poignant regret because he and his friend Hallam will lose their individuality and thus their relationship:

> And we shall sit at endless feast,
>   Enjoying each the other's good:
>   What vaster dream can hit the mood
> Of Love on earth? He seeks at least

> Upon the last and sharpest height,
>   Before the spirits fade away,
>   Some landing-place, to clasp and say,
> "Farewell! We lose ourselves in light."
>   (Tennyson 1971)

The "endless feast," and even the "light," of Heaven fill the narrator with a barely concealed horror, and the phrase "last and sharpest height" evokes a vision of some cataclysmic flood rising inexorably to drown even those who have escaped to the highest mountains.

Loss of human individuality is also the theme of Arthur C. Clarke's *Childhood's End*. The benevolent alien "overlords" who arrive to nurture and protect earth know that humanity is about to take an evolutionary step forward, losing their individuality but gaining transcendence. It is a source of sorrow to the overlords that they cannot follow the same path – indeed the overlord Karellan, who guides humanity to a higher stage of existence to which he can never himself aspire, might be compared to Dante's Virgil who, as a virtuous pagan, can never go to Heaven. However, to the old-style humans their children's transition from human to posthuman is itself reason for grief rather than rejoicing. In an unexpected twist it is revealed that the novel's "overlords" resemble devils. This fact is ascribed to a kind of reverse morphic resonance – humanity, in a sense, foretold its own "destruction":

> For that memory was not of the past, but of the future – of those closing years when your race knew that everything was finished. . . . It was as if a distorted echo had reverberated round the closed circle of time, from the future to the past. Call it not a memory, but a premonition.
>   (Clarke 1990: 190)

It is curious that the novel's transcendence, which is really closer to Heaven than to Hell, should be anticipated by the collective consciousness of humanity with such horror.

Thus once again it would seem that tragedy can be located in a movement up as well as a movement down. The contradictory status of such transcendence as a focus of both longing and despair typifies the many irresolvable dilemmas at the heart of tragedies across the ages, the paradoxically duplex *pharmakon*, for example, or such permeable oppositions as *eros* and *thanatos*, fecundity and decay, past and future – even tragedy and comedy. Another instance, discussed in more detail in Peter Hollindale's essay, is suggested by the title of Clarke's novel. Childhood is an ambiguous good. Never to grow up – either through death or, in the case of Peter Pan, though an apparent supernatural intervention – might be seen as a tragic destiny, but growing up is a motive for equally poignant regret. In this matter too science fiction lays bare such human contradictions with particular power. In Dan Simmons's loosely linked story collection *Hyperion* (1989) one of the most effective narratives focuses on the tragic predicament of Sol Weintraub, whose daughter Rachel is exposed to the mysterious "Time Tombs" and begins to live her life backwards. Every day she gets younger and younger, forgetting her earlier (but older) self, and needing to learn all over again what has happened to her until she becomes too young to be exposed to the truth. Parents may think back nostalgically to their children's lost childhood but, for Rachel's parents, the second childhood of their daughter, with its unsettling effect of juvenile dementia, is a source of tragic despair.

A similar tragic contradiction lies at the heart of David Mitchell's *Cloud Atlas* (2004). Its extended time frame, ranging from the early nineteenth century to the far future, allows humanity itself to emerge as the tragic hero of this fragmented narrative. The novel's first narrator, Adam Ewing, poses a vital question when he "questioned if such an ill as 'too *much* civilization' existed or no" (10), a question which the novel goes on to answer in the affirmative by demonstrating that the same impulses which guide humanity toward progress ensure its eventual destruction. The same drive which opens the novel on a note of exploration and creativity propels the earth's ecological and cultural decline, and humanity's apparent entropy, if not destruction. The novel's succession of protagonists, though separated in time, is linked by a shared comet birthmark, apparently indicating reincarnation. The comet can be seen as a sign of the *pharmakon*, impressive in its bright splendor, but also transitory and traditionally seen as a harbinger of bad luck. As Zachry, the narrator of the central (and chronologically final) section observes: "human hunger birthed the Civ'lize, but human hunger killed it too" (286). This tension can be traced back to Empedoclean philosophy, which presents conflict as simultaneously destructive and generative.[10]

The novel's *telos* may seem to emphasize the more destructive aspects of civilization. However, there are just hints that the novel is not so bleak after all. Zachry has a vision that a long dead corpse speaks and tells him that "We Old 'uns was sick with Smart and the Fall was our cure" (293). The corpse's words may allude to the idea of the *felix culpa*, or fortunate fall, the doctrine that man's expulsion from Eden was happy because it enabled Christ's incarnation and mankind's ultimate salvation. (The internal contradictions within the phrase differ subtly from those which inhere within the word *pharmakon*. *Felix* qualifies and subsumes *culpa* whereas the negative and positive meanings of *pharmakon* are enmeshed together.) The reader may thus hope for a happy fate for Zachry's descendants.

Another clue to the earth's future is perhaps to be found in the novel's two citations of one of Virgil's most famous lines. When Aeneas beholds the fall of Troy depicted on the walls of Juno's temple he cries out, weeping: "sunt lacrimae rerum et mentem mortalia tangunt," "here, too, are tears for misfortune and human sorrows pierce the heart" (Virgil 1999: *Aeneid* 1.462). Mitchell's first allusion to this line is located in the novel's chronologically penultimate section, dealing with a dystopian future Korea. "THESE ARE THE TEARS OF THINGS" (354) is used as a code message by the resistance. The second allusion comes later in the novel, though earlier in the story. Immediately before his suicide in 1931 the troubled young composer, Robert Frobisher, concludes his final letter to his friend Sixsmith with the phrase "sunt lacrimae rerum" (490). Because *Cloud Atlas* is a fragmented novel containing discrete narratives separated by time it is able to replicate intratextually some of the intertextual tragic effects described earlier in this chapter. If we may suspect that there is a kind of conversation going on between Weir Smyth's *Agamemnon* and *Hamlet* we can be sure that the Virgilian echo in *Cloud Atlas* is a planned effect. But how to map it onto the different possible trajectories which may be traced by tragedy in a state of transition? Does such an obtrusive repetition draw attention to the novel's status as a highly patterned fictional construct whose characters' destinies are determined not by fate or the gods but by David Mitchell? Is the tragedy, in other words, diluted and trivialized by the artful repetition? Alternatively, does the repetition of Virgil's words enact and reinforce a tragic decline from the comparatively civilized environment in which Frobisher lives to the dystopic brutality of the science-fictional future? Does the gulf between the tragic situation of one individual and the tragic fall of the whole of humanity become itself an intratextual tragic fall? Another more comforting reading of the Virgilian repetition is possible, one which sees it neither as a purely self-conscious metanarrative marker nor as a symbol of civilization's tragic decline. In its original context the line is spoken by Aeneas when he beholds a representation of the fall of Troy. And yet by the end of the poem Aeneas has founded a new and greater empire, that of Rome. Perhaps even Mitchell's post-apocalyptic future earth will eventually be renewed. In demonstrating the persistence of tragedy Mitchell in a sense ensures the persistence of hope, at least if we accept Kierkegaard's assertion that "when

the age loses the tragic, it gains despair" (Kierkegaard 1944: vol. 1, 118).
Within the context of Mitchell's novel Kierkegaard's comment resonates
with Zachry's sense of cultural loss and his capacity to communicate and
articulate that loss. "The worst is not/so long as we can say 'this is the
worst'" (King Lear 4.1.27–8).

The transhistorical sweep of Mitchell's novel allows it to stand as a kind of
emblem for the tragic tradition more generally. The sections of Cloud Atlas
are individually satisfying but the crosscurrents between them ensure that
the novel is greater than the sum of its parts. Similarly, as the essays in this
volume demonstrate, the tragic traditions of different eras may be mutually
illuminating. The complex, sometimes disjunctive, trajectories traced by key
narratives such as those of Prometheus or Oedipus over time reflect those
disruptive yet energizing transitions within and between cultures which are
themselves so often the stuff of tragedy.

Notes

1   The ambiguity of this term is discussed at length by Jacques Derrida in
    his 1968 essay "Plato's Pharmacy" (Derrida 1993: 63–171).
2   Burian 1997: 179.
3   On the metatheatricality of the play see Boyle 1997: 122–33.
4   Peter Weir, 1998.
5   See Vanda Zajko's Chapter 8 in this volume for an extended discussion of
    the play's ambiguities.
6   For a fuller analysis of the relationship between Aeschylus and Shelley
    see Wallace 1996: 166.
7   Metamorphoses 6.401–674.
8   Kill Bill, Quentin Tarantino, 2003–4.
9   A similar tension is produced in Milton's "On the Morning of Christ's
    Nativity," especially in stanza 20 which describes the decay of the
    nymphs and dryads.
10 Cf. Gellrich 1988: 27.

Chapter 1

Trojan Suffering, Tragic Gods, and Transhistorical Metaphysics

Edith Hall

The Greek, decisive confrontation with the daemonic world-order gives to tragic poetry its historico-philosophical signature.

(Benjamin 1980: vol. 1.3, 879)

The Reasons for Suffering

When Philip Sidney defended theater in the first substantial example of literary criticism in the English language, his *Defence of Poetry* (1581), he used a story from ancient Greece to illustrate tragedy's emotive power:

> Plutarch yielded a notable testimony of the abominable tyrant Alexander Pheraeus; from whose eyes a tragedy, well made and represented, drew abundance of tears, who without all pity had murdered infinite numbers, and some of his own blood; so as he that was not ashamed to make matters for tragedies, yet could not resist the sweet violence of a tragedy. And if it wrought no farther good in him, it was that he, in despite of himself, withdrew himself from hearkening to that which might mollify his hardened heart.
>
> (Sidney 1973: 96–7)

Sidney was struck that Alexander of Pherae, a wicked Greek tyrant of the fourth century BCE, was induced to weep by "the sweet violence of a tragedy." Indeed, the emotion so overpowered Alexander that he had to absent himself, for fear that his hardened heart could be made capable of pity.

The tragedy which upset the tyrant was Euripides' *Trojan Women*, as we know from the passage in Plutarch where Sidney had found it (see below). The sufferings that Alexander could not bear to watch were those of Hecuba and Andromache, women who lost their families at Troy. *Trojan Women* constitutes an extended lament and searing statement of the philosophical incomprehensibility of human suffering. Although famous in antiquity, its perceived inadequacy in relation to some of Aristotle's prescriptions for the ideal tragedy meant that it was relatively neglected from the Renaissance until 1905, when it inaugurated the tradition of using Greek tragedy to protest against establishment politics. The 1905 production was mounted at the Royal Court Theatre in London, in the translation of the Greek scholar and humanitarian Gilbert Murray, in order to protest against the concentration camps in which the British had incarcerated Boer women and children during the terrible war in South Africa.[1] Most of this chapter revolves around *Trojan Women*, but the focus on this occasion will *not* be on its political power.

For the play is also distinguished by its metaphysical complexity. It juxtaposes physically manifest Olympian gods – Poseidon and Athena open the play agreeing to destroy the Greeks as well as the Trojans – with Hecuba's explicit expressions of doubt that the gods can concern themselves with humans or even exist in their traditional form at all. At one point Hecuba appeals to the gods in an offhand articulation of "Pascal's wager" – acknowledging god may, she says, be useless, but you might as well do it just in case (469). At another point she prays to "whatever principle it is that sustains the world...whoever you are, difficult to fathom and know, Zeus, whether you are the Inevitable Force of Nature or the Mind of Men" (884–8): here she makes the (in Euripides' time) remarkably avant-garde proposal that the supreme god is actually the physical laws that govern the material universe, or human intelligence. Finally, she announces that the gods have "come to nothing" and that all her sacrifices have proved futile (1240–2).

Hecuba's metaphysical bafflement anticipates the entire future of the medium; indeed, in his recent study of tragedy Eagleton proposes that tragedy can only survive as a valid art form in the twenty-first century if marked by metaphysical openness (Eagleton 2003). Tragedy that suggests metaphysical answers derived from any single religious or philosophical perspective is unlikely to have anything profound to say to the postmodern, multicultural global village. In this chapter *Trojan Women* will therefore be used as a basis for reflection on the relationship between tragic suffering and tragic metaphysics in its broadest sense, encompassing the gods, the unseen forces that shape the universe, and tragic characters' supernatural connection with the invisible world of the dead. It will be argued that there is a relationship between, on the one hand, Greek tragedy's susceptibility to theological and metaphysical reinterpretation relative to the religious beliefs of different societies and epochs, and on the other its permanent, definitive status as a philosophical examination of suffering. Greek tragedy turned its spectators into etiolated gods, viewers with superhuman understanding of the causes of the pain being witnessed, but with no power to prevent it. These are the selfsame metaphysical contours that underlie all subsequent drama known as "tragic."

To return to Sidney, his oxymoronic phrase "sweet violence" was borrowed by Eagleton as the title of his own book on tragedy, in which he stresses that one of the few things that is central to the historically mutable medium of tragedy is its representation of specific instances of *suffering*. Some tragic victims are aware of their suffering and the reasons for it; others certainly are not, as Arthur Miller rightly insisted: "It matters not at all ... whether [the tragic character] is highly conscious or only dimly aware of what is happening" (Miller 1958: 31–6).[2] Many of the other elements that have sometimes been deemed necessary and definitive constituents of the genre (e.g., the high social class of the sufferer, or tragedy's ability to *ennoble* suffering) prove not, on consideration of twentieth-century examples including *Death of a Salesman*, to be necessary to tragedy at all. It is suffering that unites Oedipus, Hamlet, and Willy Loman, who dies after suffering as a way of life: his son Biff says that the result of the career path Willy chose is "To suffer fifty weeks a year for the sake of a two-week vacation" (Miller 1961: 16). That in Loman's life the proportion of suffering to non-suffering is as high as 50:2 is, moreover, in itself suggestive of the *concentration* on suffering implied by tragedy. As Aldous Huxley put it in a brilliant essay on the difference between tragedy and other "serious" genres, tragedy omits all the everyday parts of life that dilute its effect. Tragedy does not tell the "whole truth" about life – that even at times when you are terribly bereaved, domestic tasks must be done (Huxley 1961). Moreover, in order to build up its effect, tragedy takes a certain period of time – what Aristotle called its *mēkos*, or extension (*Poetics* Chapter 7): a joke can make someone laugh in a matter of seconds, but it is difficult to imagine what might constitute an effective one-minute tragedy. (One of my editors suggests that the screams, heavy breathing, and garbage constituting Beckett's 35-second *Breath* (1969) just might qualify.)

A tragedy that did not represent suffering in some concentration and with some sustained build-up could not be tragic, by any criterion – ancient Greek, Senecan, Renaissance, Jacobean, eighteenth-century, nineteenth-century, Modernist, or contemporary. Eagleton has emphasized the *agony* inherent in it – whether psychological or physical, whether bereavement, boredom, or bodily mutilation. Yet "the dramatic representation of suffering," although a necessary definition of tragedy, is, as Eagleton stresses, not a sufficient one. The very process of staging agony as aesthetic spectacle must in a sense be abusive.[3] There remains, however, an obvious difference between the way that suffering is represented in tragedy and the way that it was represented in ancient Roman gladiatorial displays (which often were staged quasi-dramatically as combat between mythical heroes) and its manifestation in contemporary hardcore pornographic films. Tragedies, gladiatorial shows, and pornographic movies share dramatic form, enacted narrative, and agony, but neither the sole nor central goal of tragedy is the arousal of excitement or desire.

In Joyce's *A Portrait of the Artist as a Young Man*, Stephen Dedalus ponders the affinity between tragedy and pornography. Dedalus sees pornographic art as activating *kinetic* desire, whereas the emotion that is excited by tragic drama, in contrast, is aesthetic and "therefore static. The mind is arrested and raised above desire and loathing" (Joyce 1960: 204–5). Many tragic poets have written scenes that play on this difficult borderline between arousing desire and arousing a more contemplative reaction: in Euripides' *Hecuba* (a play he wrote a few years before *Trojan Women* and which covers similar ground) the reported death of the half-naked Trojan princess Polyxena, in front of an internal audience of thousands of Greek soldiers, is a graphic example. It invites the external spectators to take erotic pleasure in the description of the young woman, who has torn her gown "from her shoulders to her waist beside the navel, revealing her breasts and her torso, most beautiful, like those of a statue" (558–61).[4] Yet the account simultaneously insists that the spectators raise to consciousness their own suspect reaction; moreover, the pornographic element in this scene is inseparable from the overriding *ethical* question it asks, which is why the Greeks had seen fit to sacrifice the young woman in the first place.

The Philosophical Signature

One working definition of tragedy, therefore, is that it constitutes the expression of an enquiry into suffering, an aesthetically articulated question mark written in pain. It was certainly this immanent interrogatory quality that led the German philosophical tradition, from Hegel to Benjamin and Adorno, to turn to tragedy in search of a response to the radical questions that Kant had raised about the nature and proper limits of the field of philosophy and its critical practices.[5] As Hölderlin put it, "the tragic is the metaphor [in the literal Greek sense of "the transposition"] of an intellectual intuition."[6] For tragedy, while representing an instance of suffering in dramatic form, asks *why* it has occurred. It is not a matter of whether the suffering is of a particular type or quality: neither the Greeks nor Shakespeare's audiences are likely to have drawn much distinction between pitiful and "tragic'" agony. Philoctetes' abscessed foot is as fit for arousing tragic fellow-feeling as Iphigenia's death sentence, Lear's isolation, or Hamlet's alienation. The philosophical interest is in the *causes* of the suffering rather than its neuropathology.[7]

The answers to the question of cause can belong to any of the branches of the emergent fifth-century intellectual enquiry that became known as philosophy: ethics and its close relations social and political theory (the tragedy was caused by an ill-considered choice, the act of an evil individual, or social forces); epistemology and the problem of knowledge (the hero had no way of knowing that the woman he married was his mother; the community at large held an erroneous opinion; language is inadequate to the requirements of framing and communicating information); metaphysics/theology (the tragedy was caused by god, the gods, fate, or some mysterious cosmic force); ontology, which was later, like theology, regarded as a branch of metaphysics (being human is to suffer and die, suffering is the definitive characteristic of the finite human being, and not to be born – not to come into being at all – is best).

Troy formed the center of the mythical map by which archaic Greeks sought proto-philosophical routes through their experiences, and Euripides' repeated use of the mythical figure of Helen of Troy suggests that he found in her a benchmark for philosophical questions. In the three surviving tragedies in which she appears, the issues raised by her presence fall under the headings of ethics, epistemology, and ontology, respectively. In *Trojan Women* (415 BCE), Helen's role is to complicate the ethical dimension of the play and its quest to find the individual – human or divine – responsible for the carnage at Troy. In *Helen* (412), she is to be found in Egypt, where she has resided throughout the Trojan War, while a substitute image of her eloped with Paris. Her presence raises epistemological questions about how the true Helen can be identified. Is she the apprehensible, material individual, subject to ordinary laws of cognition, or the mysterious embodiment of her reputation, in the discourse and imaginations of men, that was psychologically manifested in stories and songs at Troy? In *Orestes* (408), the question becomes baldly ontological and metaphysical: Helen literally vanishes in supernatural circumstances, is elevated to the machine in which only gods could conventionally appear, and is turned, finally, into a constellation. This Helen confounds any rational probing of the nature of being Human, or of the human Being.

Many tragedies suggest that several causes have combined to create the suffering that they represent. It is not always easy to distinguish the metaphysical from the ontological, or the ethical from the epistemological. Some tragedies, notably *Oedipus Tyrannus*, even make allocation of responsibility itself not only a symptom of suffering but the direct cause of more. Laying blame exacerbates the pain of the titular Trojan women, and yet it is one of their main activities, since nearly all the characters, as well as several gods, are sooner or later held responsible for the carnage at Troy.[8] Their other activity is suffering, which the play potently synthesizes with the "why" question that it also asks, especially when Hecuba's bereavements are consummated by the Greeks' murder of her grandson Astyanax. Few episodes in world theater can rival the emotional impact of the scenes in which the infant is torn from his mother Andromache's arms, and later laid out by his heartbroken grandmother, a tiny corpse on his dead father Hector's shield (709–98, 1118–251). Sidney had found his anecdote about the tyrant who fled the theater in Plutarch's *Life of Pelopidas*, published in English translation just two years before the *Defence* was written.[9] Plutarch names the tragedy, describes Alexander's crimes (which included massacring the populations of entire cities), and specifies the cause of Alexander's flight: it was "shame that his citizens should see him, who never pitied any man that he murdered, weep at the sufferings of Hecuba and Andromache" (29.4–6). This is evidence that the ancient Greeks appreciated the emotive power of this play. It also helps to explain the player scenes in Shakespeare's *Hamlet*, initiated by the arrival of the "tragedians of the city" to offer their Lenten entertainment.

In Act 2 scene 2, the player performs a speech by Aeneas describing the death of Priam and Hecuba's response to it. Hamlet wonders how the player could make himself go pale, weep, and speak with a broken voice for a woman about whom he in reality cared nothing. If he did really care about Hecuba, and have Hamlet's reasons for feeling strong passions:

> He would drown the stage with tears
> And cleave the general ear with horrid speech,
> Make mad the guilty and appal the free,
> Confound the ignorant, and amaze indeed
> The very faculties of eyes and ears.
>
> (2.2.564–8)

Hecuba's suffering, if depicted by a skilled actor, could inspire weeping and "make mad the guilty," just as it once reduced the thoroughly guilty Alexander of Pherae to an embarrassment of tears. It is this exemplum that suggests to Hamlet the very idea that "the play's the thing/Wherein I'll catch the conscience of the king" (2.2.606–7). Claudius, like Alexander of Pherae, subsequently watches in the course of *Hamlet* Act 3 scene 2 a play dramatizing actions so similar to crimes he has himself committed that he has to absent himself from the performance.

The point of this discussion of the enduring cultural impact of Euripides' *Trojan Women* is partly to offer a specific example of how ancient tragedies can shape the subsequent tragic tradition in ways that are invisible and yet of enormous significance. Shakespeare had almost certainly never read in ancient Greek the *Trojan Women* that lay behind Plutarch's influential anecdote, and no English translation became available until the eighteenth century. It is of course possible – some scholars have argued likely – that he knew Latin versions of Euripides' plays, which had appeared by 1541.[10] He may indeed have known about Erasmus' Latin translation of *Hecuba* (1506). Yet Shakespeare used translations of the works of Plutarch widely elsewhere, especially in his Roman history plays, and the whole function of the figure of Hecuba in *Hamlet* fits better with the Plutarchean anecdote, plus a knowledge of the second book of Virgil's *Aeneid*, than with either Euripidean tragedy. Hamlet is fascinated with the way that a mere player can convey the extreme grief of Hecuba, which is a direct response to Plutarch's discussion of the ancient actor; it is also through this encounter that Hamlet decides that the play is indeed the thing wherein he can "catch the conscience of the king." Claudius is induced to leave the theatrical production at the court because it hits, as Euripides' *Trojan Women* had done long ago in Pherae, far too close to home.

The Metaphysical Chrysalis

Reactions to Euripides' *Trojan Women* in subsequent centuries also provide, collectively, an excellent example of how the representation of a particular episode of suffering – the terrible ordeal undergone by the bereaved women of Troy – is susceptible to changes in the presentation of its metaphysical dimension. Indeed, the physical appearance of the gods on stage in this play seemed to epochs later than Euripides, when different religious and philosophical beliefs were held, to be an element that could simply be removed. Euripides' play was imitated in imperial Rome, in the Senecan *Trojan Women*, but this version avoided altogether the material theophany of Athena and Poseidon with which Euripides' play opens. Instead, the drama is opened by Hecuba, grief's emblem herself, who in her very first sentence poses and suggests answers to the question "why I am suffering?"

> If any man puts his confidence in royal power and rules supreme in a great palace, if he does not fear the fickle gods but surrenders his trusting heart to times of prosperity, then let him look on me, and on you, Troy: Fortune (*Fors*) never gave a greater demonstration of the fragile poise in which the proud are set.
>
> (Fantham 1982: 1–6)

In addition to the fickle gods' dislike of human greatness, and the old Roman principle of *Fors*, by the time her prologue has finished, Hecuba has also inculpated the *numen* of the gods – an almost untranslatable Latin word here approximating to "will" – and alleged her own responsibility in having given birth to Paris (28, 38–40). The Chorus later surveys different philosophical theories as they search for consolation: the belief of some Stoics in the total annihilation of the physical body at death; the doctrine of *ekpyrosis*, by which the whole cosmos or galaxy is periodically destroyed by the onset of an incendiary whirlwind; the conventional picture of the traditional Underworld (371–408).

Tragedies have subsequently been written by believers in many different Christianities. There have been attempts at tragedies by Calvinists, Jansenists, Huguenots, and Anglicans. Toward the end of the twentieth century, there have been productions of Greek tragedy that have been identifiably Confucian, Hindu, Moslem, Shinto, Rastafarian, and conflations with the rites of the African Ogun, god of the Yoruba. *Trojan Women* is no exception: it informed Robert Garnier's biblical *Les Juifves* (1583), a tragedy on the suffering of the Jewish captives in ancient Babylon; Franz Werfel's version of Euripides (1917), frequently staged in Germany during both world wars, turned Hecuba into a proleptic Christian martyr.[11] In the German Democratic Republic *Trojan Women* was reconceived by Mattias Braun in a famous production, revived several times between 1957 and 1969. Its perspective was that of a Marxist interpreting classical drama in a Dialectical Materialist revolutionary theater, where the gods were understood in terms of human agency writ large, as symbols of ideological forces at work, or allegorically. But Tadashi Suzuki's adaptation, in which Hecuba communed with the ghosts of her dead in a Japanese cemetery devastated during World War II, was opened by the indigenous Japanese Buddhist–Shinto god Jizo, the patron of children.[12] Since the Gulf War, numerous productions in both the West and the Middle East have drawn on Muslim styles of vocal performance and funeral rituals. But the most philosophically interesting example is perhaps Sartre's *Les Troyennes*, an adaptation which appeared in the spring of 1965.[13]

Les Troyennes had its première with the Théâtre national populaire at the Palais de Chaillot, Paris, on March 10, 1965, where it was directed and designed by a Greek team. It was explicitly conceived as a protest against French brutality in Algeria. Yet the adaptation is also an articulation of the central premise of Sartre's particular brand of Existentialism, that hope is life and hopelessness is equivalent to death, as Sartre's Hécube herself remarks more than once. The Trojan women are, from a Sartrean Existential perspective, already dead, since death is a permanent state of denial of choice, "an absence of the defining human characteristic of freedom" (O'Donohoe 2005: 57). It is in this sense that Sartre's version is most innovatively philosophical; his gods pass the death sentence on Greeks and Trojans alike in the opening scene, thus removing all hope, which is the Sartrean precondition of meaningful human action or existence.

Sartre's old Marxist allegiances mean also, however, that it turns out that it is the gods who do not exist at all, since they are only sustained in being through human ideological activity. In determining annihilation for the world they therefore determine annihilation for themselves. Hécube actually predicts the gods' demise, which Sartre has made quite explicit in his introduction: "The gods are created along with mortals, and their communal death is the lesson of the tragedy" (Sartre 1965: 6). Sartre seems to have reveled in the paradox of staging gods that his own philosophy and even his heroine know to be figments of the human imagination, for he brought back one of them – Poseidon – in an entirely original epilogue appended to the play. After the audience sees a flash of lightning, in lines that in print were deliberately typeset in the shape of a mushroom cloud, Poseidon delivers an apocalyptic warning of total extinction:

> Idiots!
> We'll make you pay for this.
> You stupid, bestial mortals
> Making war, burning cities,
> violating tombs and temples,
> torturing your enemies, bringing
> suffering on yourselves
> Can't you see
> War
> Will kill you:
> All of you?
> CURTAIN
> (Sartre 1969: 347)

This had a precise meaning in the mid-1960s, in the light of the appalling torture practiced by the French in Algeria, as well as the Cuban missile crisis. For Sartre, the nuclear arms race underlined his conviction that when "hope is deleted from the human enterprise, teleology gives way to eschatology" (O'Donohoe 2005: 255). Here his tragic god delivers his own passionately felt political and ethical as well as metaphysical message, in a very precise historical situation, but in a play that simultaneously sets that god up as a product of the human mind. Thus, in theatrical semiotics, a tragic god can even signify an author's atheism.

The director of the first production of Sartre's adaptation was Michael Cacoyannis, who had recently directed Euripides' own play at the 1963 Spoleto Festival. The most familiar and accessible version of *Trojan Women* is Cacoyannis's subsequent film (1971), starring Katharine Hepburn as Hecuba and Vanessa Redgrave as Andromache. Although Cacoyannis's screenplay, adapted from a translation by Edith Hamilton, was in the main much more faithful to the Greek original than the screenplays of his other Euripidean movies, the one really significant structural alteration relates to the prologue. Since the aesthetic mode of Cacoyannis's film is relentlessly realist, he deleted the scene with Athena and Poseidon which introduces Euripides' play, a scene which stages "petty-minded deities blithely arranging to wipe out thousands of mortals" (Mackinnon 1986: 84). He replaced it with an impersonal voice-over which accompanies the opening freeze-frames by providing the information that the Greeks, the aggressors in the film, are soon to die themselves. This omniscient narrator, whose tone of quiet authority resembles that of the voice of God in certain Hollywood epics, providentially suggests that the crimes that are about to be enacted will eventually be punished. No doubt this notion resonated at the time of the film's release, when it was widely understood as a denunciation of both the Greek dictatorship and American war crimes in Vietnam. In the process the version loses altogether the anarchic, arbitrary edge of the Euripidean theodicy, which implies that no peace can ever be found amongst mortals subject to the whims of warring gods.

Cacoyannis's audiences worldwide, despite being invited to respond politically in their own secular contexts, were still watching an incidence of terrible suffering and being asked to enquire philosophically into its causes. No amount of surgery, or "realist" revision, can remove from the form and tone of tragedy the fact of its genesis as a medium which in every detail was framed by the forces that lay beyond the arena materially visible to everyday humankind. In fact, the transhistorically enduring metaphysical signature of tragedy, the result of what Benjamin called the decisive Greek "confrontation with the daemonic world-order," originated in its physical inclusion of gods in its performance space. In Greek tragedy, the "metaphysical relationships between audience, gods and humans" became "sharply insistent through their concrete visualization in the coding of space" (Lowe 1996: 526). The physical, vertical axis marked "a metaphysical separation between the two planes of existence within the stage world: the groundling level of the mortals, and the supernal plane of the gods" (Lowe 1996: 527).[14] In ancient vase-paintings inspired by tragic performances, the gods inhabit the upper level of the vase, looking down on the suffering mortals as if from windows in the upper storeys of a building.[15] This convention of artistic representation in the form of a physically elevated internal audience reflected the elevated physical positioning of the spectators in tiered seats in theaters, whether temporary wooden erections or permanent stone buildings, across the Greek-speaking world. It is this vertical axis that the subsequent tragic tradition – whether it retains or dispenses with material epiphanies of gods, incorporates Christian terminology, or dramatizes an incidence of suffering in contemporary, secular suburbia – has never abandoned altogether.

The way that characters suffer in tragedy, the philosophical enquiry it invites into the causes of their suffering, and the forms of dramatic irony it uses to situate the audience in respect of that suffering, are ultimately what provides it as a literary form and theatrical medium with its sense of generic continuity. You can lose the chrysalis from which the butterfly – or moth – emerges, but its shape and nature will always remain fundamentally conditioned by the shape and nature of the chrysalis. In Marxist terms, this is called the "relative autonomy" of art forms and artworks that achieve cultural longevity. The metaphysical *dimension* is fundamental to tragedy's "relative autonomy" – its ability to outlive historical and epistemic shifts as great as those introduced by the arrival of Christianity, the English Reformation, or Modernity.[16] The metaphysical is structurally impossible to excise from tragedy without stopping it from being a tragedy, even if its ideological manifestations vary, and even if it becomes physically invisible – even if Godot never turns up, after all.

Death and Mystery

The great French director Ariane Mnouchkine has said that the dominant interest the Greek tragedians hold for her is "metaphysical . . . they did theater with that very far away part of ourselves" (quoted in Delgado and Heritage 1996: 180). This special quality of tragedy, that points continually to what lies beyond empirically, materially discernible human experience is also connected closely to its intimacy with the past, and especially the dead. Nietzsche had a point when he identified the thrilling moment when Heracles leads the veiled Alcestis back from the world of the dead to her living husband at the climax of Euripides' *Alcestis* as the scene that epitomized every spectator's experience of the tragic actor (Nietzsche 1972: 59–60). For the ancient Greeks, almost all tragic characters were such revenants, since all their surviving tragedies, with the single exception of Aeschylus' history-play *Persians*, were set in a heroic world that had existed many generations before the premières of their plays. This is no longer the case, yet the sense of communion with the dead is another aspect of Greek tragedy which has inhered in its philosophical legacy: in the tragic world the dead always return, because the tragic hero so very often *lives among the dead* – those he has lost and mourns, or those he has himself murdered (Kott 1974: ix–x; emphasis added).

Even in plays set in their author's "here-and-now," the hero has often been cast as living among the dead, like the bereaved men and women in the Irish tragedies of O'Casey and Synge discussed in an important study by Macintosh (1994). Willy Loman in *Death of a Salesman* communes with the spirit and memory of his dead brother Ben, a diamond prospector in Africa.

This aura of intimacy with the dead is another bequest of Greek tragedy, especially of Sophocles' supremely death-conscious heroes (Jones 1962: 169). It is not just that the big bereavement scenes in Greek tragedy have directly shaped subsequent plays, as Hecuba's archetypal lament over Astyanax is implicitly echoed by Maurya in O'Casey's *Riders to the Sea*.[17] It is more important that subsequent tragedy has retained some residual element of the psychological conditions under which the people who created its first examples lived. The Athenians lived in far greater emotional and ritual proximity to their dead and personally faced the strong possibility of death and bereavement on a much more constant level, whether on the battlefield to which every citizen male was regularly summoned, or the childbed that jeopardized every woman.

This chapter has used the metaphor of the metaphysical and death-focused tragic winged insect retaining the imprint of its ancient Greek religious chrysalis. It must at least address, therefore, the striking neglect of the divine, religious, metaphysical, and thanatological dimensions of tragedy in its earliest Greek critics. One of the remarkable features of the earliest discussion of Greek tragic theater, by the classical Greeks themselves, is how little emphasis is given to the medium's metaphysical tendency. The comparison of the tragic art of Aeschylus and Euripides in Aristophanes' comedy *Frogs* is interested in form, meter, style, the character of its heroes, and whether its function is to please or to educate, but there is hardly any sign of an attempt to discuss the role of the gods in tragedy, its probing of any philosophical matters more cerebral than the practical science of rhetoric, or its intense dialogue with those who are no longer alive.

In the *Republic*, however, Plato's Socrates does have a specific criticism to make about tragedy's depiction of the gods. The gods, who are changeless and perfect, should not be introduced in disguise (2.381) or be accused of speaking falsehoods (2.383). Socrates objects to tragedy's *familiar* treatment of divine figures. Tragedy breaches what, in his view, should be a great gulf of respect and awe separating mortals from immortals. Perhaps he would have admitted into his Republic tragedy that asked theological questions in a way that did not involve negative representation of gods; but it is difficult to see what kind of tragedy in a religious society could refrain from implicating the divine in the representation of human suffering. What may lie behind the Platonic suspicion of the representation of tragic gods as miscreants may have been an adumbration of the type of charge laid against tragedy several centuries later by the early Christian polemicists, who loathed theater to a man,[18] and were presciently aware that although "the Tragic Muse was born of religion" she would always remain "something of an infidel" (Lucas 1957: 69).

Aristotle's a-theological view poses more of a problem. His defense of tragedy against Plato is based on his conviction that representations of unpleasant things are educational (*Poetics* 4.1448b). He could, theoretically, have come up with a defense of the tragic representation of divinity, at least within certain criteria, but the rest of his philosophical output makes it hard to see how the intense reciprocity between gods and men so central to Greek tragedy could have interested him. Aristotle's god is the "unmoved mover," a remote non-substantial principle, the source of the human world but unaffected by human conduct or worship. And the world of Aristotle's *Poetics* is as doggedly centered on human experience and observation – as anthropocentric – as the rest of his philosophy: even the treatise that became known in later antiquity as his *Metaphysics* (simply because it concerned matters to be studied "after" [*meta-*] physical phenomena), included questions of ontology, first principles, and indeed the nature of the "unmoved" divine, but no discussion of the gods as represented in Homer or tragedy. It comes as little surprise, therefore, that in the *Poetics* Aristotle's account of the canonical heroes in tragedy discusses only their crimes against other people and ignores their relations with heaven (Chapter 13). He pays no attention to the religious context in which tragedies were produced, at festivals of the god Dionysus. His sole substantial comment on the gods comes in his famous discussion of the use of the stage crane. Aristotle associated this device particularly with Euripides, and objected to examples of its use that did not arise "organically" from the plot:

> The denouements of plots ought to arise just from the mimesis of character, and not from a contrivance, a deus ex machina, as in *Medea*. The contrivance should be used instead for things outside the play, either all that happened beforehand that a human being could not know, or all that happens later needs foretelling and reporting, for we attribute omniscience to the gods.
>
> (Chapter 15.1454b)

To Aristotle's notion of divine omniscience, and the way that the tragedians used gods in machines for revealing things in the future or "that a human being could not know," the argument of this chapter will soon return. But it is worth dwelling on the failure of the most influential text in the development of tragedy to suggest that theology or metaphysics belonged to its realm at all.

The answer, paradoxically, may be that Aristotle's avoidance of the topic has in itself been profoundly generative. When it comes to ethics, action, and responsibility, Aristotle certainly had plenty to say, and indeed argued influentially that tragedy's potential for ethical exploration of probability makes it a close relation of philosophy (*Poetics* Chapter 9). Perhaps, therefore, it is partly to Aristotle's focus on ethics and human action, rather than their larger metaphysical context, that we can attribute the *openness* and indeed the open-endedness of the metaphysics of the tragic medium as it continued to develop subsequently – its insusceptibility to exclusive appropriation by any single theological or philosophical viewpoint. The history of tragedy as it has been composed since its Renaissance rediscovery would have looked very different – much less mysterious and on that account much less powerful and fascinating – if Aristotle's *Poetics* had included any extended prescriptions for the place and function of the divine in tragedy. "Shakespeare was not attempting to justify the way of God to men, or to show the universe as a Divine Comedy. He was writing tragedy, and tragedy would not be tragedy if it were not a painful mystery," wrote A. C. Bradley, sensibly (Bradley 1904: 37–8).

Aristotle's apparent indifference to the tragic gods of his day and to specific religious viewpoints also seems echoed repeatedly by dominant trends within the criticism even of tragedy written by and for Christians, such as those by Shakespeare. Shakespearean critics have far more often than not argued along lines resembling the view that tragedy "is only possible to a mind which is for the moment agnostic," since "any theology which has a compensating Heaven to offer the tragic hero is fatal."[19] This is the case not only with plays set in pagan ancient Greek or Roman contexts, but even those with explicitly Christian medieval settings such as *Macbeth*. The very diversity of types of Christianity which critics have detected in this grim play – ranging from Calvinist determinism to the most dogmatic traditional Catholicism – suggests that Christian theological categories are an unsafe filter through which to address the presentation of suffering and its ultimate causes in Shakespeare (Waters 1994: 141–73, 247).

The Spectator Bound

When the Greeks included the gods and their immortal perspective within tragedy's visual fields, they incorporated the metaphysical – the sense of mysterious striving beyond the discernible world to guess at its ultimate causes – forever in the medium. When they raised heroes from their pale existence in the Underworld to suffer again, the spectators reminded themselves that they and their closest kin would soon face death on the battlefield or childbed, thus imbuing tragedy with what proved to be a lasting atmosphere of intimacy with the dead. One of the reasons why these fundamental qualities have proved so resistant to change across time is precisely that the tragedians' "instruction manual" inherited from antiquity – Aristotle's *Poetics* – had so little to say on the subject, allowing the religious sensibility of each time and place where tragedy has flourished to formulate its metaphysics anew.

Yet a cause of the ancients' sparse commentary on tragic gods may actually have been that their presence in serious poetry was so organic that it was self-understood and scarcely to be discussed separately from tragic humans. It was inherited from the serious poetry of the past – especially Homeric epic – and it may never have occurred to them even to question why. With the gods, tragedy inherited the presentation of "the gap between individual and cosmic value – the ways in which things that mean a great deal to individuals become futile or infinitesimal when viewed in the objective proportions of time, multitudes, or divinity" (Lowe 1996: 524). This world picture is actually the great contribution not of tragedy but of an epic, the Homeric *Iliad*, where the literally life and death decisions taken by Achilles or Hector or Patroclus are taken while the epic audience is equipped with full knowledge of the gods' preordained and often arbitrary plans.[20] It is no surprise that Plato regularly calls Homer a "tragedian."

One of the very few surviving observations on tragedy's use of the gods framed by an ancient Greek playwright implies that tragic authors themselves were thought to possess almost godlike powers. Antiphanes, a comic poet approximately contemporary with Plato, wrote a comedy called *Poetry* in which a speaker, perhaps a comic playwright, complained that tragedians have it easy. When they have run out of things to say, and plot elements to dramatize, "and have completely given up on their plays, they raise the machine as easily as lifting a finger, and everyone is perfectly happy with what they see."[21] The playwright, like God, can interfere in or curtail tragic action on account of his authorial power over narrative, instantiated in his control over the god in the machine. Yet in terms of the ancient experience of tragic theater, which dispensed altogether with the authorial voice and narrative presence that so distinguishes epic, it is the *spectator* who most conspicuously possesses godlike powers. "The spectator stands where the Gods themselves stand, in a happy position of omniscience" (Styan 1968: 365–8). Yet the happiness of that omniscient condition is painfully compromised because the spectators of tragedy can only ever be divine *epistemologically.* They can never ontologically be immortal themselves, and they have absolutely no ethical autonomy, no executive powers of agency which would allow them to intervene.

In Samuel Beckett's *Endgame* the question of tragic suffering is explored through characters called Hamm and Clov, whose names may partly reflect the hammer and nails used in Jesus Christ's crucifixion,[22] but also the terrifying opening of the Aeschylean *Prometheus Bound*, where Prometheus is nailed to the rocks of the Caucasus by the hammering gods Might and Violence. The audience of tragedy is enchained, like the Titan Prometheus who was fettered precisely for trying to wrest, from the highest authority in the universe, the means by which to intervene in human life and transform it for the better. The tragic spectators' chains mean they can never change what they see – never prevent Astyanax from being thrown from the wall of Troy. Gilbert Murray, responsible for that first modern-language staging of *Trojan Women* in 1905, said that it is a truly great tragedy because, although so "harrowing," it is also "a bearing of witness" (Murray 1905: 6). To be a witness of tragic suffering means being shackled to the seat of a god, conscious and yet completely incapacitated, to watch the mortal passion. As Lukács long ago put it in *Soul and Form*, tragedy is that particular medium in which "God must leave the stage, but yet remain a spectator" (Lukács 1973: 154).

Notes

1   See Hall and Macintosh 2005: 508–11. For an excellent discussion of the production of the play and the political causes with which it has been associated see Willis 2005.
2   See also Williams 1966: 104; for an unusually clear articulation of the view against which Miller was arguing see, e.g. Krook 1969: 39–46.
3   Žižek 2001: 87; Eagleton 2003: 175–6.
4   See Hall 2006: Chapter 4.
5   See de Beistegui and Sparks 2000: 1–2; Rocco 1997: 30–1, 196–7.
6   Hölderlin 1988: 83; see Dastur 2000: 80–1.
7   On this topic see Kaufmann 1968: 135; Eagleton 2003: 5.
8   Hall 2000a: xxvi–vii; see also Croally 1994.
9   North (1579) in Wyndham 1895: 323. See further Hall 2002: 423.
10 In the translation of Oporinus. Further Latin versions appeared in 1562 and in 1597. For discussion of their possible impact on English Renaissance drama, see Schleiner 1990 and Ewbank 2005.

11   Mueller 1980: 178–9; Flashar 1991: 131–2.

12   Trilse 1975: 144–50; McDonald 1992: 36.

13   See O'Donhohoe 2005: 251–6.

14   For a technical discussion of the staging of the gods in Greek tragedy see Mastronarde 1990.

15   For examples, see e.g. Trendall and Webster 1971: nos. III.3.24, III.3.28, III.3.44, III.4.1, III.4.2, III.5.6.

16   See the excellent remarks of Poole 2005: 27–9.

17   Macintosh 1994: 165–70; see also Lucas 1965: 181.

18   See Barish 1981.

19   Richards 1924: 245–8; for a bibliography on Christian concepts in Shakespeare see Bratchell 1990: 156–9.

20   Rutherford 1982; Gould 1983.

21   Antiphanes fragment 189.17–18 *Poetae Comici Graeci*.

22   So Steiner 1996: 543–6 and n. 9.

Chapter 2

Hardcore Tragedy

Ewan Fernie

This chapter argues that tragedy's great function throughout history is to induct human beings into what the French psychoanalytical philosopher Jacques Lacan calls "the Real": the most lively and profound plane of our experience. To see tragedy from this vantage point makes an immediate difference. For, whereas the traditional Aristotelian critic sorrows over what is lost and broken, Lacan sees the genre in terms of what is gained. Tragedy not only inaugurates new (self-)knowledge, it also proffers the existential payoff of a fuller and more vivid life. In case these sound like the familiar promises – or temptations – of religion, it's important to note that tragedy is what the late Jacques Derrida calls "religion without religion" (Derrida 2002): spirituality before it hardens into determinate dogmatic forms. Of course, to read tragedy as "spiritual" flouts prevailing critical assumptions. Contemporary critics tend to interpret tragedies as historical instantiations of ideology, and they partly are. But such readings evade the heart tragedy rips open and establishes as the truest thing in experience – as prior to, immanent in, and beyond human history considered as a series of specific social arrangements. This chapter tries to recover and adventure into tragedy's suppurating heart.

It also attempts to repossess some of the messy affective intensity of this most stirring and upsetting of art forms, and in the only way such intensities can be owned: by an embodied human self. The galloping professionalization of English Studies no doubt bars the bodily quiverings of the critic, and so does a narrowly historicist approach to literary texts, but what besides our bodily selves have we got with which to witness and explore the shocking power of tragedy? It's not just that pity, fear, recognition, etc., are bodily affects. In any really engaged response, tragedy rehearses the most piteous, fearful, and thrilling existential possibilities *as if for me*. And I take it as axiomatic that what I'm calling "hardcore tragedy" here – that is, tragedy at its most pure, uncompromising, and powerful – will as one of its most salient features seize the embodied minds of those who attend it. The critic's job, rather like that of the tragic protagonist in the theater, is in part to stand for – *to suffer for* – the shaken reading subject; no essay on, no assay of, hardcore tragedy that altogether fails to do this can hope to be convincing. Given the singularity of any aesthetic experience, critical idiosyncrasy isn't so much a barrier as the hallmark of this representative function. Only the most curiously particular response will stand for the curiosity and particularity of human responsiveness as such. Never fear – I'm not going to describe the fluctuating state of my glands or organs; but, in order to stress the primacy of tragedy's existential effect, and also as a small protest against the "science" and "business" models of objective "research" that are increasingly misapplied to "the humanities," I do hereby insist on my own shaken physical implication in what follows.

Among the array of recent critical approaches, it is psychoanalysis that has kept literature's existential flame and legacy alive, which is one reason why I take my first bearing toward tragedy from psychoanalytical thinking here. Sigmund Freud derived much of his thought from tragedy, and Lacan insists on what he calls "the tragic dimension of psychoanalytical experience" (Lacan 1999). Following Lacan, I've said tragedy transports us into "the Real." But what is real for Lacan? Certainly not the reality of the realist novel: a solid social world rendered present in each particular. Lacan contends that the social sphere is frail and delusive. He and his most important successor, Slavoj Žižek, have revived for our times the ancient religious distinction between what's really real and what we merely call "reality." Religious thinkers and artists have traditionally contrasted passing social forms with God's eternal essence; Lacan and Žižek oppose them to an original and abiding void of pure potentiality. They agree with their religious forebears that death is the place where what's contingent wears out and the ultimate is revealed. But whereas sacred texts and art best negotiate this passage from a dogmatic point of view, Lacan perceives that it is tragedy which best describes and makes manifest the kind of terrible but pregnant abyss that he and Žižek recognize as the wound gaping in the tragic heart of life.

According to Lacan, tragedy definitively differs from comedy in that it actually sets foot in the Real, which exceeds as much as it underlies ordinary day-to-day experience. The Real transcends comedy:

> the element in comedy that satisfies us, the element that makes us laugh, that makes us appreciate it in its full human dimension...is not so much the triumph of life as its flight, the fact that life slips away, runs off, escapes all those barriers that oppose it...
>
> (Lacan 1999: 314)

This slippery ineffability of the Real is borne out by Shakespeare's comic drama, where (as contemporary critics have often remarked) all sorts of anarchic energies are released into verbal and theatrical play only to be frustrated and lost in the restitution of established order at the end. But Lacan doesn't see the transcendence of the Real as a failure of comic form. Instead, he regards tracing the Real's flight as the essence and vocation of comedy; and, as he also says, if the comic hero in hopeless pursuit "trips up and lands in the soup, the little fellow nevertheless survives" (314). But there is humiliating pathos, of course, in being left in the soup with your empty butterfly net, and it is here that Lacan locates comedy's kinship with tragedy and the scope for their hybridization in tragicomedy.

Yet if earthbound comedy falls on its arse to watch the Real flutter off into some unutterable zenith, Antigone, Hamlet, and Macbeth themselves lift off, storm the Real, and incarnate it for us in their consequently transfigured persons: hence Lacan's bizarre, love-struck description of "the violent illumination, the glow of beauty" that "visibly emanates" from the eyelids of Antigone at her crisis. This "beauty effect," explains Lacan, is also a "blindness effect": a sublime recognition of what is happening to "this admirable girl" beyond symbolization (281). But such tragic apotheosis is no pristine humanist triumph, for the tragic climax of the attainment of the Real is also always accomplished by means of a *via negativa* into filth, pain, misery, and death. Whereas the traditional Aristotelian critic *discharges* our awareness of such things via catharsis, Lacan welcomes them as the painful aspect of who and what we most ultimately are.

According to Lacan's reading of *Antigone*, the heroine's violation of the social order tears a hole in her world. She performs illegal burial rights for her criminal brother, Polynices: a simple sprinkling of dust on his dead body. But what's amazing about this straightforward deed is that it's perfectly self-generated and free: "That's how it is because that's how it is," as Antigone says, with a shrug, to the outraged King Creon (278). Nothing will explain her act, not even her preexisting self. Writing after Lacan on *Antigone*, Žižek explains:

> the act is not simply something "I" accomplish – after an act, I'm literally "not the same as before." In this sense, we could say that the subject "undergoes" the act ("passes through" it) rather than accomplishes it: in it, the subject is annihilated and subsequently reborn.
>
> (Žižek 2000: 44)

Antigone's selfhood thus doesn't so much generate her act as her act generates a new, surpassingly free selfhood as a kind of epiphenomenon or blossom. In relation to Sophocles' play, Lacan proclaims "the advent of the absolute individual" (Lacan 1999: 278). This astonishing event is also discerned in Antigone's defense and affirmation of "the unique value of [her brother's] being without reference to any content, to whatever good or evil [he] may have done" (279). As Lacan puts it, "[t]hat purity, that separation of being from the characteristics of the historical drama he has lived through, is precisely the limit or *ex nihilo* to which Antigone is attached" (279). In short, *Antigone* discovers human being as such: so much for Harold Bloom's proclamation of Shakespeare's invention of the human (1998). But the perfected self which this severe attic play dramatizes is blank, perfectly disintricated from social and historical life. It's therefore extremely difficult to distinguish from the state of death, to which Antigone accordingly runs like a bride. As Lacan says, she "has been declaring from the beginning: 'I am dead and I desire death'." She ultimately paints herself as Niobe petrified. At which point, Coryphaeus sings: "You then are the half-goddess" (281). Antigone achieves an ecstatic identification with death that simultaneously inaugurates a radical and unprecedented humanism. She steps outside the circle of ordinary life and into an unearthly beyond. Nor is this paradoxical victory hers alone. "As a consequence of the tragic act," Lacan writes, "the hero sets free his adversary too." Thus it is that at the end of the play "Creon henceforth speaks loudly and clearly of himself as someone who is [also] dead among the living" (320).

Lacan's interpretation of *Hamlet* discovers the same tragic pattern of attaining the Real characterized as a strange blend of transcendence and death that he discerned in *Antigone*. The French thinker angrily castigates the immemorial critical fascination with Hamlet's supposed impotence: "Why on the threshold of the modern period would Hamlet bear witness to the special weakness of future man as far as action is concerned? I am not so gloomy and nothing apart from a cliché of decadent thought requires that we should be" (251). His more invigorating reading stresses "the hero's progress to his mortal rendezvous with his act," which Lacan portrays as ritualistically involving: it "has something in it of the moment at the end of the hunt when everyone moves in for the kill" (Lacan 1977: 29). This is because, for Lacan, Hamlet's deed – like Antigone's – emblematizes the nature and possibility of action itself; it gathers all deeds into its own queerly radiant aesthetic density. Indeed, Shakespeare expressly clothes it in what I have described elsewhere as "a metaphysics of rashness – an absolute now – wherein everything is gathered and staked upon a deed" (Fernie 2005: 209). Hamlet fulfils the paternal mandate but in so strange a way as to make his action utterly his own. His act transcends revenge; it is unprecedented, incalculable; it "defies augury" (*Hamlet*, 5.2.158).[1] Shakespeare's play casts action like a beam of light into the void. As with Antigone's act, this carries its agent with it, beyond social identity and support. The abstracted Hamlet of his own last act, who has puzzled most commentators, is therefore, quite literally, an alien. According to Lacan, authentic action is always, in Shakespeare's phrase, "dreadfully mortal" (*Measure for Measure*, 4.2.134–5): a concrete determination of the "death-drive." But "the undiscovered country" (*Hamlet*, 3.1.81), the void into which the act travels, is equally the primordial womb from which all human culture is born. Any authentic human action is tragic since it threatens death for the current order and self it departs from but it may rebound as the founding gesture of a new order and a new self. Tragedy therefore teems with a strange, undetermined incipience.

To recall Lacan's reading of tragedy seems salutary in the current critical context for a number of reasons. Where traditional criticism explains action in terms of character, historical criticism pushes back further, reading action in terms of contextual analogues and cultural factors. Lacan returns to us the possibility and seriousness of tragic action as such, in all its own proper historical, political, and philosophical ramification. Lacan also restores much of tragedy's ontological force and dignity. The ephemeral historical realities which are the main focus of current critical activity are exactly what tragedy transports us beyond. I say beyond, but the tragic reality revealed under Lacan's illumination both is and is not elsewhere. It's immanent. It haunts and hollows out all particular histories from within. It's the opposite of metaphysical inasmuch as its locus is the sphere of bodily disintegration and death. And yet, such degradation turns out paradoxically to harbor another, transcendent life. Lacan helps us to acknowledge and to think about the fact that tragedy very saliently is the genre where exaltation and degradation are braided so tightly together as to be virtually indistinguishable. According to Lacan, tragedy takes place "between two deaths" (Lacan 1999). The first, social death precedes our final biological demise, and it baptizes the subject into a new, more authentic form of being. And yet, we need to tread carefully here to avoid easing the triumph away from tragedy. Any tragic flourishing is as ineluctably bloodsoaked as the original flourishing of birth. Tragedy unites the best and worst as though they absolutely belong together – and perhaps, in some sense, they do: hence this deadly art's traditional preeminence among genres; hence the feeling that anything but tragedy just isn't the real thing at all.

I want to pause a bit over the difficult notion of "the Real" Lacan picks out of tragedy. Perhaps, instead of picturing the Real as what's paradoxically above and beneath social life, we should conceive of it as what runs together in the infinity surrounding the circle of the social. That at least removes the barrier between degradation and transcendence. The realist novel fills in the circle of the social; tragedy lays bare its eternal relationship with the disorderly beyond. Žižek tries to isolate the commonalities between abject and sacred versions of the Real by comparing two passages from Hegel.[2] The first, less known, is from the manuscripts of *Jenaer Realphilosophie*, and is about the "night of the world":

> The human being is this night, this empty nothing, that contains everything in its simplicity – an unending wealth of many representations, images, of which none belongs to him – or which are not present. This night, the interior of nature, that exists here – pure self – in phantasmagorical representations, is night all around it, in which here shoots a bloody head – there another white ghastly apparition, suddenly here before it, and just so disappears. One catches sight of this night when one looks human beings in the eye – into a night that becomes awful.
>
> (quoted in Žižek 1999: 29–30)

The hideous interiority described here corresponds very well with the image-breeding nightmare of tragedy, which always exceeds and often, in the immediacy of aesthetic experience, completely defeats cognition; indeed, the phrase "night of the world" is itself a powerful encapsulation of tragedy. Hegel's description also matches the chaos of infantile experience that, in Lacan's view, persists into and constantly unsettles more organized and reliable adult lives.

The second passage from Hegel to which Žižek points is much better known. It comes from the Preface to the *Phenomenology of Spirit* and describes the quintessentially transcendent human facility of thinking itself in terms that are strangely reminiscent of the "night of the world." For Hegel here, thought is a violent tearing-up of the sensuous manifold into "separated and non-actual" objects of thought. That such objects "should attain an existence of [their] own and a separate freedom" is, Hegel considers, testimony to "the tremendous power of the negative," which he also calls "the energy of thought, of the pure 'I'." But such violence calls for a novel and a complex aesthetic:

> Lacking strength, Beauty hates the Understanding for asking of her what she cannot do. But the life of the Spirit is not the life that shrinks from death and keeps itself untouched by devastation, but rather the life that endures it and maintains itself in it. It wins its truth only when, in utter dismemberment, it finds itself.
>
> (quoted in Žižek 1999: 30–1)

This, surely, describes the terrible spiritual beauty of tragedy, and we may now recognize in the Hegelian "night of the world" both the primordial chaos of experience *and* the primordial violence of thought which is the origin of all authentic action and civilization but which first disrupts and disorders experience again. Hamlet distinguishes the transcendent qualities of human being – "What a piece of work is a man! how noble in reason, how infinite in faculty..." – from its deadly abjection – "And yet, to me, what is this quintessence of dust?" (2.2.293–8) – but Hegel perceives that these are the intimately related predicates of a creature whose tragic essence and destiny is the violent negation of its own substance. Such negation can be achieved both in the graveyard and in the mind, as Hamlet finds out. Hegel concludes:

> It is this power, not as something positive, which closes its eyes to the negative, as when we say it is nothing or is false, and then, having done with it, turn away and pass on to something else; on the contrary, Spirit is this power only by looking at the negative in the face, and tarrying with it. This tarrying with the negative is the magical power that converts it into being. This power is identical with what we earlier called the Subject...
>
> (quoted in Žižek 1999: 30–1)

What is tragedy but tarrying with the negative to the end? And for Hegel this is the paradigm of human becoming, of subjectivity itself. Tragedy is, in this perspective, nothing less than the truest vale of soul-making.

What Lacan adds to Hegel's tragic philosophy is a specifically poststruc-
turalist understanding of the relationship between language (as the mechanism identical with thought) and negativity. According to Lacan, language
inaugurates a radical break in what he calls "the life of man" (Lacan 1999:
279). Žižek explains:

> We have reality before our eyes well before language, and what language does,
> in its most fundamental gesture, is – as Lacan puts it – *it digs a hole in it*, it
> opens up visible/present reality toward the dimension of the immaterial/
> unseen. When I simply see you, I simply see you – but it is only by naming
> you that I can indicate the abyss in you beyond what I see.
>
> (Žižek 2003: 70)

Thus, in Lacan's reading, "Antigone appears as . . . a pure and simple relationship of the human being to that of which he happens to be the bearer,
namely, the signifying cut that confers on him the indomitable power of
being what he is in the face of everything that may oppose him" (Lacan
1999: 282–3). This "signifying cut" is visible in Antigone's self-authorizing
act and in her declaration of her brother's value in spite of all he has done
and been. It is the power of human beings to *mean anything at all*. But this
power entails a kind of death: the utter erasure of all the rootedness and
specificity of Antigone's and Polynices' former selves. Lacan equally brings
the agony and the ecstasy of tragedy together in a single, specifically
linguistic formulation when he suggests that *Hamlet* ends when the Prince
of Denmark "manages to identify himself with the fatal signifier" (Lacan
1977: 30). Here Hamlet's belated action – which we will recall Lacan regards
as extraordinary and creative rather than as merely giving in to social
pressure – allegorizes the simultaneously death-dealing and life-giving
advent of human speech.

Lacan's readings of *Antigone* and *Hamlet* powerfully convey his understanding of tragedy as the art-form which arrives in the Real. But no tragedy
attains that "night of the world" more perfectly and tremendously than does
Macbeth, which the French thinker does not discuss. It even seems likely that
Hegel's description of the "night of the world" derives from the Scottish
Play, where it's literally true that "darkness doth the face of earth entomb
when living light should kiss it" (2.4.4–10), that "here shoots a bloody
head," "there another ghastly white apparition," which as quickly disappears. Consider Fuseli's astonishing renditions of the play in paint as exactly
such a dreadful phantasmagoria.

What *Macbeth* manages that *Antigone* and *Hamlet* do not is the thorough *embodiment* of the Real as a pervasive existential condition, a *terra damnata*, an entire world. We tend to think of *Macbeth* as a particularly headlong play but in fact it's full of generalizations that intensify and entrench as much as they broaden the tragic effect because of their concrete precision and resonance with the original tragic act. That act is predestined. It is waiting for Macbeth – no, not even waiting, rather it is pressing with inexorable force back into the present:

> My thought, whose murder yet is but fantastical,
> Shakes so my single state of man, that function
> Is smother'd in surmise, and nothing is
> But what is not.
>
> (1.3.138–41)

The thane's fantasy of absolute action, of all being gathered, concentrated into a single deed – "that but this blow / Might be the *be-all and end all*" (1.7.4–5, my emphasis) – speaks expressly, as *Antigone* and *Hamlet* do not, for tragedy's ambition to epitomize human life as such. As Macbeth says later, "Who could refrain, / That had a heart to love, and in that heart / Courage to make's love known?" (2.3.113–15). He speaks these words in a context which makes them a lie, but perhaps they more truthfully refer back to Duncan's murder? Macbeth can't but do that deed; it is perhaps literally irresistible. And the love of which he speaks might be the love of possibility which, according to Lacan, always inheres in the transgressive tragic act and which involves a certain murderousness in forsaking and contravening what is.

But killing Duncan throws the whole world into Hell, as the play makes clear from the very beginning. Note the extraordinarily powerful and insistent generality and essentialism – the, as it were, *reverse religiosity* – of the first witness's response:

> O horror, horror, horror,
> Tongue nor heart cannot conceive nor name thee.
>
> (2.3.59–60)

> Confusion now hath made his masterpiece.
> Most sacrilegious murder hath broke ope
> The Lord's anointed Temple and stole thence
> The life o'th'building.
>
> (2.3.62–5)

Approach the Chamber and destroy your sight
With a new gorgon.

(2.3.68–9)

Banquo and Donalbain, Malcolm awake!
Shake off this downy sleep, death's counterfeit,
And look on death itself

(2.3.72–4)

up, up and see
The great doom's image

(2.3.74–5)

Malcolm, Banquo,
As from your graves rise up, and walk like sprites,
To countenance this horror.

(2.3.75–7)

It's as if by means of Duncan's death Macbeth has scratched away the flimsy surface of the world to reveal the Lacanian void raging beneath. The sight of this new gorgon, death itself, the great doom's image drains all being from its beholders: Banquo, Donalbain, Malcolm, whomsoever else. Thus when Donalbain asks, "What is amiss?," Macbeth answers for everybody, himself included:

You are, and do not know't:
The spring, the head, the fountain of your blood
Is stopped, the very source of it is stopped.

(2.3.93–6)

Thereafter Scotland increasingly takes on the contours of Macbeth's hideous deed, and the great bard or chronicler of this is the critically underrated Ross. A falcon, towering in her pride of place, is killed by a mousing owl; Duncan's horses – beauteous and swift, the minions of their race – break their stalls, fling out, contending against obedience, as if they would make war with humankind, and end by eating each other (see the conversation between Ross and the old man in 2.4). As Ross puts it in his most agonized statement of the theme:

Alas, poor country,
Almost afraid to know itself. It cannot
Be called our mother but our grave, where nothing
But who knows nothing is once seen to smile;

> Where sighs and groans and shrieks that rent the air
> Are made, not marked; where violent sorrow seems
> A modern ecstasy. The dead man's knell,
> Is there scarce asked for who, and good men's lives
> Expire before the Flowers in their caps,
> Dying or ere they sicken.
>
> (4.3.165–74)

Here is the "death-drive" nationalized. In its own terms, *Macbeth* memorizes another Golgotha (cf. 1.2.40): one in which Christ does not rise. As Ross testifies above, all life, good, smiles, signification, and distinction fail in such a world. In the purity of its negativity, *Macbeth* goes beyond Lacan's readings of *Antigone* and *Hamlet*. And yet, no play does more to exemplify the allure of the Real at its worst; no play more strangely dramatizes and solicits the Hegelian virtue of "tarrying with the negative." The womb is a tomb in *Macbeth*, but the tomb is also – somehow – a womb, and the longed-for redemption and restoration come as a killing disappointment. Who really prefers Malcolm? In its untinctured and yet magnetic negativism, *Macbeth* seems the ultimate hardcore tragedy.

And we may well ask: what strange and terrible spirituality follows from this?

Though Ross describes the tragic cataclysm of Shakespeare's Scottish play as a specifically modern ecstasy, most modern tragedy falls short of the attainment of the tragic Real we have seen in *Antigone*, *Hamlet*, or *Macbeth*. To move from historically distant tragic art to the scope for tragedy in the present is to confront a difficult and important problem. On the one hand, the aesthetic experience of tragedy is incommensurably different from real-life tragic experience. On the other, as we have seen, tragedy is written out of and works to reveal the most terrible realities of life. It may be that the Real is generally sidestepped in contemporary Western culture. Žižek comments, for instance, on the "derealization" of the horrors of 9/11:

> while the number of victims – 3,000 – is repeated all the time, it is surprising
> how little of the carnage we see – no dismembered bodies, no blood, no
> desperate faces of dying people...in clear contrast to reporting on Third
> World catastrophes, where the whole point is to produce a scoop of some
> gruesome detail: Somalis dying of hunger, raped Bosnian women, men with
> their throats cut. These shots are always accompanied by an advance warning
> that "some of the images you will see are extremely graphic and may upset

children" – a warning which we never heard in the reports on the WTC collapse. Is this not yet further proof of how, even in this tragic moment, the distance which separates Us from Them, from their reality, is maintained: the real horror happens *there*, not *here*.

(Žižek 2002: 13)

Such repression, of course, causes considerable strain, and there are moments when it shows, as in Peter Weir's *The Truman Show* or Philip K. Dick's *Time out of Joint*, where reality is exposed as a fake to keep people happy (cf. Žižek 2002: 13). In this context, tragedy acquires a special vocation for stripping the Real.

There are a number of reasons why it has largely failed to do so. Because it tends to be historicist, modern tragedy typically conceives of and embodies the tragic in terms of the lethal conjuncture of cultural contingencies. The Dickens of *Bleak House* and Kafka are its great progenitors, and many modern novels, from Hardy's *Jude the Obscure*, to Richard Wright's *Notes of a Native Son*, to Margaret Atwood's *The Handmaid's Tale*, extend a pattern whose theoretical laureate is Michel Foucault. Such tragedy has real aesthetic conviction and force inasmuch as it gives bitter dues to the power of error and accident to post men and women to ultimate destinies. The individual becomes a suffering victim. Agency is transferred to faceless and malign historical forces. But what is lost is the power of a calamitous deed to vaporize historical conditions and reveal a more naked and profound stratum of experience: much of the lingering power of *Macbeth* is vested in the uncanny feeling at the end that "this dead butcher and his fiend-like queen" hold sway in spite of their deaths and Malcolm's historical triumph (5.11.35). To the extent that the suffering of characters like Jude or Wright's Bigger Thomas is specifically the pain of being excluded, it does light up a place beyond cultural history. Jude and Bigger dwell exactly on the supercharged fringe of ordinary existence that Lacan describes as "between two deaths," alive and yet without any positive social identity to call their own. But modern tragedy implicitly cherishes another order, one which will right the wrongs of the past and absorb such figures and their sufferings within its ethically pristine novelty. Suffering in the outer darkness is perhaps the ultimate thing in the partly atavistic Hardy but Jude, breaking his nose on the shut college gates, wants in. As we have seen, classical and Shakespearean tragedy are more radical and disturbing. Antigone, Hamlet, and Macbeth, each in their different ways, step out onto the bloodsoaked heath of hardcore tragedy, and stake all their being there.

Another reason why much modern tragedy has largely failed to match its classical and Shakespearean heritage is the tendency of late-capitalist liberal democracy to proliferate and valorize differences – and if this is obvious enough in liberal democracy, it is also seen in capitalism's spicing up the market with "ethnic" or "gay" products and cultivating cultural minorities as special-interest consumer groups. This valorization of differences makes it impossible to embody human possibility and destiny in a single figure in the manner in which *Macbeth*, for instance, reveals the sovereign individual in the actual sovereign. The solution offered by works such as Tony Kushner's *Angels in America* is to establish a range of characters diverse and open-ended enough to suggest something of the infinite possibility of human being and experience. The tragedy is that such possibility is "cabin'd, cribb'd, confined" (*Macbeth*, 3.4.23) by social organization and by mortality, experienced in *Angels in America* as the ravages of the HIV/AIDS crisis. It's true that Kushner's play confesses the limits of liberal tolerance and calls for unity and solidarity in difference, but no one character can speak for difference as such without contravening it. This sort of tragedy has kaleidoscopic range but lacks concentrated intensity, whereas *Macbeth* has both, inasmuch as each detail of its panorama reflects and reveals the original crisis.

Of course some of the best modern tragedy, like *Antigone* or *Macbeth*, does reach through cultural and historical contingency and into the heart of the Real. In J. M. Coetzee's *Disgrace*, for example, David Lurie's patrician exhaustion as a university lecturer in "the new South Africa" leads him to the profound final scene when, divested of all historical identity, he bears a sick dog tenderly towards its death as one animal sharing absolutely in the last gasp of another. This goes further than the traversal of historical, cultural, and racial differences the times require. It recalls and extends Lear's filial agony over Cordelia, and even Mary's over the dead Christ, as though the paradoxical vocation of humanity at full ethical stretch were to reach beyond the human. *Disgrace*, for all its rigorous and upsetting observation of personal and political suffering, is finally a hopeful book; it shares some of the strange incipience which Lacan discerns in *Antigone*.

Philip Roth's *American Pastoral* is more crushingly negative. The innocent seedtime and flourishing of the Levov family is epitomized in the athletic, professional, financial, cultural, and marital successes of the handsome and strikingly Aryan "Swede" Levov. It resonates with the happiness of a generation of upwardly mobile, increasingly integrated Jewish-Americans but is literally blown to bits, along with a local post office in the expensive arcadian suburb where "the Swede" has settled down with his family, by his daughter, the ironically named Merry. Vietnam's behind this, and so's the child's stutter; but Roth takes care that nothing explains it. The Levovs are acting out, with attic economy and purity, the twists and turns of the tragic destiny of their nation, a tragedy of the mutability of happiness, which reaches into the emptiness to which history always returns. *American Pastoral* retains a truthful fidelity to what is broken and doesn't perceive any life stirring or glowing in the wreckage. More plainly than any other work considered here, it insists on the intolerable cost of gaining the tragic Real. This is its sober question: in spite of the ennobling, even soul-conferring possibilities of "tarrying with the negative," who would honestly choose to do so?

I have briefly discussed these two novels because they seem to me particularly fresh and powerful modern embodiments of tragedy. And yet, both works see their respective tragedies from the sidelines, just as Tom Stoppard regards *Hamlet* in *Rosencrantz and Guildenstern Are Dead*. Levov is, as it were, someone who flourished under Duncan but lived on, unfortunately for him, to experience the devastating consequences of Macbeth's reign; Lurie is more of a Gloucester than a Lear, a cynical survivor who rubbed along all right under the old king only to be shocked into a tragic awakening when times went bad. What's missing in both books is the primal scene – the equivalent cataclysm to Lear's rage or the murder of Duncan. Merry Levov's terrorism is the counter-example that proves the point because it's treated from such a contemptuous distance: Roth refuses to endow it with any originality or even agency. To the extent that even these two powerful novels fail to capture the lightning bolt of an original tragic deed, they remain irredeemably minor compared with the great tragedies of Antigone, Hamlet, and Macbeth.

Modern tragedy has generally found it hard to realize or entertain the possibility of the tragic act. Hence Hamm's wistful quotation from *The Tempest* in *Endgame*: "Our revels now are ended" (Beckett 1964: 39). Hence, too, Estragon in *Waiting for Godot*: "Nothing happens, nobody comes, nobody goes, it's awful!" (Beckett 1988: 41). Of course "awful" here has both its demotic sense of generalized negativity and its older, more exact flavor of the sublime (p. 41). But the sublime in Beckett is a negative, ironic, and secondary sublime of endless exhaustion and belatedness. And yet this general omission of the tragic act from modern tragedy is especially curious if Alain Badiou is right that the key feature of the twentieth century is what he calls "the passion for the real [*la passion du réel*]" (see Žižek 2002: 5). Žižek explains:

In contrast to the nineteenth century of utopian or "scientific" projects and
ideals, plans for the future, the twentieth century aimed at delivering the thing
itself – at directly realizing the longed-for New Order. The ultimate and
defining moment of the twentieth century was the direct experience of the
Real as opposed to everyday social reality – the Real in its extreme violence as
the price to be paid for peeling off the deceptive layers of reality.

(Žižek 2002: 5–6)

If this is the case, then the preceding century is the tragic epoch *par excellence*,
and Žižek further suggests that "the passion for the Real" is renewed in
the fundamentalist terror of our own time (9). Why then does Lacan – why
should *we* – have to look back to ancient and Shakespearean precedents
when we want "the thing itself," that is, a really hardcore tragedy?

Perhaps the tragic act eludes us because it's too immanent and undigested
in recent experience. Where it does appear, it tends to do so in terms of the
sufferings of the victims. D. M. Thomas's *The White Hotel* is a good example
of this. And in much modern tragedy there's a certain sacralization of
victimhood. This is partly a result of the late cultural sympathy and responsibility for oppressed minorities: the marginal has become central. But it's
also because of the intimate access to the Real that goes along with historical
abjection. Toni Morrison's novel of slavery, *Beloved*, is a profound exploration
of this: the richness of the protagonist Sethe's experience is one of the chief
pleasures of the book, and *Beloved* is a bravely complex novel because any
politically progressive artist's avowal of the Real in historical sufferings runs
the risk of glamorizing the conditions she's protesting against.

But what's much rarer than suffering in modern tragedy is any real
representation of the act or agency that effects it. A number of disfigured
victims acquired an unenviable temporary publicity in the aftermath of the
London bombings on July 7, 2005 but, as we have seen, Žižek argues that
the more "original" and devastating bombing of 9/11 was softened and
obscured in the reporting. Sethe kills her baby in *Beloved*, but this is a
consequence of her victimhood: a last-ditch attempt to *save* her baby; we
certainly don't see the diabolical deed of enslavement clearly or from within.
Like Sethe, Antigone and especially Hamlet are reactive, but they are not
themselves victims as she is; and that Macbeth isn't a victim at all only
underlines the terrible purity of his tragic agency. As I observed above, Roth
keeps us resolutely outside of Merry Levov's terrorism in *American Pastoral*.
Ironically, Salman Rushdie does imagine what it's like to be a terrorist in *The
Satanic Verses*, but the furious reaction of hard-line Islamists to the novel

made Rushdie a liberal *cause célèbre* and spared his readers any real confrontation with this. In *Four Quartets*, T. S. Eliot famously suggested that humankind can't bear too much reality, but the particular reason for artistic avoidance of the "passion for the Real" that, according to Badiou, has possessed our recent history is surely the repellently demonic forms that passion has taken? Nazism is the axiomatic case. In the face of such horror, Žižek asks, "Is the 'passion for the Real' as such, then, to be rejected?" But he answers: "Definitely not, since, once we adopt this stance, the only remaining attitude is that of refusing to go to the end, of 'keeping up appearances'." According to Žižek, "[t]he problem with the twentieth-century 'passion for the Real' was not that it was a passion for the Real, but that it was fake passion whose ruthless pursuit of the Real behind appearances was *the ultimate stratagem to avoid confronting the Real*" (Žižek 2002: 24; original emphasis). And it does seem reasonable to say that, instead of confronting the abyssal negativity of the Real in themselves, and in all human culture, and taking this as warrant for a genuinely new social program, in a gesture as lazy as it was lethal the Nazis displaced it onto the Jews.

After the horrors of the twentieth century and the terrorism that characterizes the new millennium, a recoil from the Real is understandable. But we should perhaps admit the opposite reaction: to the extent that any such atrocities are, however perversely, animated by the "passion for the Real," they make that passion all the more hideously interesting. Thomas Mann's great novel *Doctor Faustus* registers a tragic and mysterious resonance between the aberrant extremity of Nazism and the artistic apotheosis of its hero, Adrian Leverkühn. And yet, the Real solicits our best instincts as well: after all, a passion for the Real is very simply a passion for truth; and, if Lacan and Žižek are right, the universality of the Real in fact is beyond "ethnic cleansing" and tribal politics and represents an immanent chance for something better. This complex magnetism of the Real in the present suggests we could be on the brink of a new era of great tragedy. But it's a rare artist that goes so far as Shakespeare or Sophocles. To my mind at least, one who does is Cormac McCarthy. The remainder of the chapter will be devoted to the peculiarly intense "passion for the Real" which shows through his astonishing novel *Blood Meridian* and perhaps exposes a certain defensive idealism or sentimentality in Lacan's and Žižek's presentations of the tragic dimension of art and life.

Blood Meridian is a late successor to *Macbeth*. It's the tragic novel that might have been written by Shakespeare's Ross: it embodies the Real as a topography – *as all the world* – with luminous and detailed insistency. In *Macbeth*, Ross's speeches reincarnate Scotland as it is revealed in Duncan's murder. In *Blood Meridian*, the reverse is true: violence emanates like heat from the landscape. To this extent, McCarthy's book isn't so much a particular tragedy as it is a voyage into tragedy's womb. For all the specificity of its mid-nineteenth-century Mexican/American borderland setting, *Blood Meridian* turns its back on the social world where history matters:

> Only now is the child finally divested of all that he has been. His origins are become remote as is his destiny and not again in all the world's turning will there be terrains so wild and barbarous to try whether the stuff of creation may be shaped to man's will or whether his own heart is not another kind of clay.
>
> (McCarthy 1992: 4–5)

The image insinuated here of clay sculpting clay brilliantly encapsulates tragedy's characteristic revelation of simultaneously degraded and exalted mortal conditions. *Blood Meridian*'s plot ultimately is the purely archetypal one of the voyage. Its narrative becomes aimless and confused and its characters are set adrift in a Wild West become the naked plain on which the Real flourishes. It does so in rocks, stones, and trees, in fire, light, and cold, and in the nameless things of the wilderness, as well as in the violence and minds of men to which all this mysteriously corresponds. McCarthy's book is perhaps the fullest expression of the Hegelian "night of the world" in literary history.

Antigone, *Hamlet*, and *Macbeth* enact stories of the terrible attainment or advent of the Real, but all of *Blood Meridian* is set there, on a transposed tragic heath which, page after page, lays bare the conditions of existence:

> They rode on and the sun in the east flushed pale streaks of light and then a deeper run of color like blood seeping up in sudden reaches flaring planewise and where the earth drained into the sky at the edge of creation the top of the sun rose out of nothing like the head of a great red phallus until it cleared the unseen rim and sat squat and pulsing and malevolent behind them. The shadows of the smallest stones lay like pencil lines across the sand and the shapes of the men and their mounts advanced elongate before them like strands of the night from which they'd ridden.
>
> (45)

Where Shakespeare proclaimed "much virtue in 'if' " (*As You Like It* 5.4.92), McCarthy's keyword is "like" and here it negotiates a typically subtle passage into metaphysical regions. In the first sentence, its usage infuses a natural sunrise with an obscene and bloody demonic body; in a way reminiscent of the tomb/womb in *Macbeth*, this rises out of nothing. Also typical of tragedy is the perversity with which the protagonists ride away from the light. In the second sentence, "the shadows of the smallest stones lay like pencil lines upon the sand" is precisely material. The next usage transposes this into "the shapes of the men and their mounts advanced elongate before them like strands of the night from which they'd ridden," but shadow hereby becomes night's substance unnaturally trespassing into day, as in *Macbeth*. In "like tentacles to bind them to the darkness yet to come," the specific darkness of night turns into something more vague and ultimate, but something that is nevertheless palpably hooked by McCarthy's now uncannily incarnate shadows. As a whole the passage embodies humanity's brief voyage under a bloody star from and to such profound and yet actual darkness. Shameless poetic assays at such revelation succeed each other in rhapsodic succession in this book, remembering and reasserting the sheer aesthetic authority and power of offering some new-minted image for all experience. The "modern ecstasy" Ross announced in *Macbeth* is amply fulfilled here, thanks to McCarthy's gift for visionary prose.

And amid such a welter of visions there is no danger of crudely hypostasizing. McCarthy's "like" enables a metonymic epistemology that's never done, and from which the Real emerges as both vividly present and beyond knowledge. Even when *Blood Meridian* dispenses with "like," it incorporates the uncertainty of simile into its importunately metaphysical conceits, as in this particularly gruesome example:

> The way narrowed through rocks and by and by they came to a bush that was hung with dead babies. They stopped side by side, reeling in the heat. These small victims, seven, eight of them, had holes punched in their underjaws and were hung so by their throats from the broken stobs of a mesquite to stare eyeless at the naked sky. Bald and pale and bloated, larval to some unreckonable being.
>
> (McCarthy 1992: 57)

Like such small pupating corpses, almost every sentence in *Blood Meridian* is ominously pregnant with the unutterable, and conveys more in phenomena than it can say. The Real is present in its inexhaustible singularity in this book, irreducible not just to any social, ethical, or political rationalization but to any of its own particular appearances. Here the real mystery of tragedy returns with a vengeance.

And yet *Blood Meridian* doesn't merely leave us foundering in the midst of an aesthetic opacity. It proclaims a certain, troubling ethics of the Real.

Nor is this just a descent into what Hamlet calls "bestial oblivion" (4.4.30) for – as is also the case in Hegel, and in classical and Shakespearean tragedy – bedrock is the wellspring of the soul. Thus is shadow, in McCarthy's visionary idiom, the mark of death which at the same time visibly leans toward a separate spiritual life. It betokens humankind's ultimate origin in and betrothal to night in the description quoted above, but elsewhere it casts out other metaphysical possibilities:

> They descended the mountain, going down over the rocks with their hands outheld before them and their shadows contorted on the terrain like creatures seeking their own forms.
>
> (65)

> the slant black shapes of the mounted men stenciled across the stone with a definition austere and implacable like shapes capable of violating their own covenant with the flesh that authored them and continuing autonomous across the naked rock without reference to sun or man or god.
>
> (139)

As before, the physical precision of this combined with the rigorous unsureness of "like" saves it from whimsy, and indeed there is no simple spiritual consolation or sentimentality in this book. For the spiritual in *Blood Meridian* is always sourced in physical humiliation and violence, and this is often almost unbelievably intense. As if the dead babies weren't enough, consider the following:

> Already you could see through the dust on the ponies' hides the painted chevrons and the hands and rising suns and birds and fish of every device like the shade of old work through sizing on canvas and now too you could hear the pounding of the unshod hooves the piping of the quena, flutes made from human bones, and some among the company had begun to saw back on their mounts and some to mill in confusion when up from the offside of those ponies there rose a fabled horde of mounted lancers and archers bearing shields bedight with bits of a broken mirrorglass that cast a thousand unpieced suns against the eyes of their enemies. A legion of horribles, hundreds in number, half naked or clad in costumes attic or biblical or wardrobed out of a fevered dream with the skins of animals and silk finery and pieces of uniform still tracked with the blood of prior owners, coats of slain dragoons, frogged and braided cavalry jackets, one in a stovepipe hat and one with an umbrella and one in white stockings and a bloodstained weddingveil and some in headgear of cranefeathers or rawhide helmets that bore the horns of buffalo

and one in a pigeontailed coat worn backwards and otherwise naked and one in the armor of a spanish conquistador, the breastplate and pauldrons deeply dented with old blows of mace or sabre done in another country by men whose very bones were dust and many with their braids spliced up with the hair of other beasts until they trailed upon the ground and their horses' ears and tails worked with bits of brightly colored cloth and one whose horse's whole head was painted crimson red and all the horsemen's faces gaudy and grotesque with daubings like a company of mounted clowns, death hilarious, all howling in a barbarous tongue and riding down upon them like a horde from a hell more horrible yet than the brimstone land of christian reckoning, screeching and yammering and clothed in smoke like those vaporous beings in regions beyond right knowing where the eye wanders and the lip jerks and drools.

(52–3)

The horror of this has everything to do with its demonic deconstruction of order. It's a vision of chaos which in its mockery of form parodies various kinds of aesthetic work: mythical ("fabled"); pictorial ("like the shade of old work through sizing on canvas"); musical ("piping"); dramatic ("war-drobed"). It's the defeat of all "dreamwork" ("out of a fevered dream"). It offends against generic decorum by blending comedy and tragedy into "death hilarious," and scrambles the national, historical, and social semiotics of dress into a sort of vomit. It also defaces beast and man, forsaking the crucial distinction between them. And yet, it remains horribly aesthetically compelling, and is even clothed in a negatively sacred aura, with McCarthy's consummating similes blending "death hilarious" with unfathomed spiritual depths ("a hell more horrible yet than the brimstone land of christian reckoning") and visionary seizures ("regions beyond right knowing where the eye wanders and the lip jerks and drools").

Part of the brilliance of the writing is to induct us into the dreadfully extended caesura that is inhabited by McCarthy's characters as they await what seems certain to be death in a curiously rapturous beholding of imminent enemies that is rendered as a seemingly unending noun phrase. Then, suddenly, they're upon us

like funhouse figures, some with nightmare faces painted on their breasts, riding down the unhorsed Saxons and spearing and clubbing them and leaping from their mounts with knives and running about on the ground with a peculiar bandylegged trot like creatures driven to alien forms of locomotion and stripping the clothes from the dead and seizing them up by the hair and passing their blades about the skulls of the living and the dead alike and

snatching aloft the bloody wigs and hacking and chopping at the naked
bodies, ripping off limbs, heads, gutting the strange white torsos and holding
up great handfuls of viscera, genitals, some of the savages so slathered up with
gore they might have rolled in it like dogs and some who fell upon the dying
and sodomized them with loud cries to their fellows. And now the horses of
the dead came pounding out of the smoke and dust and circled with flapping
leather and wild manes and eyes whited with fear like the eyes of the blind
and some were vomiting blood as they wheeled across the killing ground and
clattered from sight again. Dust stanched the wet and naked heads of the
scalped who with the fringe of hair below their wounds and tonsured to
the bone now lay like maimed and naked monks in the bloodslaked dust
and everywhere the dying groaned and gibbered and horses lay screaming.

(54)

Here the swift unmisgiving biblical narration is supplemented by similes
that work to convey the apparent unreality of such terror ("like funhouse
figures," "like creatures driven to alien forms of locomotion," "like maimed
and naked monks in the bloodslaked dust"). The whole is a visitation or
advent beyond ordinary understanding which is given a definitively and
heretically religious cast at the end:

With darkness one soul rose wondrously from among the new slain dead and
stole away in the moonlight. The ground where he'd lain was soaked with
blood and with urine from the voided bladders of the animals and he went forth
stained and stinking like some reeking issue of the incarnate dam of war herself.

(55)

Thus is the protagonist, known merely as "the kid," baptized into the tragic
morality of *Blood Meridian*.

He's a man of few words, although the words of the novel itself are often
ambiguously possessed by him according to the technique infelicitously named
by critics "free indirect discourse." I've already said that violence emanates like
heat from the desert in *Blood Meridian*, but a voice does emerge out of the
violence, the voice of one who, according to the pattern of McCarthy's brazen
nomenclature, is called "the judge." Unlike Duncan, Macbeth, Antigone, and
Hamlet, whose representative function is vested in their standing in the
symbolic order as members of the ruling family, the judge is the representative
and avatar of what goes down ineffably further than such order:

A great shambling mutant, silent and serene. Whatever his antecedents he
was something wholly other than their sum, nor was there system by which

to divide him back into his origins for he would not go. Whoever would seek out his history through what unravelling of loins and ledgerbooks must stand at last darkened and dumb at the shore of a void without terminus or origin and whatever science he might bring to bear upon the dusty primal matter blowing down out of the millennia will discover no trace of any ultimate atavistic egg by which to reckon his commencing.

(310–11)

Thus is history humiliated, and McCarthy's strange creature spins out an immanent and archly knowing tragic philosophy that accords with but also challenges that of Lacan and Žižek. In his system too, transcendence is indivisible from degradation and death, which is nothing less than the symbolic meaning of a "blood meridian" itself:

The way of the world is to bloom and to flower and die but in the affairs of men there is no waning and the noon of his expression signals the onset of night. His spirit is exhausted at the peak of his achievement. His meridian is his darkening and the evening of his day.

(147)

As Hegel and Lacan also recognized, human culture simply redoubles the violence of the Real. The judge rides with outlaws and shares in their experiences of bloody mayhem but he equally incarnates the originary violence of thought, system, civilization.

The judge tilted his great head. The man who believes that the secrets of the world are forever hidden lives in mystery and fear. Superstition will drag him down. The rain will erode the deeds of his life. But that man who sets himself the task of singling out the thread of order from the tapestry will by the decision alone have taken charge of the world and it is only by such taking charge that he will effect a way to dictate the terms of his own fate.
  I don't see what that has to do with catchin birds.
  The freedom of birds is an insult to me. I'd have them all in zoos.
  That would be a hell of a zoo.
  The judge smiled. Yes, he said. Even so.

(199)

But whereas Hegel and Lacan, and Žižek after them, maintain a certain separation between the Real's primordial violence and the humanizing and even spiritualizing violence of thought, language, and system which is indissociably related to it, the judge, by contrast, insists the consummation of humanity as it emerges from both the Real and the Symbolic is war. In this he seems the vessel of a bitter truth that has been evaded in recent Western culture:

> It makes no difference what men think of war, said the judge. War endures. As well ask men what they think of stone, war was always here. Before man was, war waited for him. The ultimate trade awaiting its ultimate practitioner. That is the way it was and will be. That way and not some other way.
>
> (248)

Any step away from the tragic Real of war in this book is therefore paradoxically dehumanizing: "If war is not holy man is nothing but antic clay" (307).

In *Blood Meridian*, violence is the only life, event, and ceremony. The world of the novel seems infinite in its vast physical panorama, and in its insistence that "every man is tabernacled in every other and he is in exchange and so in an endless complexity of being and witness to the uttermost edge of the world" (141); but it also seems appallingly narrow inasmuch as there are no women (save as victims and whores) and there is no love. And yet, the book is so powerfully realized, so full of crystalline images of life and death, that it provokes a strange resonance with experience as such. Take the case of love: troubling though it is to say so, is it not – if stripped of its sentimental aura – at least partly a creative form of violence, one which tears both lover and beloved out of context in an absolute forsaking of all else? The judge's terrible sermon finishes as follows:

> I tell you this. As war becomes dishonored and its nobility called into question those honorable men who recognize the sanctity of blood will become excluded from the dance, which is the warrior's right, and thereby will the dance become a false dance and the dancers false dancers. And yet there will be one there always who is a true dancer and can you guess who that might be?
>
> You aint nothin.
>
> You speak truer than you know. But I will tell you. Only that man who has offered up himself entire to the blood of war, who has been to the floor of the pit and seen horror in the round and learned at last that it speaks to his inmost heart, only that man can dance.
>
> Even a dumb animal can dance.
>
> The judge set the bottle on the bar. Hear me, man, he said. There is room on the stage for one beast and one alone. All others are destined for a night that is eternal and without name. One by one they will step down into the darkness before the footlamps. Bears that dance, bears that don't.
>
> (331)

It's a strange credo that endues violence with a tragic and indeed theatrical fullness and intensity that somehow burns forever; it also bleeds life without violence of all substance. And McCarthy substantially allows if he does not endorse it in *Blood Meridian*'s visionary final paragraph:

> And they are dancing, the board floor slamming under the jackboots and the fiddlers grinning hideously over their canted pieces. Towering over them all is the judge and he is naked dancing, his small feet lively and quick and now in doubletime and bowing to the ladies, huge and pale and hairless, like an enormous infant. He never sleeps, he says. He says he'll never die. He bows to the fiddlers and sashays backwards and throws back his head and laughs deep in his throat and he is a great favorite, the judge. He wafts his hat and the lunar dome of his skull passes palely under the lamps and he swings about and takes possession of one of the fiddles and he pirouettes and makes a pass, two passes, dancing and fiddling at once. His feet are light and nimble. He never sleeps. He says that he will never die. He dances in light and in shadow and he is a great favorite. He never sleeps, the judge. He is dancing, dancing. He says that he will never die.
>
> (335)

Here then, in an historical context that has weakened and diminished tragedy, is a hardcore tragedy indeed, one that tarries with the negative to the end and gives it a terrifyingly joyous new voice and presence. In *Blood Meridian*, tragedy's incipience and metaphysics is not in any way the warrant of a brighter future but is instead reinscribed in tragedy itself. This is a book of extraordinary and terrible tragic density. And, in its gesture of furiously revived essentialism, it pulls all experience back into tragedy's intense artifice. In the midst of the rather tired prejudice against essentialist thinking and almost universal liberal and academic handwashing over all forms of violence, it's a book which really confronts us with something.

Notes

1   All Shakespearean references are to *The Norton Shakespeare* edited by Stephen Greenblatt, Walter Cohen, Jean E. Howard, and Katharine Eisaman Maus (1997).

2   Žižek engages with Hegel's tragic philosophy rather than his schematic philosophy of tragedy. For the latter, see Hegel 1975.

Chapter 3

Tragedy and Disgust

Robert Douglas-Fairhurst

In *Pictures from Italy* (1846) Dickens describes his experience of attending a public execution in Rome. Having arrived in the square early in the morning, he reports, in order to be sure of getting a good view, he spent several hours observing the crowd, as they cheerfully gathered and gossiped, until with a blare of trumpets the condemned man ("Face pale; small dark moustache; and dark brown hair") emerged onto the scaffold:

> He immediately kneeled down, below the knife. His neck fitting into a hole, made for the purpose, in a cross plank, was shut down, by another plank above; exactly like the pillory. Immediately below him was a leathern bag. And into it his head rolled instantly.
>
> The executioner was holding it by the hair, and walking with it round the scaffold, showing it to the people, before one quite knew that the knife had fallen heavily, and with a rattling sound.
>
> When it had travelled round the four sides of the scaffold, it was set upon a pole in front – a little patch of black and white, for the long street to stare at, and the flies to settle on. The eyes were turned upward, as if he had avoided the sight of the leathern bag, and looked to the crucifix. Every tinge and hue of life had left it in that instant. It was dull, cold, livid, wax. The body also.
>
> There was a great deal of blood. When we left the window, and went close up to the scaffold, it was very dirty; one of the two men who were throwing water over it, turning it to help the other lift the body into a shell, picked his way as through mire. A strange appearance was the apparent annihilation of the neck. The head was taken off so close, that it seemed as if the knife had narrowly escaped crushing the jaw, or shaving off the ear; and the body looked as if there were nothing left above the shoulder.

Nobody cared, or was at all affected. There was no manifestation of disgust, or pity, or indignation, or sorrow. My empty pockets were tried, several times, in the crowd immediately below the scaffold, as the corpse was being put into its coffin. It was an ugly, filthy, careless, sickening spectacle; meaning nothing but butchery beyond the momentary interest, to the one wretched actor.

(Dickens 1957: 391)

The description of this "one wretched actor," like Dickens's later reference to the events as a "show" ("the show was over"), gives his account a theatrical cast that had long been a standard feature of execution reports, reflecting the performative nature of such public displays of justice.[1] (Compare Marvell's double-edged judgment on the beheading of Charles I: "thence the royal actor born / The tragic scaffold might adorn: / While round the armed bands / Did clap their bloody hands"; "An Horatian Ode upon Cromwell's Return from Ireland," Marvell 1972: 56). However, although there is no attempt on Dickens's part to suggest that the execution was unjust – he has already informed his readers that the pale young man was sentenced to death for beating a female pilgrim to death with her own staff – he is clearly alarmed that the other witnesses do not respond as thoughtfully or sympathetically as they should, as can be heard in that sudden switch from "the body" to "Nobody" ("the body looked as if there were nothing left above the shoulder. Nobody cared, or was at all affected"), as if there was not much difference between their reaction to the execution and the "dull, cold" corpse itself. Earlier in *Pictures from Italy* Dickens had devoted several pages to poking fun at the theatrical nature of Italian life, reporting it to be full of artifice and gaudy display, not least in the rituals of the Catholic church, which he describes with a mixture of amusement, bemusement, and sharp-tongued contempt. The execution falls into the same pattern: in a culture that cannot tell the difference between the real and the phony, Dickens implies, a beheading is not likely to stir up any more interest than the street entertainment provided by a busker or a juggler.[2] But Dickens's writing does more than criticize the audience's reactions; it also offers itself as an alternative. Notice, for example, how quickly he alters the narrative focus between general scene-painting and close-up details (flies settling on the decapitated head, or a cleaner daintily picking his way through the gore), and how quickly he jerks his tone away from the comic, with a flickering joke about the executioner's blade giving his victim the closest shave of his life, to the appalled: "an ugly, filthy, careless, sickening spectacle." Even his withdrawal into short, factual sentences

("There was a great deal of blood") registers his ambivalence about what he has witnessed, suggesting shock as well as indifference, controlled fury as well as chatty reportage. In this way, Dickens produces in his writing precisely the sort of ethical perspective his fellow-observers seem to have lacked; although "There was no manifestation of disgust, or pity, or indignation, or sorrow" from them, the uneasy switches between all these responses in his own account show the mixed feelings that such an event could and should produce in his readers.

Dickens is not alone in worrying that the spectacle of human suffering, far from provoking disgust, pity, indignation, or sorrow, might instead provoke little more than indifference. Tragic speakers, too, often find themselves wondering aloud how far they deserve the audience's concern, and whether or not they will receive it, as if half-aware that as theatrical characters it is their unavoidable fate to take pains to entertain us, to suffer for our art. "O, heavens," cries Marcus Andronicus as he watches his brother Titus collapse into the sad compulsions of revenge: "can you hear a good man groan/And not relent, or not compassion him?" (*Titus Andronicus* 4.1.122–3).[3] His appeal is to the gods, but tragedy often asks much the same question of its spectators, and of itself. How can we bear witness to events which are unbearable to the figure experiencing them? How can we be loyal to another person's pain, confronted by events which rupture the sufferer's capacity for rational and articulate thought, and at the same time make sense of it? The figure of the Auditor in Samuel Beckett's play *Not I* is described moving in response to the speaker's account of her unhappiness: a "simple sideways raising of arms from sides and their falling back," according to Beckett's stage direction, "in a gesture of helpless compassion" (Beckett 1984: 215). Both supplication and shrug, the movement is doubly a "gesture" in response to the speaker. One argument for the longevity of tragedy as a theatrical art form might be that it encourages us to consider how far we too are helpless in a world of suffering: it allows us to exercise our compassion on victims of our own making, while also teaching us how to bear witness to events in which we are powerless to interfere. And yet, as is clearly shown by Dickens's response to the execution in Rome, and in particular his description of the Italian public's lack of response, one possible danger with the theater, in which suffering is routinely depicted for our entertainment, is that it risks developing what is now commonly referred to as "compassion fatigue."[4] In the face of this threat, how has tragedy managed to remain such an enduringly lively and enlivening cultural form? My purpose here is to suggest that one way in which tragedy has successfully reinvented both itself and its audience is through its use of another piece of cultural thinking that involves similar negotiations between self and other, good and evil, life and death: the complex set of responses that cluster around disgust.

It is not surprising that Dickens's description should have gravitated toward pity, indignation, and sorrow – emotions which the theater has often been celebrated for depicting on stage and exercising in its audience. However, the appearance of disgust as the first item on his list is worth pausing over. "Disgust" is a difficult term to pin down, not least because it has been written about in such diverse ways as it has migrated across different disciplines. Appropriately for a concept that involves so much border-crossing and boundary-straddling, disgust has often found itself alternately joining and separating a broad range of ideas, from Mikhail Bakhtin's category of the "carnivalesque" (Bakhtin 1968) to Julia Kristeva's theory of "abjection" (Kristeva 1982). Particularly in the fields of anthropology and psychology, a number of writers have attempted to account for the functions of disgust and the cultural meanings it carries. Darwin devotes five pages of *The Expression of the Emotions in Man and Animals* to the topic, starting with the recollection of his "utter disgust at my food being touched by a naked savage" in Tierra del Fuego, and concluding that disgust – literally "distaste" – is inextricably bound up with our fears about being contaminated by contact with a foreign body (Darwin 1965: 256–7). Freud goes further still in arguing that disgust, like shame and morality, is one of the "reaction formations" built up by the unconscious in order to keep our desires in check: flinching away from sexual contact, he suggests, reveals the hold that repression has on our bodies as well as our minds (Freud 1985: 280). More recently, and more broadly, William Ian Miller's superb study *The Anatomy of Disgust* (1997) has made a powerful case for thinking that disgust animates many of the experiences and values that are central to human culture. From aesthetic judgments on tasteless art, through to ethical reflections on behavior that is vile or loathsome, "Disgust seems intimately connected to the creation of culture; it is so peculiarly human that, like the capacity for language, it seems to bear a necessary connection to the kinds of social and moral possibility we have" (Miller 1997: 18). If disgust is peculiarly human – and animals seem to be as immune to disgust as they are to embarrassment – it is also alone among the emotions in generating a "unique aversive style" (Miller 1997: 9), making it hard to account for the experience of disgust without one's descriptions being open to the accusation that they are equally disgusting, as if tainted by association. This style does not seem to be limited to a particular genre. Disgust shares significant points of contact with comedy, for example, which regularly turns the body's transgressions and failures into material for laughter, whether this is children finding nothing funnier than the sound of a classmate farting, or adults simultaneously displaying and displacing their sexual anxieties by telling one another dirty jokes. However, disgust is also close to the troubled heart of tragedy.

Aristotle's notion of catharsis, however incomplete it is as an account of the psychological effects of tragedy, does at least provide a helpful way of thinking about the ambivalent responses of its audience. Depicting events that are intended to evoke pity and terror, tragedy both attracts and repels; it asks us to approach with sympathy and recoil with alarm. A similar double movement is central to the experience of disgust. From diligently checking what emerges from our noses or bowels, to watching horror films which crawl with maggots and slime, we are regularly drawn toward what repels us. This is especially true of the spectacle of the human body being torn or mangled, as can be seen in Dickens's description of how he got "close up to the scaffold" but then drew back from the "sickening" sight. As the literary genre that is most centrally concerned with the vulnerability of the human body, tragedy is full of moments in which characters express their disgust at the frailties of the flesh, from the Duke of Cornwall plucking out the "vile jelly" of Gloucester's eyes in *King Lear* (3.7.81), to Hamlet's appalled fascination with the fleshy tangle of "incestuous sheets" and "the rank sweat of an enseaméd bed" (1.2.157; 3.4.82). And where tragedy engages most closely with such ideas, disgust is bound up with more than psychological or social anxieties; it is also a matter of literary style.

Shakespeare never uses the word "disgust" in his plays; it does not enter the English language until the seventeenth century, as part of a new self-consciousness over "taste" in everything from artistic appreciation to moral conduct. Even so, the concept of disgust, spread across a wide vocabulary of revulsion and loathing, is one that has always animated tragedy, a genre that is unstably situated within what Kierkegaard refers to as the "border category" between art and manners (Kierkegaard 1983). In part this is because it provides a set of ideas and a set of words for characters who are forced to come to terms with the fact that their physical capacities will never be adequate to their ideals or longings – as when King Lear responds to Gloucester's appeal to kiss his hand by saying, levelly, "Let me wipe it first; it smells of mortality" (4.5.129). But tragedy is also drawn to the beliefs and idioms associated with disgust because they are central to its own function within culture. Just as our disgust provides us with a way of coming to terms with everything which our senses find both fascinating and repellent, so tragedy allows us to finds terms for, and to come to terms with, the pain that our culture has created in the past and might create again. (Indeed, like disgust, tragedy implicitly ask us what we mean by terms such as "we" and "our culture" – terms which collapse precisely the sort of historical, geographical, and racial differences that tragedies so often seek to exploit.)[5] "What an enormous price man had to pay for reason, seriousness, control over his emotions," Nietzsche remarks, "How much blood and horror lies behind all 'good things!'" (Nietzsche 1956: 194). He is describing the barbaric and primitive urges that need to be kept in check in order for civil societies to function effectively, and suggesting that the invention of tragic characters responds to a deep-seated desire to act out all the desires and fears we normally have to repress; in Adrian Poole's words, "They represent all that we have had to overcome in the cause of culture and civilisation" (Poole 2005: 51). In this context, I want to suggest, disgust works to remind us at both an intellectual and visceral level of a past that we find both appealing and appalling. At the end of *The Tempest,* Prospero owns up to the monster he helped to create: "This thing of darkness I/Acknowledge mine" (5.1.278–9). He is referring to Caliban, but we might also say of tragedy: "this thing of darkness I acknowledge mine."

The Anatomy of Disgust

Disgust might seem an unusual choice for anyone in search of a common thread to link the diverse cultural productions collectively known as tragedy. However, there are good grounds for thinking that, like tragedy, disgust is central to our attempts to make sense of the world, both on and off the page; ethically and aesthetically, it is one of the key ways in which a culture defines its priorities, conventions, and acceptable transgressions.

Disgust provides a means of dividing up the world according to established conceptual schemes, of separating the pure from the impure, the safe from the defiling. It works like the body's radar, reminding us which physical substances we can use and which we should avoid, and at the same time it embodies our moral judgments about what is good and what is evil. According to Samuel Johnson, writing in *The Rambler,* "Vice ... should always disgust" (cited in Miller 1997: 179), and it is hard to express a moral judgment without using the lexicon of disgust, from Shakespeare's rich attraction to the language of abomination and loathing, to the more contemporary "that's revolting" or "you make me want to puke." Disgust asserts and preserves differences: the difference between me and you, which is why I can pick my nose but not your nose, and the larger differences of class and status, which is why historically it has been such a powerful political tool in encouraging discrimination, from medieval writings that linked the Jews with leprosy and well-poisoning, to Nazi propaganda that linked them with lice and excrement. Above all, disgust monitors the frontiers of the self, or what Erving Goffman calls its "territorial preserve," patrolling the precious but precarious boundaries that prevent our bodies from being invaded by what is dangerous or defiling (Goffman 1971). Disgust is therefore especially drawn to our orifices, where potentially hazardous substances can enter or exit. As Paul Rozin and April E. Fallon explain, the orifices are the checkpoints of the body, but also places of transition and magical transformation. Saliva in the mouth, snot in the nose, blood in the veins, feces in the colon, and so on, are benign if kept in their proper place, out of sight and mind, but what is safe inside us can become unsafe once it is on the outside:

> One's own body products have a peculiar status with regard to the self. Feces and urine in one's own body... do not elicit a disgust response. As soon as they leave the body, however, they become disgusting... although one is not disgusted by saliva in his or her own mouth, it becomes offensive outside of the body so that one is disgusted at drinking from a glass into which he or she has spit... The same is true for chewed food, which we accept in our mouths, but refuse to consume once we have spit it out.
>
> (Rozin and Fallon 1987: 26)

The mouth is an especially charged point of transition, not only because something that is in the mouth is in the body but can be expelled from the body, by spitting it out, but also because the mouth justifies disgust by finding separate words to account for the same substance – as Rozin's report uses "saliva" to describe what is in the mouth and "spit" for what has left it.

One way of thinking about disgust, then, is that it reflects our desire for classification and our anxiety about what threatens classification. The anthropologist Mary Douglas once famously defined dirt as "matter out of place." As she writes:

> Shoes are not dirty in themselves, but it is dirty to place them on the dining-table; food is not dirty in itself, but it is dirty to leave cooking utensils in the bedroom, or food bespattered on clothing... Dirt then, is never a unique,

isolated event. Where there is dirt, there is system. Dirt is the by-product of a systematic ordering and classification of matter, in so far as ordering involves rejecting inappropriate elements.

(Douglas 1966: 35)

To this extent, the toddler who proudly brings a full potty into a dinner party to show his mother what he has produced might make her wince, because here is a sharp example of matter out of place; but the wince helps to restore the adult systems of classification which the toddler briefly threatened: cognitively, if not physically, disgust puts things back in their place.

The fact that adults and children do not always wince at the same things reminds us that these systems are a matter of learned behavior as well as instinct, culture as well as nature. For example, Rozin reports that experiments confirm how surprisingly unpicky about their food very young children are:

The percentage of children under 2 years of age who put disgusting things in their mouths were as follows: 62% for imitation dog feces (realistically crafted from peanut butter and odorous cheese); 58% for a whole, small, dried fish; 31% for a whole sterilized grasshopper; and 8% for a sterilized lock of human hair.

(Rozin et al. 1986: 145)

However, it is not only children who remind us that our ways of dividing up the world are not all the same. Early anthropologists were shocked to discover the Sambian boys who must regularly fellate warriors in order to receive the strength of their semen, the Nuer who wash in cow urine, and the Zuñis whose rituals include eating the excrement of humans and dogs. Such examples seemed to suggest that cultures, too, grow up, and that disgust can therefore function as a way of defining and rejecting those aspects of a culture's past that it has outgrown, mixed with the fear that the roots of a culture might work more like the roots of a plant, hidden away while still sustaining visible growth. In this context, a response like Darwin's "utter disgust" at his food being touched by a savage helps to distinguish the observer from the historically as well as geographically other; it is a flinch that works in time as well as space.

Civilization and its Discontents

Tragedy often engages with this question of how much distance a particular society has succeeded in putting between itself and its atavistic earlier state, and the strength of its engagement can be gauged by the frequency with which it adopts words and concepts associated with disgust. In Aeschylus' *Eumenides*, for example, the Furies are described as "black and utterly repulsive," with "foul ooze" dripping from their eyes, and snoring "with breath that drives one back" (Grene and Lattimore 1992: 1.136).[6] When they are absorbed into the ground at the end of the play, the episode works to remind their original audience that the Athenian system of democratic justice supplanted, but was also built on, a more primitive code of blood revenge. In later tragedies, too, a lexicon of disgust is regularly used in order to enquire into the possibility that the savage and bloody past is still lurking under the surface of the supposedly civilized present, not least by revealing how often our beliefs and our words move at different speeds. For example, even a society that no longer believes literally in guilt as a form of pollution can retain a ghost of this belief in the shape of its metaphors, as one hears in Shakespeare's frequent recourse to the language of corruption and contamination, from the "damned spot" of blood in *Macbeth* (5.1.33) to the connections between lechery and disease in *Troilus and Cressida*: connections which spread out between the play's speakers like a stain. Similarly, one might notice how often Shakespeare returns to ideas of division which remain imaginatively powerful despite being intellectually outmoded. "The time is out of joint," laments Hamlet (1.5.189); "But let the frame of things disjoint," exclaims Macbeth (3.2.18). The plays take – and cause – pains to show us that it is people who do the disjointing, but the metaphor retains an unsettled echo of an earlier tragic era, a time when Athenian spectators could take more seriously than Shakespeare's contemporaries the idea that inner divisions accurately reflect outer divisions, families and bodies and minds being torn apart as a direct consequence of the gods being divided against themselves. But although an ancient language of ritual and pollution is historically "out of place" in *Macbeth* or *Hamlet*, it is also dramatically fitting, because it allows us to hear in these speakers' voices a conflict between the drag of primitive murderous impulses and the draw of more civilized values: an idea which both plays explore at the level of plot, but also build into their own language, as when Hamlet approaches Claudius at prayer ("O my offence is rank, it smells to heaven") with the intention of murdering him, and then recoils from the blunt consequences of revenge into a world of more measured reflection: "*And* now I'll do it, and so a goes to heaven,/And so am I revenged. That would be *scanned*" (my emphases) (3.3.74–5).

Even where this conflict is usurped by others within a play, disgust remains a key imaginative resource for tragic writers, because one central aim of tragedy which it shares with the workings of disgust is to affirm social values through what cognitively or physically threatens them. In *Miasma*, his account of the role played by ideas of pollution and purification in ancient Greek thought, Robert Parker describes a culture's beliefs about what is defiling as "by-products of an ideal of order" (Parker 1983: 46). The same could be said of tragedies: they too are by-products of an ideal of order, allowing us to demolish in fiction our most cherished social structures and values without committing ourselves to a similar demolition of them in fact. Tragedy, one might say, is an expression of civilization and its discontents. As a number of anthropological critics have pointed out, tragedy often attempts to enforce neat oppositions of pure/impure, good/bad, human/nonhuman, and so on, so that when Oedipus commits incest, he is expelled from the society whose rules he has unwittingly transgressed, as one might spit out a prohibited item of food. But tragedy also shows how easily these oppositions shade into one another, so dramatizing the worrying vulnerability of the civilized structures in which we place so much, perhaps too much, trust. Like disgust, then, tragedy offers itself as a response to cultural fault lines and border disputes. Like disgust, sometimes what it discovers is so shocking that it breaks down basic structures of language and thought altogether, as Lear's revulsion at his daughters' unnatural behavior makes his speech first cast around for definitions and then shudder to a halt: "There's hell, there's darkness, there is the sulphurous pit, burning, scalding, stench, consumption. Fie, fie, fie; pah, pah!" (4.5.124–5). More often still, expressions of disgust in tragedy indicate the speaker's recognition that all previous certainties about the world and his or her place in it now seem questionable and flawed. If pollution is "matter out of place," tragedy offers glimpses of a world in which it is not only matter, but also everything that matters – truth, justice, compassion – that has been shunted out of its proper place; in these contexts, expressions of disgust work like ethical signposts, allowing individual characters and their audience to check their bearings in a world where the line between good and evil, or right and wrong, starts to look simultaneously like a division and a continuum.

To take just one example: in Sophocles' *Philoctetes*, the hero has been abandoned on the isle of Lemnos because of the stench of his wounded foot – a wound he suffered when he accidentally trespassed on holy ground, and was bitten by a snake sent as a punishment by the gods. Neoptolemus is sent to bring him back to Troy, because it has been prophesied that only with Philoctetes' bow can Troy fall: in one of those slowly unfurling ironies so beloved of Greek mythographers, the man whose sufferings resulted from his pollution of holy ground must be reabsorbed into society if its own wound, opened up by the conflict in Troy, is eventually to be healed. Philoctetes' wound is described in appalled and appalling detail: it runs with pus and blood; it makes him faint with pain; it makes other people faint with nausea. No one can come near him. It is only after struggling against his feelings of revulsion that Neoptolemus manages to approach, and at this point his disgust turns inward, finally confessing that he has been sent by the scheming Odysseus:

> NEOPTOLEMUS: I do not know what to say. I am at a loss.
> PHILOCTETES: Why are you at a loss? Do not say so, boy.
> NEOPTOLEMUS: It is indeed my case.
> PHILOCTETES: Is it disgust at my sickness? Is it this
>   that makes you shrink from taking me?
> NEOPTOLEMUS: All is disgust when one leaves his true nature
>   and does things that misfit it.
>   (Grene and Lattimore 1992: 2.442)

The reference to shrinking back is there to remind the play's original audience of why, at the level of immediate physical response, Philoctetes is disgusting: he smells. The Greeks enjoyed thinking of the gods as aromatic beings, and delighting in sweet fragrances, so Philoctetes' bad smell indicates the nature and seriousness of his offense; it reduces him from a man to the status of an ill-smelling beast. But human smells also alert us to the fact that we cannot help releasing small parts of ourselves into other people's noses and lungs; they remind us on a physiological level how closely involved we are in one another's lives, that being merely a spectator isn't always an option. Philoctetes' smell, then, proves that he is not irrevocably cut off from his fellow men, just as the references to "disgust" by both Neoptolemus and Philoctetes prove that the same mouths which register divisions can also help to bridge them. The word in Greek, *dyschereia*, has a rich range of meanings, used to refer to everything from unpleasant food to offensive people and troublesome questions. When Philoctetes uses the word, he imagines that he is the source of all disgust on Lemnos; what he gets instead is a thoughtful turn upon the word, a linguistic acceptance which anticipates his own final reintegration into civilization. The slight shift of emphasis registers the need to engage critically with other people without turning away from them: always a temptation held out by Greek tragedy, with its choric structure of strophe and antistrophe (turn and counter-turn), its apotropaeic attempts to turn away trouble by the rituals of staging, its individual turns of verse. But their shared use of "disgust" also shows how easily Neoptolemus could have agreed with Philoctetes' self-assessment and turned away. Things could have happened otherwise.

"List, List, O List"

The ability to transcend disgust for another person's body could serve as one definition of love, from the mother who does not wrinkle her nose at changing her baby's nappy, to the lover who does not retch at the prospect of having someone else's tongue inside his or her mouth. This is not to say that love is simply the suspension of all the normal disgust rules. It is certainly true that the "territorial preserve" of the self will be breached by anybody we allow to get close to us, either physically or emotionally, and that part of this closeness will involve the "strippings, exposures, and knowledges upon which intense intimacies are founded, the intimacies of prolonged, close, and loving contact" (Miller 1997: 138). But even while preserving the tacit understanding that such contact will involve the other person witnessing (if not judging) our weaknesses, some of these weaknesses, such as the stench of Philoctetes' foot, are the unavoidable costs of intimacy rather than its privileges:

> It is not a privilege of intimacy to endure bad breath in the way it can be a privilege to see someone with his or her guard down, to see someone weak, vulnerable, sick, fearful, and ugly, conditions which if manifested publicly would elicit contempt and disgust in the viewer. It is a very narrow line that separates the things that disgust from the things that elicit concern, love, pity, and affection.
>
> (Miller 1997: 139–40)

Take Keats's description of Niobe, after her children have been killed:

> Perhaps, the trembling knee
> And frantic gape of lonely Niobe,
> Poor, lonely Niobe! when her lovely young
> Were dead and gone, and her caressing tongue
> Lay a lost thing upon her paly lip,
> And very, very deadliness did nip
> Her motherly cheeks.
> (*Endymion* I.337–43, Keats 1970: 135)

As Christopher Ricks observes:

> What makes the lines disconcerting is the candour with which they raise a matter that a more grandly tragic manner may be prone to forget: that a great impediment to our full sympathy with frantic grief is its being embarrassing to contemplate, especially in its physical distortion. The tear-swollen child will often get less and less sympathy as it needs more and more . . .
>
> (Ricks 1974: 9)

Niobe's children were "lovely" but, in a tiny verbal shift which finely calibrates how easily joy can be transformed into despair, she is "lonely": lonely because they have been taken from her, and lonelier still in Keats's honest refusal to assume that he can tell us what this feels like. Her gaping maw is all the more terrible in that it fails to attract an adequately articulate response: that unbridgeable divide between an open-mouthed cry of pain and the open-mouthed horror of the person observing it which Browning described with brilliant economy in *The Ring and the Book* as "the gaping impotence of sympathy" (Browning 1971: 458). But even if Keats prevents us from assuming that we can fully appreciate Niobe's grief, his lines do not leave us only speechless. His repetitions of "lonely Niobe," "Poor lonely Niobe," and "very, very," are like the repetitions of grief, and so provide some companionship to grief, so that to read his description of Niobe allows us to exercise the imagination's double responsibility: to share other people's experience while recognizing that some parts of this experience will always remain foreign to us. Curiously but cautiously, his writing treads the "narrow line that separates the things that disgust from the things that elicit concern, love, pity, and affection." A similar poise could be necessary in any writing that sets out to offer an honest account of another person's weakness, if this account is to remain alert to how easily it could topple over into either undeserved distance or equally undeserved intimacy. However, a tussle between the suspension of disgust rules and the enforcement of them is especially important in tragedy, which situates itself at just such a juncture of the private and the public worlds. By putting the hero's suffering on stage, tragedy allows itself all the license of an intimate with all the distance of a voyeur – a situation that is oddly in tune with the hero's own ambiguous status, both central to and set apart from the community in which he finds himself. But by expressing this tension in the idiom of disgust, it also reminds the audience of his steady drift toward the still larger community that the play evokes: the community of the dead.

Compare two examples from Renaissance tragedy: *Macbeth*'s witches brewing up a recipe, and Bosola's satirical treatment of old age in *The Duchess of Malfi*. In both cases, it seems that disgust is not simply an unconscious and temporary flinching from defilement, but a deliberate stance, an attitude toward the world:

> Liver of blaspheming Jew;
> Gall of goat, and slips of yew,
> Slivered in the moon's eclipse,
> Nose of Turk, and Tartar's lips;
> Finger of birth-strangled babe,
> Ditch-delivered by a drab,
> Make the gruel thick and slab.
>
> (4.1.26–32)

> BOSOLA: You come from painting now?
> OLD LADY: From what?
> BOSOLA: Why, from scurvy face-physic. To behold thee not painted inclines somewhat near a miracle...
> OLD LADY: It seems you are well acquainted with my closet.
> BOSOLA: One would suspect it for a shop of witchcraft, to find in it the fat of serpents, spawn of snakes, Jews' spittle, and their young children's ordure; and all these for the face. I would sooner eat a dead pigeon taken from the sole of the feet of one sick of the plague than kiss one of you fasting.
>
> (Webster 1996: 2.1.20–36)

The most obvious feature which both passages share is a fondness for lists, which respond to the worry that the world is falling apart with a form of grammar that is both symptom and therapy. Lists are popular in tragedy, because they set up an appearance of order and at the same time risk spreading out of all control; they suggest that there are connections in the world, meaningful patterns to be traced, but also warn us that, in language at least, anything can be connected to anything else. Passages like these draw particular attention to the need for tragedy to depict collapse without suffering from it – the model of writing that Edgar hints at in the final scene of *King Lear* when he reminds his listeners that "The worst is not / So long as we can say 'This is the worst'" (4.1.27–8). "List... list, O list!" cries the Ghost in *Hamlet* (1.5.22), and although he means "listen closely," a pun hovers, because this play rarely offers one idea where it can be set against additions and alternatives: even the Ghost himself, so shifty in person, can't be pinned down to a single origin, as Horatio describes how, at the crowing of the cock, "Whether in sea *or* fire, in earth *or* air, / Th'extravagant *and* erring spirit hies / To his confine" (1.1.134–6, my emphasis). "Or" and "and" are important words in a play which is chiefly concerned with the need to choose a course of action, and the impossibility of choosing only one course of action. But the same might be said of almost any tragedy; it is certainly true of both *Macbeth* and *The Duchess of Malfi*, where lists once again seek to provide an illusion of control over the unstable and contingent mess of the world.

Both passages make richly detailed efforts to be as disgusting as possible, rather as if some playwrights of the period, like the earlier ascetics, enjoyed a form of competitive abjection in their writing, daring one another to see who would be the first to recoil. Webster brings together witches, vermin, excrement, spit, leprosy, and syphilis, all forming part of a more general disgust with sex. Shakespeare, too, gathers up some tried and tested ingredients of disgust: suggestions of stagnant water, sliminess, dismemberment, deformity, and orifices. Both lists brood on images of the foreign, the other. The references to Jews, in particular, function as a form of theatrical shorthand. The word "Jew" is inserted into a context of loathsome substances to tap into an established politics of disgust, intended to evoke in its original audience an ethical response with a visceral, almost Pavlovian, force: Jews are bad, therefore they are on intimate terms with everything else that either is bad (such as that ever-popular Christian symbol of the snake) or has gone bad (such as a dead pigeon). These lists have other ingredients in common as well. Both are geographically wide-ranging and imaginatively far-reaching, and this is intended to add to our mixed feelings, encouraging us to admire the speaker's lip-smacking resourcefulness in discovering new ways of making us squirm, even as we worry about the disgustingness which seems to lurk even in the most intimate nooks and crannies of the world. But both speakers also calm these fears, by implicitly dividing up the world into categories of the more and less disgusting. So, "fat of serpents" is chosen rather than, say, bones of serpents, because people are likely to find the slippery and wobbly more disgusting, more unstable and unpredictable, than the dry and flaky. The phrase itself, though, seems to have one foot in this world – "fat" – and one foot in the world of myth – "serpents"; like most of these ingredients, "fat of serpents" is disgusting because it confuses the very boundaries that it invokes.

As one might expect in a tragedy, the most important of these boundaries is the one between life and death. "Finger of birth-strangled babe": but was the finger taken before or after the babe was strangled? "Liver of blaspheming Jew": was his liver removed as a punishment for being blasphemous, or was he blaspheming because his liver was being removed? "Spawn of snakes," too, muddles up life and death: the promise of new life with the assumption that, like many promises in tragedy, this promise will be unfulfilled. As Miller explains:

> What disgusts, startlingly, is the capacity for life, and not just because life implies its correlative death and decay: for it is decay that seems to engender life . . . Rotting vegetation can be nearly as gorge raising as rotting flesh, and we are still wedded to folk beliefs that such vegetable muck spontaneously generates the worms, slugs, frogs, newts, mudpuppies, leeches, and eels we associate with it. From it come some of the most piquant ingredients of [*Macbeth's*] witches' brew: "Fillet of a fenny snake,/Eye of newt, and toe of frog." . . . Images of decay imperceptibly slide into images of fertility and out again. Death thus horrifies and disgusts not just because it smells revoltingly bad, but because it is not an end to the process of living but part of a cycle of eternal recurrence. The having lived and the living unite to make up the organic world of generative rot – rank, smelling, and upsetting to the touch.
>
> (Miller 1997: 40)

In other words, what generates disgust is often generation itself, the fact that sometimes life doesn't seem to know where to stop. Think of Edgar in *King Lear*, disguised as Poor Tom and describing how he eats "cowdung for salads, swallows the old rat and the ditch-dog, drinks the green mantle of the standing pool": the final image clinches a feeling of disgust by describing what appears to be dead (stagnant water) but is still producing life (pond scum) (3.4.123–5). Or there is the world of Egypt in *Antony and Cleopatra*, where nature and people "o'erflow the measure," where Antony is unstably rooted in the "slime and ooze" of the Nile, and where, according to Caesar, a fickle populace moves to and fro like a reed upon the stream, "lackeying the varying tide/To rot itself with motion" (1.1.1; 2.7.22; 1.4.46–7). Or *Hamlet*, so choked with weeds that from time to time they spring up between the cracks of speech: Hamlet's "unweeded garden/That grows to seed"; his father's warning about "the fat weed/That rots itself in ease on Lethe wharf";[7] the poison which is a "mixture rank of midnight weeds collected" (1.2.35–6; 1.5.32–3; 3.2.245).

Such concerns are not limited to tragedy, of course; the ramble undertaken by Hardy's Tess is just one of many literary examples whose creative energy emerges from the tension between a natural fecundity that seems endless, and the necessarily end-stopped character of human lives, as she stealthily approaches the man she will end up dying for:

The outskirt of the garden in which Tess found herself had been left unculti-
vated for some years, and was now damp and rank with juicy grass which sent
up mists of pollen at a touch; and with tall blooming weeds emitting offensive
smells – weeds whose red and yellow and purple hues formed a polychrome
as dazzling as that of cultivated flowers. She went steadily as a cat through this
profusion of growth, gathering cuckoo-spittle on her skirts, cracking snails
that were underfoot, staining her hands with thistle-milk and slug-slime, and
rubbing off upon her naked arms sticky blights which, though snow-white on
the apple-tree trunks, made blood-red stains on her skin; thus she drew quite
near to Clare, still unobserved of him.

(Hardy 1978: 178–9)

And we could go further. The fact that so much disgust centers on rot and
rankness might make it seem profoundly anti-tragic: if tragedy deals in lives
which end in death, what can it have to do with ideas which seem to reverse
this trajectory, and instead deal in the life which comes out of death?
Of course, there is a rich philosophical tradition according to which because
everything that lives must die, even growth and development is really
movement in the direction of the stillness which we fear or yearn for. But
it could be that tragedy is attracted to these ambiguous images of restraint
and excess because it too is awkwardly situated on the boundary between
life and death. A play like *King Lear* satisfies two desires at once. Because the
end of the narrative coincides with the death of the hero, the play rehearses
and flatters our hope that our lives can be as shapely and structured as our
fictions. At the same time, because we know that this performance of *King
Lear* will not exhaust the play altogether, and that therefore Cordelia will
"come no more" again tomorrow night (5.3.283), the play also rehearses and
flatters our hope that even death might not be the end of the story, so long
as a life can be reshaped into narrative and then remembered on the stage.

Put another way, tragedies often deal with the troubling aftermath of what
has been done, but is not yet done with, from curses and prophecies to cycles
of murder and revenge, and this interest in an active aftermath also seems to
be part of their ambition for themselves: to linger, to survive, to endure their
own endings. It is a situation that suggests two overlapping reasons for
tragedy's repeated recourse to disgust. Most simply, disgust registers the
defiling presence of death: just as Hamlet is disgusted by the smell of Yorick's
skull, so tragedy recognizes our physical and moral repugnance to death even
as it is playing out our fascination with it. But this repugnance stretches
beyond the hero, because Hamlet's twin movements of approach and recoil
in the graveyard also provide a miniature of the ambivalent narrative drive of

tragedy as a whole. Even if a tragedy ends in the full stop of death, this is the gravitational force that must be resisted as well as acknowledged by the narrative; without the delay exacted by the hero's struggle against his fate, and the possibility that this time things could turn out differently, there would be little to distinguish a tragedy from the sort of execution witnessed by Dickens. (It would be a poor tragedy that had the hero asking "To be or not to be," before swiftly concluding that it would be better not to be and jumping out of the window.) And this ambivalence – at once seeking out the finality of death and spurning it – also appears to be written into tragedy as a genre. Think of *Hamlet*, which ends with an incomplete action and on a metrically incomplete line: "Go, bid the soldiers shoot" (5.2.357); or the last word of *Troilus and Cressida* – "diseases" – ending the play with an unstressed syllable that drifts into the air like an infected spore (Quarto text). Even tragic goodbyes don't always fare well as attempts to stop us speculating about what might come next: "Adieu, adieu, Hamlet. Remember me," Old Hamlet calls out as he fades from view, but if we remember his mournful description of the pains he must suffer in purgatory, we might also wonder about the longing and warning force of that "Adieu" to the son he has just asked to commit a murder: literally, "I commend you to God" (1.5.91). And how are we supposed to take Hamlet's celebrated last line, "The rest is silence," given his earlier response to the wandering figure of his father: "Rest, rest, perturbèd spirit" (5.2.310; 1.5.183)?

Questionable Shapes

"Thou com'st in such a questionable shape," remarks Hamlet to the ghost, "That I will speak to thee" (1.4.24–5). Much the same could be said of tragedy. Individual plays, too, regularly present themselves as "questionable shapes," not only in the questions which they implicitly raise (Can Antigone be loyal both to her brother and to her father? Is it possible for Antony to retain his honor while also preserving his place in Cleopatra's heart?), but also in those which they explicitly ask. Some of these questions are answered, swiftly and unequivocally:

> CLAUDIUS: What would you undertake
> To show your father's son in deed
> More than in words?
> LAERTES: To cut his throat i'th'church.
> (4.7.97–100)

Other questions are important precisely because they cannot be answered, but even these questions provoke later responses, like Beckett's flickering resuscitation of *King Lear* in *Endgame*:

> LEAR: No, no, no life?
> Why should a dog, a horse, a rat have life,
> And thou no breath at all?
>   (5.3.281–3)
>
> CLOV: There's a rat in the kitchen!
> HAMM: A rat! Are there still rats?
> CLOV: In the kitchen there's one.
> HAMM: And you haven't exterminated him?
>   (Beckett 1964: 37)

Such questions draw attention to how incomplete many of the plays are, how open to changing interpretations, and thus the difficulty faced by any critic who attempts to bring them into line with a definition of tragedy. Definitions suggest fixed limits (its etymological root is the Latin *de-finis*, "from the end"), but as a genre tragedy seems far too porous and provisional to be pinned down in this way. This is why drawing attention to tragedy's unmisgiving interest in disgust, whether as a narrative subject (as in *Philoctetes*) or a narrative mode (as in *The Duchess of Malfi*), is also to be brought to recognize how often tragedy educates its spectators into the limitations of theoretical models that promise to answer all of its questions. For no matter how many different theories are tested against these stubbornly idiosyncratic plays, whether singly or in ambitious combinations, none of them is capable of adequately defining what is more like an ongoing process of cultural self-definition; indeed, trying to make a tragedy fit a pet theory comes close to producing a hermeneutic version of the hero's plight, as ideals are fractured against obdurate actualities. Some theorists, from Hegel onward, have pointed out that tragedy often emerges particularly strongly at moments of historical transition, whether this is Athenian democracy anxiously considering how far it had grown out of its heroic past, or the place of Elizabethan tragedy in a world caught between feudal and capitalist values. However, it could just as reasonably be argued that tragedy and transition are natural soulmates, because tragedy is always in transition; it offers itself as a developing proof of the simple and profound remark by the Gypsy in Tennessee Williams's play *Camino Real* that "Humanity is just a work in progress" (Williams 1958: 84).

Notes

1 For an influential (if much disputed) account of such public displays, and the gradual move toward more private means of exacting retribution upon the criminal's body, see Foucault 1977.

2 Dickens's worry may have been focused by a rich tradition of staging mock-executions as comic spectacles that had lasted well into the nineteenth century: in an essay on comedy first published in 1855, Baudelaire reports seeing an English pantomime in which one of the characters, realistically guillotined, got up afterwards to steal his head back and strut off the stage.

3 Shakespeare 1986. All references to Shakespeare are to this edition.

4 *OED* "compassion" (first cited 1968).

5 For this reason, although most of the literary examples in this chapter are taken from Western culture (principally Greek and Shakespearean tragedy), the use of "we" and "our" should be understood as referring to the inner workings of any society in which tragedy, like disgust, has been used to investigate "the sorts of social and moral possibility" open to its members. I discuss below the frequent overlap between tragedy and disgust in seeking to define particular social groups against the perceived threat of aliens and outsiders.

6 All references to individual Greek tragedies are taken from Grene and Lattimore 1992.

7 This is the Folio reading; both Quarto texts have "roots" rather than "rots."

Chapter 4

Tragedy and the Sign of the Eclipse

Anne C. Henry

Julia Kristeva observes melancholy in the image of a black sun. In her study, "Soleil Noir," a title taken from Gérard de Nerval's poem "El Desdichado" ("The Disinherited"), she describes how the Saturnine metaphor "fully sums up the blinding force of the despondent mood – an excruciating, lucid affect asserts the inevitability of death" (Kristeva 1989: 151). Struggles with deeply embedded loss can seem to close down the world to representation, yet with such suffering can come a clarity and the reachings of philosophy. Kristeva writes:

> *Melancholia* belongs in the celestial realm. It changes darkness into redness or into a sun that remains black, to be sure, but is nevertheless the sun, source of dazzling light. Nerval's introspection seems to indicate that *naming the sun* locates him on the threshold of a crucial experience, on the divide between appearance and disappearance, abolishment and song, nonmeaning and signs.
>
> (151)

The subject of this chapter is another black sun: the eclipse. While darkness unsettles, the eclipse, as a sign of aberrant loss, more commonly disturbs. Existing quite literally "on the divide between appearance and disappearance," as one astronomical body disappears and reemerges, the eclipse is a paradox of simultaneous presence and absence. The sudden loss of sun or moon is both an explicable occurrence of nature and yet seemingly unnatural; on the one hand it can be predicted by rational computation, but it has also been read as an omen, something uncanny that portends political and personal discord.

Ruth Padel, who has examined images of the black sun, such as Nerval's, in relation to tragedy, has described how, "tragedy itself runs on blackness. Grief, death, failure, loss" (Padel 1992: 62). The Greek word *ekleipsis*, from which "eclipse" derives, can signify all that: loss, abandonment, failure, death, and darkness. The English word "eclipsis" (now obsolete) comes from the same Greek word and refers to a grammatical figure of omission.[1] "Eclipsis" has also been used for typographical signs of omission that mark the page visually when speech lapses into silence and words are hidden from view.[2] Eclipsis exists on that boundary between "nonmeaning" and expression, as an inability to communicate is communicated. This chapter will examine verbal and nonverbal signs of the eclipse as they figure in tragic writing: the *eclipse* as a celestial occurrence and omen of destruction; words related to *ekleipsis* as they appear in Greek tragic drama to indicate loss, especially the loss of words; finally, the *eclipsis* as a typographical sign that signifies lost words and makes literal on the page the metaphors of darkness that pervade tragic writing. *King Lear* is the focus of this study. It brings together the sign of the eclipse in its two visual forms, as a purportedly observed natural event and as a typographical sign. The analysis does not imply authorial or compositorial association between the different types of eclipse, but rather serves as a reflection upon variant manifestations of an ill-omened sign recurrent across tragic writing.

The eclipse was understood as an omen in fifth-century Greece: a sign from the gods to be deciphered by seers, but along with other spontaneous (as opposed to sought) omens, such as earthquakes, thunder and lightning, or the flight of birds,[3] eclipses were part of a collective experience and were open to the comments of laymen. Interpretations of eclipses are recorded by historians. Thucydides, known for his skepticism with regard to oracles and omens, is critical of Nikias for delaying the retreat from Syracuse following a lunar eclipse; persuaded by the fears of the Athenians and advised by soothsayers, Nikias is described as "too much under the influence of divination and omens" (Thucydides 1881: 7.50). Other references to eclipses in the *History of the Peloponnesian War* suggest that they interested Thucydides as natural phenomena and as a means of marking chronology.[4] However, in the first book, he describes an unparalleled number of eclipses, along with other devastating natural events – earthquakes, famines, and plagues – all of which "fell upon Hellas simultaneously with the war" (1.23). Later writers have debated the extent to which Thucydides believed that there was a connection between such signs and the war that followed, and this passage has been commonly seen as almost as aberrant to the historian's style, as the events he describes are "unprecedented" for Hellas.[5] Whatever the case, their symbolic role at the opening of the narrative is clear: they introduce, rhetorically if not actually, the unparalleled suffering that is to follow.[6]

In the seventh book of his *Histories*, Herodotus describes an eclipse of the sun occurring just before Xerxes' invasion of Greek lands (7.37). The sun disappears at the height of Xerxes' hubris, immediately following his lashing of the Hellespont (36) and before his grotesque dismemberment of Pythias' sons (38–9). The magi reassure Xerxes that the eclipse signifies the defeat of Greece, by transforming it into metaphorical terms: for "God meant to foretell to the Greeks the eclipse of their cities (*ekleipsin tôn poliôn*)." Herodotus elsewhere stresses the arrogance of the tyrant in failing to listen to wise advisors, and here the interpretation of the magi is noticeably deficient, especially in contrast with the Athenians' democratic discussion about how best to interpret the meaning of the Delphic oracle described later in Book 7 (140–4). No eclipse of the sun can be connected with Xerxes' presence in Sardis at this time, and it seems to have been invented by Herodotus or suggested to him through common lore. Many Greek cities did indeed fall to Persian forces, of course, but nonetheless, in Herodotus' telling the eclipse symbolizes primarily the reversal of expectations and the ultimate casting of the Persian king and his dazzling army into darkness.[7]

No astronomical eclipses are referred to in the extant corpus of fifth-century Greek tragedy. Jon D. Mikalson describes how: "In tragedy such ominous events are limited to the flight of birds, chance words, and thunder and lightning, whereas in life they included also rain, earthquakes, eclipses, sneezes, sacrilegious acts, and other such events" (Mikalson 1991: 104). We do know from Apollonius Rhodius that the third-century dramatist Sosiphanes wrote a tragedy in which an eclipse was effected by magic (Riess 1896). Related forms of the word *ekleipsis* do, however, have resonance in Greek tragedy. The verb *ekleipein* can mean to undergo an eclipse (intransitively, of the sun or moon), but also to die. Plato in the *Logics* describes the dead as the eclipsed, *eklipontes*;[8] and in the first century CE, Strabo employs *ekleipsis* to describe the extinction of a whole community (Strabo 1968: vol. 4, 417). More commonly, it means to leave or to forsake, which, in the context of tragic writing, does not augur well.

Euripides uses it most often to mean exile: for example, in *Electra*: "And what other griefs are greater than to leave (*ekleipein*) the borders of one's native land?" (Euripides 1988: ll.1314–15). Or *Trojan Women*: "Troy, unhappy Troy, you are gone and those who leave you (*ekleipontes*), are unhappy too, both the surviving and the dead!" (Euripides 1986: ll.173–5). Again, in *The Bacchae*: "Farewell, O house, farewell O paternal land. In misery I leave you (*ekleipô*), a fugitive from the chambers" (Euripides 2001: ll.1368–70). Collective suffering is described in Aeschylus' *Seven Against Thebes* when Eteocles imagines a captured city (like Herodotus' cities in eclipse) as one that the Gods have abandoned (Aeschylus 1985: ll.217–18). The verb is used with *bion*, "life," in Sophocles' *Electra* (Sophocles 1969: l.1131); and means, likewise, "to die" in its conventional conjunction with words for "light," mainly *phaos*. Helen, for example, says to Menelaus: "When you die, I will leave this light (*ekleipsein phaos*)" (Euripides 1959: l.839).[9]

The verb *ekleipein* appears in *Persians* as the messenger ends his tale: "Such is the cause of grief for the city of the Persians, yearning for the country's beloved young men. These things are true. But my words omit many of the afflictions with which god blasted the Persians" (Aeschylus 1996b: ll.512–14). Here *ekleipô* meets with speaking, in participle form, drawing attention to that which words must leave out (*polla d'ekleipô legôn*).[10] The messenger concludes a long and unhappy speech, indicating an unwillingness to afflict his audience further, or his inability to describe the extent of the devastation. This use of paralipsis (a leaving aside) is common to Greek tragedy and, as is always the case, it draws attention to that which has been omitted: the miseries of the Persians are in part hidden, but also present through the suggestiveness of that which has not been told. In *Agamemnon* the chorus shrink back from expressing the possibility of disaster, but with an aposiopesis (a breaking off) as they see the messenger approaching, to tell them the news of Troy:

> The thirsty dust, consorting sister of the mire, assures me that neither by dumb show nor by kindling a flame of mountain wood will he give sign with smoke of fire, but in plain words will bid us either to rejoice the more, or else – but God avert the omen of the contrary!
>
> (Aeschylus 1957: 493–9)

In Athenian oratory aposiopesis was understood as the suppression of ill-omened words,[11] and, as Silvia Montiglio has described in her study of silence in classical Greek texts, "ancient rhetoricians themselves did not draw any formal distinction between aposiopesis and the other figures of silence" (132). But, such figures of silence in turn act as signs of that which is to be feared. The reversal in Xerxes' fortunes is presented in *Persians* (as later by Herodotus) as a movement from brilliant light to darkness, and the play is replete with images of shade and visual contrast.[12] *Persians* also provides an example of how words can be cast into darkness as language is eclipsed by the burden of speaking. Such linguistic darkness is as much a sign of tragedy as its metaphorical counterpart; like exile and loss, reticence and interruption are forms of absence that mark the genre.[13]

There are four Shakespearean plays in which "eclipse" appears as an astronomical phenomenon (and as a noun), and these are each of the four major tragedies.[14] In *Macbeth* and *Hamlet* the eclipse is referred to in scenes of prognostication and supernatural event. *Macbeth* holds the slightest of the references, when slips of yew "Sliver'd in the moon's eclipse" (4.1.28) are thrown by the witches into their pot.[15] Both *Hamlet* and *Othello* reveal a different conventionality to the sign of the eclipse. In the first scene of *Hamlet*, Horatio, Marcellus, and Barnardo discuss how the "portentous figure" of the ghost of old Hamlet might signify the invasion of the state by Norway; in the Second Quarto, Horatio continues by describing the death of Julius Caesar as foreshadowed by the "moist star," which:

> Was sicke almost to doomesday with eclipse.
> And even the like precurse of feare events
> As harbindgers preceading still the fates
> And prologue to the *Omen* comming on,
> Have heaven and earth together demonstrated
> Unto our Climatures and countrymen.
> *Enter Ghost*
>
> (Q2. 1.120–5)

It is certainly feasible that this passage was cut for being too overt a "prologue to the omen coming on,"[16] however compelling the implied comparison between a ghost and an eclipse. The confusion of day and night has already been established in real time, as Marcellus asks why the emergency in Denmark "Doth make the night joint labourer with the day" (Q2 1.1.78) and the celestial omen remains an allusion when the crowing of the cock relieves superstitious fears, for "then no plannets strike, / No fairy takes, nor witch hath power to charme" (Q2 1.1.162–3). Horatio's skepticism, "So have I heard and doe in part believe it" (Q2 1.1.165) – as earlier, "at least the whisper goes so" (Q2 1.1.80) – suggests a half-heartedness to his own narrative of prediction:[17] an eclipse might have signaled Caesar's fall, but, as Robert Wilson's 1595 play testifies, it is also part of every "pedler's prophecie."[18]

In *Othello*, instead of foregrounding and issuing in the "fear'd events" to come, the eclipse marks the end of the play and the dissolution of the world and all that is good in it. Like *Hamlet*, it is a night scene and Othello calls to mind eclipse and earthquake immediately after killing Desdemona and on hearing Emilia's approach:

> I think she stirs again. No. What's best to do?
> If she come in, she'll sure speak to my wife—
> My wife, my wife! What wife? I have no wife.
> O insupportable! O heavy hour!
> Methinks it should be now a huge eclipse
> Of sun and moon, and that th'affrighted globe
> Should yawn at alteration.
>
> (5.2.96–102)

The speech reveals a disconcerting "alteration" as Othello, anxious about whether his wife might still show signs of life, suddenly recognizes what it is that he has done and calls immediately for those well-known signs of terrestrial disturbance.[19] But if the eclipse and earthquake are imagined as portents (or "prologues") they are belated – following Desdemona's death rather than prefiguring it – and thus anticlimactic.[20] On the other hand, they do transport her significance to the realms of the extraordinary, because the globe does indeed seem "altered" without her, as is Othello himself, with no wife but a murdered one. But Shakespeare might confront another sense of "yawn" in the employment of this trope. It is the realization that Desdemona has gone that brings about Othello's invocation, but, his hands almost still upon her, she becomes absent from his thought, as he is lost in rhetorical abstraction (his next words are "I had forgot thee," but to Emilia). Desdemona has been eclipsed, lost in the chasm that has been created between a few moments ago and now, and, though he begins to see her death, she is still lost from his mind in his "madness."[21] Realities are only slowly dawning upon him and there are more to come. Conventional tropes, even of disaster, can carry comfort with them, for Othello perhaps, but most certainly for Antony, who can posit that his own misfortunes are worthy of lunar eclipse and thus, rhetorically, he disturbs the heavens for the sake of his own conceit:

> Alack our terrene Moon
> Is now eclips'd, and it portends alone
> The fall of Antony![22]

From Polybius at least, the specific metaphor of a king in eclipse has been used,[23] though we have seen how much earlier the eclipse "perplexes monarchs."[24] Alexander, in John Lyly's 1584 play *A moste excellent comedie of Alexander, Campaspe, and Diogenes*, states sententiously that "An eclipse in the Sunne is more then the fallinge of a starre, none can conceive the tormentes of a king, unless hee be a king."[25] There is, however, an extended use of the figure in the anonymous 1606 play *Nobody and Somebody* that deserves some attention. In its prologue, an analogy is posited between the death of the king and the sun in eclipse:

> And reason *Martianus*, when the Sunne
> Struggles to be deliuered from the wombe
> Of an obscure Eclipse, doth not the earth
> Mourne to behold his shine envelloped,
> O *Corbonon* when I did close thine eyes,
> I gaue release to *Britaines* miseries.
>
> (A3r)

Appropriately, the dead king and the new share the image of the sun: the former through a suggested simile (and thus implied connective before "O Corbonon"); the latter through overt metaphor. The earth "mourns" to see the sun's shine "envelloped," as Corbonon's eyes are now closed and his body enshrouded. But homophony (sunne/son) and the images of the difficult delivery make the heir the prime subject; the father's death, the closing of his eyes, are the eclipse from which he fails to emerge and "Britaines miseries" are caused by the "struggles" of the son's succession.

The chronicle plot of *Nobody and Somebody* is concerned with the usurpation of good kingship by tyranny; tyranny succeeds through flattery, as Cornwell, the honest and wise advisor, is replaced by Sicophant, and fear sets in concerning a realm divided between brothers ("a dubble state") (G2r). Elydure, who ultimately succeeds as king (three times), holds no ambition for the crown; but he is dominated by a wife who usurps his place and who desires to cast the former queen into "shadow." The same wife has disturbing retributive imaginings when losing the crown: "Would they had burnt his eyes out / That hath eclipsd [*sic*] our state and Majestie" (E4r). Kingship in *Nobody and Somebody* is marked by a series of interruptions, which, following on from the prologue, are imagined in terms of darkness and disembodiment. The eclipse extends figuratively and linguistically to the more obscure members of society, into the comic plot of *Nobody and Somebody*, as the latter promises to "eclipse" the praise of Nobody's goodness and charity (C3r).

There are a number of intriguing correlations between *Nobody and Somebody* and *King Lear*. Luke Wilson comments, for example:

> Both rely on Geoffrey of Monmouth and Holinshed for their British pseudo history; thematically, both plays manifest a preoccupation with nothing (in particular the language of *Nobody*'s prologue plays with the idea of nothing in a way quite similar to the Fool's tormenting of Lear), and in both a king's unwillingness to rule creates a political problem with extensive social consequences.
>
> (Wilson 2000: 318)

The eclipse might be considered an addendum to this list. The play was printed in March, 1606 following the eclipse of the moon on September 17 and of the sun on October 2 of the previous year (Buckley 1962). However, *Nobody and Somebody* had been in performance for several years before the 1606 printing, which makes any such later extra-dramatic associations speculative.[26] On the other hand, *King Lear*, performed in December, 1606, refers deictically to "these late eclipses," and it is possible that Shakespeare was alluding directly to the recent astronomical events: whatever the case, the eclipse is transformed from a figurative convention into a dramatic fact, and this results in the return of its symbolic powers.

Gloucester reflects:

> GLOUCESTER: These late eclipses in the sun and moon portend no good to us. Though the wisdom of nature can reason it thus and thus, yet nature finds itself scourged by the sequent effects. Love cools, friendship falls off, brothers divide. In cities, mutinies; in countries, discord; in palaces, treason; and the bond cracked 'twixt son and father. This villain of mine comes under the prediction: there's son against father. The king falls from bias of nature, there's father against child. We have seen the best of our time. Machinations, hollowness, treachery, and all ruinous disorders follow us disquietly to our graves. Find out this villain, Edmond, it shall lose thee nothing. Do it carefully. And the noble and true-hearted Kent banished; his offence, honesty. 'Tis strange.
>
> *Exit*
>
> EDMOND: This is the excellent foppery of the world, that when we are sick in fortune, often the surfeits of our own behaviour, we make guilty of our disasters the sun, the moon, and stars: as if we were villains on necessity, fools by heavenly compulsion, knaves, thieves, and treachers by spherical predominance
>
> (1.2.91–108)[27]

Shakespeare dramatizes a contemporary discussion about the validity of eclipses as portentous signs and more generally about the nature of "planetary influence" (1.2.110). Don Cameron Allen describes how: "None of the English opponents of astrology was willing to say that the stars were without influence; at most, they denied that the planets had the governing of the human will and that the influence of the stars could either be measured or predicted" (Allen 1966: 143–4). However, Franco Moretti believes Gloucester to have "recourse to what already appeared to the Elizabethan audience an empty superstition, 'the excellent foppery of the world'" (Moretti 1988: 52) Anthony Grafton, on the other hand, in an essay on the reading of eclipses, has argued that in sixteenth- and early seventeenth-century Europe eclipses "continued to be seen as portents, moreover, not only by peasants and urban laborers, but also by educated men and women" (Grafton 2003: 218). Nevertheless, this was a time when the eclipse was changing in scientific writing from a sign into a fact, significant, for example, in the production of historical chronology (Grafton 2003: 218).

William Elton has documented satirical writing about predictions relating to eclipses and James I himself, publicly disparaging of superstitious activities, produced a mock-prognostication of court news following "this laite eclipse" of 1605: "But now will I goe to hyer maitters & and tell you ... the effectis of this laite eclipse ... for this yeare are verrie many & wondrouse ... many other prodigiouse eventis are flowid from this eclipse."[28] But prognostications did occur, serious as well as satirical,[29] and the eclipses were interpreted as signs of potentially calamitous intrigue and, more specifically, associated with the gunpowder plot. In Robert Pricket's *Times Anotomie* (1606) such political anxiety is clear:[30]

> Me thinkes there should be some thing understood,
> When heaven is cloth'd in cloudes of fire and bloud
> Before and since the heavens did never cast,
> More signes than were about this treason last.
> ...
> And if the sunne should but some signe bewraie,
> Might no man dare gainst such prediction saie.
> And now shall heaven both fier and blood presage,
> And we not thinke they chide this sinfull age.
> Eclipses strange both ... Moone and Sunne,
> When strangely they, on heapes together come.
>   (Pricket 1606: Hlr)

Whether the audience of *King Lear* was actively engaging in "celestial hermeneutics" (Grafton 2003: 215) or not, when the play was performed in

1606 the reference to "these late eclipses" was likely to have carried a certain *frisson*, as recent political anxiety, or even gossip, was remembered. Gary Taylor, looking at the textual history of the play, has considered the extent to which the political consequences imputed to the eclipses in the 1608 Quarto necessitated its censorship.[31] After making his own distaste for astrology clear, Edmund duplicitously aligns himself with his father's superstitions in order to generate a mood of anxious "melancholy" (1.2.118) for his brother's arrival. A number of Edmund's lines of prediction have been excised from the Folio, and these are indicated in the Quarto text below by square brackets:

> BAST. I am thinking, brother, of a prediction I read this other day, what
> should follow these eclipses.
> EDG. Doe you busie your selfe about that?
> BAST. I promise you the effects he writ of, succeed unhappily, [as of
> unnaturalnesse betweene the child and the parent, death, dearth,
> dissolutions of ancient amities, divisions in state, menaces and
> maledictions against King and nobles, needles diffidences, banishment
> of friends, dissipation of Cohorts, nuptial breaches, and I know not what.
> EDG. How long have you been a sectary Astronomicall?
> BAST. Come, come,] when saw you my father last?
> EDG. Why, the night gon by.
>
> (Shakespeare 2005: 265–6)

Edmund's words are understood by the audience to be satirical, but they emphasize, nonetheless, the familiar augury of political disorder. Complementing this excision, Gloucester's speech on these "late eclipses" is augmented in the Folio, so that he comments straightaway upon the immediate – and therefore fictional – context, beginning "This villain of mine."[32] Taylor concludes, however, that censorship does not seem a valid reason for the removal of Edmund's lines; rather, the passage was more probably cut for artistic purposes and because the lines had started to *lose* their resonance (Taylor 1983: 83). What is striking about this analysis is the emphasis thus laid upon the divisive effects of the eclipse in early performances. Taylor draws attention to the abrupt disjunction, created in the Folio, between Edmund's reference to succession ("succeed unhappily") and his question to Edgar: "when saw you my father last?" The Folio passage has, he argues, "a suggestion of futurity less evident in its Quarto counterpart" (87). This is appropriate for a play in which there is so little time for deliberation, as events "succeed unhappily" at a terrifying pace. More generally, it is this charged sense of futurity – the mysteries of causes and effects – that makes the allusion to "these late eclipses" an auspicious artistic introduction into the subplot of *King Lear*, in both Quarto and Folio versions.

The eclipses serve as a nexus for a number of the play's concerns. They situate it, however tantalizingly, in recent political history, with very real connotations of threat. At the same time they capture something of the pagan remoteness of a pre-Christian world,[33] while the darkening of the sun is a sign of the Apocalypse, one of the many that the play offers us.[34] Nature elsewhere is shown to reflect and inflict human suffering, in the storm especially. The "late eclipses" make an appearance at the opening of the play and they exert their influence, like those "half-realised suggestions of vast universal powers working in the world of individual fates and passions" described by A. C. Bradley (Bradley 1904: 247). Why do "all ruinous disorders follow us disquietly to our graves"? The play gives us many approaches to answering this question, but the extremity of the disorder, the scale of the suffering, are so great, that the movements of the stars seem almost as likely as anything else.

The early foreboding they establish is echoed in other predictions in the first half of the play. Both Kent and the Fool use the general insights of proverbs to suggest their sense of the troubles ahead. Kent's "Good king, that must approve the common saw,/Thou out of heaven's benediction com'st/To the warm sun" (2.2.143–5) tells of a movement from good to worse but, in figurative terms, suggests only the early stage of the king's trajectory, which leads him out of the warm sun and into the storm. And it is the storm that marks the culmination of such prognostics as it is then that the Fool delivers a prophecy of "great confusion" for Albion (3.2.84). The confusion is articulated through a series of inversions: that which should not be is balanced against that which should be, but is not. These inversions are characteristic of the whole play in which son is against father, and father against child; daughters become mothers (1.4.133–4); and Cordelia proves "most rich being poor,/Most choice forsaken, and most loved despised" (1.1.245–6). Goneril fixates on Lear's "disordered rabble" (1.4.211) – "Men so disordered" (1.4.197) – as a means of licensing her own disorder, which originates, nonetheless, in her father's own relinquishing of the expected. *King Lear* has a "proliferation of paradox" at its heart (McAlindon 1991: 171) and the eclipse as a natural phenomenon of paradox and reversal serves appropriately as its emblem.

These late eclipses also serve a pragmatic function in that they establish Gloucester as a man of superstition. Bradley emphasized this "weakness" that makes Gloucester vulnerable to Edmund's stories and machinations (Bradley 1904: 295). Criticism of Gloucester as susceptible to "the excellent foppery of the world" is, without doubt, valid, but that this criticism is first made by Edmund shouldn't be overlooked. Shakespeare doesn't here present us with real conversational exchange, but the juxtaposition of contradictory monologues. This too is an inversion, as Edmund negates his father's viewpoint, while replacing him as the object of dramatic focus on the stage, and the audience is left with the riddle of two interpretative extremes. Edmund's views on the subject of judicial astrology have been described as "exactly those of contemporary state and church" (Smith 1958: 175), but we know him already to be a dubious guide. Gloucester, on the other hand, represents a seemingly antiquated worldview; yet his ominous words have credibility, as the eclipse is so overt a literalization of a shift in the symbolic values of the court, to which the audience has been witness in the previous scene. We don't meet Gloucester *as* he ruminates upon "these late eclipses"; instead he reflects on Kent's banishment, the king's departure, and the anger of France, before learning from Edmund that Edgar plots against him – only then does Gloucester reflect, with hindsight, on facts that now seem to be signs. The symbolism of the eclipse is retrospectively activated.

Unlike the source text for *King Lear*, the *Chronicle History of King Leir and his three daughters*, in Shakespeare's play there is no glimmer of any conventional association between the king and the sun, or light.[35] The only time such an association occurs is when Kent facetiously flatters Cornwall – "your great aspect, / Whose influence like the wreath of radiant fire / On flick'ring Phoebus' front" (2.2.96–8) – which underlines our knowledge that the desire for glib accolades is an immediate source of catastrophe. Lear is only ever seen through what he is not, as the inverse of what he was and still should be. He is a king who precipitates a journey into obscurity, by announcing his ominous intentions, "our darker purpose" (1.1.31). By the fourth scene of the first act the Fool gleans from Goneril's behavior that dark times have come – "out went the candle, and we were left darkling" (1.4.177) – and the king has become "Lear's shadow" (1.4.190). Act 2 begins in darkness, as the plotting of Edmund against his brother, and Regan against her father and Gloucester, are set in motion. In Act 3, Lear is left out in the storm, "in hell-black night" (3.7.59), and Gloucester is blinded in an act that "literalizes evil's ancient love of darkness" (Cavell 1987: 47). Gloucester's first words in blindness, "All dark and comfortless" (3.7.84), will be echoed at the end of the play by Kent, with Lear and dead Cordelia before him, "All's cheerless, dark and deadly" (5.3.264).

Gloucester is also associated with darkness, but in Gloucester's case this is a much earlier and universal failing – "the act of darkness" (3.4.79) – that in

Edgar's moralizing view is the cause of his father's undoing, as he makes explicit to his brother: "The dark and vicious place where thee he got/Cost him his eyes" (5.3.162–3). But, as has often been pointed out, it is Gloucester's insensitivity with respect to Edmund that reveals his true limitations. The eclipse passes verbally from Gloucester to Edmund who, as in "the catastrophe of the old comedy," temporarily performs a role, punning celestially in his singing: "My cue is villainous melancholy, with a sigh like Tom o'Bedlam. – O these eclipses do portend these divisions. Fa, sol, la, me" (1.2.117–19). The eclipse is then transferred from brother to brother, as it is Edgar who is forced to take on the melancholy part of Tom o'Bedlam, urged on "to course his own shadow for a traitor" (3.4.54).

People all around Lear become obscured, as the play narrates a process of attenuation and loss: "a great abatement of kindness" (1.4.51–2). Cordelia's preference for speaking "nothing" causes her to be described tauntingly by Goneril as "worth the want that you have wanted" (1.1.273) and she becomes that absence in exile; the Fool, in consequence, "hath much pined away" (1.4.63). Lear is to lose half of his men through the commands of Goneril (1.4.249); and by Act 2, scene 4 there is a bleeding of numbers: "What need you five and twenty? ten? or five?" (2.4.254). By Act 4, Lear's soldiers are imaginary (4.5.85–7). Kent razes his likeness (1.4.4) and in disguise becomes like Edgar, an absent presence, a paradox: "Edgar I nothing am" (2.3.21). And Lear too loses his name: "who am I, sir?" (1.4.67). Gloucester's blinding is a grotesque process, in which he is left for ten lines, during which a fight and a death occur, half in light, half in darkness, before his life becomes fully "'nighted" (4.4.15). In Act 4 a distracted Lear meets with the blinded Gloucester and commands him:

> [LEAR:] Read thou this challenge; mark but the penning of it.
> GLOUCESTER: Were all thy letters suns, I could not see.
> EDGAR [*Aside*]: I would not take this from report; it is,
> And my heart breaks at it.
>
> (4.5.134–7)

Gloucester, while meaning to stress only his own blindness and frailty, "I could not see," focuses attention on Lear's failure of authority: the signs of his kingship – "thy letters," "suns" – can no longer be seen.

As aberrant as celestial deviations, the departure of these two men from their lives' courses, as king and earl, cannot be taken "from report," but nevertheless theirs are trajectories into obscurity that can be accurately plotted, even predicted. "Course," as in *OED* 2a., "Onward movement in a particular path, as of the heavenly bodies..." has some resonance in *King Lear*. Kent in his disguise follows an "obscurèd course" (2.2.151) once Lear has issued in the darkness. After he is blinded, Gloucester believes that he has "no way" but nonetheless he continues, literally on his path, so that, according to Regan, "Where he arrives he moves / All hearts against us" (4.4.12–13). To hold obdurately to a "course" is to obliterate those in the way: Edmund manipulates his father into running "a certain course" against Edgar (1.2.74–5); Goneril resolves to "write straight to my sister to hold my course" (1.3.21). Cornwall and Albany are contrasted revealingly by means of this term: Gloucester describes Cornwall to Lear: "You know the fiery quality of the Duke / How unremovable and fixed he is / In his own course" (2.4.85–7); and Edmund asks whether Albany in battle is "advised by aught / To change the course. He's full of alteration / And self-reproving" (5.1.2–4). To be alterable, to be obscured, to be "removed" is a fearful matter in *King Lear*, but it is only with those characters who undergo such change that our sympathies can rest.

As so many are overcome by darkness, who can reemerge? Gloucester resolves at Dover to "bear / Affliction" (4.5.75–6) – to continue rather than end his life in despair – but when he finds again the suns / sons he "could not see" he is unable to stand this return to the familiar. Edgar had led his father to "the shadow" of a tree and it is here that the audience last see him (5.2.1). After the storm and blinding of the third act, Act 4 does allow some respite: in the hope created by the news of the French forces landing and in Cordelia's promises of applying the powers of a beneficent Nature to aid her father. For Lear, "Fair daylight" (4.6.49) returns on rediscovering his child, although, again, the tragedy doesn't allow this comfort to last. It is Kent, Edgar, and Albany who survive. Albany's character has been obscured, almost invisible, through the play, being an honorable man aligned with the wrong side. Kent and Edgar have maintained their characters and convictions, seemingly "removable," but in fact only temporarily absent from view.

The play ends in the Folio with Edgar's words:[36]

> The weight of this sad time we must obey,
> Speak what we feel, not what we ought to say.
> The oldest hath borne most; we that are young
> Shall never see so much, nor live so long.
> (5.3.297–300)

In "The Great Eclipse: Tragedy as the Deconsecration of Sovereignty," Franco Moretti describes abdication as a tyrannical act which undermines

Lear himself, his counselors and, more generally, principles of reason and authority. This also means the dissolution of linguistic authority which, according to Moretti, is nowhere better seen than in this last speech of Edgar's:

> Its blind mediocrity indicates the chasm that has opened up between facts and words, or more accurately, between referents and signifieds. The close of *King Lear* makes clear that no one is any longer capable of giving meaning to the tragic process; no speech is equal to it, and there precisely lies the tragedy.
>
> (Moretti 1988: 53)

Symbolic – including verbal – codes sustain kingship. While Gloucester adheres to the conventionality of signs, Edmund chooses to question them, calling day, night; lying right to the end:[37]

> EDMOND: What in the world he is
> That names me traitor, villain-like he lies.
> Call by the trumpet: he that dares, approach;
> On him, on you – who not? – I will maintain
> My truth and honour firmly.
>
> (5.3.91–5)

Warren D. Smith writes of Edmund's defiance of his father's interpretation of "these late eclipses": "Shakespeare's villains can normally be depended upon to tell the truth about the character of the protagonists . . . Far from being merely a diatribe of the skeptic against superstition, the speech is a justifiable criticism of Gloucester" (Smith 1958: 175). It is indeed a speech that tells us a good deal about Gloucester, but also about Edmund, who articulates a visceral anger that his father refuses to take responsibility for his own actions: "An admirable evasion of whoremaster man, to lay his goatish disposition on the charge of a star!" (1.2.111–12). Gloucester adheres to the norms, and the names, of perceived social order, to which Edmund objects: "Why 'bastard'? Why 'base'?" (1.2.6). Edmund chooses to make his own destiny by scorning signs, seemingly because his father pays them so much reverence.

But it is Lear's initial desire for flattery rather than for truth that initiates the drive toward linguistic collapse. Cordelia cannot speak as she is desired to; those offering advice are unheard; Edgar adopts, as Sheldon P. Zitner puts it, "disguises of rag and ellipsis" (Zitner 1974: 17); Lear becomes trapped in the bleak repetitions of epizeuxis. Gloucester's speech on "these late eclipses"

captures the general curtailment of speech in the play: his sentences deteri-
orate, from the portentous syntax and idiom of the opening declarations –
"These late eclipses in the sun and moon portend no good to us" – to curt and
anxious command, "Do it carefully," and then elliptical mutterings to himself:
"'Tis strange." The closing lines of the play then, only moments after Lear's
death – in spite of, and also through, their ordering rhymes – show a desire to
"speak" and in some way respond. Michael Neill addresses the similar effect at
the end of *Hamlet*, where Horatio's "stolid imagination" fails to grasp in any
significant way what has taken place. But Neill asks: "Yet if we ask what more
Horatio *could* say, the answer is not readily apparent – especially since
Hamlet's own attempts to tell his story are left hanging in frustrated aposiopesis" (Neil 1997: 241). Neill describes the impulse to "tell" in *Hamlet* as one
that is perpetually interrupted and subject to incompletion.

Marks of ellipsis, like asterisks (stars) and lunulae (Erasmus' term for round
brackets), are punctuation symbols that are connected, by name, with the
heavens. Duncan Steel, in his history of astronomical eclipses, has commented
on the etymological relationship between the eclipse and ellipsis ("a dash or
three dots in a row"), the latter being a "variant" of "eclipsis" (Steel 1999: 31).[38]
In sixteenth-century English rhetoric, both "ellipsis" and "eclipsis" were used
to describe the figure of omission.[39] George Puttenham, in his *Arte of English
Poetry* (1589), refers to "Eclipsis" as a figure of "defect": "if but one word or
some little portion of speech be wanting, it may be supplied by ordinary
understanding and vertue of the figure" (Puttenham 1589: 135). The eclipsis
signals, therefore, that that which is absent is recoverable. However, in 1633,
Charles Butler, in his *English Grammar*, provides another use for the word
when he refers to "eclipsis" as a typographical sign which indicates the
"elision of words" from a citation: "Eclipsis [—] or [---]."[40] Four years
earlier Butler had used "Ellipsis" in his *Rhetoricae Libri Duo* to describe
rhetorical omission, suggesting that he might have been distinguishing between "ellipsis," used for the rhetorical principle, and "eclipsis" for the visual
signs. And these signs, the dash and hyphens, were being used not just in
citations, but also in dramatic texts to indicate hesitations and interruptions,
aposiopesis as well as eclipsis. A new punctuation mark emerged on the pages
of late sixteenth- and early seventeenth-century print, as a means of notating
more fully the incompleteness of speech.[41]

Although used infrequently across Quarto texts of Shakespeare's plays,
marks of eclipsis are employed in the variant Quartos of both *King Lear* and
Othello.[42] In the 1608 Pied Bull Quarto of *King Lear* series of hyphens indicate

interruptions on 11 occasions.[43] The first two examples occur in Edmund's speech in Act 2, scene 1 and in both cases he is interrupted because of the anxiety of his interlocutor: first his brother, then his father:

> BAST. O flie this place, intelligence is given where you are hid, you have now the good advantage of the night, have you not spoken gainst the Duke of CORN. ought, hee's coming hither now in the night, it'h hast, and Regan with him, have you nothing said upon his partie against the Duke of *Albany*, advise your---
> EDG. I am sure an't not a word.
>
> (Q 2.1.21–9)

And a few lines later on his father's arrival:

> GLOST. Where is the villaine *Edmund*?
> BAST. Fled this way sir, which by no means he could---
> GLOST. Pursue him, go after by no meanes, what?
>
> (Q 2.1.43–5)

Lear interrupts Regan to placate her, after he has cursed her sister (Q 2.1.173).[44] Gloucester, ironically, thinking of his own woes, breaks in on Edgar's dark ravings to speak to the king:

> GLOST. What hath your Grace no better company?
> EDG. The Prince of darkenes is a Gentleman, *modo* he's called and ma hu---
> GLOST. Our flesh and bloud is growne so vild my Lord, that it doth hate what gets it.
>
> (Q 3.4.147–51)

After which Edgar himself interrupts the king (Q 3.5.21–6).[45] There are three instances in the blinding scene, beginning with the first assault on Gloucester:

> CORN. To this chaire bind him, villaine thou shalt find---
> GLOST. By the kind Gods 'tis most ignobly done, to pluck me by the beard.
>
> (Q 3.7.34–6)

Cornwall cuts his wife short, in his haste to attack the earl verbally:

> REG. Wherefore to Dover? Wast thou not charg'd at perill---
> CORN. Wherefore to Dover? Let him first answere that.
>
> (Q 3.7.51–2)

And then unable to witness the further torture of Gloucester, Cornwall's servant interrupts, allowing Gloucester to "see vengeance" in his last few moments of sight; but the servant pays for this, with his life:

> GLOST. He that will thinke to live till he be old
> Give me some helpe, O cruel! O ye Gods!
> REG. One side will mocke another, tother to.
> CORN. If you see vengeance---
> SERVANT. Hold your hand my lord
> I have serv'd ever since I was a child
> But better service have I never done you, then now to bid you hold
>   (Q 3.7.69–74)

Soon after, Gloucester refuses to listen to offers of help:

> OLD MAN. O my good Lord, I have beene your tenant, & your
> fathers tenant this forescore---
> GLOST. Away, get thee away, good friend be gon,
>   (Q 4.1.14–16)

Albany cuts short his wife in the urgency of the political situation but also because he cannot bear to hear her out (Q 4.2.66–9).[46] Finally, Regan interrupts the steward in her haste to get to her sister's letter:

> [REG.] Let me unseale the letter.
> STEW. Madam I'd e rather---
> REG. I know your Lady does not love her husband.
> I am sure of that
>   (Q 4.5.22–4)[47]

Gloucester's prediction is division and discord: "Love cools, friendship falls off, brothers divide . . . discord . . . bond cracked . . . against . . . against . . ." The language of *King Lear* imitates the divisions of the time. Interruption in each instance reveals human beings under extreme stress: it signals familial and political crisis; a brother's indignation and fear; one father's anger and another's pleas; husband against wife; sister against sister; a mad beggar interrupting a king. Zitner describes how: "Important speeches in *King Lear* seem at times to break off as if through . . . inadequacy; others are brought up short by enforced silences" creating "emblems of the play's motif of nothingness" (Zitner 1974: 4–5). This is certainly so, but interruption in *King Lear* is also emblematic of violence, verbal and physical. The language of rupture permeates the play, most insistently in the breaking and cracking of hearts. But interruption is presented explicitly as an early indication of what the new regime promises. Kent, in the stocks, tells Lear that when delivering his royal letters to Regan and Cornwall, they had permitted Oswald to disturb proceedings, cutting Kent off in the midst of his deputation. Lear's train of men is to be "cut off" by his daughters (2.4.167), but the greater suffering is to come as he feels himself "cut to th'brains" (4.5.184). In addition, to "cut off" means to kill: Regan gives commands regarding "that blind traitor," Gloucester: "Preferment falls on him that cuts him off" (4.4.39–40) and her sister wants Edmund to kill her husband: "You have many opportunities to cut him off" (4.5.250–1).

Both the Second Quarto (1619) and Folio (1623) texts of *King Lear* mark textual gaps with dashes rather than hyphens; the alternative mark of "eclipsis." And whereas in the First Quarto these marks are all terminal, indicating interruption, and the transferral of speech between characters, in the two later versions they indicate speakers' own hesitations and breakings-off, mid-speech.[48] For example, in a marking of eclipsis unique to the Folio, Lear cuts himself short (in a line that is already overextended):

> LEAR: Fiery? The fiery Duke, tell the hot Duke that –
> No, but not yet, may be he is not well
>
> (294)[49]

Lear checks his rage with an aposiopesis. He does likewise in Q and Q2, but in each Quarto a comma, rather than a dash, marks that suspension.[50] While commas have many grammatical roles, the dash signifies only discontinuity, and in this instance makes Lear's self-division much more visible. The first eclipsis of the Folio is (as in Q) Edmund's; but now it introduces his own "eclipses," facilitating his change of tone and persona:[51]

> Pat: he comes, like the catastrophe of the old comedy. My cue is villainous melancholy, with a sigh like Tom o'Bedlam – O these eclipses do portend these divisions. Fa, sol, la, me.
>
> (286)

And, eclipsis no longer surrounds the blinding of Gloucester but is mimetic of it. The dash here opens up a space for the performed, or imagined, action as well as the accompanying expressions of terror and pain:

GLOU. He that will thinke to live, till he be old,
Give me some helpe. – O cruell! O you Gods.

(300)[52]

The very final instance of the mark in the Folio of *King Lear* stands for the
death of Goneril:

EDG. What means this bloody knife?
GEN. 'Tis hot, it smoakes, it came even from the heart
of – O she's dead.
ALB. Who dead? Speake man.
GEN. Your lady Sir, your lady; and her sister
By her is poyson'd: she confesses it.

(308)[53]

This is a suspenseful aposiopesis that could be caused by the Gentleman's
anxiety or shock at the news he relates; but it also indicates a reluctance to say
Goneril's name and, in consequence, the line falls short. It is fitting that
Goneril is erased from the text: "she" and her sister are finally unspeakable.[54]

There is no doubting the elocutionary and symbolic significance of figures
of omission to Shakespearean tragedy, nor the importance of characters'
disordered speech to plot, as "choked half-lines," "frustrated utterance,"
"violent aposiopesis" recur (Neill 1997: 228, 225, 238).[55] The versions of
King Lear show a printed sign of disorder developing across the texts, so as
to make observable the "frustrated utterance" that afflicts the characters.[56]
In tragedy, the punctuation of eclipsis makes forms of loss textually present:
the loss of words through emotion; the loss of accord and tolerance between
individuals; the loss of eyes; and of the whole self, finally in death. It acts
synecdochically, because the absence of words suggests the absence of so
much more. But the representation of such emptiness encourages a desire to
fill in, descriptively and sympathetically, that which has been lost. For Freud,
for example, "filling out an ellipsis" becomes the duty of the psychoanalyst
who tries to help people recover their words (Freud 1991: 106). Kent's
determination to fight against injustice is, in the Quarto texts, an explicit
striving toward completion, in life and in speech: "My poynt and period will be
throughly wrought, / Or well, or ill, as this dayes battels fought" (Q 4.7.96–7).
The eclipse marks disjunction and disconnection, but words, theatrical and
otherwise, offer some hope for continuity after the darkness: and "defects /
Prove our commodities" (Gloucester, 4.1.20–1) from which we try to learn.

Notes

1   *Ekleipein* can mean "to leave out." I am grateful to Andrew Taylor for his comments on an earlier version of this chapter.

2   The *OED* describes "eclipsis" as 1a. "An omission of words needful fully to express the sense. *Obs.*" and 1b. "a Line drawn to denote that some part of a Verse or Sentence cited, is left out," also obsolete.

3   See Mikalson 1991: 104.

4   Thucydides 1881: 2.28 and 4.52. See Gomme 1975: 88–9.

5   Simon Hornblower describes "Th.'s claim that disastrous *natural* phenomena were more frequent during the Peloponnesian War is an embarrassment to his commentators" (Hornblower 1991: 63). See also Oost 1975.

6   See Woodman 1988: 28–32.

7   Commentators on Herodotus' use of oracles likewise have argued that they are added "to give shape and meaning to human history after the event" (Bushnell 1998: 20, referring to Crahay 1956 and Fontenrose 1978).

8   Plato, *Logics* 856e. A form of this expression continues to be used in formal modern Greek to describe the dead, or "the late."

9   Other examples include *Ion* (l.1186) and *Heracles* (l.1348).

10 *Prometheus Bound*, ll.827–8, offers a parallel: "Yet most of the weary tale I shall leave out and come to the very close of thy wanderings" (Aeschylus 1996b).

11 See Montiglio 2000: 132–7.

12 See Edith Hall's commentary on the play: Aeschylus 1996: 119. Also Kakridis 1975: 145–54. Pelling (1997: 2–6) compares light–dark, day–night contrasts in the Battle of Salamis, as described by Aeschylus and Herodotus. Michelini describes the movement between night and day in *Persians* as part of the "theme of reversal" (Michelini 1982: 115).

13 On "Aeschylean Silences and Silences in Aeschylus" see Taplin 1972.

14 Shakespeare uses the verb "eclipse" figuratively in *I Henry VI* (4.5.53): Talbot: "Then here I take my leave of thee, fair son, / Born to eclipse thy life this afternoon. / Come, side by side together live and die, / And soul with soul from France to heaven fly." This is cited in *OED* as sense 3b of "eclipse" vb. "to hide, screen, *from*. Also, to extinguish (life). *Obs.*"

15 In his *Discoverie of Witchcraft* (1584), one of the sources for *Macbeth*, Reginald Scot discusses the tradition in which witches pull down the sun and moon in eclipse. Apollonius Rhodius describes it in relation to the drama of Sosiphanes.

16 One editor, Philip Edwards, has deemed it "not a strong or necessary speech, and few would find the play worse for its absence." Shakespeare 1985: 14.

17   All of these later quotations from *Hamlet* appear in the Folio in slightly
     altered form. Quotations from Q2 are taken from the facsimile prepared
     by W.W. Greg (London: The Shakespeare Association and Sidgwick &
     Jackson, 1940).
18   Wilson 1595: B2r.
19   Contemporary historians of chronology worked often "in the conviction
     that great terrestrial events should have been accompanied by great
     celestial omens" (Grafton 2003: 224). The text from *Othello* follows
     here the New Cambridge edition, ed. Norman Sanders (Cambridge:
     Cambridge University Press, 1984).
20   Don Cameron Allen writes: "Othello reverses the ordinary attitude when
     he insists that an eclipse should follow his crime" (Allen 1966: 178, noted
     in Smith 1958: 170).
21   *Othello*, 5.2.110–12: "It is the very error of the moon:/She comes more
     nearer earth than she was wont/And makes men mad."
22   *Antony and Cleopatra*, 3.13.153–5. The other use of eclipse as a participle
     occurs in *3 Henry VI* (4.6.63), where the celestial connotations have
     waned: "My joy of liberty is half eclipsed." OED definition 3. *fig.* "To
     cast a shadow upon, throw into the shade; to obscure, deprive of lustre."
23   *The Histories of Polybius*, ed. Jeffrey Henderson (Cambridge, MA and
     London: Harvard University Press, 1927), 29.16.1: "When there was an
     eclipse of the moon in the time of Perseus of Macedonia, the report
     gained popular credence that it portended the eclipse of a king."
24   John Milton, *Paradise Lost* (1667), 1.596–9: "from behind the Moon/In
     dim Eclips disastrous twilight sheds/On half the Nations, and with fear of
     change/Perplexes Monarchs."
25   John Lyly, *A moste excellent comedie of Alexander, Campaspe, and Diogenes*
     (1584), B4v.
26   See Bosman, 2004: 570 and Wilson 2000: 238.
27   All references to *King Lear*, unless otherwise noted, are to the New
     Cambridge Shakespeare (2005).
28   Letter (1605) in Hatfield MSS. 134/79/BM Microfilm M.485/30/; quoted
     in Elton 1966: 150, n.8. Frederick George Marcham writes about this
     letter as revealing James's "favorite trick...to turn astrologer" (Marc-
     ham 1931: 321).
29   See also Allen 1966: 190–246.
30   The second of the marks of ellipsis here indicates illegible text where
     there has been a manuscript cancellation.
31   The 1619 Quarto follows the First Quarto here: (London: [W. Jaggard]
     for N. Butter, 1608 [1619]).

32 The full addition to the Folio here reads: "This villaine of mine comes under the prediction; there's Son against Father, the King fals from byas of Nature, there's Father against Childe. We have seene the best of our time. Machinations, hollownesse, treacherie, and all ruinous disorders follow us disquietly to our Graves."

33 William Elton points out that in 1605 an English translation of Le Loyer's *A Treatise of Specters* appeared, in which paganism was connected with fear of eclipses (Elton 1966: 151).

34 Wittreich, 1984: 95. John Holloway describes the speech as echoing St. Luke (21.325–6). (Holloway 1961: 76).

35 *The True Chronicle History of King Leir and his three daughters.* Leir: "As doth the sun exceed the smallest star,/So much the father's love exceeds the child's" (1.3.14–15) and "I am as kind as is the pelican,/That kills itself, to save her young ones' lives:/And yet as jealous as the princely eagle,/That kills her young ones, if they do but dazzle/Upon the radiant splendour of the sun" (2.3.43–7).

36 The words are Albany's in both Quartos.

37 McAlindon sees this as indicative of the "Edmund–Goneril party" where "everything is re-named from an opposite point of view" (McAlindon 1991: 169).

38 The *OED* ventures the explanation that "eclipsis" was "perhaps confused with 'ellipsis'."

39 The rhetorical figures of aposiopesis and eclipsis differ in that the omitted words are recoverable in the latter, while in the former they are obscure. Quintilian makes this distinction (1969: vol. 3, 481).

40 Butler 1633: 63. This is the first English grammar to include a section on punctuation. The earliest example given in *OED* for "Eclipsis" as a punctuation mark is W. Mather's *Young Man's Companion* (1727), which comes almost one hundred years after Butler's *Grammar*.

41 I have discussed this elsewhere (Henry 2005).

42 The following contain marks of eclipsis: *The whole contention betwixt the two famous houses of Yorke and Lancaster* [*II Henry VI*] (London: [W. Jaggard] for T. P[avier], 1619), *King Lear* (London: [N. Okes] for N. Butter, 1608), *King Lear* (London: [W. Jaggard] for N. Butter, 1608 [1619]), *Othello* (London: N. O[kes] for T. Walkley, 1622), *Othello* (London: A. M[athewes] for R. Hawkins, 1630), *Troylus and Cresseid* (London: G. Eld for R. Bonian and H. Walley, 1609).

43 This is based on an examination of three copies: the text here follows the Gorhambury copy, reproduced in facsimile, with an introduction by W. W. Greg (London: The Shakespeare Association and Sidgwick & Jackson, 1939). Peter Blayney, in his list of First Quarto press-variants, records one further occurrence of the marks at D4v (Blayney 1982: 593).

I am grateful to Henry Woudhuysen for allowing me to read his paper "The Dash – A Short but Quite Dramatic Account" (given at the Jacobean Printed Book Conference, Queen Mary, University of London, Sept. 2004), where he notes this variant.

44   REG. O the blest Gods, so will you wish on me,
When the rash mood ---
LEAR. No *Regan*, thou shalt never have my curse,

45   Or, perhaps, Lear is unable here to complete his utterance:

LEAR. It shalbe done, I will arraigne them straight,
Come sit thou here most learned justice
Thou sapient sir sit here, no you shee Foxes ---
EDG. Looke where he stands and glars, want thou eyes, at
tral madam come ore the broome *Bessy* to mee.

46   ALB. [...] how ere thou are a fiend,
A womans shape doth shield thee.
GON. Marry your manhood mew ---
ALB. What newes. *Enter a Gentleman.*

In Q2 the placing of the stage direction before Albany's "What newes" gives the Gentleman's entrance greater emphasis as the interrupting factor.

47   *King Lear* (1608), D3v, D3v–D4r,G3v, H1v, H2r–v, H4v, I2r.

48   Q2 repeats all the eleven interruptions marked in Q and adds a further eight instances. F shares most of its nine marks of eclipsis with Q2 (two are unique to F), but in only one case do all three texts agree; that is, when Regan tell the steward to "Let me unseale the letter." With whom these typographical signs might have originated is not a matter of concern in this chapter; nor is the question of transmission, although the variation in usage across the three texts has very interesting implications. It is generally agreed that a copy of Q2 was consulted in the printing of the Folio.

49   *Mr. William Shakespeares comedies, histories, & tragedies* (London: Printed by Isaac Jaggard, and Ed. Blount [at the charges of W. Jaggard, Ed. Blount, I. Smithweeke, and W. Aspley,] 1623), p. 302. Another example occurs at the end of the second Act when Lear cannot find the words to express his rage: "No you unnaturall Hags,/I will have such revenges on you both,/That all the world shall – I will do such things" (p. 295). This repeats Q2 (2.4.283).

50   The lines in Q read:

> Fierie Duke, tell the hot Duke that LEAR,
> No but not yet may be he is not well,
>   (Q 2.4.105–6).

51   This instance is also unique to F.

52   This also occurs in Q2, but there the three interruptions of the Q blinding scene are repeated. In the same scene in the Folio, it is only the act of blinding that is marked typographically in this way.

53   Again this follows Q2, although the text has been altered:

> ALB. What kinde of helpe? what meanes that bloody knife?
> GENT. Its hot, it smokes, it came even from the heart of –
> ALB. Who man? speake.
> GENT. Your Lady sir, your Lady;
>   (5.8.222–4)

54   The other terminal interruptions in the Folio text are as follows. In 1.4.287, Oswald slights Lear, providing him with one of the first clear demonstrations of his new diminished status. Another marks an early altercation between Goneril and Albany (290), which Albany puts to an end by means of an interruption. And in the final act, Lear interrupts the news of Cordelia's return with confusion and anxious misunderstanding:

> GENT: O heere he is: lay hand upon him, Sir. Your most
> deere Daughter –
> LEAR: No rescue? What, a prisoner? I am even
> The natural fool of fortune. Use me well.
>   (304)

55   Dashes are used in the Folio *Hamlet*, but neither dashes nor series of hyphens appear in the Quarto texts of the play (1603 and 1604–5).

56   Graham Bradshaw, in his essay "Dashing Othello's Spirits," argues for a clear methodology driving the employment of triple hyphens in the 1622 Quarto of *Othello*, so as to serve characterization and to bring us closer to the idiosyncrasies of dramatic speech. In Act 1, the majority of instances mark Iago's words, contrasting with Othello's rhetorically poised speech in the early scenes. But Othello's collapse evolves typographically: "the Quarto hyphens trace a more gradual and subtle process of disintegration which begins where we would expect, in 3.3" (Bradshaw 1993: 270).

Chapter 5

Jonson's Too Roman Plays: From *Julius Caesar* to *Sejanus* and *Catiline*

John Henderson

Howsoever I cannot escape, from some, the imputation of sharpness, but that they will say, I have taken a pride, or lust, to be bitter, and not my youngest infant but hath come into the world with all his teeth; I would ask of these supercilious politics, what nation, society, or general order, or state I have provoked? What public person? Whether I have not (in all these) preserved their dignity, as mine own person, safe?

(Jonson, *Volpone*, "The Epistle")

Just one slip of a script, the *Octavia*, survived antiquity to show how Roman history could play as authentic tragedy (Boyle 2006). Roman criticism made little of the idiom, and this princess-slaughtering *jeu* featuring Seneca on stage showed the Renaissance how to read and riff on Senecan drama – or, rather, showed that, rather than how, it could be pulled off (Smith 2003). Where Athenian democracy had turned on itself myths framed in Theban, Argive, *alien* Greek palaces, the Roman Republic transplanted the classic repertoire of hard-to-take doom and dread into magisterial celebration of its own world-beating post-regal *humanitas* (Kragelund 2002): then the *Senecan* corpus showed how Neronian absolutism eventually realized in its there and then those primal paradigms of tyranny, now amplified to match the hyperbole of imperial superpower (Boyle 1997).

Classic Roman *texts*, however, served up the full range of exemplary parables saturated with multidisciplinary exploration, critical analysis, and theory-laden disputation, that pumped Renaissance-through-Early-Modern education and wired literate culture across the networks of image, stage, print. Antique stories in the Romadrome could feed hearty swash and soapish buckle in *any* modality, but the recovery and dissemination of the caustic political thought of the "satiric" historians Sallust and Tacitus showed writers how to tear into destructive mode, as their devastating performances of Rome-ripping yarns took in the grand debacles of Roman cataclysm. There had evidently been a cult of such self-laceration, and the power of its ideas was catching. In the theater, the Roman Play was a strong brand within the welter of "history plays" that roved across a more or less continuous past reaching back through to the classical patterns and axioms from which fresh drama departed and differed (Ronan 1995).

To make a hit play, a script could hype a grand exhibition of Roman nobility with lashings of stage rhetoric, all-action death-or-inglory, and characterful, ethical, daunting intimations of universal pertinence. To make a play hit home, or take a tilt at it, the script could accentuate the negative, soup up the scandal, ape and echo headline news, tap pressure-points in current power play at court. One way or another, Roman togas – the whole panoply of power represented by Rome across European culture – would inveterately get close enough but secure enough to play as "not *not* the here-now-us" (Miola 2002). So when Roman roles were set to slate their world, audiences could be, or feel, impelled to follow suit – and slate theirs. In particular, the dynamics and logic of state apparatuses were starkly on show "back then," primed for reinvention – and/or/as abomination. Some versions of savage writing could go for it – give bums on seats a real *bad* time; that would be their pitch, turning (Rome) on their public. In reclaiming this aggressive function for the genre, Jonson's brace of "Roman plays," *Sejanus* and *Catiline*, style an abrasive line of damaging goods. Tooled up, by way of "Roman Tragedy," these self-styled (poetic) *Works* would anticipate the option of high-and-mighty audience-assault available to the modern playwright (Eliot 1950: 121; "a titanic show").

The sixteenth century wound up with a box-office winner in *Julius Caesar* (1599). Here was holiday fare for a wholehearted clientele, a crowd-pleaser from the curtain-raiser: togged-up commoners cheek and pun at the cops, who try telling them Caesar's so-called triumph is devastation for Pompey's city, before minding that "today" is indeed a bona fide folk feast-day, the Lupercalia. And the carnival hams it up, too, first joining in the fertility-cult

flummery to see if Antony can whip Calphurnia's womb into playing its part
(and so give the future an heir other than the boy Octavius), and then
bringing the house down with the reported showpiece of Caesar refusing his
crown once, twice, and thrice, "every time gentler than other" (1.2.230), says
spleen. Unaccepted, unacceptable "honours" for Caesar kick Brutus and
Cassius to summarize, programmatically, "I love the name of honour more
than I fear death"... "Well, honour is the subject of my story" (1.2.91, 94).
These spoilsports (Caesar: "that spare Cassius. He reads much... he loves
no plays" (1.2.202) spoil our fun:

> CASCA: ... I am sure that Caesar fell down. If the tag-rag people did not clap
> him and hiss him, according as he pleased and displeased them, as they use to
> do the players in the theatre, I am no true man.
>
> (1.3.257–61)

But they maybe spare us, too:

> CASCA: ... it was Greek to me.... There was more foolery yet, if I could
> remember it.
>
> (1.3.286–7)

For Act 2, stormy night joins conspirators – "the noblest-minded Romans"
(1.3.121) – to plot "honourable–dangerous consequence" (123), with, first,
notice of a fake mail-shot petition by way of wake-up call for Brutus, but
then its obviation by the gang's visit to our vigilant hero, "honoured" by
them as by "every noble Roman" (2.1.93). Accepting "O conspiracy!," he's
proud to shake on it and not call for an oath; this is Rome. These braves
must "show yourselves true Romans" and "bear it as our Roman actors do"
(2.1.77, 222, 225).

There's time to show us Brutus' "true and honourable wife" (2.1.287),
who'd never leak the plot, no fear, before Caesar spurns Ides of March
warnings, unable to resist the bait that the Senate means to "give a crown to
mighty Caesar" (2.2.94), and never hearing the Sophist's notelet listing the
assassins, instead preferring to take a fatally close look and "read this
[Trebonius'] schedule." The centerpiece Act 3 barely begun, and "ambition's
ladder" (2.1.22) never climbed, the Senate on the Capitol neither scene nor
heard: cut! This play itself has "the falling-sickness": the trip over before we
really settled in. Bah. *Julius Caesar* leaves us more or less content – and
not unduly touched – to shrug or else conjecture whether said crown
had been forthcoming, or was a smear or phobia conjured up by enmity

plus tyrannicidal "virtue," while throwing down this huge gauntlet for the play to run (Miola 1985).

Stoking up the heat, the stand-out spectacular of Antony's mob oratory directed at *our* ears will surely rule out any chance of the assassins ever escaping anticlimax in the play's denouement – short of true genius. Shakespeare never lets the Globe forget this is theater, a political theater, true, but in and about otherwheres, bent on putting us through live – electric – incitement to riot; for the "issue" is at a discount, except for that Roman gang, who have, naturally, got it coming: it was going to take at least a regicide plus a civil war in England to get a London audience on anything like the same wavelength as this machine-gun burst of 33 daggers followed by the full works of classical oratory turned rabble-rousing. Brutus' genetic imperative to maintain the status quo of the Republic's founding in expulsion of kingship by his ancestor the Liberator was a world away from Jacobean anxieties.

Brutus let Antony live; now he lets him speak at the funeral; and leaves him to it. A Servant gives us due notice that this history will (take the full prerogative of the genre, and ignore any dramatic unities it pleases, and) skip the years to deliver Octavius to Antony for a showdown shootout at sundown a couple of acts and years on down the line, at Philippi. But first, we "Romans, countrymen, and lovers!" must lend our ears. Antony the least-expected orator has been handed his style sheet, must play in Brutus' wake and by Brutus' rules – no blaming "us,/but speak all good you can devise of Caesar,/and say you do't by our permission" (3.1.247–9). No problem: Citizens First-through-Fourth are our gauge, in our role as "the people." We decide Brutus lives, OK, and "This Caesar was a tyrant" (3.2.70). Until Antony corpses on us, come to dig Caesar, not to bury him, and lamely intoning Caesar's ambition versus Brutus' honor until we feel the magic. We wonder if Caesar would've taken the crown from the Senate that he rejected before/from the People, but can't resist hearing the will – "They were villains, murderers" (3.2.156) – while Antony climbs down to *our* level, and unveils "the unkindest cut of all" (3.2.181). Thus lighting the touchpaper before standing back: "let me not stir you up/to such a sudden flood of mutiny" (205–6), this fire-starter cleans up with a final lick of agitprop denials – where "I am no orator... I only speak right on" (212, 218) *means* "I predict a riot, I predict a riot on" – and we're off on the rampage, out for blood. Start with a poet wandering on, do him for his verse, for his name, "It is no matter," just "Tear him, tear him" (3.3.33, 35), and so to Rome. "Away! Go!," ends Act 3, off to torch all their houses, and bring down the house.

"O! What a fall was there, my countrymen,/then I, and you, and all of us fell down" (3.2.188–9). And we did, too, all of us. How hard is it to feel that this is "our" play, for today? Verbal sorcery, the figured pride of classical rhetoric, and direct revenge regressive as the *sparagmos* winding up any mythical *Bacchae*. But guilt must set in. Act 4 starts at once to pick up the counter-rhythm and repossess our ears, as (still in Rome, at home with Antony, for this moment) another gang teams "friend" Antony with his fellow-proscriptionist triumvirs, fiddling that inflammatory will of Caesar to make a (financial) killing on the side, so we must be sure he conned one and all, lied through his boots with every Molotov disclaimer. Lepidus will be jettisoned shortly, we're given notice: Antony and Octavius will indeed leave us hungry for their sword-and-asp *Carry On Cleo* sequel (1607), as staked out finally by the play's last lines (*Antony and Cleopatra* pits legionary Roman suicide turned *Liebestod* against an African Queen's legendary Pharaonic reginacide, for showstopping climax).

You don't have to realize that we are quitting the *Life of Caesar* for Plutarch's *Life of Brutus* to spot that a new cast is rehearsing for the fray as we jump to Brutus' tent in Asia, where Cassius comes to bond, resolving tensions arising from friction in the exchange of letters; other letters afflict Brutus – that superwife is dead; Octavius and Antony are on the march; a hundred senators – maybe seventy, but including Cicero – are dead for the bounty. Up alone at night, Brutus gets back to his book, just in time for his "evil spirit" (4.2.333), the ghost of Caesar, to come for him: Philippi!

So to Act 5, and over to DeMille, for the meeting in full rig between both armies on stage simultaneously. Jousting taunts, the challenge, and Brutus preserves his unbroken record of folly intact, by overruling Cassius' strategy. *Alarum* fireworks accelerate the tempo through a six-line scene – (Brutus) "Ride! Ride!"(5.2.1) – answered by an eight-liner – "O! look..., O Cassius!" (5.3.1, 5) – as the battle goes to blazes, and the noble-suicidal Romans pile the boards with corpses: Cassius' turn to get it all wrong, followed by Titinius for unwittingly misleading him – "the last of the Romans," quoth Brutus. *Alarum* again: *Enter fighting,* Soldiers *of both armies.* "Young and noble Cato..." *is overpowered, and falls.* But Brutus – "no enemy/shall ever take alive the noble Brutus" (5.4.21–2) – is granted his last stand, looking for help to die, before (*Alarum still*) He runs on his sword. *Alarum*: meet the winners, for the play's (self-congratulatory) benediction: "This was the noblest Roman of them all./...This was a man...According to his virtue let us use him,/.......this happy day" (5.5.67, 75, 80).

This was a drama, and a half. The Hollywood clichés throw these two macho all-action acts into the reckoning to make it worth our watching Caesar kill Brutus, so our loser can win at the death by daring hara-kiri, trump card of nobility triumphant (*and curtains*). So many indicators confirm that this is a play for the lot of us: classic *Roman* suicide! (Helms 1992). We're *not* to like being "done" by oratory, and it's Brutus who ends up being (wrong, but how wrong? and anyhow) "right on," for all his stuck-up graces, bookish fancies, and patchy comrades. Indeed, the more the merrier. There was so little played behind closed doors, reserved for the powers-that-be, decided in the wings. This playwright knew to trail texts before us – but to keep *them* under wraps; he does wave plotters plotting at us – but as foil for the true libertarian, who does no skulking, recruiting, propagandizing, jiggery-pokery, just does the bloody deed, with his: "Let's all cry, 'Peace, freedom, and liberty!'" (3.1.111). This play is effectually *inclusive*, and tells us so (Helms 1992. Universalizing/ humanizing all the way back to Attica, forsooth: Silk 2004):

> CASSIUS: How many ages hence
> shall this our lofty scene be acted o'er,
> in states unborn and accents yet unknown!
> BRUTUS: How many times shall Caesar bleed in sport
> (3.1.112–15)

The answer, my friend, is blowin' in the mind; but if there are any roads of freedom, they still do walk down to this panto-Rome. Say what you like,

Figure 5.1 *Sejanus* by the Royal Shakespeare Company. © RSC/Stewart Hemley

providing you can carry off the farce-paced choreography of those Armageddon alarmed military maneuver (a far tougher ask than the line-up for backstabbing), this play won't close theaters.

When the same company took over the same rounded playhouse in 1604, with Shakespeare playing the "upstairs" role of the running-down battered emperor who may well be running things, you'll have to stick around and figure that out, and Burbage, Jr. (son of the founder of the Globe) taking the lead role of Sejanus, as he had or would Richard III, Hamlet, Othello, Lear, Macbeth, and Catiline, to name but a few, the up-and-coming scriptwriter Jonson couldn't have imagined that it was going nowhere fast. In fact, *Sejanus*, the story of the rise and fall of Tiberius' right-hand man, hasn't ever been performed *his* way: the 2005–6 Royal Shakespeare Company version directed by Greg Doran, which opened the "Gunpowder Season" at the Swan in Stratford, was adroitly pruned and souped up, still lining up 21 actors to take a bow, and still being tarred for cumbersome wordiness; and on its only other outing, a 1928 William Poel production at the Holborn Empire, with Arruntius supposedly mocked up as Jonson, and Cordus as Shakespeare so he could recycle the immortal line "the last of all the Romans," *Sejanus* was cut by about a quarter, chopping the "Germanicans" and halving Tiberius' exorbitant letter at the *peripeteia*. We hear tell of armies of extras:

> a crowd, monks, gaolers, pages, girls, maharajahs – even Sabinus' faithful dog... There was a banquet scene in the first Act... The stage was heavily militarized: Silius was followed about by his private retinue of soldiers carrying his trophies, while five or six other regularly accompanied Tiberius. In the final Senate scene, Laco brought in a guard of "six Cromwellian soldiers," carrying guns.
>
> (Jonson 1990: 40)

The year before they went public, the King's Servants had premiered for the court. According to Jonson's address "To the Readers" in the Quarto version (1605), the script we have was purged from the original collaboration (with Chapman, it is supposed). So Jonson's authorized *Sejanus* is yet to face an audience. I shall read over now, with *Julius Caesar* for constant point of comparison.

It seems likely that he encouraged the idea that the play got him into trouble with the (Privy) Council in 1603 and with the watching public in 1604, part and parcel of the same orchestration of his launch as a celebrity worth cultivation that had seen him shadow-boxing for scandal with Dekker and Marston in 1600–1, in a conspiratorial scam for publicity that pitted his lampooning skit *The Poetaster* against their *Satiromastix*. Jonson wrote himself into the shoes of the poet Horace, facing a brazen conspiracy that put him in the dock before Augustus, with Virgil (Virgil!) for judge. For all of Jonson's hyped record as desperado and daredevil, he was busy already fashioning a laureate future when he co-designed the pageantry for James I's entry to his capital, and then landed his first of many hires for the new court's masque. *Volpone* (also 1605) was his breakthrough hit, performed at both Oxford and Cambridge, and prefaced with a brash *Preface* proclaiming his classicizing credentials ("The laws of time, place, persons he observeth"; and his affinity with Horace). For all the ups and downs that blessed *The Alchemist* (1610) and damned *Catiline* (1611), the coup in producing his collected *Works* raised him to "Poet Laureate" status – celebrated by *The Devil is an Ass* (his last play for a decade), marked by an honorary MA, Oxon, and sealed by a royal pension (all 1616). Both in the paraphernalia of the folio edition preliminaries and on other, later, occasions for self-styling, Jonson's spin combined his Horatian aspirations to the rank of poet and theorist of poetics (translating and, he said, commenting on the peculiarly *drama*-oriented *Ars Poetica*) with enough reminiscences of early high jinks, back when he could still hit and run, to keep the legend of (Juvenalesque) satiric bravado alive. And it's true that both his "Roman plays" do manage to collide with the flashpoints of his times – though Catiline and his incendiaries menaced Rome a good half-dozen years after Guy Fawkes' Catholics composed their plot of Gunpowder Treason, and *Sejanus'* spectacular *Fall* told of a succession of court favorites whose crashes linked "Sejanus" Leicester of the 1580s, through the crises of Essex and Raleigh (1601, 1603), to Somerset ahead (his trial in 1616, the year of the folio) and Buckingham still to come in the 1620s. As has been shown in detail (Perry 2006: 229–75), the paradigm of the Upstart minister, who is buffer, scapegoat, instrument, medium, and menace to his variously humane, naïf, devious, aloof, wise, or paranoid boss, played within an endlessly permutating political discourse that discovered its own Machiavellian prehistory in the recovered works of Tacitus, Roman historian of the first two dynasties of Caesars, from Tiberius onward (covered in *Annals* I–VI).

Even when news stories threw up nothing of the kind, the "Sejanus" model of political instability at court worked on readers of Tacitus the First World over, stimulated, intensified, and extended by the availability of full-length commentary and translation (Lipsius, 1574, and, into English,

Greneway, 1598). Tacitus' (melo)dramatized narrative notoriously contrives to seed its unfolding events with multiple partial perspectives, techniques of suspending authorization and figures of innuendo, to the point where reading consists in participating along with the Roman characters and groupings caught in the textual web. Which fiendish mimesis has won him the aura of *éminence grise*, on the money at second-guessing all and sundry.

That a Caesar might become, or prove to be, a tyrant was one parable that could never be pinned to *Julius*, thanks to Brutus's preemptive strike. And since Augustus was the self-inventing founder of Roman autocracy, he too was strictly nonreplicable – so undercutting all *his* rivals to come. But Tacitus' emperors *begin* from succession, from Tiberius' succession, and continue with the evolution of dynasty (leading to implosive interregnum, before reinvention of terms of continuity). And Tacitus' *Annals* feature an incipient cult of receding republicanism, and its varieties of nostalgia. Hence his Tiberius comes close *enough* to the contemporary "legitimate" monarch – not excluding the Scots. Yes: Tiberius, Caligula, Claudius, Nero – *they* were the monsters patterning spite and fear of every "tyrant" on the globe. And if you had an education or plenty of determination, you could get to grips with the whole story, without needing to turn scholar.

When Jonson tooled an elaborately "Romanized" layout for the quarto, he insisted on Latinate "Actus Primus," etc.; he had the substantial pieces of writing which he included in the script laid out "epigraphically"; and, in the Eliotic waste land of his margins, he planted an onward-marching column of references to passages in the primary classical texts interspersed with sec-ondary works (in severe abbreviation) that gave the punchiest accounts of the various formulae, ceremonial procedures, and social customs on display in the lines adjacent. In truth, Jonson's citations are, necessarily, for the most part either the obvious chief source in Tacitus, in Suetonius' *Life of Tiberius*, or Dio's fragmentary history (Book 58), or else routine identifying testimo-nia attached to proper names. Access to Justus Lipsius' great commentary would put virtually all this archive in your hands, ready assembled *ad loc* (Worden 1994).

The insistent claim to write from on high, on a level with the controlling powers that be within the story as well as among the ancient "author(itie)s," sets the tone for aggressively caustic exposure of the cannibalisms endemic to a court. Jonson chooses to draw laughably scant attention to his framing of his script by studded gems taken over from the succinct tableau in Juvenal, *Satire* 10, where Sejanus stars as *the* exemplum of Roman ambition

(vv. 58–107); nor does he advertise his use of Senecan machinery, set-pieces, and strenuous conceits that pin the unfolding delusions of Sejanus to Atreus' in *Thyestes*, as his disgusting sadism triumphs over his victim brother for the duration of his – their – play (Schiesaro 2003). (*Atreus*' "Fall" lies ahead, in tomorrow's revenge. *Medea* serves up more key monomaniac touches. So, too, the Caesar of Lucan's "Senecan" epic.) This classy craftsman knew the ropes, how to shape prose narrative into dramatic poetry, just as he could call on a wide repertoire to supply stock materials for a wrenching atrocity. (Claudian's Rufinus hands him the full tableau for Sejanus' dismemberment, *un*signaled.) He's not about to spotlight his toolbox. The parade of references indicating prose hunks transformed to jagged verse has very different ambitions.

When the Acts are formally divided by a *"Chorus of musicians,"* performance montage is being given the same up-market "classicist" glossing as is signaled by the paraded "Latinate" diction, featuring translationese, heavily etymologizing usage ("insolent" = not customary, *et sim.*), and the whole syntactic profile of mock – "Tacitism" (antisymmetrical inconcinnity, staccato parataxis, agitational hustle [Mulryan 2000]). All of which presses into loaded salience this theater's comprehension of the tokens, moves, symbology, and psychodynamics of bedchamber and bodyguard, star chamber and council (Sweeney 1985). Arch, knowing, insider-dealing, this was a fit first offering to the king from His Majesty's servants. Indeed, a real Latinist then or now knows, before a word forms, that this artisan was taking on the Annalist's mantle – and literally rewriting history. As we shall see, in his second "Roman tragedy," he'll try on a still more audacious intervention on the Roman scene – if not *quite* so heralded.

On page or stage, *Sejanus* flattens its crowd flattered by Shakespeare. Every move *Julius Caesar* made to exhilarate "us," Jonson turns into a lever for alienation. Let's see. The stage fills for Act 1, in two groups apart, Sabinus and Field-Marshal Silius cursing a rotted Rome and smearing the clients of Sejanus opposite, on silent watch. They are joined by the historian Cordus and gruff survivor Arruntius – who gets the line "'Tis true, that Cordus says,/'Brave Cassius was the last of all that race'" (1.1.104), while the Others are no sooner joined by a fifth-columnist than he is quizzed sotto voce on Cordus as they slink off; living proof of deplorable Times. Two major players parade past them (and us): first Crown Prince Drusus is escorted on his way, variously assessed by our band of worthies, aside, acting as supplementary spectators: he is an opportunity for them to lament the elimination of Germanicus, the good emperor that never was. Next comes

Sejanus, doing business with more cronies on the wing, but instantly alert to the main chance, of access through her personal physician to Drusus' wife. Our huddle of Germanicans groan in the wings at the sycophancy, then, as some of the clients hang behind, ears flapping, their expostulations at Sejanus' fiendish plotting toward his own far distant success at succession turn to risky threats duly accepted by the snoops. We have touched down in the Babylon of Juvenal, *Satire 3*, sat beside the catwalk of perverted senators of *Satire* 4, watched spies work the forum, heard the vending of office and "honours" conducted in inane formulae of virtue – "He's the noblest Roman" (267) – this Upstart – "where he takes – " (1.1.267) (as beautifully self-canceling as it is self-confuting).

Our worthy bystanders somehow fade into the shadows without actually exiting while barter with the doctor swells to the scale of a skit: the villain we love to hate manages to coarse it up with woman-baiting body banter sliding seamlessly into open bragging of his command of what "the world" styles "honourable," before launching into the first of his "Atreus" mono-mania-logues, clarifying for us that power rush is better than sex. Just the ticket, so far?

Our onstage match commentators next resume their soundtrack of snide asides to undermine Tiberius' promising rejection of flattery, *almost* spurring themselves, at last and at length, to stick their necks out and open his eyes, while he busies himself with a pile of letters, before delivering a peach of Tiberian dissimulation. The counterpart gang of toadies ooh and aah till Tiberius' second wind switches instantly into accepting mode, lapsing into approval of Sejanus, and his statue for Pompey's theater, while (over-) elaborating denials of flattery but then refusing to have his princely motives examined by such as us: "above the poor low flats of common men" (538). Our never-never whistleblowers manage a "Caesar!" to his disappearing back, canceled at once with their own "Peace" (541), but interject spirited loud bravos into Drusus' overheard soliloquy of indignation. This time, his delay throws the choreography, and upon Sejanus' entry this town is suddenly not big enough for the both of them, and "Take that! *Drusus strikes him*" (565). Clear the stage, meaningfully leaving Sejanus in control, and swearing covert (Senecan) revenge. "Brave, brave Drusus!," squeal the Roman resistance (biff), then "Good! Brave! Excellent brave prince! . . . A noble prince!" (565, 574) That is, and so say all of us, "A Castor, a Castor, a Castor, a Castor!" (575) – his bratpack nickname after . . . a hulking *gladiator*.

Watch the play diffract around all the dislocation, channeling all we see and hear through our surveillance team of interceptors. They'll never stop the slide or spring the plot. Their morale is the product of the demoralized Times they bemoan: draggy defeatism beckons. As those musicians play through the first intermission, stop-start dramaturgy puts impetus in its place: only Sejanus can pull us out of this stall, and in Act 2 he brings us a treat of adulterous seduction and buggery, while Dr. Druggist mixes poison and cosmetics for his princess, and the concoction brewed from Ovid's *Ars Amatoria* confected with Juvenal *Satire* 6 (add a dash of Martial, because he's worth it) in a trice has made over-tedious hand-wringing into knockabout prinking fun worthy of Plautus. Tiberius' partner in empire certainly enjoyed it, taking time out for a third monologue (more on the sweet – Atrean – prospect of revenge) before answering Tiberius' summons for a tête-à-tête with his prospective partner in crime.

In *this* play, the "conspirators" hold all the cards on high, and mark down all the cast. Between them, Sejanus, you would say/see, takes control, planning ways and means, and settling a fiendish pecking-order for the victims and running-order for the play – "that discontented list" (2.221): Silius' card is marked for first up = for Act 3, venue the Senate sitting as court. A perked-up Tiberius at least spoke the (metatheatrically implosive) words "We can no longer/keep on our mask to thee, our dear Sejanus" (2.278–9), act it the way you feel you must, and for his flourish of an exit-line even dares venture on Anglo-Greek rhyme in the fee-fi-fo-fum slogan: "While I can live, I will prevent earth's *fury,/emou thanontos gaia michthêtô puri*" (2.329–30)! (Just a saw in the wind – but still *Greek to us*.) The spies set to entrap the Germanicans draw a blank, but no matter – they can make stuff up in any case. Monologue four sets Sejanus' sights on Germanicus' heirs, since, as the foregathering Germaniclan now discovers, while the would-be vultures circle, Prince Drusus is expiring fast: Silius reads ahead to the Senate awaiting him past the second musical chorus, "No tree, that stops his prospect, but must fall" (2.500).

Enter both gangs – "we,/that are the good-dull-noble lookers-on" (3.16) versus "my subtle whisperers" (3.15) – as the set shifts to formal session. Sejanus' ostentatiously scripted show trial winds up the puppet magistrates and stately ceremonial formulae gild the cynical play of *Realpolitik* (Miller 1983). But the emperor interrupts: his only son Drusus dead, "this Sphinx" would commend Germanicus' boys to the protection of the Conscript Fathers (aka the Senate). Commentators Arruntius & co., whispering from the backbenches, remind us this isn't necessarily face value – "Well acted, Caesar" (3.105) – and encourage us to join in giggling at the rigmarole of abdication tendered, poisonously staining Tiberius' whole performance as poisonous poison – "Why, this doth render all the rest suspected!" (118) – as the House rises as one, to belt out the national anthem in unison. So to the agenda – short-fuse Generalissimo Silius is meted out "justice," not "law," trapped by the classically trained inquisitor – "Well worded, and most like an orator" (283) – but beats the rap by "falling" on his sword: cue the real tussle, disputing the right to damn the traitor/canonize the martyr, either side of one verse caesura: "O desperate act! – An honourable hand!" (340). Our benediction "'Twas nobly struck" (341) is at once outbid by (crocodilian?) regrets from the throne, "We...intended to preserve thee, noble Roman" (343–6). The loose ends tied, enter under arrest item number 2, "Noble Cordus" (371), the annals of Rome brought to life, indicted for the treason of praising Brutus, and underwriting "that 'Cassius was the last of all the Romans'" (392). Cool under fire, this one, we acclaim his rebuttal as "Freely and nobly spoken" (461) and (conceivably?) a spanner in the works: "He puts 'em to their whisper." They *disappear* this prisoner, burn his books, and leave "us" holding the fort, to lament the reign, as us-ual. But was noble Roman suicide a blow struck for undying freedom or a fit of histrionics? And does Cordus matter or does what's in his books? Either way, Jonson spoils, good as dismantles, "the Roman frame of mind" he has invoked (Maus 1984).

Trust our privileged inside-track of fly-on-the-wall "subtitles," and we'll know exactly what we've witnessed. That our panel of experts spin instant opinionation, but none of us, but none, can read the ruse of power in operation. So now *does* it help to go behind the scenes? In private conclave we watch Sejanus overreach by asking Tiberius for his newly widowed princess's hand. Can the Favorite make the jump into royalty? Is he pulling the emperor's strings – was he, will he, could he – *ever*? Does Tiberius dangle "better to come and soon" for real, or has he been waiting all along for the moment when the minion landed on this square? There can be no better conditions for observing the secrets of empire...And the next secret soon arrives when the ruler departs to read his unruly minister's written reasons (his "charms") why the cat best leave Rome for his rat to play with the mice. The sixth manic monologue of glee is capped when Sejanus leaves us alone – but this time Tiberius reenters, to remind himself to "hold a certain space/ between th'ascender's rise and thine own flat" (3.644–5). When in doubt, call in a stooge, clone the next Sejanus: on his way up, Macro can stand in securely as his absent master's eyes and ears. This new spymaster "engine" concludes, from the off, "his fall/may be our rise" (3.47–8). And – *Chorus of musicians.*

Meantime, the company are still in the toils of Sejanus' scheme to remove all obstacles, Germanican, senatorial, or princely, and miss the news. These micro-success stories set each other up, line themselves up, *as* a succession. For our benefit, the Favorite Saga is herewith granted a rerun by royal appointment, from the top for this next take. Before, we only came in after Sejanus'd got his start. But, more to the tragic point, the rerun with his rising successor Macro will *also* put us in the picture, so we'll never again obsess on our Bismarcks one at a time: the system is up and running, the personnel come and go, because, no less than any Kaiser, (a) Sejanus is a function of government; not a one-off, but programmed on serial obsolescence and replication. Now Tiberius has taken his bow, his surrogate will play the obedient instrument, executing his plot by executing his own discard predecessor and (briefly) debutant plotter. And no one notices: as if *Sejanus* was still showing, and two acts to go.

The Germanican sheep muster again, count losses, make juicy targets for Act 4. Silius' partner at the outset, Sabinus, is bugged, trapdoored into loose talk by a hefty dose of his own brand of complaints ("When to be high, or noble, are made crimes" (4.129)). Accelerating tempo denies him a passion scene (Fido still by his side in the Tiber is *reported* to us!), and we *only* hear tell of the fourth victim, done for in a trice, in one single Macro co(s)mic verse ("feasted today by Caesar, since committed!" (4.236)). Already bent on preemptive strike as "preparation to his fall" (4.88), Macro makes a move, to save one darlin' princeling (*Caligula!*) for later and for posterity. But our ranting commentator Arruntius' record teams up with the best ally on offer, that "prodigy,/a great, a noble Roman, and an honest" (4.274–5), whose "arts" (creed? secret? shame?) are "to suffer, and be silent" (295). The pair are preoccupied with the expulsion of a further trio of Germaniclans, 1–2–3, by Sejanus. Arruntius *still* supposes that "our night-eyed Tiberius doth not see/his minion's drifts" (363–4), away in debauched retirement, "acting his tragedies with a comic face" (379). Yet waves of teasing imperial letters now make the running and the reading, alternately and oracularly raising and sinking Sejanus' stock, until our ringside commentators assure us and each other that Tiberius "hath some scent/of bold Sejanus' footing" (446–7), while the other gang is equally reassured that their guy "is still in" good "grace" (479), and register but discount Macro's odd emergence as his prince's champ.

(The final *Chorus of musicians*. Let Act 5 commence:)

Sejanus' ninth monologue of his dozen puts him up there with Seneca's exultant Atreus, deaf to signs of his bandwagon falling apart, and blind to

Macro's variation on his own earlier orchestration of the grand Senatish Inquisition. Using Tiberian letters and his own to suborn, summon, and station magistrates, courtiers, and soldiers, the waxing Favorite organizes another comprehensive governmental conspiracy, this time targeting the first minister, lost in his own megalomanic balloon. Along with a stageful of dysfunctional groups and gangs all throwing their babble track of asides, confidences, chants, and exclamations into the mix, our tin Caesar is lured to the meeting by promises of crowning elevation onto Tiberius' pedestal. Through these scripted shreds Jonson plants his own satiric asides on the "honourable men" working those corrupt corridors, as suspense builds for the herald's amplified reading of the "huge, long, worded letter/from Capreae" (5.796–7).

For these packed benches on stage and in the auditorium are treated to strictly literate denunciation from a literal dictator, as the tone modulates (as in Antony's demagoguery) from the expected boost of preferment to progressively less veiled condemnation for treason, and increasingly open desertion of the Favorite out of favor. Sejanus' failure to scotch and halt the epistle is completed by Macro's strong-arm arrest and frogmarching him away to face what he has coming. To this point, boos and catcalls from groundlings or boxes would represent a welcome response to comeuppance for the execrated "insolent Monster... Typhoeus, Prodigy, Traitor" of the piece (5.669, 673, 696, 697). But *Sejanus* has a sting in its tale, in its triple–treble messenger speech. First "the eager multitude" tear down – savage – the statues; and then the "herd" of "beasts... these very rascals... the rude multitude" (808) rip head from body, limb from limb, and detail by detail. Had enough? A bonus third narrative socks it to us with the disgusting disposal of the children (and the princess). "My monster,/the multitude..., rogues" at once repent their own barbarity, they "grieve,... wish him collected, and created anew" (879–88). The perfunctory call home appealing to "this example" (namely, "to move th'insolent man") seals the script, but surging audience antipathy must figure in the calculation. When *Sejanus* turns round to lash out at its populace, let loose as mindless horde for the finale of orchestrated *sparagmos*, it is all of a piece. Having trounced the power-merchants, the play makes mugs of the people: surely mass rage at the stage is *invited* by this script. (As per the ads in the *Works'* paratextual preliminaries.)

This Roman Play's polished talkers have recited centos patched from canonical Latin prose into quality verse; they declaimed just the way guaranteed to rile a public. From on high. All makes for an extreme case of classicism traduced, as these flumps prove time and again how literate education sponsors sarcastic cynicism voided by denunciatory sermonizing. To cap all, as Act 5 ventures past the rise of Sejanus between January 23 and early 29, Jonson dares plug the wicked lacuna in our manuscript tradition for the *Annales*, which has engulfed the *Fall* from the exile of the Germanican royals onward, right through Macro's coup de théâtre on October 18, 31, and that month's immediate fall-*out*. From November onward, we can read Tacitus again, through to Tiberius' demise (at Caligula and Macro's hands) in 37 CE/*Annals* VI. The (Greek) account in Dio Book LVIII comes to us holed and reliant on Byzantine excerpts, though one substantial chunk does carry much of the all-important crisis; and Suetonius has his cracked crack at it. But schooled classes knew all along that Jonson was of set purpose bidding to take on Rome's greatest historian at his own game, patching and writing over the edges of the hole till it will never show; filling in a convincing *peripeteia*, as if to the manner born. (Senecan) Tragedy conspired with this poet to usurp his Roman author's realm, emptying out self-determining agency, reason, and context in favor of double-bind positionality, syndrome, and cycle (Braden 1985). And the telling hermeneutic impasse of Tacitus' Tiberius and "his" narrative makes for a disconcertingly rough ride for every participant observer (Williams 1990). But *Jonson's* obeisance to killer textuality performs *self*-adulation for all to see, through his marvelous repair to the damaged classic – crowning the episode's withering tale of Roman tragedy (Santoro L'hoir 2006). This for the one time that imperial inscrutability lifted the veil, to keep Tacitus' whole sick crew steam-rolling, no prisoners taken. *The day the emperor wrote sense* straight through Roman paranoia.

By implication, *Julius Caesar* must, in both senses, be a sell-out. Where *Sejanus* sears and sneers: "That's anti-~~entertainment~~. . . . "

Tacitus' affiliation of his Sejanus to Sallust, through displayed intertextuality between his introductory fanfare at *Annals* IV.1 and Catiline's debouchment where the *Bellum Catilinae* launches into narration, cements Jonson's return to Rome, with *Catiline* as prequel to fallen *Sejanus* (Woodman 1988: 180). This second time round (at) the Globe, the script parades processions of re-pointed writing from Cicero's prize consular orations (*De Lege Agraria* prominent besides those first-grade set texts, *Catilinarians* I–IV) as jewels ostentatiously restored to the saga, whence Sallust had made a point of "excising" them (Worden 1999).

Diverting for initiates, the bulk of *In Cat.* II will be diverted to Act 5, scene 1's Unto the Breach speech from the stand-in career General on location.

As response to *In Cat.* III, Latin tiros will applaud the Meanest Mobster's alternative script, with feeling:

> Consul..., your part
> had not then bene so long, as now it is;
> I should have quite defeated your Oration;
> and slit that fine rhetoricall pipe of yours,
> in the first Scene.
>
> (5.4.171–5)

Last laughs *for Latinists*, and one in the eye for every Juvenal, when at the death *Cato*, "voyce of Rome," unremarkably blesses Cicero's worst line in all classical verse (5.9.4–6): "So, Marcus Tullius, thou maist now stand up,/and call it *happie Rome, thou being Consul*" (*O fortunatam-natam me consule Romam*, *Satire* 10, 122, next in line after Sejanus; the Catilinarians will soon lose their heads, at vv. 286–8). Every Roman in his Humor, folks, and Everyman written right Out of it. You'll soon pick up the plot – Jonson's plot, out to discomfit any theater audience by exploding Catiline's *literary* plot to bring down Rome.

Caustic denigration of the fallen author along with the society that had spoiled, then ruined, him (turned him into symptom and analyst, aka *writer*) trained reformed rake Sallust's scorn on conspirators and government alike, indeed on conspiracy narrative as such (Pagan 2005: Chapter 1). Voiding bites of language as so many mystificatory scraps (Batstone 1986). In his wake, Jonson, too, is picking now (on) an(other) aborted flash-in-the-pan coup that could have spelled curtains for Rome. Degrades the sleazeball desperadoes and deflates their flopped revolution; yet portrays the self-promoting figure representing the "authorities" as the sultan of spin. This opportunist upstart in charge Cicero stage-manages drama into crisis, stampeding self-incriminating malcontents into isolated rebellion (under the demonized "Insolent Monster, Fiend, Fury" of *this* piece, Act 5, scene 4) while conniving at ratted-on big fry (Crassus and Caesar-before-he-invented-*Caesar*), and, naturally, *les girls*. Hardened colleagues get the score as it racks up (yes, Caesar and Crassus again, obviously, Act 3, scene 1):

> Popular men,
> they must create strange monsters, and then quell them;
> to make their artes seem something. Would you have
> such an Herculean Actor in the Scene,
> and not his Hydra? ...

> Treasons, and guiltie men are made in States
> too oft, to dignifie the Magistrates.
>
> (96–100, 102–3)

Gilding grubby spooks and blackmailed moles, man of the moment Mr. SPQR grabs the mike to declaim that perennial box set of orations forever dinned into the establishment in short trousers. (*"Quousque tandem . . . ?,"* indeed, quoth Sallust's Catiline, ahead of this opening gambit in Cicero's lengthy "oration or high language," become Act 4, scene 2's "Whither at length . . . " (4.2.116). For Cicero's orchestration of the forum: Krostenko 2004).

Again the script *starts* with crowd-pleasing fireworks ("A strange, unwonted horror...As at Atreus' feast!" (1.311–14)) and rabble-rousing kneejerks ("We, all this while, like calme, benum'd Spectators,/sit, till our seates do cracke...?" (1.404–5)). Revs up with a first act pulling in the Cry Freedom-fighter gangsters to stockpile their less-than-principled motives for insurrection and take the pledge Brutus disdained, only quaffing from a punchbowl laced with fresh human (a surplus slave's) BLOOD..., while the antihero's much-lusted wife drums up girl power to do their bit, and keep mum, in character until "the Scene shift[s], in our Theaters" (1.185). (One sister, The Brains, will later even cite *Thucydides* on (Greek) diplomats, "aka spies" (4.5.12–3). In Act 2 Cicero's own female interest (agent Fulvia) plays all too convincing an Ovidian-Martialic-Juvenalian scrubber when we catch her, not face-painting, but shuffling tedious loverboys through the comic-cuts boudoir, before she gets to play Mata Hari no sooner in bed with her ickle plotter than on the phone to the consul (Boyd 1987). Comic travesty is owned when the weakest link cuts up rough before turning worm ("I must...plucke/the tragicke visor off" (2.277–8)) and Mellowdrama, when the premier moves straight to red alert ("It so far exceedes/all insolent fictions of the tragicke Scene" (3.2.24–5)).

These bedraggled rebels have no Caesar, no cause; the counter-conspiracy, the Ciceronian Plot, gets under way early, steadily recruiting motley members from assorted minnows, stoolpigeons, and moral crusaders, until our outed nocturnal hoodlums in the final act invert into a perversely brave regiment of what to the naked eye look just like rank "noble Romans" fighting to the last man ("A brave bad death,/had this bene honest now" (5.9.84–5)). Socking it to us with embedded *Into Battle* speech exercises (live and livened up by self-ironization, "I never yet knew...that a Generals oration made/an Army fall, or stand" (5.5.1–4)) and *Reports from the Front* (via courier, souped up with overwhelming odds, virtuous wounds, the full works). Alack as well as alarum: these coulda-been heroes bad lads of the Upper Fifth are crushed, so, by the massed forces of their world state. (Eat your heart out, Cassius.)

But this Sallustian finale is shot through with intimations of what is to come. *His* spectacular Senatorial Courtroom had already convened to hear, at length, the thinking of Caesar and Cato on fit punishment for the Enemy Within; and *that* pairing (atavistic severity versus improvized reinvention) was, Sallust knew, soon enough to stand for the end of the Republic. (For the synkrisis of rhetorics played false: Batstone 1988.) And that thought beggars this whole tempest in a tea cup, the Catilinarian plot, the last occasion when elected magistrates would utilize their might to put paid to a might-have-been. The Field-Marshals turned on Rome and the legions caved in the whole system, soon enough, for good (Henderson 1998). By contriving to survive, we knew all along, the Republic had proved it was already dead in the water.

Now Jonson takes care to sabotage *all* the players, with lashings of split-stage muttering and fraction, and with them goes the hollowed Roman rhetoric of honor, faith in the electoral process, ruling class esprit de corps, as every page in the script sprays lousy "Noblest Romanes..., Noble confederates..., Brave, Valiant...Vertue" salutations around like yester-year's confetti. The saviors of the day are *all* throwback, or sinister, or sordid, posers, and worse. In this *authentic* Rome, none more so, Jonson dresses up the fake triumph of The System in the weeds of Senecan Tragedy – with bloodwhetting ghost for sullen prelude à la *Thyestes* (or *Agamemnon*). And his later-but-earlier Roman Play will give up on interval music, and distribute Sallust's rhetoric of despair spiked with execration out of Lucan's book *through a full-blown classical Chorus* to commence each act with ampli-ficatory reflections on menaced polity, voters' pietism, cosmic doom.

Where Shakespeare only ever ventured just the one half-ways proper Chorus, for *Henry V* (1599) – and *then* to commandeer him for whipping up to the rafters patriotic participation "within this wooden O" (*Eng-er-land...*: Mason 2002: 180), Jonson heads straight for this most stylized, least lubricant, dinosaur of a scene-shifter, to peg his script to the mighty (testing) set-piece extravaganzas of oratory he insists on inflicting on Senate and theater-people alike. Out to show the lessons don't work any more, this time, true, our poetaster points up the uniquely damning status of the signed and sealed letter short of ~~dramatized~~ recitation – within the frame of loudly delineated mani-pulation by the "authorities" of timing, discretion, entrapment. Instead we are foregathered to bear the brunt of Jonson's full-blown impersonation of the greatest public address system known to civilization (4.3, 5.4). In verse, mouth on legs Tully is in his element, proclaiming crisis management solved, as he *speaks* those texts from the diaphragm (Konstan 1993). But the effect is nullified by the Sallustian smear of verbal glitz seizing fifteen minutes of fame, while the real heavyweights fight it out for real. ("Shall we withdraw into the House of Concord?" (5.9.20), i.e., for *In Cat.* IV: "No, happy Consul, here" (21). Instead, Caesar vs. Cato has it.) It's goodbye from a cruel world, then, to Cicero's imaginary closed set, the *Orationes* where the premier is at the controls, editing his one-man show, starring The One single-handedly saving the State from itself, as insider cells plot to torch the capital, fetch in handy tribesmen insurgents, liquidate officials and establishment (Batstone 1994). A presidential dream-ticket, politics minus the mess. But Theater says no. Instead, Jonson fouls his own nest and ours, in an evening of audience-baiting where everything hits the fan. All that made Brutus's heroization satisfyingly "tragic" is wiped by total cynicism.

To give the play bite despite nonpertinence to the Jacobite autocracy, the postcript was added to the quarto, "This we do advance as a marke of Terror to all *Traytors*, and *Treasons*" Like the consul ("H'has strove to emulate this morning's thunder/with his prodigious rhetoric" (4.2.405–6)), before retreating a while, Jonson needed a storm of popular displeasure to ride out. An emergency retrieved; the nick of time; fanfare in the closing act. But crisis – what crisis? Well, everything that was wrong *still* needs fixing, and fixing insurgents was itself a fix. And (so) this second of two Roman Plays of hauteur and humiliation could make you hate most of what you're sitting through. What you came to see, the theatricality of power crumbling into hearty showbiz, instead sprays nihilistic acid, out to transfix the good audience with phony lecturing and hollow hectoring. This Poet insists on counting, *through* dislike of his play – a strategy for Tragedy with a prolific future.

After Shakespeare, it seems hard to miss: there is no formula, but uppity Jonson takes tragic drama on the offensive, to (hack at) the root of literary authority. It wasn't going to be exactly *popular*, this top-down stagecraft – not *yet*. (Presently, it would be The (second) Globe that burned to the ground, in 1613, not still pupating Parliament.)

A Note on Editions

For *Julius Caesar*: Shakespeare 2004. For *Sejanus*: Jonson 1990 so far outperforms the current crop sown by the *RSC* revival. For *Catiline*: Jonson 1973. Tacitus' *Annals* IV is best read with (the involuntarily dialogic) Martin and Woodman 1989. Cicero and Sallust on Catiline await scintillating commentary.

Chapter 6

Neoclassicisms

Raphael Lyne

Neoclassicism in art and criticism is associated with restraint and appropriateness.[1] This might give the term an inherent resistance to being stretched and tested beyond its usual scope. Nevertheless, the aim of this chapter is to investigate its boundaries, an exercise in literary taxonomy that proves instructive, not least because some of the key tendencies of Neoclassicism are persistently evident elsewhere, including in works that from certain perspectives are antithetical in their approach. Furthermore, the core characteristics of Neoclassicism come under pressure as its purview broadens. What might sometimes seem like a restrictive, conservative set of principles comes to seem energetic even to the point of perversity. This is particularly true when tragedy is the focus of Neoclassical theory and practice, because the affinities between the two are both productive and tense.

Neoclassicism, broadly, is based on reverence for the classical world. It is justly thought of as in many ways conservative, not least because a preference for past models and derived rules tends against innovation. The idea of decorum is often central: in art and morals there are rules to live and work by. These rules are derived from established practice but fundamentally from nature – things have a proper relation to one another and each thing's or each person's integrity depends on that relationship being preserved. This can manifest itself as a protest against the political or social or indeed artistic *status quo*, or as a defense of it. Of course the definition of the *status quo* in any of these fields is contentious, and, as will be seen, there is often a contentious element in Neoclassical writing even as it seems most confident.

Tragic theory has returned again and again to the relationship between extreme content and the stability of the form in which it is represented. This goes back to Aristotle's *Poetics*, where hugely influential artistic principles, concerned with the need for decorum in representing reality, are set out. One could polemically call this a Neoclassical work: it originates classical theory but it describes the practice of a century or more before. Aristotle surveys the achievements of the Greek tragedians in retrospect and extracts lessons from them. For us, the *Poetics* seem more simultaneous with Aeschylus, Sophocles, and Euripides than with the lost works he was trying to correct by past example.[2] This obscures the fact that even the first exposition of what became core principles of Neoclassicism was an act of recovery. Whether in the light of Aristotle or not, tragic theorists, including those who could not be accommodated within any broadened sphere of Neoclassicism, return to forms of the idea that tragedy involves formal control (and problems therewith) over dangerously energetic subject matter.

Neoclassicism's interest in decorum overlaps, then, with a repeating theme in the theory of tragedy. Each is concerned with the reconciliation of extremity and proportion, of vicissitude with constancy. The mention of constancy evokes Stoic thought; the shared interests are notable and at numerous points below Stoic behavior and Neoclassical art will overlap. There is not space here to probe the various frictions between them.[3] It is natural, then, that Neoclassical writers tend to recognize, or to impose, qualities of tragedy that reinforce decorum as an artistic and moral principle. Other genres are equally amenable to their aims. Satire is often revived from classical predecessors (Horace and Juvenal in particular) and then used to criticize the inconstant vices of the present. Tragedy, however, poses particular problems and opportunities. If a tragic character is fully accommodated within Neoclassical principles, he/she can become a powerful embodiment of ideal representation and behavior. However, there are gaps between theory and practice – tragic heroes who do not actually show sufficient likeness to the ideal in question, and plays that break unbreakable rules. In practice, one of the intriguing things about Neoclassicism is its resourcefulness when faced with the fact that past models do not do what they should.

The main Neoclassical period in English literature centers on the careers of Dryden and Pope, but is perhaps best seen as bounded by Ben Jonson in the early seventeenth century and Samuel Johnson in the later eighteenth – preceded by the relatively liberated energy of the Renaissance and followed by another kind of liberated energy in Romanticism. A vital and often animating reference point for English Neoclassicism is its French seven-teenth-century counterpart, exemplified in the work of Boileau, Corneille, and especially Racine. These writers were better able than their English counterparts to take the central cultural ground. The reasons for this are beyond the scope of this study in their variety and complexity, but Dryden's *Essay of Dramatick Poesie* (Dryden 1964) shows how earlier English drama (especially Shakespeare) impinged on English taste and tempered attempts to reform its stage. In addition to this literary heyday, Neoclassicism is the term applied to a tendency in art and architecture of the late eighteenth and early nineteenth centuries.[4] This derived some of its energy from a new experience of the classical world gained from archaeology and travel, but it also had a close association with the French Revolution, which was styled not only as an innovation, but also as a return to Roman values. This was not by any means solely a French phenomenon but Jacques-Louis David, who held political office under the Revolution, was its greatest exponent.

Two of David's paintings serve as examples of Neoclassical treatments of tragic, or potentially tragic themes. The Homeric scene *Andromache Mourning Hector* was painted in 1783, and is now in the Pushkin Museum of Fine Arts, Moscow. It depicts three figures: Hector lies peacefully on his back, with blackness behind him. Andromache sits by his bed, her hand adjacent to his, her eyes looking upward and away from her husband. Their son Astyanax is holding his mother's other hand in his right and reaches up to her with his left. In profile, and shadowed, his facial expression is not clear, so all the more emphasis falls on Andromache. Her grief is evidently enormous but it does not appear to be being vented. The family group is united, dignified, but restrained. A brilliant touch is the presence of Hector's sword and helmet (the latter most prominent) in the lower left of the picture. While this scene of mourning is not part of the *Iliad* – Andromache's lamentation in Book 24 is part of the public reception of the corpse – the intimacy recalls Book 6, where we do indeed see Hector's family in private, and where the boy is scared by his father's helmet.[5] There is scope for poignancy and sentiment in the juxtaposition. David's solution – the helmet is present, but nobody pays it any regard – capitalizes on the connection but does not slacken the heroic restraint of the scene. The helmet makes the Neoclassicism of the painting evident as a process. The scene's decorum has to be recognized – it is inherent in the majestic story – and maintained – since stories gather details that might lead a response away from the proper path.

Figure 6.1   Jacques-Louis David, *Death of Marat*, 1793, Musées Royaux des Beaux-Arts, Brussels. Photograph IRPA

Another work, *The Death of Marat*, 1783, now in the Musées Royaux des Beaux-Arts, Brussels, also creates the impression of Neoclassicism as recognition, discovery, and maintenance. This is not a classical scene, but a very recent event. As a subject for a Neoclassical painting the subject matter is unpromising. David's friend Marat, a leading revolutionary, was obliged to spend time in his bath owing to a skin complaint. A royalist assassin, Charlotte Corday, managed to gain access to his room, where she stabbed him and he died. The scene, then, is one with potential for indignity, and difficult to transform into the kind of restrained splendor of *Andromache Mourning Hector*, or one of David's various paintings of noble classical events (in particular *The Death of Socrates*, and *The Oath of the Horatii*). Though bloodstained water can be seen, the wound itself is not prominent. The assassin's knife lies on the floor – rather like Hector's helmet, it reminds us of what this painting is not. Marat's head and upper body incline toward the foreground of the picture, but the face is fairly serene and the torso uncontorted. The rest of his body is shielded by a board and a green cloth, placed over the bath so he can continue working. On this desk and the packing case to the right are his ink-bottle and some papers; his pen is still in his hand. We can read two of the documents: one is a piece of small-scale official business, the other the deceptive petition from Corday herself. The scene is elevated by its simplicity, dignity, and proportion – the ignominy has been downplayed, while the figure's apparent earnest dedication to revolutionary duty diminishes the incongruity further. In addition, the scene's allusive qualities are subtle but telling: Marat's posture recalls Christ after being taken down from the cross – and it is possible, though fanciful, to link the drapery around the bath with his shroud, and the bath itself with a tomb, so the painting even suggests a kind of resurrection. This is a curious association, perhaps, but it helps explain the discovered majesty of the scene. Further, it is perhaps not too fanciful to think of Marat's fate not as a few seconds of frantic, bloody action, but as something more like a suicide. The philosopher Seneca (as Tacitus reports) commits suicide by cutting his wrists in a bath – but in his case it proves painful and protracted. The poet Lucan also commits suicide in this way, more effectively and calmly, and his last words are his own poetry.[6] Neither of these is a close analogy for Marat but their Stoic deaths in the face of tyranny help contribute to the dignity and proportion of the scene, where now the quill and the letters resemble a kind of suicide note.

In these paintings by David, then, Neoclassical principles govern the way in which a tragic scene is represented, but they also determine (in the guise of describing) the behavior of the characters within the scene. There is, therefore, a double moral opportunity for the viewer, who can appreciate the value of both kinds of decorum. In the plays of Racine too there can be observed this same doubling-up of restrained dramatic style and admirably constant behavior – and of course their opposites, where the technique and morals can be decorous and complementary in their extremity.[7] In Racine's *Andromaque* and *Phèdre* the author's prefatory comments present artistic contrivance as discovery or resolution. There is not space in this chapter for a fuller account of Neoclassical drama, but these prefaces are remarkable instances of its forcefulness, coherence, and ingenuity. In *Phèdre* Racine explains a stark difference between his play and that of Euripides. His Hippolytus-figure is not an entirely chaste follower of Artemis, but has an illicit love. The justification is that without this transgression (against morality and paternal authority) Hippolytus would be too blameless to suffer his dreadful fate.[8] Without asserting that this is a fault in the Greek play exactly, Racine appeals to classically derived principles of decorum while varying drastically from his classical example. In *Andromaque* the preface makes revealing concessions to modern times:

> Although my tragedy bears the same name as his [Euripides' *Andromache*], the subject is entirely different. In Euripides, Andromache fears for the life of Molossus, a son she had borne Pyrrhus and whom Hermione wishes to kill,

Figure 6.2   Jacques-Louis David, *Andromache Mourning Hector*, 1783, Musée de Louvre, Paris. Photograph akg-images/Erich Lessing

together with the boy's mother. But in my play, Molossus does not come into the picture. Andromache has never had any other husband except Hector nor any other son except Astyanax. In taking this line, I felt I was conforming to the idea which we have nowadays of this princess. Most of those who have heard of Andromache hardly know of her otherwise than as Hector's widow and Astyanax's mother. It is not felt proper that she should love another husband or another son. And I doubt whether Andromache's tears would have made the impression they did on my spectators if they had been shed for another son than the one she had from Hector.

It is true that I have been forced to make Astyanax live a little longer than he did. But I write in a country where this liberty could hardly be taken amiss. For, quite apart from Ronsard, who chose this very Astyanax as the hero of his *Franciade*, everyone knows that our kinds of olden times are supposed to be descended from this son of Hector's, and that our ancient chronicles save this young prince's life after his country is laid waste, so as to make of him the founder of our monarchy.

How much bolder was Euripides in his tragedy, *Helena*. In it, he openly flouts the common belief of the whole of Greece. He supposes that Helen never set foot in Troy, and that, after that town was set on fire, Menelaus finds his wife in Egypt, from which she had never stirred. All this founded on an opinion which was accepted only among the Egyptians, as may be seen from Herodotus.[9]

The point of this part of the preface is to justify points where Racine departs from the example of Euripides. For the modern reader, it seems likely that the role of Molossus is the result of the Greek dramatist's characteristic testing of the hinterland of mythology, and of his iconoclastic tendency. For Racine, to deny his model prized characteristics such as decorum and consistency would be a bold step. Instead, there is something deceptively guileless about "I felt I was conforming to the idea which we have nowadays of this princess" – pandering to capricious modern taste seems a contentious decision. The self-justification continues as he strikes a patriotic note: Astyanax is special to the French because he is the hero of Ronsard's national epic, and thus must not be marginalized. Here, then, decorum depends on immediate context rather on the continuity of nature. The third part of the quotation points testily at the transgressions of Euripides himself, and sets up a double-edged affinity between "common belief" and suitability.

The crucial tension to remember is that this willingness to vary is part of a rich and sensitive processing of the classical source. Susanna Phillippo's study of Racine's annotations in a copy of Euripides, for example, describe a "susceptibility to the effectiveness of what Euripides achieves in *his* [i.e. Racine's] own terms," but also an ability to value "a poetic idiom which is in a number of ways quite distinct from his own" (Phillippo 2003: 131). The maneuvering in these two prefaces does not represent a Neoclassical writer being hypocritical. Rather, it shows how a key exponent has to work hard to reconcile central principles with the examples from which, in theory, the principles were derived. These writers were innovators who aimed to be most up-to-date and in tune with modern needs by means of an allegiance to ancient literature. The paradox here is clear, and it is also ubiquitous as writers confront anachronism. Jonson's *Art of Poetrie*, a translation from Horace, encounters this paradox in the ancient source itself:

> Our Poets, too, left nought unproved here;
> Nor did they merit the lesse Crowne to weare,
> In daring to forsake the *Grecian* tracts,
> And celebrating the home-borne facts;

> Whether the guarded *Tragedie* they wrought,
> Or 'twere the gowned *Comoedy* they taught.
>   Nor had our *Italie* more glorious bin
> In vertue, and renowne of armes, then in
> Her language, if the Stay, and Care t'have mended,
> Had not our every Poet like offended.
>   (Jonson 1925–53: vol. 8, 405–14)

Jonson's allegiance to classical principles, and his antipathy toward modern lapses of moral and artistic judgment, run very deep.[10] When he translates Horace so faithfully, there is no discernible disruption in the writing even as he praises "our Poets" and "our Italie" for not following the received models. Neoclassical writers had to find a way of accommodating novelty and difference, especially when these are advocated by classical authorities, within their theory and practice. In the *Art of Poetrie* Jonson does this, in effect, blankly: the translation seems undisturbed by the paradox. In his *Discoveries* – a collection of aphorisms and distilled commentary – Jonson approaches these issues from another angle:

> I am not of that opinion to conclude a *Poets* liberty within the narrowe limits of lawes, which either the *Grammarians*, or *Philosophers* prescribe. For, before they found out those Lawes, there were many excellent Poets, that fulfilled them. Amongst whom none more perfect then *Sophocles*, who liv'd a little before *Aristotle*. Which of the *Greekelings* durst ever give precepts to *Demosthenes*? Or to *Pericles*, (whom the age surnam'd *heavenly*) because he seem'd to thunder, and lighten, with his Language? Or to *Alcibiades*, who had rather Nature for his guide, than Art for his master?
>
> But, whatsoever Nature at any time dictated to the most happie, or long exercise to the most laborious; that the wisdome, and Learning of *Aristotle*, hath brought into an Art: because, he understood the Causes of things: and what other men did by chance of custome, he doth by reason; and not only found out the way not to erre, but the short way we should take, not to erre.
>   (Jonson 1925–53: vol. 8, 641)

The first paragraph here echoes my earlier point about the secondariness of Aristotelian precepts. The artistic "liberty" of the Greeks is seen as the product of "Nature" in the role of "guide." The second paragraph turns to the modern world and becomes less pugnacious: now "wisdome, and Learning" must be recognized as something more than the pedantry of "Greekelings." Precepts now have extra force because in a less "happie" age, or for less "happie" individuals, the path of nature is a very arduous one. Jonson implies a sort of belatedness, wherein people need Aristotle's map to give them some chance of catching up. This highlights the earnest effort that is evident at times in Neoclassical writings: while the claim of nature remains strong, what should be natural has become a regulated struggle for which few have the appetite.

Broadly speaking, Racine and Jonson encounter classical models (of art and life), and the version of nature that they see behind them, as a principle of order. Formal principles and moral values are characterized by consistency and constraint, which can offer a salutary framework for the modern world. In European culture since and indeed before the Renaissance, the classical world has often offered solace from the chaos of existence. However, this is by no means the only kind of intervention Roman and Greek themes have made. In this chapter there is space to explore two phenomena in classical reception that are not primarily Neoclassical, but which have significant contiguity with it (whether in time or in outlook). Here the classical world intervenes as a principle of disorder. On the one hand, in Shakespeare's plays, which are contemporary with Jonson, characters look to Stoic constancy as a means of resisting the tyranny of fortune or appetite, but when they do so, the gesture seems hollow or even perverse. In *Hamlet* and *Antony and Cleopatra* values dear to Neoclassical thought are disruptive or alien. In a very different context, Tony Harrison and other modern writers (Donna Tartt's novel *The Secret History* will feature briefly below) look to the classics for artistic models and ways of understanding modern predicaments (so far so Neoclassical) but the recovered texts are energetic and assertive in ways that disrupt rather than foster order. As with the truly Neoclassical artists considered thus far, the interaction with the classics is a combination of discovery and imposition, a close encounter with historical distance alongside moments of affinity, and ultimately a spur to creativity rather than a retreat from it.

Shakespeare is in many ways the antithesis of the idea of the Neoclassical, as he varies constantly from the perceived classical ideals of form and moral content. Nevertheless his plays reveal many hints of a close encounter with Neoclassical possibilities. At a climactic moment in *Hamlet*, the hero announces his imminent death and hands over the burden of storytelling to Horatio. Grief-stricken, his friend tries to refuse the task and to join Hamlet in death. For a brief moment, Horatio's name, shared with more than one great hero of the Roman Republic who died nobly to save Rome, looks like it will resonate with significance:[11]

HAMLET: Horatio, I am dead,
Thou livest. Report me and my cause aright
To the unsatisfied.
HORATIO: Never believe it;
I am more an antique Roman than a Dane.
Here's yet some liquor left.
HAMLET: As th' art a man,
Give me the cup. Let go! By heaven, I'll ha't!
O God, Horatio, what a wounded name,
Things standing thus unknown, shall I leave behind me!
If thou didst ever hold me in thy heart,
Absent thee from felicity a while,
And in this harsh world draw thy breath in pain,
To tell my story.[12]

The "wounded name" mentioned is Hamlet's own, but the brief possibility that his friend is falling short of his own name (perhaps by offering a travesty of Roman self-sacrifice) appears in the same ghostly way that the significance of "Horatio" itself does. This character never quite contributes anything very substantial to the play, and it is fitting that we get one last hint of his significance waiting to happen.[13] The important thing for considering Shakespeare's relationship with Neoclassicism (broadly conceived) is that *Hamlet* invokes the potential of model classical behavior to bring form to a disordered scene. However, although the motives he cites are self-centered, Hamlet may have a broader sense that an attempt at noble suicide would bring only meaningless excess to the bloody end of *Hamlet*. The gesture looks insubstantial within the plot, but the code it embodies also looks unstable, curious, in the context of such a heavily scrutinized tragedy as *Hamlet* – its central character being the most avid scrutineer.

Things get more edgy when the complexities of the text are addressed. First, the word "antique" is tantalizing. Is this "antique" Roman anything to do with the "antic" disposition taken on by *Hamlet* earlier? The word is almost the same – in Folio the words are actually "antike" and "anticke," respectively.[14] Can this extend even to Priam's "antique" sword at 2.2.469? These questions cannot properly be answered – this is a shadow of a wordplay, not a revealing ambiguity. It does testify, though, to the edginess of the idea of the decorous "antique" in this play. There is more textual difficulty around Horatio's name. The Folio text actually has "live" rather than "leave": "what a wounded name . . . shall I live behind me?" This seems to need the amendment found in the Riverside text. The First Quarto text, however, has "thou leave" rather than "I leave." This gives a little more impetus to the notion that the "wounded name" might be that of the noble Roman Horatius, now replayed in lesser form in a problematic new setting. The First Quarto text, though, has many slips, of which this may be best seen as one.

Hamlet engages with ideas close to the heart of Neoclassicism not only in its characters' choices, but also in its internal examination of dramatic practice. The rules Hamlet imparts to the players in 3.2 are clearly post-Aristotelian. The assertion that the purpose of playing is to "hold, as 'twere, the mirror up to nature" (3.2.21–2) paraphrases the idea of mimesis. It is worth noting that Hamlet's twitchy "as 'twere" might indicate some anxiety about the glibness of the mirror metaphor, or a deeper anxiety about this theory of representation itself. He goes on to give advice about keeping performance in proportion: "in the very torrent, tempest, and, as I may say, the whirlwind of your passion, you must acquire and beget a temperance that may give it smoothness" (3.2.5–8). This is summed up by due reverence to "the modestie of Nature": so the dramaturgical pose taken on by Hamlet here clearly has Neoclassical sympathies. The play does not disprove these wise thoughts, but it does not show them having any consequences. When the players, who seem to accept Hamlet's teaching, perform "The Mouse-trap," there is no way of determining whether this advice has had an effect, although any production could feature actors conspicuously failing to follow it. In the broader context of the play, the hero who wants to drink "hot blood" often strives to take on a more excessive style, in direct contradiction of his dramaturgical advice. The "modesty of nature" sounds like something anyone could agree on, but in Shakespearean tragedy the question of what actually is "natural" is unresolved.

In Hamlet, then, there are moments where the style and behavior typical of Neoclassicism are invoked as the right thing to do in the play's fraught situations. In practice these solutions have little to offer, and the action of the play resists being processed into an orderly form. In Antony and Cleopatra, in theory, classical values should be more at home.[15] The play's structure offends decorum with its broad geographical and temporal scope, but pointed reflections on Neoclassical ideas also result from the problematic opposition of Caesar and Antony. In particular, ideas of natural order and constancy seem to add to the chaos when they are introduced. The point is not whether, in Antony and Cleopatra, the Roman view (in favor of duty and restraint and Caesar, against pleasure and changeability and Antony) fails to win through. Rather it is that these ideals do not even seem truly natural to the most upright Romans, let alone the Egyptians. At one key moment, this is the result of Shakespeare following his main source, Plutarch's *Life of Antony*, but with stark differences. Caesar regrets that Antony, in Cleopatra's thrall, has forgotten his former virtues:

> Antony,
> Leave thy lascivious wassails. When thou once
> Was beaten from Modena, where thou slew'st
> Hirtius and Pansa, consuls, at thy heel
> Did famine follow, whom thou fought'st against
> (Though daintily brought up) with patience more
> Then savages could suffer. Thou didst drink
> The stale of horses and the gilded puddle
> Which beasts would cough at; thy palate then did deign
> The roughest berry on the rudest hedge;
> Yea, like the stag, when snow the pasture sheets,
> The barks of trees thou brows'd. On the Alps,
> It is reported thou didst eat strange flesh,
> Which some did die to look on; and all this
> (It wounds thine honour that I speak it now)
> Was borne so like a soldier, that thy cheek
> So much as lank'd not.
>
> (1.4.55–71)

> And therefore it was a wonderfull example to the souldiers, to see Antonius that was brought up in all fineness and superfluitie, so easily to drinke puddle water, and to eate wild frutes and rootes: and moreover it is reported, that even as they passed the Alpes, they did eate the barcks of trees, and such beasts, as never man tasted of their flesh before.
>
> (Bullough 1957–75: vol. 5, 267–8)

Caesar embraces this model of behavior with curious fervor. Read alongside the source, his version includes a series of strange amplifications: the "Stale of horses" is new, the stag simile is an addition with an almost visionary tone, and instead of meat "as never man tasted of their flesh before," there is "strange flesh, / Which some did dye to looke on." The fact that this source is well known, and especially well known as a source of the play, makes it perhaps viable to take into account this embellishment as part of Caesar's activity as well as Shakespeare's. Within one structural account of the play, Caesar's Roman point of view represents a way of living that clashes with Antony and with Egypt. It also represents a point at which Stoic philosophy can offer an ordering principle for the play's morals. As in *Hamlet*, however, the decorum and constancy that are central to Stoicism and Neoclassicism arise not as a product of nature and order, but as something unnatural and disruptive, obsessive rather than reasoned.

This may not simply be an absolute contrast, in the light of the interpretations of David, Racine, and Jonson offered above. Although the classical world operates as a principle of order in their works, it does so under pressure. So those texts where the classical world operates instead as a principle of disorder may join conventional Neoclassical writing as part of a broader history of classical reception in which the gap between the present and the past is at issue. A further set of examples will develop this possibility. Shakespeare writes in a period where classical examples were fundamental to education and where their potential to regulate modern art and morals was considerable. Writers in the late twentieth century faced very different circumstances, where the place of classics in education had become marginal, and where there was no widespread allegiance to the notion that Greece and Rome offered especially strong examples. Nevertheless, the prevailing view was that if classical learning and classical literature operated anywhere in the culture, they operated within the establishment. For these writers, then, any attempt to revive classical forms and ideas was less likely to appear like prevailing orthodoxy policing standards (since the material was less familiar), but more likely to seem like a particular conservative world-view harking back. There are, of course, numerous cultural and philosophical factors weighing on this new attitude toward classical authority. The important thing here is that in works arising from this intellectual environment, Greek and Roman texts and ideas often make strangely and dangerously assertive interventions, arising unnaturally rather than naturally.

In Donna Tartt's *The Secret History* the narrator Richard Papen joins an ancient Greek class at his new university. He finds himself in a close-knit group of students who revere their teacher, Julian, a mysterious figure who is both subversive (in that he resists professional conventions) and of the old school (in that he stands for a classical education). Richard becomes embroiled in tragedy when first, his classmates re-create a Bacchic ritual which results in the death of a farmer, and worse, when they kill one of their number, Bunny, who cannot keep the secret. Not surprisingly, this novel was very popular among classics students: in it, their subject appears dangerous and sexy. Despite the horrific consequences of indulging one aspect of their subject (encouraged by Julian's emphasis on the dark mysteries of Greek literature), the novel does not represent the classics themselves negatively, and it incorporates features of Greek tragedy.[16] Richard is a noncommittal narrator who does not make sweeping judgments: though he witnesses cracks in Julian's confident exterior, the content of his classes remains substantial. However, classical ideas operate as a principle of disorder in the life of the college, rather than performing their Neoclassical role, promoting decorum. Thus the paradoxical position of classics in a late twentieth-century American university (not part of the established order in practical terms, but nevertheless deeply identified with the old order) is reflected in *The Secret History*. The combination of conservative attitudes in teaching with chaotic consequences in learning may be a kind of neo-Neoclassicism: the place of the classics and their relationship to the prevailing ideology are different – less secure – and so the contribution they make to contemporary life is disruptive rather than corroborative.

Tony Harrison's writings return repeatedly to the place of the classics in his life and his culture. His experiences in the Classical Sixth at Leeds Grammar School are essential to his identity as a writer: in "Them & [uz]" he explicitly deals with the incongruity between Latin words and a Yorkshire accent (Harrison 1995). His work is often influenced by classical and indeed Neoclassical writers, and he translated the *Oresteia* and Racine's *Phèdre*.[17] In many ways, then, Harrison is a modern version of the Neoclassical writer, returning to Greek and Roman themes again and again, attributing them authority in understanding the modern world. However, the texts and ideas evoked are not those of order, restraint, and decorum, challenging modern practices with underlying standards. Instead, the disruptive power of the classical world is felt; it reveals the underlying contradictions rather than resolving things into a coherent form. Some of Harrison's works have this as their explicit subject as well as their implicit content. *The Trackers of Oxyrhynchus* is partially a retelling of Sophocles' *Ichneutae* (*Trackers*), but dramatizes also the discovery of the papyrus of Sophocles's text by the Edwardian scholars Grenfell and Hunt. With the recovery of the text comes the rebirth of its characters, who are full of bitterness at their neglect. The god Apollo faces up to what he has lost over time:

> I'm a god, Apollo, but I was tipped
> on a rubbish tip inside this manuscript.
> I've spent 2000 years asleep
> on an Oxyrhynchus rubbish heap.
> Till 1907 I had to wait
> when Grenfell and Hunt came to excavate.

Covered in rubbish! But what's much worse is
being resurrected with scarcely half my verses.
Converted into dust and bookworm excreta
riddled lines with just a ghost of their metre.
(Harrison 1990: 92)

The Sophoclean characters sometimes speak in the fragmentary words of the papyri, and Apollo also laments the degradation of his divine presence at the hands of classical education. The clash between a stolid Edwardian view of Greek culture, and the resistant, chaotic voices of Apollo and the satyrs, allows Harrison to hint at a new Neoclassicism – where the complacency and ignorance of the modern era has to encounter the things which won't be assimilated.[18] This is very different from earlier versions, but it is one that (perhaps) emerges from a cultural environment in which the truth of the classical world is neglected – as one of the satyrs says:

SATYR 2: You, you gormless grovelling sod
being so servile to that sodding god
got us stuck here in Great bloody Britain
where nowt about satyrs'll ever get written.
(129)

When classical texts intervene in conventional Neoclassical writing they have less cause to complain, but in Harrison and in, say, Jonson, there is a parallel feeling that the present is neglecting an important source. The pivotal difference is that here the satyrs will not offer a cultural anchor, and certainly not a moral one. My suggestion in this chapter is that this is a difference of degree, not of kind.[19] Harrison relishes the ways in which they cannot, and will not, be assimilated into modern life, but the contact is still necessary and enlivening.

The Trackers of Oxyrhynchus is not a tragedy; it is based around a satyr play – a raucous and often comical kind of play that was performed at the Athenian Great Dionysia festival, after the tragic trilogy. Although satyr plays are distinct from tragedies, they were very much part of the Greek tragic experience, to an extent Neoclassical and indeed modern conceptions of tragedy sometimes find it difficult to imagine. The other Harrison play to be discussed here, The Common Chorus, is also no tragedy – it is about a performance of Aristophanes' comedy Lysistrata by protesters at the US Air Force base at Greenham Common in the 1980s. Because the onstage audience of policemen keep the audience at a distance from the play itself, it has very sharp edges. At a climactic moment the central character connects past and present under the pressure of nuclear holocaust:

> There's no confusion. My mind's clear
> and there's no difference between there and here.
> Since Hiroshima what we've done
> paradoxically's to make the whole earth one.
> We all look down the barrel of the same cocked gun.
> One target, in one united fate
> nuked together in some hyperstate.
> So Greece is Greenham, Greenham Greece,
> Poseidon is Poseidon, not just for this piece.
>   (Harrison 1992: 49)[20]

This is a retort to the guard's criticism that a Greek comedy has nothing to do with a nuclear air base. The continuity that is the basis of what are usually thought of as Neoclassical works arises from the constancy of nature, which provides everlasting rules to live and write by. In *The Common Chorus*, this continuity is replaced by simultaneity resulting not from nature, but from an aberration against nature. Nuclear weapons create affinity between the present and the past by assuring mutual destruction. The essential contrast may be the product of context, whereas the Neoclassical impulse (to look back, to compare, to recognize similarity and difference, to encounter paradoxes) may be intact. The problem with literary-historical taxonomy is that any term has a dangerous potential. They get more useful as they expand beyond their safest environs, since they challenge other texts and are challenged by them. But that usefulness comes at a cost – particularity and definition are lost. In some cases, though, as in Neoclassicism, I argue, the resources revealed in the term and its adherents are good compensation.

Notes

1   For orientation, the entries on "Classicism" (pp. 136–41) and "Neoclassical Poetics" (pp. 559–64) in Preminger 1974 are both compact and wide-ranging.
2   For the *Poetics* see Russell and Winterbottom 1972: 85–132.
3   Inwood 2003 introduces the key features of Stoic thought in Greece and Rome. Shifflett 2004 discusses some of its later influence.

4   Irwin 1997 is a beautifully illustrated account of this movement. It
     includes plates of both the David paintings discussed here. Eitner 1970
     includes many of the key texts.

5   See Homer 1924: 6.466–93, 24.723–45.

6   Tacitus 1999: 15.60–4 (Seneca), 15.70 (Lucan).

7   See Parish 1993: 135–62, on the "ordered disorder" of *Phèdre and Andro-
     maque*. See also Maskell 1991: 198–204 on the importance of morally
     ambiguous characters in Racine (especially Phèdre herself), and how this
     is featured in prefaces.

8   See Racine's preface in Racine 1963: 145–7. For the French text see
     Racine 1950: 763–5.

9   Jean Racine, second preface to *Andromache*, in Racine 1967: 43–4. See also
     Racine 1950: 260–2.

10   See Mulryan 2000.

11   The three sons of Horatius (the Horatii) are part of an archetypal story of
     loyalty toward the State overcoming loyalty toward the family – as depicted
     in David's painting *The Oath of the Horatii*. See also Corneille's *Horace*
     (1640). Another Horatius fights alone on a bridge to keep the Etruscans
     away from Rome, and then bravely swims the Tiber. Livy's history *Ab Urbe
     Condita* is the key source for both stories. (Livy 1919: I.xxiv–xxvi, II.x)

12   Shakespeare, *Hamlet*, 5.2.338–49 (Shakespeare 1997). All quotations from
     Shakespeare are taken from this (Riverside) edition.

13   This is a considerably more negative reading of Horatio than most.
     Monsarrat 1984: 135–47, approves Horatio, more or less uniquely in
     Shakespeare, as a representative of Stoic virtue. Here his virtue and
     constancy are not in question, but their effectuality and appropriateness
     (what the play allows the character to do) are.

14   The question is posed by Ronan 1995: 6.

15   Miles 1996 is an excellent account of the Stoic influences on Shakespeare,
     and consequences in his Roman plays. He emphasizes not only the
     weighty classical voices promoting such virtues, but also more skeptical
     voices that read the stories of Cato et al. more irreverently: Montaigne is
     a key example.

16   See Melvin 1996 and Arkins 1995.

17   See Astley 1991: 174–94 for Harrison's preface to *Phara Britannica* (1975)
     and revealing reviews ("It is now the turn of a Racine masterpiece to be
     pillaged and packaged for the modern audience" [192]). This collection
     has much useful material on Harrison's other classical interactions. See
     also Kelleher 1996 and Huk 1993.

18   A resonant phrase from an interview in Astley 1991: 245: "There's a lot of
     vested interest in the Classics as being a rather aseptic foundation of our
     culture."

19 For a different, but more or less complementary perspective on *Trackers*,
    see Forsyth 2002. Forsyth focuses on the creative potential of rewriting
    and rethinking classical texts and the fixed values they embody.
20 Harrison's introduction, entitled "Hecuba to Us," rephrases Hamlet's
    question about what a classical heroine can signify to a later reader: in it
    he develops the ideas represented in Lysistrata's speech. He also discusses
    the fact that the play was never performed – politics moved faster than
    the theater, and "the tension of a topical present and a tragic past had
    leached away into oblivion" (xvi).

Chapter 7

Tragedy and Exile

Jennifer Wallace

On September 26, 1940, in a lonely hotel room in the town of Port-Bou on the French–Spanish border, the German-Jewish philosopher Walter Benjamin took a fatal overdose of morphine pills, aged 48. He had spent the last seven carefree years in Paris, having fled the Nazis in Germany in 1933. But when France fell to Hitler, he was forced to move once again. Escaping south with friends, he attempted to walk over the Pyrenees to freedom, clutching only a briefcase containing the manuscript of his most important but unfinished work, the Parisian *Arcades* project. However, when he reached Port-Bou, on the Spanish side of the mountains, and presented his transit visa to the border police, he was told that the Spanish leader, Franco, had made an agreement with Hitler just a few weeks before and that these visas were no longer valid. As a refugee, Benjamin was ordered to be sent back over the border to Vichy France. Unable to face the likely prospect of falling into the hands of the Gestapo, he committed suicide on the border, in the no-man's-land between incarceration and liberation.[1]

Walter Benjamin was just one of millions of displaced people in Europe during the World War II.[2] But the enforced migration of people is something we are also familiar with in modern times. In recent years, we have witnessed the tragic movement of peoples on a large scale. In 1994, for example, approximately two million Hutu and Tutsi refugees arrived at different camps to escape the massacre in Rwanda. Five years later, in 1999, more than half a million Kosovo Albanians streamed out of Kosovo into neighboring Macedonia to avoid Serbian ethnic cleansing. In the summer of 2006, a quarter of the population of Lebanon (about one million people) have been forced to leave their homes to avoid Israel's bombing campaign. If and when they manage to return, there may not be any "homes" left standing.

Yet the last decade has also been a period of mass voluntary immigration, where millions of people risk their lives in order to leave their homes and escape to the promised prosperity in the West. The Spanish Canary Islands, lying off the west coast of Africa, attract boatloads of immigrants attempting to get into Europe; 7,000 people arrived there in 2003 alone. If the makeshift boats leave the coast of the Western Sahara at dusk, they can hope to reach the lighthouse of one island, Fuerteventura, by dawn. But many do not make it. Their fragile boats are dashed apart by the Atlantic waves and the drowned bodies are washed ashore a few days later, bloated by seawater. The Reuters photographer, Juan Medina, documented this "desperate story of human tragedy unfolding on the shores of the Canary Islands" over a period of five years for his exhibition, *Cruel Sea*, capturing the bitter irony of dead bodies washed up onto the idyllic beaches peopled by sun-seeking tourists.[3]

Europe is also the golden utopia for thousands of people from the former Soviet Union and Eastern bloc countries. Depressed by the harsh economic fallout following the introduction of capitalism, Europe appears to offer dreams of Western materialism – the health, wealth, and happiness to which everyone feels entitled. But while some lucky immigrants make the transfer successfully, thousands fall prey to the cynical mafia networks which exploit

Figure 7.1   Juan Medina, *The Cruel Sea*. Photograph REUTERS/Juan Medina

the gullibility of the desperate.[4] Cut off from family, friends and all the traditional social structures afforded by "home," women are forced to put their trust in strangers who promise to befriend and assist them, only to find themselves all too frequently sucked into the clutches of the sex industry, experiencing the worst, darkest side of shining Europe. The Swedish film, *Lilya 4-ever* (2002), dramatized this tragic narrative most graphically, with the story of Lilya enticed by her Swedish boyfriend, Andrei, to leave her life of misery in the former Soviet Union with a fake passport for a job with him in Sweden. Once there, she is taken by her "employer," imprisoned in an apartment, and forced to perform sex for clients while her pimp takes all the money. The film opens and closes with her suicide, jumping from a motorway bridge, but set against the sordid reality of the film is Lilya's fantasy life. The conclusion shows her as a ghost or angel, playing with her old, dead friend, who has also committed suicide, on the roof of an apartment building, in what is clearly her idea of heaven.

In the twenty-first century of globalization, travel and movement are supposedly highly desirable. Popular culture bombards us with images of tropical pleasure afforded by relocation. You too can have a "place in the sun"; sell up, buy quick, properties in Croatia or Turkey are going cheap. Go on the trip of a lifetime. In the academy, the message is similar. To be rootless, "hybrid," or "liminal" is the goal of the postmodern age. "We find ourselves in the moment of transit where space and time cross to produce complex figures of difference and identity, past and present, inside and outside, inclusion and exclusion," wrote the cultural critic Homi Bhabha, who gave the terms hybridity and liminality wide currency (Bhabha 1994: 1). Liminal means staying on the threshold, belonging to neither one state nor the other, like Benjamin at the Pyrenees. But for Bhabha, this is a joyous, carefree situation. The talk is all of "mobilization" and liberation, no longer being weighted down by historical expectation, fixed identities, crushing responsibilities, the burden of history. Indeed, Bhabha writes of the experience of the exile or the "unhomely" as being quintessentially and paradoxically the state of "belonging" to the modern era:

I have lived that moment of the scattering of the people that in other times and other places, in the nations of others, becomes a time of gathering. Gatherings of exiles and *émigrés* and refugees; gathering on the edge of "foreign" cultures; gathering at the frontiers; gatherings in the ghettoes or cafes of city centres; gathering in the half-life, half-light of foreign tongues, or in the uncanny fluency of another's language ... In the midst of these lonely gatherings of the scattered people, their myths and fantasies and experiences, there emerges a historical fact of singular importance ... The emergence of the later phase of the modern nation ... is also one of the most sustained periods of mass migration within the West, and colonial expansion in the East.

(Bhabha 1994: 139)

To live, exiled, chatting in the cafés of the world, becomes, according to Bhabha, the cosmopolitan image for our times. Indeed, for one anthropologist, the idea that there might be an alternative, demarcated sense of home, in which one doesn't "gather" but remains "rooted," is outmoded. In *Routes*, James Clifford challenges the old model in which a Western anthropologist jets into a "primitive" culture and studies its way of life, assuming it never changes, while being in transit and not implicated himself. Instead, he argues, both the culture studied and the culture from which the anthropologist hails are equally in transit, hybrid, subject to change. Culture, he writes, "comes to resemble as much a site of travel encounters as of residence." It is necessary to focus on "hybrid, cosmopolitan experiences as much as on rooted, native ones" (Clifford 1997: 25).

But the tragedies at the borders I have described teach us that life today is far from Bhabha's or Clifford's depiction, that it is far from carefree, mobilized, and liminal. We need to think, as Bhabha himself put it, about "that element of people caught in that margin of non-movement within an economy of movement."[5] The bloated bodies on the beaches of the Canary Islands or the female sex-slaves living a shadowy existence in seedy hotel rooms in Europe's red-light districts point out the proximity of pleasure and tragedy at Europe's boundaries. Sun-kissed beaches and sexual fantasy offer not hope but death and disillusion to thousands. For while virtual borders are disappearing as capital moves around the world, paradoxically real borders – fences, security walls, immigration controls – are rising up. Just when people are able and desperate to migrate, then it becomes more difficult than ever before. The barbed-wire fence around Europe (around Spanish Ceuta or "Europe in Africa," for example[6]), or the military- and vigilante-patrolled security barrier between the United States and Mexico: these are tragic sites where dead, shot, and wounded bodies reveal the limited capacity of the West to share its declared ideals of universal freedom, prosperity, and happiness.

Tragedy, as a dramatic genre, traditionally raises questions about rules and constraints. The rules become apparent as they are blown apart by tragic events; paradoxically, constraints are desired precisely when they appear to be absent and when anything – violence, exploitation, injustice – consequently becomes possible. In other words, regulation and freedom enjoy an ambiguous relationship in tragedy, just as leisured travel and enforced migration might both be said to involve mobility, but with very different, equivocal implications. What, then, is the purpose of constraint? "Tragedy's function is to get under control life's most chaotic and difficult parts," observed the psychoanalytic critic, Roy Morrell (Morrell 1956: 24). Or to put it another way, "the creation of order is directly related to the fact of disorder," according to Raymond Williams in *Modern Tragedy* (Williams 1966: 52).

But to the exile, what does order or disorder mean? Whose order? Whose rules? It's a question which lies behind Coriolanus' scornful challenge to his detractors, before he is "banished" from Rome and joins his enemy, Aufidius. Cutting himself off from his roots in Rome, Coriolanus "banishes" the Romans, implying that Rome's values or "order" are encapsulated within his own identity rather than represented by the ordinary citizens:

> You common cry of curs, whose breath I hate
> As reek o'th' rotten fens, whose loves I prize
> As the dead carcasses of unburied men
> That do corrupt my air: I banish you . . .
>   Despising
> For you the city, thus I turn my back.
> There is a world elsewhere.
>
>   (3.3.124–7, 137–9)

To ponder Coriolanus' challenge, and the question of the exile's ethical system, we must go back to Walter Benjamin, with his briefcase and his invalid visa, at the border. For Benjamin spent his life speculating on the order or meaning of things once they have been torn from their familiar contexts, or undergone a process of "ruination." For example, works of art, he argued, traditionally acquired their value from their use and provenance; their "aura," derived from their provenance, continued to imbue the art with value, even when the context was stripped away (Benjamin 1973: 211–44). Meanwhile, the *flâneur*, who walked around the city looking at the spectacle of life, found his gaze was liberated by the particular nature of the metropolis, with its anonymous, freely available arcades (Benjamin 1978). Each of the objects in the arcades, like archaeological remains in a museum, spoke of a time and a context which had now been lost. Most importantly, Benjamin was interested in the complex relationship between the individual and history. To understand an individual, he maintained in his essay, "Fate and Character," one should remove the narrative structures afforded by notions of history and fate which support him or her. But one finds that in fact the individual is permeated by history: "Between the active man and the external world all is interaction, their spheres of action interpenetrate; no matter how different their conceptions may be, their concepts are inseparable" (Benjamin 1979: 125).

So Benjamin at the French–Spanish border finds himself living his own intellectual dilemma: free-falling without the consolation of community, uprooted with only a suitcase, but also freighted with a past, oppressed by prejudice, burdened by the fact of his race in antisemitic Europe. He suffers both from being isolated from supporting structures and also from being constrained by them, being still judged by them. He carries the exilic identity of a Jew upon his shoulders, the *unheimlich* of modernity. For George Eliot, of course, Judaic identity meant that the roots of a nation, so elusive in her complex novel *Daniel Deronda*, might survive not in deadening institutions and capricious economies, to be gambled and lost, but kept alive within each individual, dispersed around Europe, to be reignited at the right time. "Let my body dwell in poverty, and my hands be as the hands of the toiler; but let my soul be as a temple of remembrance where the treasures of knowledge enter and the inner sanctuary is hope," says her proto-Zionist character, Mordecai, to the hero, Daniel Deronda (Eliot 1986: 555). But W. G. Sebald's Jewish emigrants fleeing Nazi Germany find themselves prey to the obsessive demands and even fickleness of memory in the loneliness of their immigrant status. One character, Ambros Adelwarth, who ends his days in a psychiatric sanatorium, appears to be suffering from "an illness which causes his memories to be replaced by fantastic inventions" (Sebald 1997: 102). And another, Max Ferber, blots out painful memories of leaving his parents behind in Nazi Germany to be evacuated to safety in London. His "ruined" state of mind infects the narrator, himself an emigrant, so that even his writing project recording the lives of these exiles comes to seem pointless and fragmentary:

> These scruples concerned not only the subject of my narrative, which I felt I could not do justice to, no matter what approach I tried, but also the entire questionable business of writing. I had covered hundreds of pages with my scribble, in pencil and ballpoint. By far the greater part had been crossed out, discarded, or obliterated by additions. Even what I ultimately salvaged as a "final" version seemed to me a thing of shreds and patches, utterly botched.
> (230–1)

The "scruples," which dog Sebald, about the fragmented and deracinated nature of enforced displacement, have not always troubled writers. The Romantic critics, for example, viewed exile as a positive, rather than a negative, experience. According to writers such as Schelling or Schlegel, the state of alienation – or being "indifferent" to Benjamin's "external world" – is actually central to tragedy and to be welcomed. Schelling maintained that tragedy involved "a real conflict between freedom in the subject and objective necessity" (Schelling 1989: 251). This meant that not being at home in the world both produced the tragic conflict but also was paradoxically to be celebrated, desired as "freedom in the subject," like Bhabha's mobilized exile, crossing continents. A. W. Schlegel also, in his lectures on Greek tragedy, viewed tragic protagonists as heroic individuals, unrecognized by their own society but with a higher confidence of their own. Prometheus, for example, was, for Schlegel, a classic depiction of heroic defiance and alienation: "It is an image of human nature itself: endowed with a miserable foresight and bound down to a narrow existence, without an ally, and with nothing to oppose to the combined and inexorable powers of nature, but an unshaken will and the consciousness of elevated claims" (Schlegel 1815: 112–13). To be exiled from society – literally on the Caucasus but also psychologically – was to suffer short-term hardship, misunderstanding, and oppression in this life, but to gain long-term transcendental freedom and moral satisfaction.

Ibsen appeared to share Schlegel's complex view of exile as a state to be celebrated rather than shunned. Brand voluntarily leaves his community, exiling himself like Coriolanus for a "world elsewhere," because he believes his individual notion of God to be more valid than that of the whole village. "Away from this place! God is not here. His kingdom is perfect freedom" (Ibsen 1986: 55), he tells the crowd. Dissatisfied with the church the villagers have built according to his instructions, he sets off up into the glacier on the high mountain, seeking a more transcendental church of his own fantasy. Similarly, among Ibsen's later plays, one could point to the suicidal, self-exiling of Ruben and Irene out onto the mountain avalanche at the end of *When We Dead Awaken*, or Rebecca West and Rosmer leaping from the bridge into the millstream in *Rosmersholm*. Admittedly, some of the declarations of social alienation by Ibsen's protagonists are greeted with a degree of ironic skepticism. Dr Stockmann, for example, declares that the common people are their own worst enemies, rather as Coriolanus banishes Rome, because they don't appreciate his leadership. He is driven so much by his own personal vision of what is in his people's best interests (the hygiene of the town's Baths) that he cannot actually relate to the people he wishes to lead or understand their perspective (the commercial need to keep the Baths open). "I love this town so much that I'd rather destroy it than see it prosper on a lie," he declares before being dubbed an "enemy of the people" and suffering the destruction of his home by the townspeople (Ibsen 1971: 82). The irony evident here, in Stockmann's declarations of love for a town he simultaneously derides as ignorant and common, might make us want to question retrospectively how we are to interpret Brand's solitary idealism. But nevertheless, it can be argued that in Ibsen, the underlying tragic condition of the world, in which each individual is necessarily isolated from his community, becomes transformed into a positive celebration of detachment as the mind accesses some transcendent reality.

Existential writers such as Camus and Sartre similarly idealize the individual consciousness at the expense of the environment. As Sisyphus continually goes back down the hill to collect his rock again in the Underworld, he "surmounts" his "fate with scorn" (Camus 1975: 109), gaining a perspective upon his absurd predicament by rising above it. In *The Outsider*, Meursault's sense of alienation precedes his actual incarceration and isolation from the community, following his killing of the Arab. Unable to cry at his mother's funeral, he is exiled in spirit long before he finds himself literally shut away from society. "The hero is condemned because he doesn't play the game," commented Camus. He is "an outsider to the society in which he lives, wandering on the fringe, on the outskirts of life," because he "refuses to lie" (Camus 1983: 118). So again, Meursault supposedly has some individual purchase upon truth (that life is meaningless) which the rest of the world is just incapable of understanding.[7]

In contrast to these post-Romantic tragedies, Greek tragedy supposedly presents each individual as defined within his community. To be exiled is to become nobody. Students often point out that Oedipus and Creon are punished not with death, like the women in the stories, but banishment from Thebes. "Take me away, quickly, out of sight. I don't exist – I'm no one. Nothing," says Creon, at the end of *Antigone*, after hearing that his son, wife, and niece have all committed suicide because of his actions, and the chorus reply that this is indeed a wise idea: "Good advice, if there's any good in suffering" (Sophocles 2000: ll.1445–7). Oedipus meets with a similar response to his plea to Creon at the end of *Oedipus Tyrannus*:

> OEDIPUS: Drive me out of the land at once, far from sight,
> Where I can never hear a human voice.
> CREON: I'd have done that already, I promise you.
>
> (ll.1571–3)

To be exiled in ancient Greece was indeed to become a "no one. Nothing." Aristotle observed that man was a political animal (a *zoon politikon*), naturally designed to reach his full human potential in the city-state or *polis* (Aristotle, *Politics*, 1253a3).[8] The city provided the social bonds which formed an individual's identity. Civic ideology in Athens was apparent everywhere, from the iconography on public buildings to religious processions and rituals, designed to bolster city pride. In this case, to be exiled was to be *apolis*, outside the city and, by implication, outside humanity. Indeed, so shameful was the state of exile that it was introduced as one of the ultimate sanctions in the Athenian constitution. Each year, the citizens were given the opportunity to vote for one person to be banished or "ostracized" from the city for a period of ten years. The measure was designed to prevent the city falling back into the tyranny of the previous century, and it lasted, as a practice, for just 70 years, in the early years of the democracy.[9] But it meant that there was a heightened awareness of the perils of individualism amongst the Athenians, since it was an individual's personal development of extraordinary talents and the consequential influence and power which were accorded him that usually provoked the citizens' envy and his banishment. There was no debate; no accusation, and no defense. Citizens merely wrote their chosen names on potsherds, without accountability or scrutiny. They could be motivated by jealousy, peer pressure, or even corrupt manipulation.[10] They would also be reminded annually of the horror of exile, as they watched one of their number forced to leave. Blessed with a little more *hubris*, this could have been the fate of any of them. So the chorus of women in *Medea* articulate a widely shared and very relevant fear for Greeks when they sing of the misery of banishment:

> O my fatherland, O my home,
> may I never be without my city,
> trudging on life's difficult path
> of helplessness –
> the most pitiful of sorrows.
> Before that may I have done with this light of life
> laid low by death, by death.
> Of all miseries none is worse
> than to lose one's native land.
> (Euripides 1998: ll.644–52)

But the portrayal of exile in Greek tragedy is actually more complicated than this declaration by the Corinthian women in *Medea* suggests. For one thing, Oedipus has made a distinction, at the beginning of *Oedipus Tyrannus*, between acceptable and unacceptable states of exile. If the murderer of Laius owns up to the killing, he will be spared capital punishment, and simply sent away from Thebes, suffering "no unbearable punishment, nothing worse than exile, totally unharmed" (ll.260–1).[11] But if anyone hides either his own or another's guilt, then he will be banished with shame and vindictiveness: "never shelter him, never/speak a word to him, never make him partner/to your prayers . . . Drive him out, each of you, from every home" (ll.271–3; 275). Moreover, in *Antigone* and *Oedipus Tyrannus*, Creon and Oedipus actually ask to be exiled. Like existential heroes, they want their punishment visibly to match their own internal sense of transgression and alienation:

> CREON: Enough
>   You've wept enough. Into the palace now.
> OEDIPUS: I must, but I find it very hard.
> CREON: Time is the great healer, you will see.
> OEDIPUS: I am going – you know on what condition?
> CREON: Tell me. I'm listening.
> OEDIPUS: Drive me out of Thebes, in exile.
>   [*apoikon*, "homeless," in Greek]
> CREON: Not I. Only the gods can give you that.
> OEDIPUS: Surely the gods hate me so much . . .
>   (ll.1661–9)

Indeed, at the end of *Oedipus Tyrannus*, Oedipus probably exited back into the palace or *skene*, rather than wandering out to the wilderness of Cithairon, represented by the *eisodos* (side exit). Creon has initially demanded that he get inside, for the abject horror Oedipus poses should best be dealt with indoors, between kinsmen, rather than shamefully in the open, before the city. And, having told Oedipus not to try to control his fate now that he is nothing before the gods, Creon might be seen to get his way at the end.[12] Oedipus does not even get the satisfaction of knowing that "the gods hate me so much" (l. 1669). At the end of *Antigone*, Creon also is told not to direct his own fate. Praying for the certainty of banishment is a luxury not extended to the utterly abject like Creon. So he is left in the no-man's-land of confusion: "Take me away, I beg you, out of sight . . . Wailing wreck of a man,/whom to look to? where to lean for support?" (ll.1459, 1462–3).

Secondly, as Simon Goldhill has argued, Greek tragedy actually interrogates what it is to be *politikos*, what it is to live in the city (Goldhill 1986: 57–78). In other words, the order of the city, from which one might be exiled, is questioned during the course of the tragedy. Philoctetes, lured back from long-term exile to reintegration within the Greek army, believes at first that his island represents "absolute loneliness," in Seamus Heaney's words (*eremos*, in Greek, or "deserted"), and that Neoptolemos offers him the chance to return "home," to family, *polis*, society.[13] But during the course of the play, as Neoptelomos tricks him, he is reminded of the treachery of a civilization which ten years earlier betrayed him. Now the island comes to stand for civilized values and the society to which he is departing in the ships seems a murky world of deception and abandonment: "Everything that made me my own self, you've stripped away," he tells Odysseus in Heaney's version. "And now you're going to take away my second self. This boy. He's your accomplice but he was my friend. Here I am, like a lost soul bound for Hades, being led away out of the house of life and light and friendship" (Heaney 1990: 56). On the one hand, life on the island, scratching out an existence among the birds and wild animals, has been a shadowy, unreal existence: "My whole life has been/Just one long cruel parody" (18), Heaney interpolates into his version. But on the other hand, Philoctetes' island existence seems more authentic and reliable than the "Hades" of fictions and lies – the world of politics – to which he is returning. No wonder Neoptolemos comes to echo Creon's – and indeed Meursault's – state of confusion: "there's no way out."[14] "I am an affliction to myself," he declares, unconsciously taking on Philoctetes' identity. Who is the exile? Who is at home?

The wandering Oedipus, in *Oedipus at Colonus* (*OC*), finds himself at the borders of Athens. He is careful to position himself precisely in the space demarcated for him by the chorus: "Here, no farther. This base of native rock, never lift a foot from this firm threshold" (211–12). The Greek text is filled with repeated images of feet shuffling up to boundaries, suggesting the mental borders which are explored and tested as well as the physical borders. Like Walter Benjamin, Oedipus at the border is asked by the chorus to reveal his story, like his ancient transit visa, in order to be given sanctuary. But unlike Benjamin, the legacy he carries with him, like a physical *miasma*, has the power to transform any place for good or ill: "a blessing to the hosts I live among,/disaster to those who sent me, drove me out!" (ll.113–14). Creon, his brother-in-law, and later Polyneices, his own son, try to persuade him to return "home" to Thebes, where his presence can supposedly give a divine boost to his allies. But instead, Oedipus prefers to die abroad, in a marginal, mysterious place outside Athens, granted protection, if not complete assimilation, by the king, Theseus:

THESEUS: Your father...
          ... commanded me
that no one may go near that place,
not a living voice invade that grave:
it's sacred, it's his everlasting rest.
And he said that if I kept that pledge
I'd keep my country free from harm forever.
                                              (1975–85)

Oedipus' significance depends upon the community which judges him. To the Thebans, he is hateful and therefore he brings curses down upon the city; to the people in Colonus, outside Athens, he is mysterious but they accept him, and therefore he blesses them, warding off future harm. Through this negotiation between the individual and the collective, a nebulous, shifting notion of being "at home," or at least, being given a stable point of rest, is established. The sense that this is a matter for negotiation and debate, rather than a given, is enhanced by the fact that the chorus is itself made up of marginal figures (old men in this case), rather than central, powerful city leaders.[15] There is not a fixed, unambiguous representation of the "city," from which the individual, Oedipus, is banished or into which he can be integrated; rather that centrality must be imagined, discussed, the consequence of exchange. Exile, therefore, like so many aspects of Greek tragedy, becomes a state of mind as much as a physical condition. As such, it can be transformed through new acts of social interaction and interpretation: the threat of deception (*Philoctetes*), the kindness of strangers (*OC*).

The postmodern ambivalence about exile can be seen to have continuities with Greek tragedy as well as disjunctions. In Greek tragedy as well as in modernity, the borders which demarcate safety from danger, civilization from wilderness, blessing from curse, or belief from skepticism, are shown to be extremely permeable, vulnerable products of the cultural imagination. Yet to breach them, in ancient and modern times, is to incur very real distress, disturbance, and personal tragedy. The opening shot of Anthony Minghella's film *The English Patient* (1996), appears to be of a desert landscape. The camera moves slowly over what seem to be the mounds and dips of a vast sand-dune. But then the camera pulls back and we realize that we have been following the curves and hollows of a woman's naked body. It's a telling visual pun, for the film – and the novel on which it is based – explore the tensions between the private imagination, which acknowledges no borders, and public politics, which is fighting a war over land and boundaries:

> We die containing a richness of lovers and tribes, tastes we have swallowed, bodies we have plunged into and swum up as if rivers of wisdom, characters we have climbed into as if trees, fears we have hidden in as if caves. I wish for all this to be marked on my body when I am dead. I believe in such cartography...We are communal histories, communal books. We are not owned or monogamous in our taste or experience. All I desired was to walk upon such an earth that had no maps.
>
> (Ondaatje 1993: 261)

Thus Almasy, the "English patient" in the novel, declares his desire for an earth without maps. But his wish is rebuffed by a world at war, in which he elects to help the Germans, on the opposite side from his friends and former colleagues in the desert. His aspiration for a new kind of "cartography" collides with an old world of national allegiances, social responsibility, accountability to one's past. His passionate love affair with Katherine Clifton was doomed by external events, the jealousy of her husband, the war which prevented him from returning to rescue her. And his morphine-assisted efforts to forget his past are punctured by Caravaggio identifying him as the German double or triple agent, ultimately responsible for his torture.

The English patient's body is carried on a wandering course, across Africa and up through Italy, until he is given sanctuary in the Villa San Girolamo in northern Italy, cared for by the Canadian nurse, Hana. In many ways like Oedipus, Almasy dies with no fixed home or identity but blessed by the disparate community that has gathered around him: Hana, Caravaggio, Kip the Indian sapper. His guilt, tragic loss, and transgression are modified, partly by his own drug-induced amnesia, but mainly through their capacity for little acts of kindness and their need to hear his story. In a move reminiscent of Oedipus's sanctification, Hana even grants him saintlike status, as she tends his blackened, burned body: "Hipbones of Christ, she thinks. He is her despairing saint" (3). The exilic condition, the novel suggests, is the product of the "ruination" (Walter Benjamin's word) of Europe, after World War II, as old structures exploded and peoples, dispersed around the world, were drawn into the conflict. But it also allows these new types of communities to gather, the incongruous group around the English patient, with their capacity for a different kind of grace.

Far bleaker is Ondaatje's more recent novel, *Anil's Ghost*, which explores the atrocities of civil war in Sri Lanka (now, in 2007, more pressingly relevant again).[16] In the search to investigate the alleged organized campaign of murder by the government, the novel brings together two characters, one, a Sri Lankan-born forensic anthropologist, Anil, now living in America, and the other, a local archaeologist, Sarath. They come across a body which has clearly been murdered and moved to a new grave site, and Anil decides to investigate it for the sake of justice and human rights. Sarath is reluctant, because he knows the terrible dangers of this kind of investigation. But at the crucial moment, after Anil is arrested and all her data seized, he comes to her aid, ensuring that she has the skeleton again to collect her evidence, even, as it turns out, at the cost of his own life. The novel contrasts Anil's facility to dip into a country's troubles and escape again, with the difficulties which Sarath faces in belonging to this community. Telling the truth about the past is not an academic exercise for him; after Anil has left the country, he is abducted, tortured, killed, his hands broken above the wrists. Anil, the emigrant, believes like Philoctetes that truth is absolute and unambiguous and can be "broken apart" from its context; Sarath recognizes that life in a community is more complicated than that and that truth is nuanced by the pressure of political forces, the fear of reprisals, and the memory of past atrocities:

> "You like to remain cloudy, don't you, Sarath, even to yourself."
> "I don't think clarity is necessarily truth. It's simplicity, isn't it?"
> "I need to know what you think. I need to break things apart to know where someone came from. That's also an acceptance of complexity. Secrets turn powerless in the open air."
> "Political secrets are not powerless, in any form," he said.
>
> (Ondaatje 2000: 259)

So Anil leaves, unharmed, with her skeleton and her tape recorder retaining the evidence of government murder and cover-up, while Sarath ends up being tended by his brother Gamini in the mortuary. To be the Western émigré, jetting back to the States, seems the superior option. Yet Ondaatje leaves the question open. Anil is torn between her freedom as an exile and her yearning for the land of her childhood. We last see her the night before her departure, still drawn to Sarath's voice on the tape recorder, to the tragic world of love, sacrifice, belonging, and betrayal in which he was held fast, to the instinctive, embodied world from which the logical, abstract analysis of the cosmopolitan exile – and, indeed, the academic – is excluded:

> At one point that night, she remembered, they spoke of how much they loved their country. In spite of everything. No Westerner would understand the love they had for the place. "But I could never leave here," Gamini had whispered.

"American movies, English books – remember how they all end?" Gamini asked that night. "The American or the Englishman gets on a plane and leaves. That's it. The camera leaves with him . . . He's going home. So the war, to all purposes, is over. That's enough reality for the West. It's probably the history of the last two hundred years of Western political writing. Go home. Write a book. Hit the circuit."

(285–6)

Notes

1 More details of this story can be found in Benjamin 1973: 23–4.

2 One estimate puts the figure at around 40 million displaced people in Europe in 1945.

3 Juan Medina's photographs won a 2005 World Press Photo Award. They were published as a feature in *EI8HT* (2005), 4:3.

4 Precise statistics on sex trafficking and illegal immigration from Eastern Europe/the former Soviet Union are not known. The London Metropolitan Police have estimated that 70 percent of women working in off-street prostitution in London are foreign nationals.

5 Homi Bhabha, in "Discussion," following Clifford's paper, "Traveling Cultures" (Clifford 1997: 43).

6 See Smith 2006.

7 Jonathan Dollimore points out the unexpected similarity between a Romantic and an existential interpretation of tragedy in his book (Dollimore 2004: 193–5, 262–4).

8 The full context of this well-known aphorism is as follows:

> Therefore, if the earlier forms of society are natural, so is the state, for it is the end of them, and the nature of a thing is its end. For what each thing is when fully developed, we call its nature, whether we are speaking of a man, a horse or a family. Besides, the final cause and end of a thing is the best, and to be self-sufficing is the end and the best. Hence it is evident that the state is a creation of nature, and that man is by nature a political animal.
>
> (Aristotle 1996: 13)

For a discussion of this passage see Cartledge 1993: 107–14.

9 The first ostracism was carried out in 487 BCE, and the last in 417 or 416 BCE, roughly the golden age of Greek tragedy (Vernant and Vidal-Naquet 1988: 415).

10   Archaeologists have unearthed a cache of 190 potsherds, all bearing the name of Themistocles, who was ostracized in 471 BCE, and, from the handwriting, clearly written by only 14 individuals. This indicates that the potsherds with the designated name already written were intended for distribution to the voters and has therefore caused some to fear foul play.

11   H. D. F. Kitto translates this line even more neutrally, and closer to the original Greek: "no punishment shall fall on him, save only to depart unharmed from Thebes" (Sophocles 1994).

12   Although the audience, and we, know that, according to the myth, Oedipus left Thebes and eventually came, as exile, to Athens, nevertheless, in the play, he finishes going back into the palace. See Wiles 1997: 177–9 for an analysis of the dramatic exits in OT.

13   The Greek word *eremos*, meaning "deserted," used to describe Philoctetes' island, Lemnos, shares a common root with the Greek word, *ereo*, meaning "I ask" or "I explore." So it is tempting to see the island as both literally deserted and also psychologically a metaphorical space for questioning and self-questioning. See my discussion in *The Cambridge Introduction to Tragedy* (Cambridge University Press, 2007).

14   Meursault mentions the fact that there is "no way out" twice in *The Outsider* (Camus 1983: 22, 79). The word that is used in *Philoctetes*, *aporos* (897), which literally means "no way out," is the same term which Socrates uses at the end of his dialogues to indicate the state of confusion and impasse the interlocutors have reached: the state, in theoretical terms, of *aporia*.

15   The extent to which the chorus represents the city is much debated among critics. For an example of one exchange, see Gould 1996 and Goldhill 1996.

16   Ondaatje's novel, published in 2000, was set during the worst of the civil war violence in the early 1990s. By mid-2000, there were estimated to be more than one million internally displaced people in Sri Lanka. There was a formal ceasefire between 2001 and 2006, but from July 2006, the civil war flared up again.

Chapter 8

Narratives of Tragic Empathy: *Prometheus Bound* and *Frankenstein*

Vanda Zajko

Tragedy as an artistic form, as drama or narrative, could be said to rely on the idea that it is possible to enter into the experience of another and gain a different perspective on the world. Whether this is potentially a beneficial or a dangerous process for either individuals or communities is a question that has been debated from antiquity onward, and a variety of vocabularies have developed that attempt to describe and explain how it might occur. The philosophical and psychoanalytic discourses preoccupied with these issues tend to stress the inevitable incompleteness or impossibility of fully encountering the "other"; literature, we might argue, is somewhat more optimistic. For the purposes of this chapter, the estimation of the impact of certain literary and dramatic narratives on their readers and viewers forms the basis of a construction of "tragedy" as a phenomenon which bridges periods and cultures. As such, it works with what Andrew Laird has recently described as a "pragmatic" conception of literature whereby disparate literary productions "can be conceived and judged in terms of their effects (emotional, educational, social, etc.) on readers or audience" (Laird 2006: 27). From this perspective the potential of *Prometheus Bound* and *Frankenstein* to provoke a response of empathy becomes more significant than their obvious generic differences.

Mary Shelley's choice of "The Modern Prometheus" as the alternative title for her novel *Frankenstein* makes it probable that some readers at least would look to the ancient myth for help with its interpretation. In particular, the three most detailed accounts from antiquity, Hesiod's two poems *Theogony* and *Works and Days* and Aeschylus' eponymous play, are likely to be cited as potential intertexts. In some senses the similarities between Prometheus and Frankenstein are obvious – both figures can be character-ized as hubristic manufacturers of a new life form – and, indeed, within the contemporary popular imagination the name "Frankenstein" is frequently used of both scientist and Monster, compounding the idea of their connec-tion. But there are other ways in which the ancient representations of the Titan can be linked with the nineteenth-century novella, ways that involve the tracing of more complex patterns of identification. Commenting on the significance of the surrogate title, Muriel Spark suggests that the theme of Prometheus helps to establish Frankenstein and his nameless monster as simultaneously complementary and antithetical characters:

> That casual, alternative *Or* is worth noting, for though at first Frankenstein is himself the Prometheus, the vital fire-endowing protagonist, the Monster, as soon as he is created, takes on the role. His solitary plight – " . . . but am I not alone, miserably alone?" he cries – and more especially his revolt against his creator, establish his Promethean features. So, the title implies, the Monster is an alternative Frankenstein.
>
> (Spark 1951: 134)

From the outset, then, readers are alerted to different possible focuses for their sympathy and attention, and the nexus of stories associated with the Titan provides a tool with which to interrogate Shelley's own contribution to the myth. In laying claim to a Promethean aspect to her story, Shelley situates it within a tradition that encompasses Greek tragedy and opens up a space for comparing her novelistic version with the theatrical one. This comparison, as suggested above, may profitably be considered in terms of potential audience response. Since Aristotle revitalized the discussion with his mention of *katharsis* (he did not *initiate* the discussion, as sometimes is implied – both Aristophanes and Plato were extremely interested in the subject), the nature and scope of the affects of tragedy have been animatedly debated and the role of the public spectacle of suffering in the fifth century has been interrogated from a variety of perspectives. The debate has con-tinued to resonate in the modern world – the appropriate response to the staged, televised, or cinematic suffering of another and the interplay of intellect and emotion that shapes such a response remains a contentious subject in artistic and political fields. We might think, for example, of debates about the current television series *The Sopranos* and *24* or differing responses to the 2004 film *The Passion of The Christ*. *Prometheus Bound* can be seen as a forerunner of recent controversial dramas in that its sympathies are not univocal and its sites of identification by no means secure.

The ambivalence that attends the figures of both Frankenstein and the Monster is a striking feature of Shelley's novel, but it is also a quality that over the years has haunted responses to Aeschylus' play. E. R. Dodds has recounted how debates in the nineteenth century about its date and authenticity and its possible relation to a trilogy were prompted to a large extent by concerns about the moral ambiguity of its portrayal of Zeus. The contrast between the supreme being of the *Supplices* and the *Agamemnon*, whose sense of justice is praised, and the vindictive tyrant of the *Prometheus* led many scholars to conclude that the surviving *Prometheus* is itself a child of uncertain parentage since, based on the evidence of his other work, Aeschylus would not have created it. Dodds attributes this conclusion to the "extremely conservative and monarchist tendencies of nineteenth-century universities, especially in Germany" (Dodds 1973: 33) and makes a strong case for retaining the play within the Aeschylean corpus. He rejects the argument that the devout playwright would not have represented the king of the gods behaving cruelly by pointing to the poet's emphasis on the newness of the regime, suggesting that the progress of the divine establishment toward justice and equity is properly the play's subject:

> Far from attempting to whitewash Zeus, Aeschylus appears . . . to have gone out of his way to exhibit him in the most unfavourable light. All that he has added to the Hesiodic tradition – Prometheus' new status as son of Themis, the goddess of Justice, and as inventor of all arts and sciences, his services to Zeus in the war against the Titans, and his frustration of the plan to destroy mankind, not to mention the Io scene – all this tends to exalt the character of Prometheus and to blacken that of his divine adversary. Had Aeschylus meant to think of Zeus as "stern but just," of Prometheus as (in the words of a German textbook) "an impertinent reformer," he could and presumably would have written the play otherwise.

Dodds is right to highlight the particularity of Aeschylus' version of the myth, but perhaps overstates the clarity of Zeus' depiction as villain. In Hesiod, Prometheus is wily and calculating, but in the end his attempts to outmaneuver Zeus are ineffectual and his resistance fails. In *Prometheus Bound*, however, the same epithets are used repeatedly of both Zeus and

Prometheus and neither god nor Titan can be straightforwardly identified as virtuous within the terms of their dispute. Both are endowed with knowledge and insight and with prophetic skill and they cling to their mutual enmity with comparable intransigence. According to the mythological tradition, the conflict eventually ended when Heracles shot the eagle that had been devouring Prometheus and he in turn revealed the secret of the threat to Zeus, ensuring that the god would not be overthrown. The possibility and/or inevitability of this reconciliation is mentioned at various points throughout the drama and the prediction of the future is one of the themes that helps to unite its disparate scenes. But by the end of the play the violence of Prometheus' opposition to the god has intensified and he has attempted to enlist the compassion of his various interlocutors by recounting the story of his suffering and the grievances he holds against Zeus. The dramatic tension lies not in action (the play has often been criticized for being too static for modern tastes, although in Aristophanes' *Frogs* Dionysus explicitly claims that he enjoyed Aeschylus' immobile characters), but in the question of whether the protagonist will succeed in persuading those who come to stare at him to sympathize with his torment.

The response of the chorus of Ocean nymphs is crucial here. They alternate between expressions of sympathy for Prometheus and of fear that he has said too much and been too brazen in his defiance. Mark Griffith, in his commentary on the play, comments thus (the line references are all to the Greek text in his edition of the play):

> The choral odes of *Prom* . . . are relatively short and limited in their scope and emotional range. The frequent addresses to P. . . emphasize the Chorus' sympathy, and the odes effectively convey the pity, not only of the Oceanids, but of the mortal world (160–3, 406–35, cf. 545–51) and even of the elements themselves (431–5, cf. 88–92, 1091–3); they powerfully reinforce the sense of shock and outrage aroused by the Io scene (687–95, 887–907); and in every ode we are reminded of the terrifying threat of Zeus' anger – or even of his love (692–5, 887–907). But seldom in these odes are larger questions raised, or opinions offered, about the nature of Zeus' rule and the prospects of his downfall, about the propriety, or otherwise, of P.'s generosity to mortals, about the hope of reconciliation between P. and Zeus. Those questions and opinions that *are* voiced (183–5, 543–51) merely repeat themes and viewpoints from the preceding dialogue. Thus the Chorus, even in their songs, maintain their timid and passive character.
>
> (Aeschylus 1983: 22)

Although the last words of the Chorus (ll.1063–70) indicate their willingness to stand by Prometheus and to share in his suffering, the complexities of the staging of the end of the drama mean that it is uncertain whether they are in fact swallowed up with Prometheus or whether the earthquake and whirlwind sweep him away before they act so that their resolve is never really tested. Griffith inclines to the latter view for reasons of consistency in character and motivation, and it is certainly true that the dramatic potency of Prometheus' last speech is increased by the overwhelming sense of isolation that leads him directly to address the elements, as he has done throughout the play, but not to call upon any of the other characters:

> Word now to deed
> World cracks/Earth rocks
> I hear Thunder. Deep
> Echoes answer my cries
> Lightning curls spears of light
> Dust dances with the wind
> Winds/blow after blow
> Battle winds
> The sky drowns the sea
> I see the storm of Zeus
>
> Come close to me now my terror
>
> O my mother, holy mother mine
> O sky light eternal that revolves
> The common light of all
> Look on me, see how I am wronged.
> (Aeschylus 2005: ll.1080–93)

The loneliness of Prometheus and the provocation of his final words suggest that the challenge of the play for the audience, as for the chorus, is to find some way to comprehend and share in the extremity of his suffering. In this way *Prometheus Bound* can be seen as exemplary in its construction of a role for the audience that explores the affective dimension of tragedy. As Charles Segal has claimed, "it is a deeply held assumption among the Greeks of the archaic and classical periods that the sharing of tears and suffering creates a bond of common humanity between mortals" (Segal 1996: 149), and the ritual dimension of tragic performances, particularly when it is invoked, as so often, at the play's end, can be seen as enacting a movement from individual suffering to communal grief. In the discussion of *Philoctetes* (a play that depicts another isolated hero who converses with the elements and nature), which forms part of her monumental exploration of the cognitive structure of compassion, Martha Nussbaum argues that it is the compassionate emotion of the chorus of common soldiers and sailors for the isolated and tormented hero that drives the plot as it forces Neoptolemus to reconsider his decision to steal Philoctetus' bow and instead to treat him justly and humanely. The chorus begin to imagine what it is like to be Philoctetes before they meet him, and in this "they stand in for the imaginative activity of the audience, for whom the entire tragic drama is a similar exercise of imagination and compassionate emotion" (Nussbaum 2001: 304). Although the precise psychosocial mechanisms through which the bond between character and audience member is created are cloaked in invisibility and invoked by such terms as *katharsis*, or "identification," the expansion of sensibility brought about by the imaginative participation in the suffering of another can reasonably be seen as one of the benefits that tragedy offers to its audiences and readers even today. Margaret Reynolds has recently written compellingly about the importance of the role of tragedy in "speaking the unspeakable," in telling the stories of those who have suffered, even, or perhaps especially, to those who find them too hard to bear. Addressing the central question of the origins of empathy, she suggests that "feeling begins with a kind of art. It begins with imagination," and she cites the words of the contemporary novelist Ian McEwan: "It is hard to be cruel once you permit yourself to enter the mind of your victim. Imagining what it is like to be someone other than yourself is at the core of our humanity. It is the essence of compassion, and it is the beginning of morality" (Reynolds 2005: 135).

McEwan's is a very optimistic vision of the power of the imagination, and it is not one that is shared by all cultural commentators. The question of whether literary texts can effect change in the world is bound up with the similarly vexed question of how they are seen to represent worldly characters and events – in Aristotelian terms, whether their representations are of "the real" and "the probable" or "the specific" and "the general." The debate can in fact largely be figured as a reception of Aristotle's *Poetics*, in particular of the use of the term *katharsis* in that text (*Poetics* 1449b: 24–8) and in the *Politics* (1341b 32ff). And Aristotle himself can be represented as principally responding to Plato, who argued that poets must be banished from the ideal city because they tell lies and stir up irrational emotion (see, for example, *Republic* 398a). Crudely speaking, the argument centers around this idea of what happens to emotion when it is aroused by poetry, and

Aristotle counters Plato's position by suggesting somewhat enigmatically that there is a constructive "discharge," or "purification," or "clarification" of such emotion, all three terms being possible translations for *katharsis*. The possibility that something dynamic might happen to the audience member who engages with a dramatic text, something potentially benefi- cial, both for that person and for their community, was debated and acknow- ledged in the ancient world and the ancient debate shaped and fed into the modern. Adrian Poole summarizes the conflicting positions as follows:

> There is a strong and continuing tradition of hostility to tragedy from Plato onwards. This hostility comes from what we would call in political terms, both the Right and the Left. The former worry that tragedy gets people too excited; the latter, that it doesn't excite them enough . . . From Aristotle there derives the traditional case for the defence. This seeks to rebut the charge that tragedy presents the world as dark, violent, and incomprehensible, and that it arouses in spectators analogous feelings. The prosecution argues that tragedy falsifies the truth, exciting thoughts, ideas, and passions that endanger the security of the state, established law, political power, and the sovereignty of reason. The response of Aristotle and his successors in the 16th and 17th centuries is that tragedy is morally, politically, psychologically, and theologic- ally sound, a loyal and faithful servant to established power, in the state and the individual. This is never entirely convincing.
>
> (Poole 2005: 18)

The linking of the reaction of the chorus within *Prometheus Bound* to that of its spectators follows a tradition of seeing the collective presence depicted by the play, as opposed to its portrayals of heroic individuals, as to some extent representative of the fifth-century audience. This aspect of the theorization of the response to tragedy is not indebted to Aristotle as he, famously, conducts his discussion of the genre without emphasizing the role of the chorus, but it became popular in the nineteenth century to identify the point of view of the chorus with that of the "ideal" spectator for whom the play was written. This idea has subsequently been adjusted to accommodate a more politically charged perception of the chorus as expressive of the Athenian citizen body (see, in particular, Vernant 1991), and this perception also has been developed in favor of a more nuanced and diverse sense of the multiple roles of the chorus and its functions within different plays. But, however its task is conceived, the undeniable collective presence of the chorus insists that we consider the relation *between* human beings as one of the dynamics constructed by, and responsive to, the tragic:

The collective experience and the collective voice of the chorus may oppose that of the individual tragic agent in an almost bewildering variety of ways. The choral experience may constitute an image of stability and rootedness, of threatening disorder, of human vulnerability, to stand against the experience of the protagonists; the axis of its opposition to them can be shifted at will. But it cannot be removed. The sense of difference, the sense that the human condition embraces both the individual and the group, and that all experience, even the ultimate, all-consuming experience of "the tragic", is to be lived through, perceived, and recollected collectively as well as individually, is so essential a part of the Greek tragic theatre that, in this context at least, we cannot perceive "the tragic" otherwise.

(Gould 1996: 233)

Gould here is specifically talking about tragedy in its fifth-century incarnation, but this specificity raises questions about the use of tragedy as a generic term for texts from different periods and in different forms. Any survey of what constitutes the tragic in a broad cross-cultural frame, if it is to give space to considerations of emotional power, must consider a range of theoretical models of representation and the self. Some of these models are ancient, as in the case of Plato and Aristotle, and some are modern, as in the case of the psychoanalytic versions that are frequently utilized in conjunction with Shelley's *Frankenstein* and its afterlife. In each case either the historical particularity of performance or reading contexts or more generalized and dehistoricized depictions of what responding to a text involves can be emphasized so that the perennial question of the possible grounds for a comparison of an ancient and modern text becomes significant, this time with a distinctive psychological twist. What is it possible to reconstruct or suppose about shared or individual responses to tragedy that may enliven a sense of the intertextual relationship between Aeschylus and Mary Shelley?

It is often assumed that dramatic texts evoke emotional and intellectual responses in their audiences more easily than literary texts do in their readers due to the immediacy of a performance context. The novel, on the other hand, is associated with the development of a sense of interiority that encourages the idea that responses to it are somehow personal and internal to the subject and therefore less likely to have collective significance. But most recent discussions of Aeschylus' play take place on the basis of the written text, and the cultural authority of *Frankenstein* has expanded far beyond the limited circumstance of the printed page and, these days, is most probably associated with the medium of film. The processes of reception that have enabled both these texts to transcend the contingency of the original moments of their production break down the distinction between public and private reactions to them. And no individual "reader" is in a position to react in a purely solitary way, outside of broader social discourses. The continuum that is being argued for here between the ancient Greek drama and Mary Shelley's novel depends on establishing a similarity of potential in both texts to transform the perspectives of their "readers," a term used here in its broadest sense, and this potential exceeds the obvious differences of both period and form.

Martha Nussbaum uses the term "eudaimonistic judgement" to describe the way in which a person comes to recognize that the suffering of another has implications for the possibilities of her own life and this, she suggests, is an indispensable requirement for compassion in human beings, since "imagining one's own similar possibilities aids the extension of one's own eudaimonistic imagination." She goes on to discuss the special role of "narratives of tragic predicaments" (this category includes, but is not restricted to, classic tragic dramas) in promoting compassion in their audiences by "inviting both empathy and the judgement of similar possibilities" (Nussbaum 2001: 319). She implies that this potential for promoting compassion should be what leads to the designation of any text as "tragic," regardless of historical age or generic type, and she points out the capacity of many such narratives to disturb the complacencies of their audiences in profoundly unsettling ways:

> tragedies promote concern for someone different from oneself, through the compelling resources of poetry and drama. Although it is of course possible for tragedies to support the view that certain groups or classes are not fully human, and thus not worthy of the spectator's compassion, it is significant that they tend, on the whole, to be in advance of their surrounding cultures in recognizing the similar humanity of different groups of vulnerable humans. Thus the highly hierarchical and misogynistic society of ancient Athens created tragedies involving subtle forms of sympathy for the suffering of women; the slaveholding United States created *Uncle Tom's Cabin*, the animal-exploiting society of Victorian England created *Black Beauty*. Tragic fictions promote extension of concern by linking the imagination powerfully to the adventures of the distant life in question. Thus, while none is per se eudaimonistically reliable, tragedies are powerful devices promoting the extension of the eudaimonistic judgement.
>
> (Nussbaum 2001: 352).

Nussbaum's is a particular view of the role of literature, one that can be regarded as "neo-Aristotelian" in its emphasis on the heuristic working-through of ethical issues. If we return to *Prometheus Bound*, we find that the attempts of Prometheus to elicit compassion from the different individuals and groups of people who are forced to witness his suffering can easily be seen as conforming to this model of the tragic. His attempts fail with the tyrannical Zeus who does not appear onstage; with the single-minded bullies who act for the god, Kratos and Bia; and with Hermes, who appears at the end of the play and is more verbose, but is taunted by Prometheus throughout the scene for being nothing more than a jumped-up lackey. However, those with Hephaestus, who is a most unwilling jailer, with Oceanus, Io, and with the chorus are more successful. The appearance of Io, in particular, stages in miniature the promotion of compassion that is thematically important to the play so that Griffith can comment: "the bond of friendship which is established between Prometheus, Io and the Chorus affords a touching, though fragile, sense of community in a play which otherwise emphasizes the lonely struggles of individuals" (Griffith 1983: 12). The introduction of Io appears to be an Aeschylean addition to the myth and, as such, might be said to indicate the priorities of the dramatist in his telling of the story. So what, then, are the points of comparison with *Frankenstein* and the way that Mary Shelley chose to tell her story?

We have established already that the choice of the alternative title for her novel highlights Shelley's positioning of both Victor Frankenstein and the Monster as possible Promethean figures. Let us consider first how Victor might fit this description. According to his own account, even as a boy, the would-be scientist was motivated by the desire to divine the causes of things. His curiosity propelled him in a particular direction, toward discerning the hidden laws of nature, and there were many areas of human activity that held no fascination for him:

> I confess that neither the structure of languages, nor the code of governments, nor the politics of various states, possessed attractions for me. It was the secrets of heaven and earth that I desired to learn; and whether it was the outward substance of things, of the inner spirit of nature and the mysterious soul of man that occupied me, still my enquiries were directed to the metaphysical, or, in its highest sense, the physical secrets of the world.
>
> (Shelley 1831: 37).

In selecting "the physical secrets of the world" as his object of study Victor displays what might be described as a Promethean desire to acquire the knowledge and power of the divine. Indeed, his very name might be regarded as a modern version of the word "Prometheus." In Aeschylus' play, the crimes for which the Titan is punished are the aid he gave to mortals and, more specifically, his gift to them of fire, and yet it is the knowledge he possesses about the future threat to Zeus which makes him such a potent and menacing rival. The defiant attitude with which Prometheus refuses to accept the limits of his position and with which he endures his torture can be paralleled in Victor's determination to pursue his scientific studies, no matter what the cost. And the symbol of fire is surely translated into its contemporary equivalent when it is utilized to provide the spark of electricity that animates the Monster. But the most obvious point of comparison between Frankenstein and his ancient predecessor, the illicit creation of a new life form, has no parallel in Aeschylus or indeed in Hesiod, since the figure of Prometheus *plasticator* is familiar to us only from later Roman versions of the myth. The act of creation which corresponds most interestingly to that of Frankenstein is in fact that of Shelley herself, who put together bits and pieces from the corpus of Western myth and literature, both pagan and Christian, to fashion a literary work that looked startlingly quite like nothing that had been written before.

Frankenstein is often cited as the forerunner of a whole new genre belonging to modernity, that of science fiction, although, as Genevieve Liveley has reminded us, historians of SF might also utilize the alternative title of the novel to push back the genre's origins into the ancient world (Liveley 2006: 278). In its explorations of the limits of what it means to be human and its preoccupation with the responsibilities associated with new technology, the novel does seem to be prescient of the concerns of later eras and to comply with the definition of science fiction as "a cognitive literature which has as the basis for its vision of creation man's new knowledge systems" (Fredericks 1980: 94). As knowledge systems develop, so do the narratives that explore them, and part of the reason for the continuing energy of Shelley's issue may be that its principal theme of the ethical responsibility of the human creator is one that seems endlessly relevant to every epoch's attempts to develop its capacities. Indeed, in the words of Jasia Reichardt:

> The problems that beset man's relationship with his creations are increasingly recognized as a subject of central importance . . . The tragic story of Victor Frankenstein's nameless creation, who for better or worse has become known by the name of his maker, touches on several topical preoccupations. These involve monsters and the travesty of what we assume to be natural laws; our attitude to automata and robots; and, finally, what it means to create life artificially.
>
> (Reichardt 1994: 138)

But however much the obsessions of *Frankenstein* appear to match those of our own age, part of its modernity (the *modern* Prometheus of the alternative title) must be the relentless secularity which locates accountability in the hands of mortals and not of the divine, and this is a quality which typifies a certain nineteenth-century worldview:

> The characteristic tension between an impinging, conditional, and time-bound world and a dream of something freer and better makes the central subject matter and form of the nineteenth-century novel and, ironically, of nineteenth-century science as well... Thus, though it would be absurd to claim Mary Shelley as a direct "influence" on the dominant literary and scientific forms of the century, we can see that in her secularization of the creation myth she invented a metaphor that was irresistible to the culture as a whole... In writers as central and various as Feuerbach, Comte, Darwin, Marx, Frazer, and Freud we can find Victor Frankenstein's activity: the attempt to discover in matter what we had previously attributed to spirit, the bestowing *on* matter (or history, or society, or nature) the values once given to God.
>
> (Levine 1979: 7)

In some ways, then, the novel is an emblematic child of its time, and Shelley herself admits as much in her introduction to the 1831 edition when she categorically declares: "invention, it must be humbly admitted, does not consist in creating out of void, but out of chaos; the materials, must, in the first place, be afforded: it can give form to dark, shapeless substances, but it cannot bring into being the substance itself" (Shelley 1831: 8). She draws on existing ideas and preoccupations to furnish her imagination and, just as Aeschylus' *Prometheus* can be allegorized as a meditation upon the injustice of the tyrannies contemporaneous with his time, *Frankenstein* can be read as a symptom of its own historical period, expressing profound dissatisfaction with the limitation of traditional concepts of morality. From the same introduction comes the phrase that more than any other has come to be associated with the author's relation to her work, the "hideous progeny" that positions her as the mother of the unnatural offspring whom she urges prophetically to "go forth and prosper." There is a clear link here between the author's theory of creation and the process carried out by Victor Frankenstein, the reputation of the novel pursuing Shelley in life and death just as the Monster pursues Victor. But, as we might expect from a work which shifts the direction of its reader's empathy backwards and forwards between scientist and his creature, there is also a connection between Mary Shelley and the Monster, particularly in relation to the connotations of her name:

> The most important "coincidence" uniting Mary Shelley and the monster is to be found in the absence of a proper (*propter*) name. Mary Shelley had no Christian or family name that was her own. She was Mary Wollstonecraft Godwin Shelley, that is to say, her name was composed of the disparate parts of other identities, just as her monster was composed of the disjointed sections of other bodies. The "nominal" fragmentation of Mary Shelley did not incite her to adopt a pseudonym but to write using her "own", that is, other people's names. The very fact of becoming a novelist not only entailed self-affirmation but also acquiescence to a particularly onerous parental heritage... However, it is the affirmation that will prevail over any acquiescence as Mary Shelley simultaneously created a literary genre and two categories of character new to fiction, both of whom possessed a demoniacal will and strength. In a sentence Mary Shelley, in order to infuse a spark of life into her own unnarratable "dark shapeless substances", created a monstrous text that murdered her mother, her father and her husband. Little wonder that she called *Frankenstein* "my hideous progeny".
>
> (Olorenshaw 1994: 169)

The designation of the text itself as monstrous recalls the disreputable standing of *Prometheus Bound* as a play that has sometimes (although not in antiquity) been considered unworthy of Aeschylus, the progenitor of tragedy. Griffith outlines how a number of scholars conclude, from the structure and style (and, in a few cases, the conception) of the play, that it is not the work of Aeschylus at all, or that it was left unfinished by him, and completed by a member of his family (Griffith 1983: 32–3). If this were indeed the case, we might relish the thought that Aeschylus' son or nephew, like Mary Shelley, created a monstrous text which murdered his father or uncle. The repudiation of the play reminds us of the cultural work of "monstrosities" in fortifying bodily norms at the same time as expanding the possibilities of what might be considered "normal": the desire to designate *Prometheus Bound* as an improper tragedy leads inevitably to a recantation of the qualities that characterize a drama of worth, but simultaneously those who argue for the opposite position, as did Dodds in the passage cited above, adopt a strategy of inflating the category of the "Aeschylean" so that it can include the renegade play. The fact that the Monster is alive is not enough to ensure his acceptance by the human beings he meets because his bodily deformity causes them to react with

violence and horror. It might seem, therefore, that when it comes to
Frankenstein only the first part of the above statement is true, and monstrosity serves merely to reinforce the boundaries of the decorous and maintain
the status quo in terms of what is human. But the enormous sympathy
invoked for the Monster by parts of the narrative and the emphasis placed
on the motivation for his change from "love of virtue" and "the feelings of
happiness and affection" to the "bitter and loathing despair" which results in
murderous brutality (Shelley 1831: 221) suggest a more complex and challenging agenda. In the words of Paul Youngquist:

> That monstrosities have a life of their own is the true moral of Shelley's tale,
> one understood best by those deemed unfit, on the basis of physical differ-
> ence, for full participation in liberal society. The monster speaks violently on
> their behalf, demanding companionship by virtue of monstrosity. He knows
> viscerally that posthuman bodies incarnate new possibilities.
>
> (Youngquist 2003: 56)

This way of reading the novel enables it to be considered a "narrative of
tragic predicament" along the lines of Nussbaum's definition, with the
Monster joining the ranks of those other protagonists whose suffering
promotes the extension of the eudaimonistic judgment in their readers.

His status as spectacle is something the Monster shares with the Prometheus of *Prometheus Bound*. For from the moment of his vivification the
former is renounced, not for his behavior or character, but for the way he
looks:

> How can I describe my emotions at this catastrophe, or how delineate the wretch
> whom with such infinite pains and care I had endeavoured to form? His limbs
> were in proportion, and I had selected his features as beautiful. Beautiful! – Great
> God! His yellow skin scarcely covered the work of muscles and arteries beneath;
> his hair was of a lustrous black, and flowing; his teeth of a pearly whiteness; but
> these luxuriances only formed a more horrid contrast with his watery eyes, that
> seemed almost of the same colour as the dun white sockets in which they were
> set, his shrivelled complexion and straight black lips.
>
> (Shelley 1831: 57)

It is the appearance of the being he has created that leads Frankenstein to
reject him, and the scientist's claim that "no mortal could support the
horror of that countenance" (Shelley 1831: 58) is justified by the reactions
of those others who later react to the Monster with similar vicious revulsion.

The only person who fails to respond in this way is De Lacey, the old man whose family is the source of the Monster's education in what it means to be human. De Lacey's blindness means that he has to rely on other senses to form an impression of his visitor, an impression which, until the interruption of his sighted children, is altogether benign, since the tutelage has been effective and the Monster's speech is sincere, eloquent, and credible. The latter has deliberately sought to introduce himself to the father when the other members of the family are absent, since he has become conscious through studying his own image in water and in shadow of the horrifying effect his form is destined to have. In the absence of a favorable aspect, the Monster has recognized that he must depend instead on his capacity for language to win over the cottagers, and in his solitude he has tried to convince himself that the personality he has developed will be compensation enough: "When they should become acquainted with my admiration of their virtues, they would compassionate me and overlook my personal deformity" (Shelley 1831: 130).

Peter Brooks has described the opposition between sight and speech as central to the novel's preoccupations and emphasized the importance of Shelley's decision to make the Monster the most eloquent being in the novel:

> This hideous and deformed creature, far from expressing himself in grunts and gestures, speaks and reasons with the highest elegance, logic, and persuasiveness. As a verbal creation, he is the very opposite of the monstrous: he is a sympathetic and persuasive participant in Western culture. All of the Monster's interlocutors – including, finally, the reader – must come to terms with this contradiction between the verbal and the visual.
>
> (Brooks 1993: 202)

Just as Prometheus' brutalized and tortured body, displayed on stage for the duration of Aeschylus' drama, cannot be disassociated from the voice that so urgently solicits compassion, either by those who coinhabit the mythological landscape of the play or by its audience, so the Monster's poignant rhetoric must be juxtaposed with the hideous deformity of his features and frame. The deviant flesh of the two protagonists undermines any idea of a natural connection between physical integrity and emotional truth since the plausibility of their arguments forces consideration that, despite their afflictions, right might be on their side, or, at least, not exclusively the property of their opponents. The "contradiction between the verbal and the visual" that Brooks describes challenges the reader of both *Prometheus Bound* and *Frankenstein* to see beyond corporeal limitations, and the entailments of entering into an empathetic relationship with characters whose experience is so extreme is partly what drives the narratives of both texts.

As Brooks points out, far from being illiterate and inchoate, the Monster is an active participant in Western culture, at least as it is represented by the canonical texts from which he has been learning: *Paradise Lost*, a volume of Plutarch's *Lives*, and Goethe's *Sorrows of Werter*. The account of his self-education once he has been rejected by the human world is the centerpiece of the novel and has been criticized as a rather obvious contrivance, but it can also be read less cynically and its poignancy developed. The Aeschylean Prometheus who challenges his audience to overcome their revulsion at his plight and feel some compassion might be identified here with the isolated Monster who peeps through a chink in a cottage wall and learns about language, lost love, and what it means to be human. He studies the books he finds effectively and, in a process that directly mimics the larger-scale interaction between the reader of *Frankenstein* and his own example, he uses the characters portrayed within them as models for the expansion of his own imaginative sensibility:

> I can hardly describe to you the effect of these books. They produced in me an infinity of new images and feelings that sometimes raised me to ecstasy, but more frequently sunk me into lowest dejection . . . As I read, however, I applied much personally to my own feelings and condition. I found myself similar, yet at the same time strangely unlike to the beings concerning whom I read, and to whose conversation I was a listener. I sympathised with, and partly understood them, but I was unformed in mind; I was dependent on none and related to none. "The path of my departure was free;" and there was none to lament my annihilation. My person was hideous, and my stature gigantic: what did this mean? Who was I? What was I? Whence did I come? What was my destination? These questions continually recurred, but I was unable to solve them.
>
> (Shelley 1831: 127–8)

The combination of familiarity and alienation with which the Monster responds to the literary personages he happens upon might be put down to the uniqueness of his own situation, composed as he is from parts of human beings but not quite adding up to one himself. It could also be seen as a description of the process of encountering alterity which lies at the heart of any attempt to enter into the experience of another. We have seen how

Nussbaum has evolved a vocabulary to expound this process and developed it particularly in relation to the impact of certain literary and dramatic narratives on their readers and viewers. There are other vocabularies available, and indeed the search for recognition of and by the other has been one of the principal concerns of both psychoanalysis and ethical philosophy for the last 50 years: how is it possible to conceptualize the influence of the other on the self without domesticating or annihilating its radical "otherness"? What does it mean to claim that subjectivity is strictly relational, that a subject must bear the traces of every encounter with the external world? These huge questions which are also so central to any pragmatic conceptualization of literature continue to be the focus of contemporary debates that conclude, on the whole, that empathy necessarily involves either a denial or appropriation of the distinctiveness of the other: the possibility of understanding someone else's mind or emotions must always be limited and partial. In such circumstances a significant role for literature might be to undermine this kind of cynicism and to continue to insist on the importance of the project of imagining the impossible. In a spirit of defiant optimism, then, the voice of Aeschylus' Prometheus reaches us across the centuries, both pleading and challenging in his final words: "Look on me, see how I am wronged."

Acknowledgments

I would like to thank Paul Cheshire, Genevieve Liveley, and the editors of this volume for their help with this chapter. Particular thanks to Pantelis Michelakis for his numerous insightful comments.

Chapter 9

Tragedy and Childhood

Peter Hollindale

Susan Hill's novel *I'm the King of the Castle* (1970) has a genuinely tragic child protagonist, a boy who attains full consciousness of his tragic predicament without ceasing to be a child. It concerns two 11-year-old boys, Edmund Hooper and Charles Kingshaw. Edmund has a prosperous father, who has just inherited a large country house called Warings; his mother is dead. Charles has an impecunious mother, who has just accepted a post as "informal housekeeper" at Warings; his father is dead. While mother and father ease their way self-centeredly toward a new relationship, the boys are left to their own devices. They are required to become friends. Instead Edmund, who from the outset enjoys social and territorial advantage, bullies and persecutes the trapped and helpless Charles until he finds escape by suicide.

This is an impressive and tragic novel, but it is of its time – our time – depending on what Christina Hardyment terms "the separate world which children occupy in our society today," one in which mothers "may...be distracted and distant – 'emotionally unavailable' is the chilling phrase coined by the new family therapists" (Hardyment 1992: 84, 93). Kingshaw's mother, ambitious for profitable remarriage, is indeed "emotionally unavailable." Hill's novel requires belief in an autonomous child world, insulated from adults, and it assumes that childhood is a significant phase of life, with legitimate needs and entitlements which, for Kingshaw, are missing. It also assumes that children, as well as having value, are capable of evil. It rests, that is, on an ideology of childhood which would not be current at all times, and the space for childhood tragedy exists within that context.

Childhood is both a concept and a lived experience. Every society at every period, it can be argued, enacts through its social practices, expectations, and tolerances a theory of childhood, sometimes two or more conflicting theories. They are not necessarily well understood by the adults who apply them, since they are not a constant but evolve, often rapidly, in response to broader social conditions. Pioneering historical studies of childhood, notably those of Philippe Ariès in *Centuries of Childhood* (1962) and Edward Shorter in *The Making of the Modern Family* (1975), though still much admired, have ceded ground to more recent research and new understandings in a field which is always contentious. (For example, in Britain at the time of writing there are perceptible recent changes of attitude due in part to the problem of drug abuse, fear of pedophilia, children's mastery of the internet, and more cautious attitudes to risk.) Childhood is therefore an unstable term, historically conditioned. It is open to question whether changing theories of childhood cause or are caused by changes in the nature of actual children, or whether, as Keith Thomas assumed, "the development of the child's mind and body is essentially a biological constant" (Thomas 1989: 70).

Embedded in the changing theories of childhood and status of children over history lies the place of childhood in tragedy. Children themselves have usually been marginal figures in tragic drama and tragic fiction, accessory victims whose significance lies not in their own but an adult's tragic suffering. Medea kills her children to punish their father, Jason, but in so doing sacrifices their future performance of due rites at her own death: she, not the children, is the tragic figure (Euripides 1998). That future moment is the present for King Lear, for whom childhood, in the child–parent relationship, does not cease at maturity but is bound into lifelong ownership; he, not Cordelia, enjoys tragic primacy. When the Duchess of Malfi is shown the bodies of her murdered children, they participate in the tragedy through her feelings for them. Even in an age quite different in its attitudes to children, Ibsen's eponymous *Little Eyolf* (1894), crippled and then drowned, is less important than the corrosive compound of negligence, guilt, vicarious ambition, and sexual failure that his life and death cause his parents. Childhood is always exposed to potentially tragic ambiguities of feeling, role, and status. Sandra L. Bertman discusses Picasso's painting *The Tragedy* (1903), depicting mother, father, and child. (The painting is also known in English as *Poor Folk by the Sea*.) She asks: "Is the child to be the consoler? Caretaker to the parent? Is he about to tug at his father's clothing for the attention and support he needs? Is the child a personification of what Irving Goffman calls 'non-persons' who are there but not there?" (Bertman 1991).

Figure 9.1   Pablo Picasso, *Tragedy*, 1903, National Gallery of Art, Washington, Chester Dale Collection. Image © 2007 Board of Trustees, National Gallery of Art, Washington, 1903; oil on wood, 105.3 × 69 cm ($41\frac{7}{16}$ × $27\frac{3}{16}$ in). © Succession Picasso / DACS, London 2007

These very questions, with many others, surface, often unanswerably, when children appear in tragic literature.

Tragedy can spring from discrepancies between prevailing theories of childhood and the actualities of being a child. It can lie in the entrapment of children in a world which simultaneously, for its own purposes, both fuses their status with that of adults and exploits the differential offered by their immaturity. It can arise from disturbances of temporal process and natural growth which either propel a child into grotesqueries of premature adulthood (the *puer senex*), or conversely into incapacity for growth and refusal to surrender childhood (the *puer aeternus*). It can be traced most starkly of all to the denial of human contact in early years, the isolated animal survival of the feral child, for whom lack of quasi-parental stimuli at crucial stages of growth causes maturational lacunae that can never be corrected.

I'm the King of the Castle is relatively unusual in that its action is clearly tragic yet its central figures are unmistakably children. (The same is true of Ralph in William Golding's *Lord of the Flies* (1954), another work where childhood is autonomous.) Except where children are mere ancillary possessions of adult figures, confusions of role and status are more common. The late twentieth and early twenty-first centuries are well equipped to appreciate the potential tragedies of childhood, because we live with such confusions in our social discourse. As the historian Hugh Cunningham observed:

> The peculiarity of the late twentieth century, and the root cause of much present confusion and angst about childhood, is that a public discourse which argues that children are persons with rights to a degree of autonomy is at odds with the remnants of the romantic view that the right of a child is to be a child. The implication of the first is a fusing of the worlds of adult and child, and of the second the maintenance of separation.
>
> (Cunningham 1995: 190)

There are issues here which set childhood apart from the usual terms of reference for tragedy, and in the rest of this chapter I shall examine four categories which serve to illustrate them.

Shakespeare's Children: The Child in History

A. P. Rossiter once described the vision of Shakespeare's history plays as "obscure tragedy." He was referring to the historical process itself, where the endless unfolding pattern of events, the narrative of nationhood, is set against the individuality and fate of even the "greatest" persons by whom this narrative is written. He argued that "there is a 'Doubleness' here: in the conflicting values set by the Greatness (the Triumph) of the National Destiny, and the Frustration, the inadequacy, of the Individual (the frail man within the robe)." He contended: "These kings and great persons are all sub-tragic. They lack a degree (or some degrees) of freedom; are caught in nets of events by which they are frustrate [*sic*] and less than their potential selves" (Rossiter 1961: 42).

Although he was referring to the frail empowerment of adult kings, queens, and nobles, he could equally have been describing the children in Shakespeare who are trapped and usually destroyed by historical processes to which they are born. Their plight is caught with singular exactness in a studio photograph used in publicity for the 2006 Royal Shakespeare

Company production of *King John*. It shows a boy, half-hidden by a curtain, wearing a robe and coronet but naked to the waist beneath it. Although it may represent the condition of the boy Prince Arthur in the play, it could also stand as an image for the vulnerable human frailty imperfectly concealed by all political empowerment. The children of Shakespeare's histories and tragedies are all, in Rossiter's term, sub-tragic: they have status without freedom, and are entangled in the nets of their own dynastic importance.

Shakespeare needed nothing more than recent Tudor history by way of contrary examples of the whims of history. Edward VI, the boy king succeeding Henry VIII, had enjoyed a brief precocious reign of Protestant fervor and authoritarianism before dying of natural causes in his mid-teens. His sister Elizabeth, daughter of Henry's executed second queen, had survived a perilous childhood needing all her youthful political skills before gaining, and retaining, long monarchical success. The child in history was a political phenomenon made urgent by Elizabeth's own childlessness. Nothing could free certain royal children, when occasion arose, from a weight of circumstance that both buried the fact of their childhood beneath their dynastic status, and exploited it through their immaturity. Sub-tragically helpless, they were the playthings of history; yet introduced by their position to premature awareness, they were also individuals, doomed to unavailing use of the courtly arts that would destroy them. In a series of such figures, Shakespeare depicted "childhood" as a component in political or military conflicts where juvenile persons competed equally and undifferentiated from adults in the struggles of status and power, but were also, simultaneously, children, seen in moving efforts to overcome the weakness of their immaturity.

The moment in *King John* when the King enlists Hubert to kill the young Prince Arthur, the inconvenient young nephew whose claim to the throne is better than his own, sums up in five lines the doubleness set out above, where childhood is both abolished and exploited:

> Good Hubert, Hubert, Hubert, throw thine eye
> On yon young boy. I'll tell thee what, my friend,
> He is a very serpent in my way;
> And where soe'er this foot of mine doth tread
> He lies before me.
>
> (3.3.59–63)

The subsequent scene (4.1) in which Prince Arthur pleads for his eyes and life when Hubert, his erstwhile friend and guardian, comes to blind him, is

one of the strongest in the play. Arthur, who later dies in a desperate attempt
to escape imprisonment, is a sub-tragic figure in a sub-tragic world, but it is
the meticulous delineation through his speech of his status as both child and
not-child that makes him all but a tragic figure. The doubleness is as well
summed up by Arthur himself as by his uncle in a mere two lines:

> I doubt
> My uncle practices more harm to me;
> He is afraid of me, and I of him.
> (4.1.19–21)

The exchange of the word "afraid" brings together two coexistent contexts
of "childhood," one political, the other psychological and biological, and the
boy's sub-tragic status lies precisely in that division. The rest of the scene is
one long and moving extension of it, as the boy seeks to defend himself
through a desperate eloquence which alternates between a courtly sophis-
tication of argument through metaphor and directly childlike emotional
appeal, between resort to public rank and resort to private friendship,
between assertions of manly fortitude and collapse into childlike protest.
He looks for advantage *in extremis* one moment in being, the next in not
being, a child, and his behavior in both roles is simultaneously real and
expertly performative.

A single scene in *Richard III* straddles the same divide. When the future
"Princes in the Tower," the boy Prince of Wales and his younger brother
the Duke of York, are brought to London, meet their Machiavellian "Uncle
Gloucester" and are dispatched to the Tower, Buckingham overrules Car-
dinal Bourchier's objections to the forcible removal of the young York from
the religious sanctuary in which his mother has placed him. He does this by
exploiting childhood's irresponsibility to argue that the boy is not old
enough to have either deserved or asked for sanctuary: "Oft have I heard
of sanctuary men / But sanctuary children never till now" (3.1.55–6). Childhood is here used as a political weapon to suppress a danger to Gloucester's
self-advancing cause which has only arisen because child and adult are equal
and undifferentiated in the workings of dynastic statecraft. The politicized
child is thus trapped in a bi-colored net; and is both child and not-child. In
King John these twofold states were embodied in Prince Arthur alone. In
Richard III they are neatly divided in this scene between the Prince of
Wales (the short-lived Edward V) and the younger York. The Prince is
shown precociously adopting the mature tones, dignity, and interests of his

kingship. He recovers from his obvious reluctance to be lodged in the Tower, where Gloucester plans to place him, by an enquiry into the Tower's origins and a neat distinction between written record and oral history, ending with the regal ambition to emulate Julius Caesar and regain British territorial rights in France. All this is an "adult" way of suppressing a child's disquiet. York, on the other hand, cleverly teases and provokes Gloucester, stretching the latter's forced avuncularity to the limit, ending with a little astute self-mockery to turn aside possible wrath: he is a shrewd and witty child, but still a child. Again they are sub-tragic figures, but their two voices express the fatal strandedness of their politicized childhood.

Kings and princes are not the only victims among Shakespeare's political children. In *3 Henry VI*, the young Earl of Rutland is similarly entrapped between the vulnerability of physical childhood and the ruthless dynastic conflicts that nullify its claims to pity. Rutland's tutor pleads with the vengeful Clifford, come to kill the boy, to "murder not this innocent child/Lest thou be hated both of God and man" (1.3.8–9), and the boy pleads for his life with every serviceable argument, however desperate, but Clifford's implacable dynastic revenge is impervious to childhood's claims: "The sight of any of the house of York/Is as a fury to torment my soul" (1.3.30–1).

The Shakespearean pattern is thus clear across a range of sub-tragic children. Most famous of all, of course, is the murder of Lady Macduff and her children in *Macbeth*. This atrocity has obvious significance beyond itself. It exemplifies Macbeth's precipitous degradation, and the infection of all Scotland by his evil; and it inaugurates fulfillment of the witches' prophecies and hence of predeterminism, prompting Macduff to revenge. What is striking in Shakespeare's treatment, however, is his refusal to treat Macduff's family as token sacrificial figures in the tragic pattern, and his care instead to humanize the domestic circle, giving to Macduff's son that quality of doomed precocity that was evident also in more princely children. Like theirs, his childhood is brutally annulled in the very act of audibly growing and maturing. Two elements of childhood – its experience and its significance – are deliberately staged in ways that powerfully enact the sub-tragic status of the children.

Long after the history plays comes in some respects the strangest instance of Shakespeare's sub-tragic children, that of Mamillius in *The Winter's Tale*. In the opening scenes he is the object of Leontes' unstable affection, and is shown with the Queen and her ladies as another child in the attractive early stages of precocious challenge to grownups. It is the news of his death that in one explosive moment cauterizes his father's psychic disorder. Yet after the "wide gap of time" has eventually, in Act 5, reunited Leontes with his "dead" wife and lost daughter, the appealing but long-dead Mamillius is forgotten and unmentioned, a human object erased by time and circumstance. He is both an engaging child and the dispensable property of adult lives, and in this way follows the established pattern.

In his life's brief scenes Mamillius also opens up another perspective on childhood's place in tragedy. For Leontes, Mamillius (like the absent Florizel for Polixenes) is a means of vicarious reentry to a lost and preferred state of childhood innocence. In causing Leontes to "recoil/Twenty-three years" he compounds his father's neurotic suspicions of adulthood, and activates nostalgic memory of the condition I examine next, recalled here by Polixenes:

> We were, fair Queen,
> Two lads that thought there was no more behind
> But such a day tomorrow as today
> And to be boy eternal.
>
> (1.2.62–5)

Puer Aeternus, Puella Aeterna

The classic instance of the eternal child in literature and drama is J. M. Barrie's *Peter Pan* (1928). The play is subtitled, both in the original 1904 theatre program and the belated 1928 printed text, "The Boy Who Would Not Grow Up," but might easily have been rephrased "Could Not." The first line of the 1911 novelization of the story famously reads, "All children, except one, grow up"; in so far as Peter is depicted as both living and immortal, this is true, but in other respects the play and novel contradict it, as do the facts of the dramatist's own life. Jacqueline Rose observes of the 1982 Royal Shakespeare Company production that "The programme and accompanying commentaries recognise the centrality of death as a motif in the play but invariably divest it of its psychic meaning for children by reducing it to a fact of Barrie's personal biography" (Rose 1984: 114), and it is true that much comment on the play has centered on Barrie's life, notably the disastrous family results of the accidental death on the eve of his fourteenth birthday of Barrie's elder brother, David. The facts of Barrie's life and physical self – his evident failure to mature sexually, his complex involvement over many years with the five Llewelyn Davies brothers (see Birkin 1979) and other matters – while illuminating the strange inter-meshing of life and art, have certainly over-influenced much commentary, but they do point the way to important truths about the play.

It is not true that "All children, except one, grow up," either in life or art, or more specifically in *Peter Pan*. Some fail to do so for various reasons – for example, because they are incapable of sexual maturity, because they refuse or repress it, because of other psychological factors deriving from excess of happiness, injury, or shock in childhood – but the commonest is simply that they die. In *Peter Pan* death is omnipresent. The earlier story, *Peter Pan in Kensington Gardens*, closes in whimsical morbidity, first with the idea that "house-swallows are the spirits of little children who have died," then with the metamorphosis of parish boundary-markers in Kensington Gardens into the tombs of babies who have "fallen unnoticed from their perambulators" (Barrie 1906: 123, 125). In *Peter Pan* we have the supposed death of Wendy, shot by Tinker Bell, and the creation of the tomblike "Little House"; the near-death of Tinker Bell; the declaration by Peter, who cannot die, that "To die would be an awfully big adventure"; the ticking crocodile which hunts and finally eats up Captain Hook, as time hunts and (Peter excepted) finally gathers all. This is a work replete with potential tragedy, which yet (with intentional irony) invests "tragedy" not in growth and death but in the incapacity to grow and die.

Hence Barrie's idiosyncratic usage of the term "tragic." The word, and the vision underlying it, surface early in *Peter Pan in Kensington Gardens* when the infant Peter, having escaped from the nursery, is stranded between the bird-stage and the child-stage of human life as he is physically stranded on an island in the Serpentine. Solomon Caw the crow tells him he must live on the island always: "'And never even go to the Kensington Gardens?' Peter asked tragic-ally" (Barrie 1906: 29). His "tragedy" is that, stranded in the fantasy between two stages of growth, he gains immortality but must remain a "Poor little half-and-half," a "Betwixt-and-Between" (Barrie 1906: 28, 29).

At the end of *Peter and Wendy*, in the final chapter, "When Wendy Grew Up," itself derived from a surprise dramatic coda added by Barrie to one performance of the play in 1908, the word is still extant, still fused with irony. Wendy has flown home from the Never Land, grown up, grown older, had a daughter of her own, until one night the timeless, time-blind Peter returns to the nursery, heralded by Barrie with the sardonic statement "And then one night came the tragedy." Before she lets him see her, Wendy "let her hands play in the hair of the tragic boy" (Barrie 1911: ch. 17). Peter is still a "Betwixt-and-Between," perpetually entrapped (like the memory of a dead child) in limbo between mortal and immortal, frozen in the very condition of growing, and as Birkin notes, "'a tragic boy', who seems to be perpetually engulfed by an immense sense of loneliness that stems from the mortal in him" (Birkin 1979: 117). This state of strandedness, of ambivalence, extends to the playing of the part. Birkin cites Barrie's first biographer, Denis Mackail, who saw the first Peter, Nina Boucicault, and said: "She obtruded neither sex nor sexlessness... Above all she had the touch of heart-breaking tragedy that is there in the story or fable from beginning to end" (Birkin 1979: 117). The repeated ironic and playful reductiveness of references to death in *Peter Pan* points indirectly but insistently to the ironic tragedy of inability to die through growing – the condition of the *puer aeternus*.

That this is a dilemma at the heart of life, that stasis and growth have equal costs, is more somberly articulated in Barrie's last major play, *Mary Rose* (Barrie 1924). The heroine here is *puella aeterna*, a Peter Pan figure with a difference. As a girl of eleven Mary Rose disappears during a family holiday excursion to a Hebridean island, returning just as inexplicably twenty days later with no evident harm done. But some years later, when she is a very young woman, her mother confides the truth to Mary Rose's would-be fiancé, Simon: "I have sometimes thought that our girl is curiously young for her age – as if – you know how just a touch of frost may stop the growth of a plant and yet leave it blooming – it has sometimes seemed to me as if a cold finger had once touched my Mary Rose" (Barrie 1924: 48). The metaphor is brilliantly exact not only for Peter Pan and more so Mary Rose, but for the general condition of the child-adult: it is not stasis, but energy-in-paralysis, which characterizes the entrapment. Mary Rose does marry Simon, and has a baby son. Then the three of them fatally return to the island, and Mary Rose again disappears, this time not for days but many years. She herself, like Peter, is unchanged, but her husband is middle-aged and grey, her son fled overseas. The darkness of the play lies in the fact of a child-mother overtaken in time by her own child, whose eventual return to his birthplace as a veteran soldier is finally the means to release her from ghostly imprisonment in her girl-mother self as she searches for him.

Mary Rose is a disconcerting blend of Wendy, the girl who grows up to motherhood and natural aging, and Peter, trapped in a timeless childhood dynamic. In early drafts Barrie cast Mary Rose's island as the Never Land, revealing the conscious connection, but abandoned it for something more ethereal and enigmatic. Mary Rose reveals in herself alone, as Peter and Wendy had done in their difference, the treachery of eternal childhood and its lure, whatever form it takes. Leonie Ormond observes of the play that:

no satisfactory philosophical outcome can be deduced from it. The love of a
mother for a son is an adult emotion, and a heroine who does not grow up is a
child. Mary Rose is, on the one hand, suspended in girlhood, and on the other is
a wife and mother who seems likely to spend eternity searching for her "baby."

(Ormond 1987: 135)

As such, Barrie gives his play "a dimension common to human experience"
(Ormond 1987: 135). This is, in the end, the impossibility of having it both
ways, the ruthless exposure in both these plays of human desire to retain or
recover a lost childhood, doomed to an ironic tragedy of failure which is far
exceeded by the tragic pathology of any "success," regardless of its form.
For Barrie, childhood and adulthood form a human dialogue with no
solution, built on illusions of felicity. R. D. S. Jack correctly observed:

Barrie does not pit youth against age, as ideal against lost vision; he invites us
to consider the fantasy of eternal youth as an impossible, flawed but attractive,
view of the human dilemma and thus highlights, by contrast, the equally
flawed reality of mutability and death.

(Jack 1991: 170)

Puer Senex

If it was unsurprising in the sixteenth century to find an interest in politicized children, it is equally predictable in the nineteenth century to find a
tragic or sub-tragic locus in the operations of education and schooling. This
is the century of "education, education, education," the massive state-
sponsored advancement of universal literacy and numeracy, with their
contexts of institutional entrapment for the child. But it is also the great
post-Romantic century, heavily influenced by doctrines representing childhood as an autonomous life-phase of unique experience and value. Between
these two positions there were manifest risks of conflict in both theory and
practice, with potentially calamitous consequences for the child. At a more
fundamental intuitive level the doctrines that celebrated childhood as a
separate pre-adult time provoked an almost superstitious recoil from the
child who seemed to bypass childhood and exhibit infant adulthood and
even advanced age, the *puer senex*. Two spaces for tragedy thus coexist in
close relationship – the child who appears to be born old, and the child who
is made prematurely old by misguided educational pressures that distort
natural growth and filch childhood from the child.

It is in Dickens that we find the classic fusion of these questions. Although the novels are full of memorable children, including sadly orthodox "tragic" deaths like that of Little Nell, attacks on brutalizing education like that in *Nicholas Nickleby*, or more pertinently the childhood-denying utilitarian educational procedures of *Hard Times*, the most powerful sub-tragic synthesis of the century's theoretical contradictions lies in the fate of 6-year-old Paul Dombey in *Dombey and Son* (1848). The most sinister element in Paul's story is the total absence of intentional cruelty in it: everyone who has dealings with him – father, sister, teachers, schoolmates – has or forms affection for him, and the program for his educational dissolution is ruinously well-meaning.

When nearly five, before he goes to school, Paul already exhibits the features of the young-old child, the *puer senex*, unforgettably depicted as he sits with his father by the fireside after dinner:

> He was childish and sportive enough at times, and not of a sullen disposition; but he had a strange, old-fashioned, thoughtful way, at other times, of sitting brooding in his miniature arm-chair, when he looked (and talked) like one of those terrible little beings in the fairy tales who, at a hundred and fifty or two hundred years of age, fantastically represent the children for whom they have been substituted... They [Paul and his father in their armchairs] were the strangest pair at such a time that ever firelight shone upon. Mr Dombey so erect and solemn, gazing into the blaze; his little image, with an old, old face, peering into the red perspective with the fixed and rapt attention of a sage.
>
> (98)

Paul, then, is innately an old child; not only is he physically delicate, but he was born to that geriatric infancy which Dickens represents, with a detectable blend of compassion and aversion, as deformity. But this is mortally compounded by his enrolment in Dr Blimber's Academy, where the clear joint purposes of both his father and teachers are to expedite by well-meant educational force-feeding his growing-up to that condition which is already genetically inscribed. Paul's unconscious wisdom and self-knowledge, and by contrast the benign stupidity of his carers, are definitively summed up in an exchange during his first interview at Dr Blimber's establishment:

> "Ha!" said Dr Blimber. "Shall we make a man of him?"
> "Do you hear, Paul?" added Mr Dombey, Paul being silent.
> "Shall we make a man of him?" repeated the Doctor.

"I had rather be a child," replied Paul.
"Indeed!" said the Doctor. "Why?"

(154)

Paul is destroyed, as Dickens presents him, by both perversion of nature
and perversion of nurture. The first is an aberration beyond human aid, but
the second is a benignly lethal intensification of its consequences. In this one
case-history, more powerfully because it is free of all intended human
malignity, Dickens positions himself in relation to the competing beliefs
and theories of his time, and creates their definitive sub-tragic victim.

Where nurture and not nature are to blame for the pathological results of
childhood – denial, perhaps the most persuasively didactic text is *The Prodigy*
(1905), by the German (later Swiss) novelist Hermann Hesse. The novel is an
indictment of the competitive German system at that time for entry to the
state-subsidized seminary by way of the *Landexamen*, a route to the priest-
hood for the most talented boys. This is one example among countless
others in literature of the ruthless intellectual forcing of gifted children,
motivated primarily by the vicarious ambitions of their parents and teachers:
the desire for glory by proxy which in life and art has destroyed innumerable
children. Early in the novel there are signs of the physical damage, notably
the ominous headaches, caused in the gifted adolescent Hans Giebenrath by
the all-consuming academic pressures to which he is subjected. Before his
examination Hans is given a rare work-free evening and walks down to the
place where the local river forms a lake: "He now realized how many half
and whole holidays he had spent here, how often he had swum, dived,
rowed and fished at this place. Oh, the fishing!" (Hesse 1973: 10). Before his
recent three years of unrelenting confinement, Hans has enjoyed a Words-
worthian childhood. In a passage of Dickensian irony Hesse describes the
teacher's pride in completing the state-imposed task which:

> requires that he shall subdue and extirpate untutored energy and natural
> appetites and plant in their place the quiet, temperate ideals recognized by the
> State. Many a person who is at present a contented citizen and persevering
> official might have become an undisciplined innovator or futile dreamer but
> for these efforts on the part of the school.
>
> (Hesse 1973: 43)

Giebenrath's experience is the amputation of childhood, the forced imposition
of age on youth in body and brain. Jill P. May noted that "Most adolescent
heroes are ironic heroes because they must learn to accept an unfriendly

society's patterns and beliefs. While they are not tragic heroes, there is something tragic in the reshaping of their ideals" (May 1995: 21–2). In one sense this is true of Giebenrath, but Hesse's irony is directed not at the boy but the society itself, which receives no endorsement for its self-serving piety and rigor. While most "tragic" children are indeed sub-tragic, their status mitigated by irony, there is a case for seeing the long-drawn-out breakdown and eventual death of Giebenrath as authentic tragedy, produced by an irreconcilable war of consciousness between selfhood and human environment.

At the opposite extreme of *puer senex*, and needing little comment beyond its own notoriety, is the figure of Little Father Time in Hardy's *Jude the Obscure* (1895). He is the child who, misinterpreting a conversation with his stepmother and applying to it the morosely implacable logic that he mixes fatally with ignorance of the world, hangs himself and his siblings, leaving behind a note reading "Done because we are too menny" (325). This episode has attracted much criticism, not to mention some macabre laughter, but it stands as an essential example here because Hardy, from his late nineteenth-century standpoint, clearly gave it high tragic status, relating it through Jude's self-taught scholarship to *Agamemnon*. Little Father Time is explicitly *puer senex*. He is "Age masquerading as Juvenility, and doing it so badly that his real self showed through the crevices" (266). His face, according to his stepmother, is "like the tragic mask of Melpomene," and he is not unique, but "one of these preternaturally old boys" (270). His place in the spectrum of child tragedy is clarified in Jude's relaying of the doctor's view: "The doctor says that there are such boys springing up amongst us – boys of a sort unknown in the last generation – the outcome of new views of life. They seem to see all its terrors before they are old enough to have staying power to resist them" (326).

Puer senex, on this reading, is a mutation of human life, and so intermingled with equivalent mutations in prevailing thought and environmental conditioning that it faces children with a new existential relationship between heredity and experience, making their lives a dark confusion. Hardy's grotesque scene may be flawed, but the historically conditioned thought behind it opens up new space for childhood tragedy.

Feral Children

In the categories examined above, the tragic or sub-tragic fates of children have arisen because the child fell foul of the border crossing between child and adult. They were not inherent in the condition of childhood itself, except in so far as childhood is always in the situation of being provisionally defined by historical, cultural, and biological factors, so that children's fates are always at the mercy of current adult beliefs. There is another no man's land, however, into which children may occasionally fall, with similar potential for tragic or sub-tragic outcomes, similarly governed by the shifting ideologies of adult societies. This is the boundary zone not between child and adult but between child and beast, the predicament of the feral child.

Feral children have a long ancestry in myth and literature, with many eminent examples including Oedipus and the twins Romulus and Remus. The history of childhood has always included the practice of abandoning children, whether for principles of ethnic self-preservation, as in classical Sparta, or from poverty, or parental callousness and ineptitude, or other reasons. Life and literature abound in stories of children lost, abandoned, or stolen, including young children stolen by animals. Likewise there are stories of children found, and "rescued," sometimes after years of living alone, or with animals, deprived of all human contact. Sometimes these stories are of twins, or at any rate siblings, separated in infancy and later reunited, one having received an "orthodox" upbringing, the other some form of "wild" childhood. Michael Newton, in his study *Savage Girls and Wild Boys*, suggests:

> Perhaps stories such as this are fables of the necessity for civilization and the wild to be reconciled with each other. It is as though the contradictions that sustain each person – that tension between our primal, animal natures and our civilized, social selves – are here acted out, embodied in identical and yet utterly different selves.
>
> (Newton 2002: 7)

That same contradiction can be witnessed, and tested, in the cases of individual children recovered by society from feral existence. Some examples are famous, and are well – though not necessarily reliably – documented. Four in particular, spread across three centuries, have attracted lasting attention. The first is Peter the Wild Boy, "a silent and savage child, an inhabitant of cold Germanic woods" (Newton 2002: 16), who was brought to London to the court of George I in 1726, rousing intense interest among the aristocracy and intellectuals of the day. These included Defoe and Swift, whose own imaginations had already engaged with the issues that he raised. Then came the case of the Wild Boy of Aveyron in France, the subject of François Truffaut's film *L'Enfant Sauvage* (1970), who was captured in 1800 three years after being first observed, and thereafter subject to the dedicated scientific study and educational mentorship of Jean Marc Gaspar Itard. Then came the notorious history of Kaspar Hauser, beginning in Germany in 1828. And in 1920, perhaps most controversially of all in an always contentious area, was the capture in India of two girls later named Kamala and Amala, supposedly raised by wolves, and the much-discussed involvement in their subsequent lives of the Rev. J. A. L. Singh. (See, for example, Maclean 1977.)

What is striking about all these cases is that the personality, motives, and behavior of those who "rescued" them, or at least sought them out with voyeuristic fascination, are almost equal in interest to the children themselves. Wild children supply educated humankind in varying societies with living laboratory specimens on whom can be tested ideas of what it means to be human. Among all the characteristics which these (and other) feral children customarily displayed, the most important was their lack of language and their inability to speak, an absence which in general proved impossible to rectify. In his study *Feral Children and Clever Animals*, Professor Douglas Keith Candland put the problem exactly: "Without speech with which to communicate, how are we to imagine the experiences, the minds, of these silent subjects? The silent minds of feral children, whether human or animal, remain intriguing but awesome to us" (Candland 1993: 73).

When their situations are detached from the manifold scientific and ideological concerns of their finders, it is clear that most if not all feral children are tragic figures, and that they are so not because they have lived a "wild" existence (however unfulfilling of their human potential) but because (usually well-meant) human rescue and later efforts towards rehabilitation have stranded them between two ways of being. They are in all conceivable respects "lost" children, finally stranded in some nightmare place between what in the wild they have irretrievably become, and society's view of what a child should be. And the central element in that division is their lack of language. The finest of modern "feral child" stories, Angela Carter's "Peter and the Wolf," expresses unforgettably the unbridgeable division between the feral and the socialized child, when Peter sees his feral girl cousin for the last time, across a river, and the impossible dilemma is summed up in one definitive sentence: "Language crumbled into dust under the weight of her speechlessness" (Carter 1985).

With this brilliant exception, literature has in general stepped back from this central tragic potential of the feral child, and instead explored its fascination indirectly, permitting the feral child some entry to its own domain of language. Even so, this is enough to represent the sub-tragic or potentially tragic status of these people. The most celebrated of literary feral children is Kipling's Mowgli, and the feral child's tragic space, the necessity and impossibility of dual citizenship in the worlds of humankind and beast, is finely expressed in the last Mowgli story, "The Spring Running." Mowgli is now nearly seventeen. When spring comes to the jungle, and the animals are busy with the sexual drive of the season, Mowgli is alone and unaccountably sad, and also plagued by a strange fever, the source and cause of which he does not recognize. To cure himself he undertakes a night run through the jungle, which brings him at last to a human village, and a chance reuniting (for the second time) with the mother he lost when stolen as a baby. Leaving his mother's house to return to the jungle, he encounters "a girl in a white cloth"; hiding from her in the crops, he then "parted the stalks with his hands and watched her till she was out of sight" (Kipling 1987: 171).

"The Spring Running" works on several levels. It is a flawlessly discreet articulation of the onset of sexual maturity and the unrecognized arrival of sexual need: the mystifying, troubled physicality of adolescence has rarely been caught more exactly. More generally, it expresses the end of childhood, the last playfulness, the outgrowing of parental figures, the assumption of adult power, all attended by restlessness, desire, and loss. But over and above these images of maturation is the sub-tragic pain of the feral child, torn between jungle and village, animal and human life, alleviated only because Mowgli is excused the crisis of speechlessness, and instead is literally as well as biologically multilingual: "Man goes to Man! He is creeping in the Jungle./He that was our Brother sorrows sore!" (155).

One of the greatest and most explicit depictions of the feral child in literature, although not usually interpreted in these terms, is Emily Brontë's Heathcliff. It is done with such economy, mostly in a single sentence, that we can easily miss how many features of the feral child's predicament are there:

> we crowded round, and over Miss Cathy's head I had a peep at a dirty, ragged, black-haired child; big enough both to walk and talk: indeed, its face looked older than Catherine's; yet, when it was set on its feet, it only stared round, and repeated over and over again some gibberish, that nobody could understand.
> (Brontë 1990: 28–9)

Heathcliff the child is "it." He has no provenance. He is set on his feet, as if (like many feral children) an upright stance is not natural to him. He lacks language, and according to Mr Earnshaw, is "as good as dumb." His quickly formed close relationship with Catherine (the only significant human relationship he ever has) is fuelled by the strong atavistic urges that his presence activates in her wildness, and is not so much love as a mutual recognition of primitive creaturely kinship. Mr Earnshaw's thankless task, like that of many actual guardians of such children, is to be his devoted mentor, aided by the curate's teaching. Like many feral children, Heathcliff is both taught and unteachable. His single name is a lifelong conferred and preferred exclusion: he is human and not human, then and always. He is anomalous only – but crucially – in developing full language, but it is this one compromise with an otherwise convincing representation of the feral child that allows Brontë to follow through the logic of an early catastrophic deprivation.

In the second half of the novel, the process is reversed with Hareton and the younger Cathy. By way of revenge on Hindley Earnshaw for past grievances, but also revenge on "civilization" itself, which he mocks and parodies, Heathcliff seeks to reduce the young Hareton to a feral state, but despite his efforts he cannot engineer the primordial recessiveness that he possessed himself and released in the elder Catherine, so that Cathy is able to do what many mentors (including Heathcliff's own) had failed to do: to civilize by the arts of teaching and love. Heathcliff is a truly tragic figure, as much in this strange defeat by Cathy as in anything else, but although the tragedy is an event of adult life, it is already inscribed in the child (the "imp of Satan," as Hindley both rightly and wrongly terms him) that Mr Earnshaw brought home from Liverpool.

Newton's comment on feral children is applicable to Heathcliff, but could equally serve in its essential point as a verdict on the plight of all four groups of tragic or sub-tragic children whose place in drama and fiction I have considered in this chapter: "Always the position of abandoned children is inherently tragic in potential. They are persons without a place in the world, with no knowledge of themselves or of their relation to the world in which they live" (Newton 2002: 180–1).

From boy kings to feral children, from beings deprived of childhood to those locked into it, the history of childhood in tragedy is one of boys and girls in states of maturational dysfunction, incongruity of self and world, desynchronization in the natural processes of growth. Most, however, are sub-tragic. There are many children in tragedy; many children whose fates are tragic; but very few tragic children.

Chapter 10

Parricide versus Filicide: Oedipus and Medea on the Modern Stage

Fiona Macintosh

It's 1947: Jocasta appears on the stage, rope in hand, ready to hang herself. Tiresias strides slowly across the stage, rhythmically beating his staff, as if tolling the bell of doom. Yet as the blind priest goes to remove the rope from Jocasta's hands, we realize that it is not to prevent her suicide; it is merely to postpone it. For here, in Martha Graham's dance drama, *Night Journey*, based on Sophocles' *Oedipus Tyrannus*, Jocasta has become protagonist; and she is forced (Noh-like) to relive the horrors of her life as she stands on the threshold of death.

Graham's work owes as much to Yeats's Plays for Dancers as it does to psychoanalytic theory; and like Yeats's Noh-inspired plays, it hovers between the realms of life and death; reality and other layers of consciousness. The "night" of this particular journey refers as much to the dream world as it does to familial descent into lugubrious chaos. As Graham's Jocasta falls upon the schematic bed by the renowned Japanese designer, Isamu Noguchi, more rack-like than canopy, her dream world begins to unfold before our eyes.[1]

Graham's dance version of Sophocles' *Oedipus Tyrannus* is interesting for a number of reasons. First, it is important to note the several ways in which *Night Journey* departs from its ancient source: most obviously in its focal shift from Oedipus to Jocasta; but also in its un-Sophoclean insistence upon the erotic nature of the incestuous encounter between mother and son, and its concern with the act of incest to the exclusion of the parricide. The inclusion of a female chorus and the centrality of both Jocasta and the traditionally bisexual Tiresias to its structure bring a decidedly feminist reading to the ancient text. Indeed, these departures from Sophocles' tragedy are especially significant in hindsight because we can now see them as emblematic of a general shift in attitudes that becomes commonplace in many late twentieth-century reworkings of the Sophoclean tragedy.

Graham's *Night Journey* was the first of numerous feminist reworkings of Sophocles' tragedy for the stage.[2] Its première took place on May 3, 1947, at Cambridge High School, Cambridge, Massachusetts, just one year after Graham's version of Euripides' *Medea, Cave of the Heart,* her first dance drama based on an ancient Greek tragedy. Initially entitled *Serpent's Heart,* Graham's refiguring of Euripides' play focuses on a Medea who dominates the stage in a searing performance of reptilian and then raging revenge.[3] That Graham's feminist sympathies should have attracted her to the spurned wife and child-killing mother was hardly surprising in the aftermath of World War II, when settling scores was high on the public agenda and Medea seemed to catch the mood on both sides of the Atlantic.[4] Further-more, no more surprising was the fact that working with *Medea* led Graham the following year to Sophocles' paradigmatic ancient Greek tragedy.[5]

Indeed the modern reception histories of these two very different Greek tragic figures, Oedipus and Medea, are in many ways interrelated. Con-joined as the two tragedies are in Martha Graham's creative *oeuvre,* this is the traditional pattern from the Renaissance until well into the twentieth cen-tury. Sophocles' *Oedipus Tyrannus* and Euripides' *Medea* have enjoyed the most lively and extensive production histories of all the ancient plays; and their prominence and, to some extent, their rivalry within the modern theatrical repertoire constitute an important aspect of theater history as well as the history of ideas.

Just as Medea provides her own *deus ex machina* in the final part of the play and secures a safe haven for herself in Athens, so in her reception history she has successfully negotiated her path through very diverse cul-tural and political contexts: either by being radically recast as "exemplary" mother and wife, or by being seen as proto-feminist wrongly abandoned by a treacherous husband. Oedipus, by contrast, has very often found it much harder to survive the blows of fate bequeathed him by his own reception history. In uncanny resemblance to his experiences within Sophocles' play, the vagaries of Oedipus' *Nachleben* have very often entailed punishments that far outstrip the crimes that he committed without intent. As regicide, he has endured comparisons with Judas, Cromwell, and Charles II; and as perpetrator of incest, he has suffered ostracism in the form of censorship.

More recently, after some decades of unparalleled prominence on the stage, Oedipus has experienced a new form of ostracism: the ignominy of being linked with imperialism, and the repressive and oppressive powers of the bourgeois state by his anti-Freudian adversaries in France.[6]

Medea has now begun to enjoy precedence over Oedipus in the theater, at the very time when her ambiguity can be explained in psychoanalytical terms, and when her status as outsider has become wholly topical in a world of mass migration. With the second wave of feminism, she has been construed as the archetypal Kleinian mother-figure; and like Klein vis-à-vis Freud in the history of psychoanalysis, Medea has succeeded in challenging and then, in many ways, usurping for herself the position that she formerly shared with the Freudian son in the international repertoire. If Oedipus continues to enjoy a place in the repertoire, it is often only secured by making the protagonist more like Medea – more East End than West End;[7] more representative of a minority than a majority voice;[8] more sentient than cerebral man;[9] or, as with Martha Graham's pioneering ballet, it is by radically rewriting the Sophoclean text in order to allow the mother-figure, Jocasta, to come center stage.

Mothers versus Sons

The longstanding rivalry between the two ancient tragedies in the modern theater has much to do with the fact that they both provide perfect vehicles for the star performer.[10] The central-figure tragedy is, in fact, fairly atypical of the thirty-two extant Greek tragedies; and it is often speculated that, given the broadly similar dates of these two plays, they may well have been written with a particular ancient actor in mind.[11] Although there is only one modern star – the celebrated Japanese actor, Mikijiro Hira – who has performed the feat of taking the roles of both Medea and Oedipus during the course of his career, there is no reason why this should not happen again (Fiona Shaw, say, would make a very fine Oedipus to match her celebrated Medea of 2000).

However, it is not just that both tragedies share single central characters. These two seemingly very different plays turn out on close inspection to have certain important things in common; and to explore broadly similar concerns, albeit from different perspectives. First, both protagonists are uncommonly intelligent – a gift that turns out to be a burden rather than a blessing; and they are each already guilty of kin-killing at the start of the plays – Medea her brother; Oedipus, albeit unwittingly, his father. They are also both perceived as "outsiders" in the cities in which they find themselves: Medea as barbarian Colchian in the Greek state of Corinth; Oedipus as the *tyrannos*, the nonhereditary ruler of Thebes. And their marginal status brings with it considerable insecurity, material in Medea's case, but more importantly, psychological for both.

But, of course, it is really the different handling of similar material that matters: that Medea knowingly kills kin (her brother previously, and her children at the end of the tragedy), even though she knows it is wrong; whereas Oedipus is unaware of being a parricide. She kills her brother for love of another; he kills his father just when he is seeking to avoid killing him and loving his mother. Although Oedipus is an outsider, like Medea at the start of the play, this in no way affects his perceived status among the Thebans. Although Oedipus is not hailed as godlike at the beginning of the play by the supplicating citizens (31–2), despite many claims to the contrary,[12] he is nonetheless revered by them from the outset as savior of his new people; and his enforced exit into the palace at the end of the play is one of utter abasement – a form of incarceration in a world where the inscrutable gods direct events from afar. He is, say the chorus, paradigmatic precisely because of the magnitude of his fall (Sophocles 2000: ll.1193–4). Medea, by contrast, is abject at first, a powerless woman forced to prostrate herself before the Kings of Corinth and Athens, respectively, because her husband has abandoned her in an alien land. By the end of the play, however, she suffers no humiliating incarceration within; instead she escapes, with her guilt, into the sky above, with the help of her divine ancestor's chariot, to a safe haven in Athens.

However, despite these numerous points at which Oedipus parts company with Medea, there are equally important points at which his mother/ wife can meet her; and the links between Jocasta and Medea are provided by the mediation of the part-woman-part-animal of the Theban legend, the Sphinx. There has been considerable fascination with the Sphinx in the modern world from at least the Romantic period onward, in the wake of Ingres's painting of 1808 in particular. Ingres's interrogatory Oedipus is the archetypal cerebral Enlightenment figure, and was to exert an enduring fascination over Freud.[13] If Ingres's Oedipus is more cerebral thinker than sentient man in his encounter with the winged monster, that other famous modern painting of the encounter by the French symbolist, Gustave Moreau, makes the scene highly sexually charged. The Sphinx never appears in the Sophoclean play (in marked contrast to those Freudian and post-Freudian versions by Hofmannsthal, Cocteau, Gide and, more recently, Berkoff, where she plays a major role); she is merely referred to tangentially in the Sophoclean text (Sophocles 2000: ll.44ff., 1198–1202).

The intriguing similarities between the child-eating monster and the incestuous mother have not escaped structuralist and feminist psychoanalytical theories. Both the Sphinx and Jocasta commit suicide through their encounters with Oedipus; and Jocasta is designated the "Good" mother and the Sphinx the "Bad" Mother of Kleinian pre-Oedipal psychoanalytic theory.[14] Once Jocasta/Sphinx are assimilated to the Kleinian split "Good Mother/Bad Mother" composite, they are readily aligned with the archetypal "Good/Bad Mother" Medea, who is both adoring mother and monstrous infanticide. Moreover, the fact that in at least one ancient version Medea doesn't herself kill the children, and that in many modern versions Medea kills her children in order to prevent them suffering a worse fate at the hands of others, she is often more like Jocasta than the Sphinx, more excessively "Good" than "Bad" Mother.[15]

Crimes and Punishments

The early reception histories of these plays run parallel, especially as they were mediated through the influence of Seneca. Seneca's primacy over the Greek tragedians in the early modern period was guaranteed in England by the appearance of a number of vernacular translations of individual Senecan plays from 1559 onward (which formed part of a collection of translations of the ten plays in 1581), and a complete Latin edition of the tragedies in 1589. By contrast, there were no vernacular translations of the Greek tragedies, as opposed to loose adaptations, until considerably later. And although the Latin version of Euripides' Medea by the eminent classical scholar, George Buchanan, appeared in print as early as 1544, there was no Latin edition of Sophocles' Oedipus the King available before 1641.[16]

While the Senecan models predominated during this period, this is not to say that they did not themselves present problems. In Seneca's Medea, we find an alarmingly forthright and defiant witch, who bares both feet and breast and slashes her wrist in a ritually bloody commingling of essences with her grandmother, Hecate. Infanticide for Seneca's protagonist is a means of recovering her former, supra-human self. Stepping into the serpent-drawn chariot at the end of the play, she tosses out the corpses of her sons, and is free to ascend into the stratosphere, liberated from Jason and humanity itself. In an age that advocated the superiority of tragedy on account of its edifying subject matter, poetic justice would have to be seen to be done in any modern rewriting of this Senecan tragedy.

Indeed Medea's crimes of fratricide, murder, and filicide proved deeply problematic to early modern audiences. One way of understanding her act of infanticide, and her escape without punishment at the end of the play, was to adopt the misogynist rhetoric of the witch hunts.[17] When Pierre Corneille's *Medée* was staged in 1632 against a background of the witch hunts at Loudin, it challenged the stereotype by providing a more human reading of the Senecan witch. Even though Corneille's version only enjoyed two performances, it went on to exert considerable influence when it served as the basis for his brother, Thomas Corneille's libretto to Charpentier's operatic treatment (1694).

More generally, however, Medea could only receive sympathetic treatment by meeting with more traditional images of femininity. As early as 1566, Studley's vernacular translation of Seneca's *Medea* had changed the ending so that Medea did not escape without penalty; and in the preface to his own radical rewriting of the Euripidean tragedy of 1698, Charles Gildon maintained that Medea's infanticide is "contrary to all the Dictates of Humanity and Motherhood" (Gildon 1698: Preface). We therefore find very little Euripides or Seneca in the late seventeenth- and early eighteenth-century versions of Medea: we find instead a humane and suffering mother in keeping with the tragic heroines of she-tragedy.[18]

Although the impassive incestuous parricide stumbles his way into the wilderness at the end of Seneca's *Oedipus*, it was less difficult to find the requisite poetic justice here. The frequent association of Oedipus with Judas in the early modern period meant that he was routinely made to atone for his sins at the end of his life. We therefore regularly find versions of Oedipus, which translate the myth into a medieval mystery play;[19] or, at the very least, they insist on placing the discoveries of the *Oedipus Tyrannus* within the context of Oedipus' whole life as it is told within the narrative span covered by Euripides' *Phoenician Women*, Aeschylus' *Seven against Thebes*, and Sophocles' *Oedipus at Colonus*.[20]

How and when Oedipus dies was to remain equally important to neoclassical theorists as well: this was a major problem, in Dryden's view, with Corneille's *Oedipe* (1759), in which the blind Oedipus never appears on stage at the end of the play (on the grounds of taste), and was therefore never seen to atone fully for his sins (Dryden 1984: 115–16). This critique of the Cornelian Oedipus is somewhat surprising coming from Dryden, who himself went on to push the boundaries of taste and decorum in his own version co-written with Nathaniel Lee in 1678. Their Oedipus appears at the end of the play with full knowledge of his parentage, and yet is fully prepared, on Jocasta's exhortation, to override convention and resume his incestuously passionate relationship with her. Indeed, throughout the Dryden and Lee version, incest is granted a new prurient predominance. So tantalizingly close to the bounds of decency do Oedipus and Jocasta stray here, that their boldness has to be curtailed at the end of the play by the authority of the dead king himself, whose ghost appears in order to prohibit further pollution. In this scene, as in Oedipus' final suicidal farewell speech, Dryden and Lee's main debt is to Seneca; and even though we have a contrite Oedipus in the last few lines, we also have a thoroughly defiant one who rails against the gods who have set him upon his incestuous path (Dryden 1984: 213).

However prominent the moral issues surrounding the incest motif remain during this period, in political rhetoric Oedipus' crimes acquired different kinds of meaning. From the Tudor period on, incest served as a metaphor for political corruption in general; and in Elizabethan Homilies, the link (as in the ancient world) between incest and civil war was made explicit (McCabe 1993: 120–1). Furthermore, in republican discourse, the monarch is tainted with incest: when Parliament, the mother, is prevented from bringing about any Act without "Masculine coition" from the King by the *Eikon Basilike* of 1649, the incestuous longings of the ancient tyrant, according to Milton, are realized.[21] If incest was assimilated to political chaos and corruption, the Oedipal parricide – at a time when the King was head of the Family of State – became readily synonymous with regicide. In Dryden and Lee's *Oedipus*, with the regicide of Charles I in very recent memory, Oedipus recalls both Charles II and Cromwell himself.[22]

While the content of *Oedipus Tyrannus* proved less problematic than *Medea* on the seventeenth- and early eighteenth-century stages of Europe because political circumstances enabled his crimes to be read symbolically, by the late eighteenth century such symbolic readings were hard to sustain in England. With the Dryden and Lee play still firmly in the repertoire and with its overtly incestuous parricide center stage, audiences in the age of sensibility found *Oedipus* an affront to human decency.[23] But while Sophocles' *Oedipus Tyrannus*, as it was mediated through Dryden and Lee, suffered occlusion on grounds of its content, the Sophoclean tragedy proper never lost its place as an aesthetic paradigm.

From 1692, with the publication of André Dacier's commentary on the *Poetics* (translated into English in 1705), came the standard view throughout the eighteenth century in Europe that the supreme examples of tragedy were to be found in Sophocles' *Oedipus* and *Electra*. Dacier followed Aristotle in commending the coincidence of recognition (*anagnorisis*) and reversal (*peripeteia*) as the hallmark of the Sophoclean success with *Oedipus Tyrannus*; and given the fact that Corneille's unwieldy five-act play – and later Voltaire's *Oedipe* of 1718 – had made the discovery of regicide occur in Act 4 and the discovery of Oedipus' parentage come in Act 5, Dacier was able to appreciate the demonstrable effectiveness of the Sophoclean formal structure on account of its very absence from French neoclassical example.

Voltaire followed Corneille in this respect, but less for aesthetic than thematic reasons: How could Oedipus implausibly forget about the regicide following his discovery of his identity? But the political climate also meant that regicide could not be relegated to a secondary role. Indeed, just as the Oedipal regicide had been of uppermost importance in the Restoration period in Britain, it was to prove central again to the eighteenth-century French readings of Sophocles' play. The links between incest and the *ancien régime* were long-standing; and now in the eighteenth-century versions of Oedipus, we find a new interest in the *tyrannos* of the title as the monarchy itself comes under increasing scrutiny. While the Senecan version had denied Tiresias divine insight and so excluded the scene between Oedipus and Tiresias, now it is this scene in the Sophoclean text that gains prominence. Here we witness a new Oedipus in many French and English translations, which follow Dacier, and the Jesuitical commentators, Rapin and Brumoy, in their sharp scrutiny of his conduct. Oedipus is now the nonhereditary monarch with tyrannical tendencies; and in the French republican versions, we also see the return of the chorus, who had been excluded for so long from the modern stage on the grounds that they worked contrary to the dictates of verisimilitude.[24] Now, in a world where monarchical excesses needed to be called to check, the chorus (under the influence of the radical readings of Rapin and Brumoy) increasingly assume an interrogatory function akin to their role in the democratic drama of fifth-century Athens.

As transgressive, countercultural figure, Medea too enjoyed new freedom during the revolutionary period, especially on the operatic stage; and in Cherubini's *Medée*, she is clearly likened to the spirit of the revolution (MacDonald 2000: 114). Indeed, the Romantic period's fascination with transgressive conduct in general meant that both Medea's and Oedipus' crimes could be construed as part of a collective act of social defiance. Oedipal themes appear regularly in English drama and fiction at this time, and these are matched by an equal fascination in the German-speaking world with Medea's crime of filicide.[25] The neoclassical preoccupation with poetic justice was shown to be thoroughly tainted and compromised; and the neoclassical rules over which the court of Louis XIV had presided under Mazarin were to be rejected: a return to the Greeks now meant a complete break with the aesthetic and moral strictures of the moribund *ancien régime*.

Hero(in)es and Performers

Although the nineteenth century has been described as "the age of Oedipus,"[26] in terms of performance histories, it would be more appropriate to describe the century as belonging to Medea. The most important version of Euripides' tragedy was the Austrian trilogy by Franz Grillparzer, *Das Goldene Vliess* (1821), whose third play was based very closely upon Euripides and which became (for reasons of economy, without its trilogic partners) the main *Medea* throughout the German-speaking world and very often in the English-speaking theater as well in the nineteenth century.[27] When Freud refers to Medea, for example, in *Dora; An Analysis of a Case of Hysteria*, it is Grillparzer (not Euripides' version) that he has in mind.[28] Grillparzer's trilogy was written against a background of antisemitic riots in Austria in 1817–18; and with its emphasis on Medea as outsider – in the first play she appears in Hassidic dress – and as abandoned wife, Grillparzer's version provided the basis for what we can now see as the quintessentially "modern" reading of Euripides' tragedy.

The other Medea who dominated the nineteenth-century stages of Europe was the refiguration by the French playwright, Ernest Legouvé. As with Grillparzer's version, Legouvé's feminist reading of Euripides was to provide further sympathy for Medea's plight as victim of personal and political oppression. The French play was translated into Italian in order to accommodate its star, Adelaide Ristori; and as she toured Europe and the Americas to enormous success in the role, Legouvé's play prompted translations, new versions, and numerous burlesques.[29] The strength of Ristori's performance was made possible through Legouvé's realistic and psychologically convincing depiction of Medea. In the preface to his translation, Legouvé draws on recent Germanic studies of Black Sea peoples claiming that these had illuminated Euripides' protagonist for him, making her both more terrible and less atrocious to the modern imagination (Legouvé 1854). Legouvé was an ardent feminist, who went on to publish three serious accounts of the history of the position of women in France;[30] and his

Figure 10.1   Adelaide Ristori as Medea (c. 1856). Biblioteca e Raccolta Teatrale del Burcado S.I.A.E.-Roma

Médée was his first public statement in support of the cause of women's emancipation. When the play opened in Britain, it struck an especially topical chord at a time when rudimentary divorce legislation was being debated in Parliament: Legouvé's concern to make Medea primarily a victim of marital abuse, rather than perpetrator of filicidal revenge, spoke to a generation of campaigners whose support of the wife's cause in the event of marital breakdown was eventually enshrined in law the year following the Legouvé production's première in London.[31]

That the political climate of the period suited the Legouvé version, in particular, is certain; but there was another important factor that guaranteed both its durability, and its eventual leading role in the dramatic repertoire of Europe as a whole. This was the centrality of the character of Medea, as well as the performance of Ristori in the play. The modern star-system in the theater that replaced the old established companies was well established in the second half of the nineteenth century. In addition to having a deleterious effect on the theater in general – it resulted, for example, in the long run and the consequent decline in the number of new plays – it may nonetheless be said to have played a major role in the revival of certain Greek plays. Neoclassical readings of the *Poetics* had exaggerated the role of the single central tragic figure in Aristotle's prescriptions, and it is from these readings that the ancestry of the modern tragic hero(ine) can ultimately be traced.

Legouvé's *Medée* followed neoclassical dictates in avoiding a chorus altogether; and it is surely by no means fortuitous that the only other Greek tragedy to gain such prominence in the European repertoire from the 1850s until the end of the century was that other atypical central figure Greek tragedy, Sophocles' *Oedipus Tyrannus*, in the version of Jules Lacroix.[32] When Lacroix's version was mediated through the supreme performative powers of the tragic actor Mounet-Sully from the 1880s onward, it played an instrumental role in shaping early twentieth-century critical readings of Sophocles' tragedy.[33]

Unlike Legouvé's essentially neoclassically shaped tragedy, Lacroix's *Oedipe Roi* includes a chorus, albeit a non-Sophoclean marginal one of four consisting of two young girls, a woman, and an old man. But like *Medée*, it demands a large cast of extras, who come and go from the scene in the company of the major characters and grant the single central figure even greater prominence. In this sense, these two major mid-nineteenth-century reworkings of Greek tragedies merely extended the European neo-Aristotelian tradition of the tragic hero(ine) that can be traced in practice from Shakespeare *via* Racine and then *via* its more recent German examples from Schiller and Goethe. In 1841 Thomas Carlyle's lecture entitled *On Heroes, Hero-Worship and the Heroic in History* was published; and in an age of hero-worship, the stars of the stage were definitely not excluded. Both Grillparzer's and Legouvé's Medeas are abandoned and alone; and the postrevolutionary Oedipus of Lacroix is the lonely modern hero par excellence.

With Lacroix's version the French stage was able to witness the blinded Oedipus for the first time. Both Corneille and Voltaire had omitted the final scene for reasons of decorum; and it is significant that it is this part of Lacroix's version that seems to have captured the minds of the reviewers. The part of Oedipus was taken in 1858 and in the revival of 1861 by the tragic actor, Geffroy, who had succeeded the famous French revolutionary actor, Talma, at the Comédie-Française. Geffroy's performance received unanimous acclaim especially for this final, hitherto unseen, act. By 1861 Geffroy had become so closely identified with the role of Oedipus that one reviewer feared that in the event of his imminent retirement, there would be no one to take over the role.[34] Indeed, the ancient Oedipus now had to wait until the star-system

Figure 10.2   Mounet-Sully as Oedipus, image on cover of *Le Théâtre*, revue mensuelle illustrée, October 1901. © Private Collection/Roger Viollet, Paris/The Bridgeman Art Library

could produce Jean Mounet-Sully, the exemplary tragedian of the next generation, who was deemed worthy of donning Oedipus' heroic mantle.

When Mounet-Sully speaks of his understanding of the character of Oedipus, he extends the Cornelian view that Oedipus is Promethean in his rebellion against the gods. Oedipus is representative of "the revolt of instinct and intelligence" against blind fate and the terminal defeat of man.[35] In this sense Mounet-Sully's Oedipus is very much part of a broader French tradition in its focus on the tragic figure in an unjust cosmos. When he is asked in an interview in 1888 what he thinks about the role of fate in the play, he replies: "I've only seen a man, an unfortunate king. I don't know the secrets of the gods and I don't believe in oracular predictions when they don't conform to justice. I'm always on the side of humanity."[36] This is an Oedipus for the modern secular world, with the religious dimension of the original being subsumed into the performance. According

to Mounet-Sully, as he performs the role, he feels that "a sacred responsibility weighs upon me"; and he maintains that he always has "a religious
respect" for the role: "I arrive on stage each time like a priest going to the
altar."[37]

This deeply religious reverence that the actor feels for his role is
frequently echoed in reviews of the production. A reviewer's account of
his attendance at *Oedipe Roi* in the open-air theater at Cauterets in 1910
converts theatergoing into participation in a religious ceremony. He recalls
Oedipus' clamor echoing round the Pyrenees, the tripods on the turfed
mounds wafting incense into the air, the trees groaning a dirge in sympathy,
the fateful blind man wending his lonely way, far from the palace, toward
the unknown mountain tops beyond.[38] This Senecan-inspired ending is, of
course, a very far cry from Sophocles, and indeed far indeed from Lacroix's
own text (which is much closer to Sophocles) where Oedipus, trying to
cling on to his children, is separated from them; and, supported by a slave,
and leaning on a stick, starts on his way (and we presume) back into the
palace. The 1881 revival included numerous other changes to the original
production; and there appear to have been even more noticeable cuts to
the choral odes in the 1880s with the result that the emergent lonely
modern hero of Lacroix's text becomes the unerring focus of the new
production.

That audiences were being offered a newly psychological reading of
Oedipus is clear from Mounet-Sully's comments in his interview of 1888.
People often noted an increase in Oedipus's humanity since Mounet-Sully
took over the role, and he was either aware of Stanislavsky's work in
Moscow or at least was working along similar lines. He speaks like a Method
actor *avant la lettre* in his account of his preparations for his role. He makes
the character enter inside him and live under his skin: "I am with him in
complete intimacy. I question him, I discuss with him."[39] By stripping off the
layers of self and text, Mounet-Sully is of course anticipating the parallel that
Sigmund Freud so eloquently expressed between the experience of watching
Oedipus Tyrannus and the practice of psychoanalysis. If Freud found the
source of his psychoanalytic theory in Sophocles' treatment of the Oedipus
myth, it is hardly surprising that Mounet-Sully's interpretation of the role
made such an impact on him when he saw it in Paris in 1885.[40] When
Mounet-Sully included Hamlet in his repertoire in 1886, one is tempted
to infer that this prompted or possibly confirmed Freud's linking of
the Sophoclean and Shakespearean tragedies in relation to his theory of the
Oedipus complex.

Kleinian Mother versus the Freudian Son

In the first part of the twentieth century, both Medea and Oedipus continue to dominate the stages of Europe. The suffrage movement and the translation of Gilbert Murray gave the trials of Medea new powerful resonance in Britain; and in France her status as outsider shed new light on the position of colonial subjects (Macintosh 2005). In Europe as a whole, Oedipus' prominence was granted through the wide dissemination of Freud's theory of the Oedipus complex. A major theatrical highlight of the pre-World War I European stage was a Nietzschean-inspired production of *Oedipus Rex* directed by Max Reinhardt, which Freud himself enjoyed. But the interwar Parisian stage was dominated by Oedipuses of an overtly Freudian kind; and again it was the vestiges of the star-system that made these central-figure adaptations of Sophocles' tragedy possible.[41]

While the interwar Medeas have survived the test of time – indeed these Medeas, which explore, exoticize, and occasionally celebrate alterity seem strikingly prescient – the solipsistic Oedipuses from this period, by contrast, seem thoroughly dated. Postwar scholarship on the *Oedipus Tyrannus*, in a move strikingly evocative if not directly inspired by the eighteenth-century Jesuitical readings, sought, not surprisingly, to reinject the political dimension of Sophocles' play back into the Freudian familial romantic drama.[42] These critiques were coincident with the counter-moves in psychoanalytical theory, in which Oedipus began to come under sharp attack. If the eighteenth-century Oedipuses were insouciant tyrants, by the end of the play they were very frequently at odds with the tyrannical side of their own nature.[43] Now in postmodern Paris, and in Foucault's terms in particular, Oedipus is a tyrant through and through: his search for truth is but one stage in the repressive pan-optic society that western liberal democracies have become. Now Mounet-Sully's victim of an unjust world has himself become the prime cause of social injustice. Foucault's critique gains even greater force and prominence in *L'Anti-Oedipe* of Deleuze and Guattari (Foucault wrote the Introduction to the English translation), where Oedipus is a symbol of restraint and repression, racist, capitalist, patriarchal, and imperialist (Deleuze and Guattari 1983). The Anti-Oedipus/"antihero" of Deleuze and Guattari turns out to be another mythical construct, a joyous (misunderstood Laingian) schizophrenic, who has much in common with Nietzsche's Dionysiac boundary-breaking chorus.

The Nietzschean terminology is not fortuitous here. Much of French
psychoanalytical theory is (consciously or not) indebted to Nietzsche: Kristeva is but one such example in her distinction between (Apolline) symbolic
male phallic discourse and the (Dionysiac) semiotic, pre-Oedipal, feminine/
maternal world of the pre-lingual (Ellmann 1994: 25). In many ways, Oedipus has suffered in the late twentieth century because he is just too Apolline
for the post-1960s world: too much associated with the light, with knowledge, with the *polis*. By contrast, Medea has survived because, despite all
eighteenth- and nineteenth-century efforts to assimilate her to the Apolline,
she remains woman, outsider, witch, murky – the Dionysiac incarnate.

In Heiner Müller's trilogy, *Medeamaterial* (1982), Medea is aligned to the
Earth, which exacts a terrible revenge after years of abuse. In the first part of
this pre-unification German trilogy, *Verkomenes Ufer* (*The Despoiled Shore*), set
in an East Berlin suburb some thirty years earlier, the environment is being
destroyed (just as Jason is to abuse Medea); and the action culminates in a
moving scene in which the consequences of the ultimate act of self-destruc-
tion, fratricide, are presented on stage as Medea cradles the brother she has
killed in her efforts to help Jason. Part Two, *Medeamaterial*, is loosely based
(like Grillparzer's middle play) on Euripides, while the third part (*Landschaft
mit Argonauten* – *Landscape with Argonauts*) returns to the contemporary
world among the detritus of civilization and war and ends with the extermination of the voyagers. The Argonautic tales here (as in the earlier Roman
tradition and in previous German versions) provide a commentary on
postlapsarian decline; and the quest for the fleece within this tradition
symbolizes the perils of the colonial endeavor. Müller builds upon this
tradition by making his Medea exact revenge not just upon Jason, but
upon all those who despoil the land and its progeny.

It's four years earlier, in 1978; it's France, not Germany. Two Jocastas
dominate the stage: one is literally singing "Song of the Forbidden Body,"
which serves as the subtitle to André Boucourechliev's opera, *Le Nom
d'Oedipe*; the other speaks, albeit in highly-wrought, heightened verse.
In Hélène Cixous's libretto, *Chant du corps interdit*, Oedipus' life is told by
Jocasta in the last few days of her life, as she relives her own experiences both
with him and in her childhood. Her song is really one long lament for the
loss of the pre-Oedipal state she enjoyed with her son; but it is also a
celebration of that union between them.

The bipartite title *Le Nom d'Oedipe: chant du corps interdit* encapsulates the
two worlds within the opera and their contrapuntal relationship. Here it

is not self-discovery that determines the breakdown of the mother/son relationship, but Oedipus' discovery of his public self: Thebes, "La Ville," which becomes his "lover," who woos him away, and provides him with his Name in a thoroughly quotidian world. In the Kleinian, pre-Oedipal timeless state that life with Jocasta represented, sentient experience collapses the boundaries between self and other, "je"/"lui," "toi"/"moi." It is a world of the body, blood, the sea ("mer/mère" are played upon), song, without gender ("l'enfant") and without linear time; where present, future, and past are collapsed: "Tu étais là, tu serais là, l'avenir/est arrivé" ("You were there, you will be there, the future has arrived").[44]

The intrusion of La Ville and the Plague lure Oedipus away: first metaphorically as he sits on stage refusing Jocasta his life-sustaining gaze; and later literally when his departure from the stage leads to her physical collapse and her sense that she has changed body. Now lying on her deathbed, hearing only silence, Jocasta vainly tries to hear again the song of peace they made together; and now proclaiming that "La danse est morte" (73), she has nothing to do except turn to the wall herself and die. The androgynous Tiresias, father and mother here, sings Jocasta back in time into her childhood sleep of death; and as he does so, she reenters imaginatively the world of pre-Oedipal peace at a genderless, giant breast.

Oedipus arrives too late to enjoy any union with Jocasta in life; but now in a beautiful sequence of free indirect style, his voice, her voice, and a mediating narratorial third person merge in the linguistic equivalent of the Dionysiac eternal unity: "Je suis là/Ma bien aimée mon enfant/Il est revenu pour toi!/ Oedipe est là. Je t'avais dis" ("I am here, my [female] lover, my son. He has come back for you. Oedipus is there. I have told you" [81]). The Cixous/ Boucourechliev's baritone Oedipus is very far from Sophocles' cerebral tragic figure, whose blinding is the one independent act possible in a world circumscribed by oracles; here his flesh and body combine with Jocasta's own once he feels her again, himself now encompassed by "ma nuit," "mer."

Just as psychoanalytical theory from Rank and Klein onward has emphasized, so it is the mother/child relationship which is primary in *Le Nom d'Oedipe* as it was in Martha Graham's *Night Journey*; and Jocasta's perspective predominates in both these representative rewritings of the Oedipus myth. Forty years after Graham, Cixous's libretto is able to articulate Graham's intuitions in order to participate in a widely contested intellectual debate concerning France's late twentieth-century identity.

There may be considerable consolation to be had in the fact that parricide has been relegated to secondary consideration in the postmodern western psyche. The focus is no longer unerringly upon sons who enter into perpetual conflict with their patriarchal forebears. But what does it leave in its stead? A world of absconding, absent (Jason-like) fathers and/or monstrous (Medean) mothers, whose act of filicide is yet more terrifying than the crime it seems to have replaced? Perhaps we have only witnessed round one of the *agon* between these two towering figures of Greek tragedy.

Notes

1 A 1961 recording of *Night Journey*, produced by Nathan Kroll, is available on DVD (*Martha Graham in Performance*, Kultur, USA), with Martha Graham as Jocasta, Paul Taylor as Tiresias, and Bertram Ross as Oedipus.

2 For other recent feminist treatments of Sophocles' *Oedipus Tyrannus*, see Foley 2004: 80–9.

3 *Serpent Heart* (with music by Samuel Barber) premiered at McMillan Theater, Columbia University (NYC), before being revised and retitled *Cave of the Heart* for performance at the Ziegfeld Theater on February 27, 1947. It was then frequently revived under different titles (*Medea's Meditation* and *Dance of Vengeance*).

4 Cf. Anouilh's *Medée* of the same year (although not performed until 1953); and Robinson Jeffers' *Medea*, which opened the following year in New York and remained in the repertoire for many years with Judith Anderson in the title role.

5 For landmark productions of the *Oedipus Tyrannus* in the immediate postwar period (including Olivier's 1947 performance at the Old Vic) see Macintosh 1997: 309–12.

6 Deleuze and Guattari (1983) marks the high point of an anti-Oedipal tradition that can be traced from the Kleinian ascendancy onward (on which see Chodorow 1978, Spillius 1983, Benjamin 1988, and Hughes 1990.

7 So Berkoff's Eddy in *Greek* (1980), on which see Macintosh 2004.

8 Witness the postcolonial reworking by Ola Rotimi, *The Gods are not to Blame* (1968), and the Deep South African-American version by Rita Dove, *Darker Face of the Earth* (1994).

9 E.g., Pasolini's *Edipo Re* (1967).

10 A list of Medeas reads like a roll-call of leading actresses and singers across the centuries: Mlle Clairon, Mme Pasta, Sophie Schroeder, Adelaide Ristori, Sarah Bernhardt, Sybil Thorndike, Judith Anderson, Maria Callas, Diana Rigg, Fiona Shaw, and Isabelle Huppert. A list of stellar Oedipuses would include: Thomas Betterton, Thomas Sheridan, Mounet-Sully, John Martin-Harvey, Laurence Olivier, and Franco Citti.

11 *Medea* dates from 431 BCE. We do not know the precise date of the first production of the *Oedipus Tyrannus*, although attempts have been made to date it to 425 BCE, after the city of Athens had endured a series of plagues following the outbreak of the Peloponnesian War in 431 BCE (Knox 1979). See Newton 1980 for an attempt to highlight its influence on Euripides' *Hippolytus* (428 BCE), which would indicate a slightly earlier date, around 429. There is even some chance that Sophocles' tragedy was originally performed in the same year as *Medea*, in which case the rivalry dates from their first performances in the dramatic contest at the festival of Dionysus in Athens in 431 BCE.

12 The most influential recent source of this misapprehension is Vernant 1988: 119–20. For comment on the wider implications of this misapprehension in a French context, see Leonard 2005: 41–2.

13 It was, however, Otto Rank (1924), not Freud, who identified the encounter with the Sphinx as central to the myth because it articulated the primary trauma of birth (the Greek verb *sphingo* meaning literally "I strangle"). For comment on the impact of Ingres's painting and on Rank's relationship to Freud, see Armstrong 2005: 52–8.

14 See especially Rudnytsky 1987: 239–40 for Lévi-Strauss's adoption of Rank's reading of the Sphinx.

15 This is especially true of nineteenth-century versions; see further below. For the diverse ancient sources, see the essays in Clauss and Johnston 1997.

16 Studley's vernacular translation of Seneca's *Medea* dates from 1566; Alexander Neville's Senecan *Oedipus* from 1560. These appeared in Newton 1581. See Palmer 1911.

17 See, generally, Roper 1994.

18 See Hall 2000b.

19 So Neville's *Oedipus* (1560).

20 So William Gager's neo-Latin playlet *Oedipus* (1578) and Thomas Evans' *Oedipus: Three Cantoes wherein is contained: 1) His unfortunate Infancy 2) His execrable Actions 3) His Lamentable End* (1615).

21 "Eikonoklastes" (Oct. 6, 1649), in Milton 1962: 467; and Boeher 1992: 113 for comment.

22 For detailed commentary on the political allusions in the play, see Hall and Macintosh 2005: 24–9.

23 See Scott 1808: vi, 121; and on the censorship of the play generally, see Macintosh 1995.

24 For the French versions and Rapin and Brumoy, see Biet 1994; for English Oedipuses at this time, see Hall and Macintosh 2005: 215–42. Rudnytsky 1987 erroneously dates the "discovery" of Sophocles' tragedy to the

German Romantic period, whereas both the earlier English and French proto-revolutionary Oedipuses show that this comes considerably earlier.

25   See, e.g., Horace Walpole's play *The Mysterious Mother* (1768) and William Godwin's novel *Caleb Williams* (1794). Representative of the German fascination with Medea and her crimes at this time are Gotter's *Medea* (1775), set to music by Benda in the same year; Heinrich Leopold Wagner's *Die Kindermörderin* (1776); and Soden's *Medea* (1785).

26   Rudnytsky 1987: 96–7 *contra* Steiner 1984, for whom it is the age of Antigone.

27   See Burkhard 1961 for its impact in the United States and Britain.

28   Freud says that Medea is "quite content that Kreuse should make friends with her two children." Cited by Corti 1998: xi.

29   See Hall and Macintosh 2005: 391–429.

30   Legouvé 1864, n.d., 1881.

31   The Divorce and Matrimonial Causes Act was passed in 1857. For the topicality of productions of *Medea* in Britain at this time, see Hall and Macintosh 2005: 391–429.

32   The Mendelssohn *Antigone* of 1845, which had a huge impact on both of these plays, was rarely performed as drama toward the end of the century. The music, which had at first been found obscure and difficult, was regularly given concert performances.

33   Jones 1953: 194 refers to the impact Mounet-Sully's performance had on Freud. There is, however, some debate as to whether Freud actually saw the star perform in the role. See Armstrong forthcoming.

34   A. Escande in *Union*, Aug. 8, 1861, cited in Lacroix 1874: 309.

35   Mounet-Sully 1914: 127: "Oedipe représente la révolte de l'instinct et de l'intelligence contre la aveugle fatalité et la défaite terminale de l'homme." (All translations from the French are my own, unless otherwise stated.)

36   Vernay 1888: 140: "je n'ai vu qu'un homme, qu'un roi malheureux, j'ignore les secrets des dieux et je ne crois pas aux prédictions des oracles quand elles ne sont pas conformées à la justice. C'est le côté humain qui m'occupe toujours."

37   Mounet-Sully 1914: 127: "une responsabilité sacrée pèse sur moi"; and he maintains that he always has "un respect religieux[.] J'entre en scène, chaque fois, comme un prêtre monte à l'autel."

38   Armand Praviel, " 'Le théâtre en plein air," in *Le Correspondant*, 204, July 25, 1910, cited in Nostrand 1934: 183.

39   Vernay 1888: 138: "Je suis avec lui dans la complète intimité, je l'interroge, je discute."

40   See n.38 above.

41   The interwar Parisian Oedipuses are: *Oedipe, roi de Thèbes* (1920) by Georges du Bouhélier, dir. Firmin Gémier at Cirque d'Hiver; *Oedipus*

Rex (1927) by Stravinsky/Cocteau, Ballets Russes, Théâtre Sarah-Bernhardt; *Oedipe* (1932) by André Gide, dir. Georges Pitoëff, Théâtre des Arts; *La Machine Infernale* (1934) by Jean Cocteau, dir. Louis Jouvet, Comédie des Champs-Elysées; and *Oedipe-Roi* (1937) by Jean Cocteau, dir. Cocteau, Théâtre Antoine.

42 For the postwar period, see Leonard 2005.

43 See, e.g., Marie-Joseph Chénier's *Oedipe-Roi* (1818).

44 Cixous 1978: 62. Subsequent references appear in the text.

Chapter 11

"Suffering into Wisdom": The Tragedy of Wilde

Alison Hennegan

I awoke the imagination of my century so that it created myth and legend around me.

(Wilde 1990: 95)

For much of his life Oscar Wilde meditated profoundly on one of Tragedy's deepest preoccupations – the relation between Suffering and the attainment of Wisdom.

Time after time Greek tragedies chart the journey which its protagonists must take, and which the audience also must try to take with them: the things they learn (*mathemata*) through their sufferings (*pathemata*) make them wise (*sophos*). The more fortunate will attain a state of moral and emotional awareness (*sophrosuné*) which enables them to face the fact and meaning of their pain. The most fortunate will come to recognize that in some sense their sufferings have become part of a complex form of Justice (*diké*), whereby a flaw in the universe has been corrected: the scales of justice are once again evenly balanced.

In 1895 Wilde took the disastrous decision to bring a private prosecution against the Marquess of Queensberry for criminal libel. The Marquess had left an insulting card at Wilde's club: it bore the legend "for Oscar Wilde posing as somdomite [*sic*]".[1] In the ensuing trial, it soon became clear that Queensberry's counsel intended to call a damning array of male prostitutes who would testify against Wilde. Wilde withdrew his case against Queensberry, but was himself then charged for homosexual offences. He was convicted, and sentenced to two years' hard labour.

Those events of 1895 and the imprisonment that followed tested to the utmost the theories of Tragedy which Wilde had been elaborating for decades in his published and unpublished work. Both Wilde and many of his contemporary commentators came to see him as the protagonist of a tragedy; and indeed if we take some of the basic and recurring concepts and themes of classical tragedy, Wilde might appear to fit them with uncanny completeness. Such a narrative might begin with a man of outstanding abilities, set apart from his fellow citizens by his remarkable achievements: he is the man who stands above the rest, just as Aristotle suggests a tragic protagonist should. In the process, he earns both admiration and envy – sometimes human, often divine: yet, at the last, when riding at his highest, he is toppled from his lofty position by a mixture of other people's enmities and his own ill-considered actions. His was the fall of a "great" person, also an essential ingredient of classical Tragedy: and when a great man falls he brings others down with him – one of the reasons why the misfortunes of the great are worthy of our attention – because they involve more people than themselves alone. The trials of 1895, in which Wilde's own role switched dramatically from plaintiff to defendant, culminated in his own conviction and imprisonment: so complete a reversal of fortune (or *peripeteia*) might well rouse in bystanders the "pity" and "fear" which Aristotle said Tragedy should evoke. Let one contemporary commentator speak for the many who expressed sentiments such as those at the time. This is how *The Illustrated Police Budget* of June 1, 1895 reported Wilde's conviction and sentencing, in language heavy with theatrical metaphor:

> The final scene in the Wilde trial was enacted at the Old Bailey on Saturday afternoon. The scene will be for ever a memorable one, and will remain in my brain as a vivid picture of a talented man, a learned scholar, and a great dramatist, going to his doom – a doom to him more horrible than the gallows to an ordinary murderer. At the close of the case, and at the time when the jury brought in their verdict of "guilty", the court was crowded to suffocation, and the silence was so deep – a silence that could almost be felt – that no one, not even the Marquis of Queensberry, who was in court, could help in his heart pitying the prisoner when he looked at the awful agony depicted on his face when he heard his fate. No matter how one might deplore the criminal actions for which he was justly found guilty, it was impossible to keep down a certain amount of pity.

> (Goodman 1988: 128)

Wilde's release led not to rehabilitation but to social ostracism, impoverishment and enforced exile until his death in 1900. His last few years were lived in that state which for the ancient Greeks constituted the worst of fates – dishonoured (*atimos*), a figure of mocking scorn (*geloios*), exiled (*echthros*), and stripped of full citizenship (*apolis*). These are the words that echo through Greek Tragedy.

Greek tragedy is replete with the words and concepts which articulate the shape of such a life. Some pertain to notions usually translated as "fate", "doom", "destiny" (*moira*, *telos*), the inescapable, seemingly pre-set pattern of a human life. Others concern sacrifice and sacrificial victims, sometimes linked to the idea of the scapegoat (*pharmakos*). Wilde himself occasionally saw his trial, and the widespread social hostility which preceded it, as a form of scapegoating: he was to pay for the unforgivable "sin" of forcing his age, through his plays and epigrams, to look upon its own hypocrisies and cruelties.

Greek tragedy also abounds with words which concern the part humans play in their own downfall – *hubris*, for example, an act of overweening pride which arouses the wrath of the gods; or an *hamartia*, an error, a mistake, a bad miscalculation, a word often unhelpfully translated as "sin", which is a rather different matter. There were those of Wilde's contemporaries who argued that his worldly success had made him arrogant, and that his arrogance was largely responsible for the failure of judgment which led him to bring the initial prosecution against Queensberry. Both *hubris* and *hamartia* may arise from being *thrasos* (having a certain rash, presumptuous arrogance). Or they may be the product of bitter strife (*eris*) or an intransigent, vengeance-seeking hatred (*até*), of the sort which Queensberry himself felt for Wilde, and which Bosie and his brothers felt for Queensberry, their father. The desire of the Douglas family en masse to humble their much hated relation led them to spur Wilde on to prosecute, and to offer funds for legal costs. In Greek tragedy, violent acts prompted by violent emotions often "pollute" the perpetrator, and bring pollution, too, to those who aid him or come into contact with him (just as Thebes, which harbours the unwitting parricide and incestuous husband, Oedipus, is devastated by plague, *miasma* or *nosos*). To many of Wilde's contemporaries, he himself was a "pollutant", spreading moral "sickness" through his subversive works. After his sentence *The Pall Mall Gazette* (April 6, 1895) wrote: "We begin to breathe a purer air" and described Wilde and his circle as "the infamous gang with which London and other great cities are infested" (Goodman 1988: 79). *The News of the World* for May 26, 1895 wrote: "Society is well rid of these ghouls and their hideous practices. Wilde practically confessed his guilt at the outset, and the unclean creatures with whom he chose to herd specifically owned that the charges were true. It is at a terrible cost that society has purged itself of these loathsome importers of exotic vice" (Goodman 1988: 132). Here so many of the words are resonant with associations from Greek tragedy: according to Aristotle, "purged" – of pity and terror – is what every tragic audience should be at the play's end. The fear of the "exotic" echoes loudly the Greek fear of the *barbaros* or barbarian (the Greekless foreigner whose speech simply sounds like an incomprehensible babble of "barbarbarbar"). Wilde, the dubious Celt in the land of the Anglo-Saxons, the ambiguous Francophile Irishman who had brought Paris to the Thames, filled the role all too well.

Long before the disastrous events of 1895 Wilde had constantly engaged in his writings with tragedy and the tragic. One of the outstanding classicists of his generation, he had a wide and subtle knowledge of Greek tragedy. The notebooks which he kept as an undergraduate at Magdalen College, Oxford from 1874 to 1879 reveal how fully he wrestled both with the tragedians themselves and with many later critics and theorists of tragedy's value and function, including Schopenhauer and Nietzsche. They reveal his constant insistence on inquiring into and arguing for connections between the ancient dramatic form and the present, all part of that vital inquiry into the relationship between Art and Life which was to underpin his own aesthetic theory and practice until his death. The notebooks also show the young Wilde already pondering the relations between Pain and Thought, Unhappiness and Memory, Emotion and Action.[2] They are themes which, years later, would help to structure *De Profundis*, the lengthy letter which he wrote, in prison, to "Bosie", Lord Alfred Douglas, once his lover, all too often his adversary.

Wilde's thinking on tragedy was shaped by his engagement, sustained over many years, not only with the literature and thought of Ancient Greece, but also with the demanding paradoxes of Christianity, the blood-stained history of Irish Nationalism, and the contradictions and dangers posed by same-sex desire. From these sometimes conflicting, often overlapping elements, he eventually fashioned his own understanding of what it might mean – and what it might exact – to "suffer into wisdom". For many readers, Wilde's supreme distillation of that wisdom is to be found in *De Profundis*. Eventually he would reach a position where he would feel able to argue "For the secret of life is suffering. It is what is hidden behind everything" (Wilde 1990: 106).

Yet long before *De Profundis*, as Wilde himself pointed out, themes of martyrdom, self-sacrifice, redemption and purification through suffering, and the wisdom it is believed to bring, are found throughout his work (Wilde 1990: 108–9). Such themes occur constantly in the earliest of his poetry, much of it published when he was only 27. They are prominent in the fairy stories which he wrote originally for his own two young sons, Cyril and Vyvyan, then polished and published in 1888 for a wider, adult audience. Consider, for example, "The Rose and the Nightingale", "The Happy Prince," and "The Selfish Giant" (Wilde 1980). Wilde notes that such themes are present in "The Young King", "notably in the passage where the Bishop says to the kneeling boy, 'Is not He who made misery wiser than thou art?'" (Wilde 1990: 109). In "The Critic as Artist" they are "set forth in many colours: in The Soul of Man it is written down simply and in letters too easy to read" (Wilde 1990: 109). They are to be found in his drawing-room comedies, such as *Lady Windermere's Fan* (1892), where a mother allows her own moral reputation to suffer in order to prevent her daughter's being compromised, and in his last completed play, *Salomé* (1894), in which John the Baptist pays with his life for his devotion to Christ, and where they form, in Wilde's words, "one of the refrains whose recurring motifs make Salome so like a piece of music and bind it together as a ballad" (Wilde 1990: 109).[3] Wilde's preoccupation with suffering was something he shared with his time. It was indubitably one of nineteenth-century literature's great subjects – what the remarkable Italian scholar Mario Praz dubbed "The Romantic Agony". In his book of that name he offers a polyglot journey through the literatures of Europe, charting in them an obsessive and sometimes pleasurably masochistic concern with pain in all its manifestations (Praz 1933). So ubiquitous is the theme that subsequent generations of readers have begged leave to question the reality of the sentiments. And Wilde's own language, which is to modern tastes so often overblown or florid, has made many readers suspicious of his sincerity when he writes of suffering and pain. For Wilde, however, life and literature were often difficult to separate. He was pre-eminently a man who lived, recorded and interpreted his life through books. Wilde's utterances often resound with echoes of other writers. This makes some critics impatient or scornful, because they see it as a proof of Wilde's shallowness or insincerity. They miss the point, however. Literature created the fabric of his thought, it was to him his native element, being, as he himself said in *De Profundis*, "the Lord of language" (Wilde 1990: 84). Two literary sources which did most to shape him were the pagan writings of Ancient Greece and the Authorized Version of the Bible, the translation commanded by King James VI. Wilde's struggle to resolve the perceived conflicts between Christian and Greek pagan values began early and continued to the end of his life.

In common with many thinkers of his day Wilde often set the Pagan Greek against the Christian. For him, ancient Greece represented a culture which loved and celebrated human achievements of mind and body, worshipped physical beauty, in all its manifestations, and accorded a special place to the beauty of the male body, and to the emotions of love and desire which it may evoke. By contrast Christianity was and is often figured as a faith which fears the body and despises desire, elevates denial above fulfilment, pain above joy. Sentiments such as those are familiar from a wide range of nineteenth-century writers: as Swinburne memorably insisted, in an address to Christ, "Thou hast conquered, O pale Galilean / And the world has grown grey with thy breath" (Swinburne 1914: 77).

Yet in some senses these distinctions were more apparent than real. For all its love of the body, and its exalting of the joys of Aphrodite, Athenian culture also insisted on the value of suffering as the necessary pathway to wisdom; indeed, some of the most eloquent statements of the value of suffering are to be found in the sweeping choruses of Greek tragedy. And the proverbial folk wisdom of Greece concurs: "to learn is to suffer, to suffer is to learn", says one ancient axiom. We might read that as a version of "we learn from experience"; but it often seems as though more is being suggested. It is not simply that wisdom is the fruit of past suffering, but rather that the condition of being wise is one that entails present suffering. It hurts to know the things that wisdom knows. Just as aspects of Ancient Greek thinking might seem to come close to a Christian elevation of suffering, so too Mediterranean Christianity retained many connections with Greek and Roman paganism, and can in some senses be seen as a continuation rather than a severance from it. (Wilde, the classicist, makes one of many such connections in De Profundis, when he writes "it is always a source of pleasure and awe to me to remember that the ultimate survival of the Greek Chorus, lost elsewhere to art, is to be found in the servitor answering the priest at Mass" (Wilde 1990: 112).

Wilde's early poetry often addresses the apparent conflict between pagan Greek and Christian values; poems whose earlier stages appear to elevate the pagan at the expense of the Christian reverse that movement in the final lines. So, for example, the sonnet, "Ave Maria, plena gratia" (the opening line of the prayer known as the "Hail Mary"), meditates on how best an artist might represent the "coming of Christ". Surely, says the poem, it would be a moment of high and spectacular drama, figured, perhaps in the way the Greeks thought of Danaë, the mortal woman who receives Zeus as a shower of impregnating gold? Or it might be a moment full of awe and terror, as when Semele conceived the god Dionysos but died at the same moment, destroyed through the force of Zeus's thunderbolt? (Wilde 1997a: 27). It is with expectations such as those that Wilde has come to view one of the great Florentine painters' vision of the Annunciation:

> With such glad dreams I sought this holy place,
> And now with wondering eyes and heart I stand
> Before this supreme mystery of Love:
> Some kneeling girl with passionless white face,
> An angel with a lily in his hand,
> And over both the white wings of a Dove.
>
> (Wilde 1997: 27)

Religious mysteries – "the white wings of a Dove", the Holy Spirit – and the vulnerably human – "some kneeling girl" – are equally important here, something typical of Wilde's writings on religion. However much Wilde might sometimes reject or condemn certain aspects of organized Christianity, his love and tenderness for its central figures remain constant. This is especially true of Christ himself, whose manhood is at least as important for Wilde as his Godhead. Another early sonnet, "E Tenebris ['Out of the Shadows']", reflects this: here an anguished poet, wracked with guilt and self-loathing, and calling upon a Christ elevated high above him, seems to fear Christ will reject or abandon him. The poem ends with a more reassuring certainty:

> Nay, peace, I shall behold before the night,
> The feet of brass, the robe more white than flame
> The wounded hands, the weary human face!
>
> (Wilde 1997: 26)

Once again, it is the human face of divine love that speaks to Wilde. The importance of human love is central both to Wilde's Christianity and to his veneration for the classical. Love inspires the Gospels, but it also drives much of Plato's philosophy, especially in those early dialogues where a fictionalized Socrates brings his followers and disciples to recognize Love as the supreme force which creates and governs both the universe and human life when lived at its best. In the world of Plato and Socrates, the highest form of human love is love between men. Some of the most powerful articulations of this belief are to be found in Plato's two Socratic dialogues, *The Symposium* and *The Phaedrus*. Both are constantly evoked in nineteenth-century writings on love between men.

A great irony of nineteenth-century English cultural life is that it so much admires, and tries to emulate, ancient Athens, even though that society was in large measure built upon a model of human love outlawed in England – a love between men which often included frank appreciation of physical beauty and its expression. The extent to which physical expression was accepted between adult men, rather than between men and younger males being socialized into adulthood, continues to be hotly debated by scholars. What matters in this context is that, increasingly in the nineteenth century, it becomes one of the tenets of homosexual apologist thought, that love between men, including sexual love, was not only accepted but honoured in Greek culture, and central to it.

In late nineteenth-century England we often see conflicts between those who admire Ancient Greece, but insist that any version of it which includes sexual love between men is a perversion of historical truth; and those who maintain that any attempt to emulate Ancient Greece whilst condemning its most important emotion is doomed to failure. John Addington Symonds (a fine scholar of Greek poetry, a lover of Plato, and a homosexual) crossed swords with Benjamin Jowett (Master of Balliol, Regius Professor of Greek at Oxford, and eminent translator of Plato), on this very subject. On February 1, 1889, Symonds wrote Jowett a lengthy and troubled letter in which he pondered on the difficulties and dangers of using Plato's Socratic dialogues, with their passionate endorsements of same-sex male love, as the most important teaching texts for generations of young English schoolboys and male undergraduates. Passions which in ancient Greece provided the infrastructure for the transition from boyhood to adult manhood and full citizenship were, Symonds argues, the same passions which would bring his present-day equivalent into conflict with the law, at risk of conviction and imprisonment. Symonds, writing just four years after the passing of the Criminal Law Amendment Act and some six years before Wilde's trials, details the inconsistencies and dangers of such Platonic teachings offered to today's youth. He, too, makes his own link between Plato and Christ, the pagan world and the Christian:

> Put yourself in the place of someone to whom the aspect of Greek life (which you ignore) is personally and intensely interesting, who reads his Plato as you

would wish him to read his Bible – i.e. with a vivid conviction that what he
reads is the life record of a masterful creative man-determining race, and the
monument of a world-important epoch.

Can you pretend that a sympathetically constituted nature of the sort in
question will desire nothing from the panegyric of paiderastic love in the
Phaedrus, from the personal grace of Charmides, from the mingled realism and
rapture of the Symposium? What you call a figure of speech, is heaven in hell to
him – maddening, because it is stimulating to the imagination; wholly out of
accord with the world he has to live in; too deeply in accord with his own
impossible desires.

(Symonds 1984: 101–2)

More recently, in his play The Invention of Love, Tom Stoppard has created his
own wickedly informed version of Jowett's view. Jowett speaks here:

A Platonic enthusiasm as far as Plato was concerned meant an enthusiasm of
the kind that would empty the public schools and fill the prisons where it is
not nipped in the bud. In my translation of the Phaedrus it required all my
ingenuity to phrase his depiction of paederastia into the affectionate regard as
exists between an Englishman and his wife. Plato would have made the
transposition himself if he had had the good fortune to be a Balliol man.

(Stoppard 1997: 22)

To which Walter Pater, the outwardly timid but intellectually inflammatory
Fellow of Brasenose, whose writings had such influence on a younger
generation of Oxford men, including Wilde himself, replies: "And yet,
Master, no amount of ingenuity can dispose of boy-love as the distinguishing
feature of a society which we venerate as one of the most brilliant in the
history of human culture, raised far above its neighbours in moral and
mental distinction" (Stoppard 1997: 22).

Stoppard sums up here with wonderful economy one of the most bitterly
debated intellectual questions of the second half of the nineteenth century.
This is not the place to detail that struggle.[4] Suffice it to say here that by the
1880s, the increasingly confident articulation of the case for male same-sex
love was creating anxiety and resistance. It is in that context that we need to
see the passing of the 1885 legislation under which Wilde would be tried and
convicted. To many it seemed as though from the early 1890s, when his
extremely public association with Lord Alfred Douglas began, he had
been actively courting prosecution under the terms of that Criminal Law
Amendment Act.

Decades before he was engulfed in the events of 1895 which so many figured as Tragedy in Action, Wilde had had an overriding concern with tragic protagonists, whether encountered in literature or life. As a very young man he found one in the figure of Socrates, that charismatic teacher tried and executed by the Ancient Athenians for allegedly teaching impiety and corrupting the young of the city; he found a second in another charismatic teacher, Christ, tried and executed for his subversive influence and ceaseless challenge to the Roman state and Jewish status quo.

Wilde, the classicist, would have known that the pagan Socrates and the founder of Christianity were linked by a common "agony". "Agony" comes from the Greek word *agon*. It occurs in many contexts but its primary meaning is "a contest" or "struggle". It can refer to a competition, whether athletic or artistic, as when orators or singers compete with each other. It can refer to a court case, and to the "battle" which occurs when the opposing parties compete to establish which side, defence or prosecution, shall win. *Agon* also becomes the name for those passages in a Greek tragedy where two characters conduct an often desperate argument which will end in the defeat or death of one of them – Antigone disputing with Creon; Pentheus with Dionysos in Euripides' *Bacchae*. And the dramatic and legal meanings of the word fuse in the climax of Aeschylus' play, the *Eumenides*, where the Eumenides, or Furies, are locked in bitter, and ultimately hopeless, argument with the goddess Athene. Here, in the final play of the *Oresteia*, the only complete trilogy to have survived intact from Ancient Greece, we witness one of the earliest dramatic representations of a trial scene. In the *Oresteia*, matters of life and death are at stake; but as Wilde himself was to remark, so many centuries later, "All trials are trials for one's life" (Wilde 1990: 156). Within a Christian context, "agony" is the word reserved for Christ's desperate hours in the Garden of Gethsemane. In those hours while He awaits the betrayal which He knows will come, must come, in order to set in train the sequence of events which will lead to His necessary crucifixion, He undergoes his own *agon*, struggling to accept and embrace the sufferings that lie ahead. Among them will be a show trial.

During the spring and early summer of 1895, Wilde himself sometimes seemed to have been caught up in a series of show trials. Certainly they – and he – became a spectacle, a drama "reviewed" by the journalists who covered them. The court was a perfect stage set, peopled by actors in the costume of wig and gown, working to the scripts provided by the traditional patterns of formal responses between judge and counsel. And for much of the time, Wilde was the leading actor, the protagonist, conducting his own *agon* against the jabbingly insistent counsel, Edward Carson, whose apparently contemptuous questions and comments frequently goaded Wilde into dangerously incautious replies. For though Wilde might have been the leading actor, he was not the dramatist. Despite his best efforts to assert himself, this was not a drama he could direct. That would have to wait, until *De Profundis*, where he could take back control of his Tragedy by writing it himself and restoring to himself the full dignity of the tragic protagonist: no longer Wilde the convict, Wilde the criminal, but Wilde, both tragic hero and tragedian. Socrates and Christ become the models for Wilde's self-construction as a tragic protagonist. All three aroused the hostility of powerful elements within their societies. All three stood trial; all three were found guilty, and two of them were condemned to death. And although Wilde was given no formal death sentence, we now know, from Home Office papers recently released, that the authorities of the day believed a sentence of two years' hard labour constituted an effectual death sentence for men of Wilde's class: few survived their release by more than a few years.[5]

Although it is in *De Profundis* that we find one of Wilde's fullest identifications with Christ, the links between Christ, the Poet, the Prisoner, and the Martyr were already long familiar to him from his own mother's poetry. Speranza, Lady Wilde, was a formidable champion of Irish Nationalism, and had herself stood trial for her beliefs. In her widely circulated poems she sanctified past Irish nationalist heroes, imprisoned, exiled, or executed, and called upon those who survived them to offer themselves up for similar fates. Constantly those "martyred" in the struggle for Irish freedom are compared to Christ. "The Brothers: A Scene of '98", for example, is a narrative poem based on actual events in which two brothers stood trial for treason ("Speranza" 1871: 7).

Elsewhere in the poems we find repeated emphasis on the suffering of Christ, and an elision of it with the suffering of all who fight for justice or truth, especially those whose weapon is poetry. Speranza's work is suffused with an extremely elevated notion of the Poet, a figure of effulgent glory, enormous power, and correspondingly great responsibility. And he, too, often seems to fuse with the figure of Christ. "The Poet at Court" offers a particularly grandiloquent version of the Poet which places him, by virtue of his poetic gift, above any earthly ruler, and, in the phrase "the Anointed One" (5, v.2, 1.4), even suggests he is synonymous with Christ. But in Speranza's work poets not only have responsibilities; they, too, must accept suffering as the price of achieving poetry:

Deepest sorrow, scorn, and trial
Will but teach us self-denial;
   Like the alchymists of old,
Pass the ore through cleansing fire
If our spirits would aspire
   To be God's refinéd gold. [verse 4]
    . . .
We must bend our thoughts to earnest,
   Would we strike the idols down;
With a purpose of the sternest
   Take the Cross, and wait the Crown.
Sufferings human life can hallow,
Sufferings lead to God's Valhalla;
   Meekly bear, but nobly try,
Like a man with soft tears flowing,
Like a God with conquest glowing
   So to love, and work, and die! [verse 6]
       ("Speranza" 1871: 26, verse 6)

And sometimes poets, too, must face the possibility of martyrdom. The second verse of "Forward!" includes the lines:

And one heart within you boundeth
   With a martyr's faith, engaging
Each to bind upon his forehead cypress wreath or laurel crown.
       ("Speranza" 1871: 31)

Here martyrdom is linked with the poet ("laurel crown") who dedicates his verse to the fight for freedom, and loses his life in it.

Not surprisingly, Speranza sought to instil in her two young sons, Willie and Oscar, an exalted vision of the Poet as a martyr in the making. The second, 1871 edition of her poems carried the printed dedication "To My sons/Willie and Oscar Wilde," which is followed by this epigraph:

I made them indeed
Speak plain the word COUNTRY. I taught them, no doubt,
That a country's a thing men should die for at need!

Whatever the truth of Wilde's own political position on Irish Home Rule, what seems incontestable is that from his earliest days he absorbed an exalted notion of Poetry and the Poet, which involved glory, danger,

death, martyrdom and a constant identification with the figure and
fate of Christ.

Much later in his life, Wilde would invert his mother's notion of Poet as
Christ to present Christ himself as Poet:

> I see a far more intimate and immediate connection between the true life of
> Christ and the true life of the artist; . . . the very basis of his nature was the
> same as that of the nature of the artist – an intense and flamelike imagination.
> He realised in the entire sphere of human relations that imaginative sympathy
> which in the sphere of Art is the sole secret of creation. He understood the
> leprosy of the leper, the darkness of the blind, the fierce misery of those who
> live for pleasure, the strange poverty of the rich.
>
>   Christ's place indeed is with the poets. His whole conception of Humanity
> sprang right out of the imagination and can only be realised by it.
>
> (Wilde 1990: 109)

For Wilde, the gospel stories of Christ's Passion come to represent the
supreme tragic narrative:

> his entire life also is the most wonderful of poems. For "pity and terror" there
> is nothing in the entire cycle of Greek Tragedy to touch it. The absolute
> purity of the protagonist raises the entire scheme to a height of romantic art
> from which the sufferings of Thebes and Pelops' line are by their very horror
> excluded and shows how wrong Aristotle was when he said in his treatise on
> the drama that it would be impossible to bear the spectacle of one blameless
> in pain. Nor in Aeschylus nor Dante, those stern masters of tenderness, in
> Shakespeare, the most purely human of all the great artists, in the whole of
> Celtic myth and legend, where the loveliness of the world is shown through a
> mist of tears, and the life of a man is no more than the life of a flower, is there
> anything that, for sheer simplicity of pathos wedded and made one with
> sublimity of tragic effect can be said to equal or even approach the last act
> of Christ's Passion.
>
> (Wilde 1990: 110)

Though Wilde will not say so explicitly in the context of De Profundis, the
figure of Christ has an additional resonance in Wilde's tragic narrative: many
homosexual men in the late nineteenth century saw in Christ's love for
St. John – the disciple "whom Jesus loved" and who, according to tradition,
"lay in Christ's bosom" during the Last Supper – a divine model for
love between men, and one whose authority was clearly greater than any
man-made law.[6]

That conflict between divine and human laws, here figured in a Christian context, has an earlier analogue in Ancient Greek notions of the relations between the cosmos and human societies. The Greeks recognized two versions of "law": *nomos*, human custom concretized in legislation; and *Themis*, both an abstract noun and a cosmic force, which represents "law" rather in the way that a chemist or physicist might talk of the "laws" of nature. *Themis* takes its force and rightness from the cosmos itself (earlier versions of this word link it etymologically with the Greek word for "earth").

Wilde's trials can be read as a battle between *nomos* and *Themis*, that older form of legitimacy which comes from the workings of nature herself. Carson, Queensberry's counsel, and the full panoply of the Court, might be seen to represent *nomos*; Wilde was being tried under the provision of a very recent piece of legislation, the Criminal Law Amendment Act of 1885, originally intended to raise the then age of female consent from 12. Those sections of it (added late at Committee stage) which dealt with sexual relations between males were loathed by many lawyers and police alike. Because it offered immunity to those who informed against their sexual partners, the new law was widely condemned as "a blackmailer's charter, a charge whose truth became abundantly clear in Wilde's own trials, where most of those who testified against him were male prostitutes who had turned Queen's Evidence. So much for *nomos*. Nineteenth-century medical efforts to identify and understand same-sex desire did not, however, always pathologize or seek to criminalize it. Already there were those who argued that same-sex desire was simply one of a variety of sexual responses, and not one confined to human beings. Other members of the animal kingdom appeared to share it. To that extent it was clearly natural, since it occurred within nature, and thus could be seen as part of the workings of *Themis*. The laws of the cosmos are not, it seems, necessarily those of human legislatures. It could even be argued that such legislatures "fly in the face of nature" by seeking to outlaw "natural" behaviours. They also inflict great suffering on those whose natures are deemed unnatural, or "inverts," in the terminology of the day. Inversion theory maintained that those who desired members of their own sex did so because they had the soul of one sex trapped in the body of the other. It is one of the world's oldest explanations for same-sex desire, and we find versions of it as far back as Plato's *Symposium*, where a witty but moving account of the first inverts is given by Aristophanes, the great comic playwright of Athens. That account would become a key text for homosexual men of later centuries, and many far more sober and "scientific" nineteenth-century medical theories would in fact echo that playfully serious explanation from fifth-century Athens.[7]

Wilde wrestles constantly with the perplexing nature of the natural and unnatural in his writings. In them Nature is often an ambiguous entity, sometimes an authority to be invoked, sometimes an enemy of Art and Civilization. As he said in "The Decay of Lying", "One touch of Nature may make the whole world kin, but two touches of Nature will destroy any work of Art" (Wilde 1945: 23). Such ambiguities are not uncommon in homosexual writings of the period. So, for example, civilization may be appealed to as a force for good, one which encourages tolerance and enlightenment; or it may be abhorred as a force which distorts and mutilates by imposing false "unnatural" values on humanity. Tellingly, in 1889, Edward Carpenter, the early homosexual apologist, called one of his books *Civilization: Its Cause and Cure*. Equally tellingly, Carpenter called another of his books *Love's Coming of Age* (1896). The maturity he described and called for there was one in which human societies would at last recognize and respect the full diversity of human sexual response; would recognize that homosexual love may perform a benign evolutionary purpose; and would, indeed, feel able to allow the word "love" to be used of emotions and deeds presently outlawed and persecuted.

Male homosexual love's "ineligibility" to be called love created many of Wilde's problems in the dock. He and Carson, Queensberry's Counsel, could not actually use the same language in their exchanges with each other. What Wilde sees as love Carson sees only as perversion or corruption. And there is no place in their exchanges, other than a shameful one, for the language of desire or the body. We see it very clearly in Carson's lengthy questioning of Wilde about passages in *The Picture of Dorian Gray* and about letters he had written to Bosie (Holland 2003: 77–111). There is, for example, the letter that begins "Dearest of all Boys" (Holland 2003: 108). In the transcripts of the trial we can almost hear the sneering quotation marks which Carson's voice is putting round the words "Dearest of all boys", "My own boy", "love", "adore" and "proper". We can also hear Wilde's attempts to rehabilitate those words, and to restore proper value to them when he repeats them. So, for instance, after recording Carson's exhaustive questioning about one particular letter, the transcript continues:

> CARSON: Did you ever write any other letter expressing that he was your "own boy" and your love for him in the same style or way?
> WILDE: I have often written to Lord Alfred Douglas "My own Boy." He is much younger than myself. I write to him as "My own Boy", and that I have

expressed, and feel great and, I hope, undying love for him as I say I do. He is the greatest friend I have.

CARSON: Do you think that is a proper kind of letter to write?

WILDE: I think it is a beautiful letter.

CARSON: To a young person?

WILDE: I think it is a beautiful letter.

...

CARSON: ... you have written, as I take it, many of these letters to Lord Alfred Douglas?

WILDE: I don't know what you call "these letters"?

CARSON: Of this particular class.

WILDE: There is no class in that letter. That is a beautiful letter. It is a poem and I have written other beautiful letters to Lord Alfred Douglas.

(Holland 2003: 108–9)

During the course of his second trial, Wilde made a magnificent and seemingly genuinely spontaneous speech in which he defended love between men, the "Love that Dare Not Speak its Name", and pleaded in evidence some of the greatest names of Western civilization – Plato, Michelangelo, and Shakespeare (Millard 1914: 271). The speech is sometimes dismissed as a set of fine rhetorical flourishes deployed in the hope of distracting the jury from less lofty concerns, such as semen-stained sheets.[8] Similarly, Wilde's ceaseless identifications with Christ in De Profundis irritate or anger those who see only a distasteful or blasphemous self-aggrandizement. But if we are to read him aright we need to understand that this is not Wilde posing. We need to recognize what is true in these self-identifications; and to recognize, too, that in the official language of his time, their truth could not be acknowledged. Carson could not accept that love between men may be physical and still rightly called love. Neither could he accept that physical pleasure, even when provided by male prostitutes, has a value beyond the financial transaction. The Ancient Greeks, with their more abundant lexicon of terms to describe love, did better: philia, for deep affections between both family and friends; eros for love rooted in the force of desire, but able to transcend it. Not for them the crude distinctions of "love" and "lust" which underpin so many exchanges in Wilde's trials.

Later, while in prison, Wilde would write to Bosie Douglas, in words which carry echoes of King Lear, "The gods are strange. It is not of our vices only they make instruments to scourge us. They bring us to ruin through what in us is good, gentle, humane, loving" (Wilde 1990: 61). Ruin for Wilde had come in part because official attitudes to male same-sex desire could see only vices in exchanges which, though commercial, could still include elements of the "good, gentle, humane, loving". Not every rent boy turned Queen's evidence; some refused to testify or withdrew their testimony. Decent conduct was not necessarily, it proved, the monopoly of "decent" people.

During his two years in prison, Wilde returned again and again to the question of suffering and the part it may or may not play in the attainment of wisdom. He had many hours in which to consider it. Much of his day was spent in solitary confinement, and talking to other prisoners was officially forbidden, whether he was working on the treadmill or picking oakum or taking his hour of compulsory exercise in the prison yard. The language of *De Profundis* is Wilde at his most allusive; phrase after phrase carries echoes of other works – the Gospels, the Psalms, Corinthians, Dante, Shakespeare, Sophocles, Goethe, Balzac, Baudelaire, on and on goes the litany of names. Yet, once more, amongst this chorus two strains predominate: that of the Greek tragedians, and of Christ. Time and again the words which shape Greek Tragedy recur: doom, destiny, ruin, catastrophe, ill-starred, fate, fatal, pollution, suffering, resolution, shame. But they are now part of a work in which the dominant note is the necessity of a redemptive love whose supreme exemplar is Christ; the supreme lesson has ceased to be "the Pleasure of Life and the Pleasure of Art" (Wilde 1990: 158) and has become instead "something much more wonderful, the meaning of Sorrow, and its beauty" (Wilde 1990: 158).

Before prison, Wilde had had ambivalent feelings about the putative value of pain, and of sympathy with it. In "The Soul of Man under Socialism" he had argued that:

> sympathy with pain is not the highest form of sympathy... It is tainted with egotism. It is apt to become morbid. There is in it a certain terror for our own safety. We become afraid that we ourselves might be as the leper or the blind, and that no man would have care of us. It is curiously limiting, too. One should sympathize with the entirety of life, not with life's sores and maladies, merely, but with life's joy and beauty and energy and health and freedom.
>
> (Wilde 1990: 33)

He disliked intensely the easy praise of suffering and the comfortable glorification of pain which he associated with "Shallow speakers and shallow thinkers in pulpits and on platforms" (Wilde 1990: 34). He not only argued that "Pain is not the ultimate mode of perfection. It is merely provisional and a protest. It has reference to wrong, unhealthy, unjust surroundings" (Wilde 1990: 36). He also went further to insist that "Pleasure is Nature's test, her sign of approval. When man is happy, he is in harmony with himself and his environment" (Wilde 1990: 36). Dangerous sentiments to voice in a world where pleasure was far more often associated with vice, and pain with duty or virtue.

In "The Soul of Man under Socialism" Wilde is particularly disturbed by what he sees as a quintessentially mediaeval obsession with the physical agony of Christ's Passion. Wilde's brave new world, when it is finally achieved, will be "the new Hellenism" (Wilde 1990: 35–6). The word "Hellenism" here is usually seen as an indication that Wilde is taking much of his thinking from Matthew Arnold's earlier 1867–8 essay, "Hebraism and Hellenism": but by the end of the nineteenth century Hellenism is becoming in part a coded term to indicate male same-sex love; of the sort which Plato is argued to have commended. I think it is legitimate to consider the possibility that Wilde is offering some of his readers the opportunity to envisage a future world in which homosexual men may be able to express their true selves, and their sexuality, in "beauty" and "joy", rather than guilt, fear and pain.

By the time Wilde came to write *De Profundis*, tears and sorrow seem often to have regained their older, redemptive function. Pater, whom Wilde so much admired, placed a particular emphasis on pain and suffering as in some ways a form of feeling which is superior to happiness. Wilde himself seems to distinguish between "good pain" and "bad pain". There are distinctions to be made between pain, as externally, arbitrarily, and seemingly unjustly inflicted; and pain which comes from a true "recognition" (a form of moral *anagnorisis*, one might argue) of one's own errors. That second type of pain has value.

In the early pages of *De Profundis* he writes of pain in prison as the thing which proves to prisoners that they are, that they exist. Pain here becomes an aspect of the self, indeed, the very proof of self. In that sense, pain is Life:

> we who live in prison, and in whose lives there is no event but sorrow, have to measure time by throbs of pain, and the record of bitter moments. We have nothing else to think of. Suffering, – curious as it may sound to you – is the means by which we exist, because it is the only means by which we become conscious of existing; and the remembrance of suffering in the past is necessary to us as the warrant, the evidence, of our continued identity.
>
> (Wilde 1990: 54)

(Even here, it seems, Wilde plays with words to serious purpose: note the overtones of judicial language, "evidence", and the pun on "warrant", a warrant for arrest, and a warrant as proof of something's value.)

Throughout *De Profundis*, we watch Wilde, "Like the alchymists of old" (to borrow one of his mother's phrases), struggle to transmute raw Pain (a wordless cry) first into Suffering (pain articulated) and then into the higher form of Sorrow, the fruit of suffering, transformed into wisdom, and something very close to the supreme ancient tragic virtue of *sophrosuné*. Intellect alone could not effect the transformation:

> Reason does not help me. It tells me that the laws under which I am convicted are wrong and unjust laws, and the system under which I have suffered a wrong and unjust system. But, somehow, I have got to make both of these things right and just to me...I have got to make everything that has happened to me good for me. (Wilde 1990: 99)

What Wilde aspires to here is a fully integrated vision of his life in which past and present always coexist. A little later he will bring together past, present, and future: "At every single moment of one's life one is what one is going to be no less than what one has been." There is an ancient Greek proverb: "The past lies all before us." In the final paragraph of *De Profundis*, Wilde offers his own reworking of it: "What lies before me is my past" (Wilde 1990: 109). Greek tragedy insists constantly on the links between past, present, and future; the Christian notion of eternity collapses the differences between them, as Wilde recognizes: "The past, the present and the future are but one moment in the sight of God, in whose sight we should try to live" (Wilde 1990: 158).

For much of his life Wilde had wrestled with various models of Tragedy, of which far the most important were those of Ancient Greece and Christianity. It seems fitting that at the close of his most sustained meditation on Tragedy, with its so hard-won conclusion, he should achieve a synthesis of the two.

Notes

1 It is usually assumed that Queensberry's misspelling of "sodomite", and his curious syntax, were the result of rage rather than illiteracy. The use of the word "posing", however, was very carefully calculated, and used on the advice of his lawyers. It was that word which would make it possible for Wilde to be tried later for his opinions (and those of his fictional characters) and general demeanour, as well as for his actions.

2 For a sense of both the breadth and intensity of Wilde's thinking during those undergraduate years, see Smith and Helfand 1989.

3 Wilde originally wrote his play in French and called it *Salomé*. He then wrote, and published it, in English, as *Salome*, but he was not always consistent in whether or not he gave the final "e" of *Salomé* its acute accent.

4 Dowling 1996 offers a particularly interesting interpretation of these tensions as manifested in the struggles surrounding Oxford University reform during the nineteenth century.

5 Wilde had been sentenced to "hard labour," rather than to the less arduous "penal servitude". Hard labour was carefully calculated "to break a man in body and spirit", as evidenced by the contemporary judicial documents and attitudes described and analyzed by Montgomery Hyde 1963.

6 On the endpaper of one of my own copies of *Iolaüs: Anthology of Friendship*, Edward Carpenter's compilation of extracts relating to male same-sex love, someone has written this inscription which makes the point perfectly, albeit not about St. John, but about another young man whom Christ encountered: "Cecil. New Year. 1917. Then . . . beholding him, loved him; St Mark 10. v.21". The ellipses tease: the Bible says "Then Jesus beholding him, loved him." Has the writer of the inscription simply omitted Christ's name? Or was the recipient to fill in the giver's name? Or does the absence of any name make possible the fusion of Christ and the giver? By the same token, the man of whom it might be said, "to see him was to love him" may be both that young man of the Gospels, and Cecil. And, finally, by letting St. Mark speak for him, the giver of the book borrows something of the saint's (and, by implication, Christ's) authority in the voicing of his love.

7 Inversion theory survived well into the twentieth century and, in much popular thinking, survives still. It underpinned the work of another author destined to find herself in conflict with the law – Radclyffe Hall. Her novel *The Well of Loneliness* – often called "the Bible of Lesbianism", and characterized by the relentless suffering of Stephen Gordon, her inverted female protagonist – would fall foul of the judiciary in 1928 and be banned in Britain for the next 20 years.

8 See the evidence given by Jane Cotter, a chambermaid at the Savoy Hotel, during the first trial in which Wilde was the defendant (Montgomery Hyde 1948: 220). That trial ran from Friday April 26 to Wednesday May 1, 1895. The Jury failed to reach agreement, so a new trial began on Monday May 20, and Wilde was found guilty on Saturday May 25, 1895.

Chapter 12

Tarzan of Athens, Dionysus in Africa: Wilson Knight and Wole Soyinka

Neil Rhodes

Since the late 1970s Greek tragedy has enjoyed a popularity unprecedented in the modern era. Not since antiquity have these plays been so regularly performed or so widely adapted by poets and dramatists for new creative purposes. In many cases those purposes have been politically radical, and the source of the modern renaissance of Greek tragedy in the political events of the late 1960s has been charted in Hall, Macintosh, and Wrigley's fascinating collection, *Dionysus since 69* (2004). Yet in the world of academic English Studies the very concept of tragedy has for much of this time been treated with suspicion. Certainly, any interest in myth and ritual – and Greek tragedy is both more mythic and closer to ritual than the drama of Shakespeare and his contemporaries – has been viewed as hopelessly conservative. But with the opening up of multicultural and postcolonial perspectives in recent years, this position itself seems somewhat naïve, or limited, since it is clear that some cultures which are rather different from the advanced Western democracies are different partly because they are more closely attuned to myth and ritual, and to dismiss these as hopelessly conservative hardly seems the right response. What I want to do in this chapter is to reexamine these issues in the light of the relationship between the Shakespeare critic, G. Wilson Knight, and Wole Soyinka, the first African writer to win the Nobel Prize for Literature, whose work includes a postcolonialist version of Euripides' *Bacchae*.

First, though, a word on the origins of modern academic hostility toward tragedy. In English Studies, and in Shakespearean criticism especially, this was generated by the turn toward a new materialist and historicist criticism impatient with the notion that tragedy reinforced a fixed moral order. The principal target here was not Wilson Knight but E. M. W. Tillyard. Indeed, at the high point of the Cultural Revolution of the 1980s, it seemed that all books in Renaissance English Studies were required to begin with a fierce denunciation of Tillyard's *Elizabethan World Picture* as proof that the scholar had been thoroughly reeducated. Looked at in anthropological rather than political terms, this might itself be seen as a kind of cleansing ritual, like the flogging of the old man at the start of Soyinka's version of *The Bacchae*, a play to which we shall return. Yet it was Knight rather than Tillyard who was the leading Shakespeare critic of the 1940s, when Tillyard's work first appeared. Author of *The Wheel of Fire* and other studies of Shakespeare's poetic symbolism, Knight was Professor of English first at Toronto and later at Leeds. Not only was he an arch-formalist, the true precursor of the formalist criticism of the 1950s and 1960s, in fact, who believed that great art transcended history, but also an arch-royalist, author of *The Sovereign Flower*, which was subtitled "On Shakespeare as the Poet of Royalism" and which contained essays on "This Sceptred Isle," "Literature and Nation," "The British Genius," and "A Royal Propaganda."

So we might wonder why it was Tillyard rather than Knight who came to be demonized in the 1980s. One reason is that Tillyard had produced what was thought to be a misrepresentation of history, whereas Knight simply ignored it or transformed it into a story of succession which he saw as a "golden thread . . . symboliz[ing] the nation's soul life" (Knight 1958: 29). But another reason might be that Knight's work can be located within Modernism, as Hugh Grady has persuasively demonstrated. (It has to be said that Grady also tries to recruit Tillyard as a Modernist, though with some significant qualifications: Grady 1991: 158–89.) Knight's Shakespeare criticism is Modernist principally because it is concerned not with character and plot in Bradleyan mode, but with deep structures: symbol and archetype in poetry, ritual as drama. *The Wheel of Fire* (1930) is rooted in a period that spans Frazer's *The Golden Bough* (1890) and Maud Bodkin's *Archetypal Patterns in Poetry* (1934), and includes *The Waste Land*. It was Eliot, in fact, who got *The Wheel of Fire* accepted by Oxford University Press, writing an introduction to the book where he praised Knight's intention of "taking Shakespeare's work as a whole," and adding that "our first duty as either critics or 'interpreters', surely, must be to try to grasp the whole design, and real *character* and *plot* in the understanding of this subterrene or submarine music" (Knight 1949: xviii–xix). Eliot's reference to "interpreters" acknowledges Knight's distinction between "criticism" and "interpretation": "Criticism is a judgement of vision; interpretation a reconstruction of vision," Knight says on the first page of *The Wheel of Fire* (Knight 1930: 1). This is why so much of Knight's work is dedicated to reenactment, both in the poetic metalanguage of his books on Shakespeare and in his Shakespearean productions where he often took a leading role, most famously in *Timon of Athens*, as we shall see.

It is also why his principal interest is in form and pattern, and in unity rather than diversity. "Perhaps it is what Aristotle meant by 'unity of idea'," he continues in the opening chapter of *The Wheel of Fire*: "Now if we are prepared to see the whole play laid out, so to speak, as an area, being simultaneously aware of these thickly-scattered correspondences in a single view of the whole, we possess the unique quality of the play in a new sense" (Knight 1949: 3). Knight's understanding of drama as space, rather than as a temporal sequence of events, is a point that Grady quite rightly makes central to his explanation of Knight's Modernism, and we shall return to this later. Knight himself, though, sees it as one of *four* principles of interpretation, the others being the importance of regarding "each play as a visionary unit" and preserving "absolute truth to our own imaginative reaction to it"; the importance of analyzing "the use and meaning of direct poetic symbolism"; and, finally, the importance of understanding that Shakespeare's plays from 1599 "fall into a significant sequence" and that "in detailed analysis of any one play it may sometimes be helpful to have regard to its place in the sequence" (Knight 1949: 15). The use of the term "sequence" does of course imply a development through time in addition to spatial organization, but the point is clear enough, and it is also clear that Knight's principles chime perfectly with many of the principles of Modernism regarding deep structure.

Knight's views on Shakespearean interpretation ultimately converge on an ideal of *synthesis* (the term itself is not one that he emphasizes), and here he was hugely influenced by his reading of Nietzsche – not just *The Birth of Tragedy*, but also, more crucially, *Thus Spake Zarathustra* (1887). *The Wheel of Fire* is largely a Nietzsche-free zone. Later work, however, was saturated in Nietzsche, much to the dismay of critics such as René Wellek, who complained of "the flattening out of any distinctions, the reconciliation of everything with everything, the monotonous conclusion that the world is pervaded by dualisms" (Wellek 1986: 132). Wellek was referring to *Christ and Nietzsche* (1948), but Knight's enthusiasm for Nietzsche certainly predates this. He wrote to his friend Francis Berry in March, 1939:

I am writing [a new book] now on literature in relation to the _forces_ at work in Europe today & I use Nietzsche's _Zarathrusta_ [sic], one of the supreme books of the world. I think I understand it through and through. He integrates fullest power into a conception itself finally chivalrous, gentle, mystical. He sums up the whole of Renaissance poetry in one short book.[1]

Knight's commentary on that masterwork eventually surfaced in "The Golden Labyrinth," the fifth chapter of _Christ and Nietzsche_, which takes as its epigraph a couplet from Pope's _Essay on Man_:

> The surest virtues thus from passions shoot,
> Wild nature's vigour working at the root.
>
> (II, 183–4)

Pope's lines, which are certainly an unlikely source, serve Knight not only as an introduction to Nietzsche, but also to the Dionysiac. Dionysus is the divine being at the heart of the golden labyrinth. Knight used that title again, for his 1962 study of British drama, and this time his epigraph came from Euripides' _Bacchae_, translated by Henry Milman (Euripides 1865):

> This say I, of no mortal father born,
> Dionysus, son of Zeus. Had ye but known
> To have been pious when ye might, Zeus's son
> Had been your friend; ye had been happy still.

Here Dionysus speaks to the family of Pentheus, the man of law and order, and denier of the god, whom Dionysus has just destroyed. On the Dionysiac theme in general, Knight comments: "We shall also find an important and recurring opposition of i) some power-impregnated man or woman against ii) some figure of youthful and seraphic, bisexual grace." On Euripides' _Bacchae_ in particular, he comments: "So Euripides drives home the dangers of ethic unrelated to deeper sources. The sexual and Dionysian powers must be accepted" (Knight 1962: 7, 13).

Knight's concept of the Dionysiac derives from both Euripides and Nietzsche, and it permeates his Shakespeare criticism. It is also responsible for his ideal of synthesis. The most obvious illustration of this is "The Transcendental Humanism of _Antony and Cleopatra_" in _The Imperial Theme_, which is also the essay that Grady takes as being representative of what he calls Knight's "spatial hermeneutics" (Grady 1991: 94–7), and we certainly don't need to labor the point that a sense of space, geography, opposed worlds is much to the foreground in that play. Knight comments, very much in the vein of which Wellek disapproved, "Within this whole vision the dualisms so starkly divergent in the sombre plays are all resolved, dissolved, melted into a sublime unity. We must be prepared to see all elements herein of sordidness resolved in a total beauty" (Knight 1951: 255). This is the Shakespeare play that most completely enacts the Dionysian principle of synthesis. As Edith Hall puts it in her introduction to the Bacchae, "Dionysus confounds reason, defies categorisation, dissolves polarities, and inverts hierarchies" (Euripides 2000: xxi). It is also the play that, for Knight, is the most perfect expression of Nietzsche's teaching in Zarathustra that "instinct ... must be accepted," that "such a self-acceptance matures into universal acceptance," and that, as a result, "'Passions' become 'virtues'" (Knight 1962: 293, 295).[2]

But Nietzsche can also provide us with a different kind of commentary on both Shakespeare's play and Euripides' Bacchae. His earlier work, The Birth of Tragedy, is of course all about the conflict between the Apollonian and the Dionysiac, a frame that can fit easily onto Antony and Cleopatra. What he says at the end, however, about state formation and empire-building is of equal relevance to both Shakespeare's Octavius and Euripides' Pentheus, opponents of the Dionysiac. Nietzsche speaks of "the Dionysiac release from the fetters of individuation" which are responsible for "political feelings" and goes on to say that:

> just as clearly, Apollo, the founder of states, is also the genius of the *principium individuationis*, and state and patriotism cannot live without the affirmation of individual personality... When a people unconditionally endorses the political impulses, it is just as necessary that it should take the path towards extreme secularisation, the greatest but also the most frightening expression of which is the Roman empire.
>
> (Nietzsche 1993: 99)

Nietzsche's discussion here applies perfectly both to Octavius' ruthless exercise of individual will in the forging of the imperial state and to Antony's erasure of self as in what Nietzsche calls "this gulf of oblivion" where "the worlds of everyday and Dionysiac reality become separated" (Nietzsche 1993: 39). In the Moralia Plutarch calls Dionysus hygra physis, the element of water, and this is where Antony's individual identity and political will dissolve (5.82). Antony and Cleopatra is in fact about state formation – the foundation of the Roman Empire – and if Knight had not been so indifferent toward history beyond the English royal lineage he would have realized that this point was also quite central to his Dionysiac reading of the play.

Antony and Cleopatra is one kind of Dionysiac space in Shakespeare, but the play that provided Knight with the fullest expression of his own Dionysiac impulses was *Timon of Athens*. He wrote various essays on it as a neglected masterpiece, and duly invoked Nietzsche's *Zarathustra*, but these are perhaps of less interest than Knight's performances as Timon himself. Playing this role was in many ways the consummation of all his ideas on Shakespearean interpretation. The actor, he writes in *The Golden Labyrinth*, "deliberately casts off [his ordinary social self] touching a deeper spring from which he recreates himself as another, experiencing a kind of possession ... Acting is itself a plunging from Apollonian individuality into the Dionysian otherness" (Knight 1962: 3, 7). And it was not just the social self that Knight cast off. In his first performance as Timon at the Hart House Theater, Toronto, in March, 1940, he appeared at the end of the play, when Timon goes back to nature, wearing nothing but a loincloth. This garment now resides in the Brotherton Library at the University of Leeds alongside Knight's literary papers. Knight sent a photo of himself in this state of undress to Francis Berry:

> Just a line to send you this of me as Timon. The production was a magnificent success artistically & in the reaction of many individuals with whom I have talked – some people were thrown into a state of awe and semi-mystical delight, a reaction quite new in my experience. The "intellectuals" however were not so easily moved, & audiences might have been bigger.[3]

When he performed the part in London the following year as part of his patriotic Shakespeare recitations in London, "This Sceptred Isle," there was a rather different reaction. One spectator wrote to Knight accusing him of turning the stage "into a psychological clinic."[4] As a result, when he moved to the University of Leeds and produced the play again, in 1948, he is said to have added a kilt to his wardrobe. This legendary production was commemorated by a bronze statuette made in 1980 (with loincloth rather than kilt) which now stands on a shelf behind the issue desk in Special Collections at the Brotherton.

While it is easy to make this sound ridiculous, the stripping-off was clearly very important to Knight. In another letter to Berry he compared Eugene O'Neill's play *The Emperor Jones* with *Timon*, saying that "in both savagery is significantly revealed under – or above – a trivial civilisation ... Only

O'Neill and Shakespeare have made <u>deliberate</u> use, significantly, of the clothes-nakedness contrast & it is a powerful and if properly used a deeply beautiful contrast."[5]

It is worth pointing out that perhaps the most famous of all formalist essays on Shakespeare, Cleanth Brooks's "The Naked Babe and the Cloak of Manliness" (1947), nowhere acknowledges the influence of Knight. Yet Knight's perception about clothes and nakedness, though it was made in a private communication, is exactly the kind of point that underlies much of his symbolic interpretation of Shakespeare, and it shows quite precisely how his work fed directly into the formalist criticism of the 1950s and 1960s, which was in turn challenged by the new historicist and materialist criticism of the 1980s and beyond. For Knight himself, though, stripping off in the Timon role was a personal expression of the Dionysiac. The 1948 *Timon* at Leeds was his last full-scale Shakespeare production, but he continued loincloth performances of the role as part of a series of recitals called "Shakespeare's Dramatic Challenge," when he was in his eighties. In an interview with the *Sunday Independent* around the time of his eightieth birthday, he said, "I don't like wearing too many clothes when I'm acting. I'm more at ease without clothes than with."[6] This certainly struck a chord with John Van Domelen, author of a biography of Knight, who called his work *The Tarzan of Athens* (1987). Knight's own comment, a few years before his death, was *"Tarzan of Athens*, a very neat title."[7]

The centrality of the Timon role to Knight's work, and of the Dionysiac more generally, is explained clearly enough by his remark about savagery being revealed under – or above (the qualification is interesting) – a trivial civilization. What this might also suggest is that, despite his being in many ways a very conservative figure, Knight's work has the potential to open up multicultural perspectives in a way that a style of discourse more firmly rooted in a Western rationalist tradition might not. The evidence for this is provided most strikingly by Knight's relationship with Wole Soyinka, to whom I shall now turn.

Soyinka had studied Greek at Ibadan University College, Nigeria, from 1952 to 1954. He then did an English degree at Leeds University from 1954 to 1957 where he took Knight's World Drama course and got to know him personally. Knight was to describe Soyinka as "a personal friend, in that he showed me stories etc. and came and talked," adding later that he was "an excellent bridge diplomatically. He understood things from a European viewpoint. He was also committed to his own people, culture etc." (Gibbs 1984: 258).[8] (Soyinka would not have had the opportunity to see Knight as

Timon, but he would almost certainly have seen him, in dubiously cross-cultural mode, blacked up as Othello, which Knight performed in his first year.) The intellectual affinity between them is indicated by the remarkable acknowledgment Knight makes in the preface to *The Golden Labyrinth* to an "examination answer" (actually an MA thesis) by Soyinka, the point in question being that Lear is "most royal" when on the heath (Gibbs 1984: 258).[9] It is a point that would have had an obvious attraction to someone whose most cherished acting role was the stripped and outcast Timon. The substance of *The Golden Labyrinth* itself undoubtedly reflects Knight's teaching on the World Drama course: it contains much reference to Nietzsche, as we have seen, and Knight also records his debt to the ritualistic theories of Frazer and Cornford in his preface. Soyinka's own response to these ideas came in an essay he contributed to a festschrift for Knight in 1969 (Jefferson 1969). The essay was called "The Fourth Stage," and Knight was surely thinking of this when he subsequently said: "I admired and liked Soyinka greatly and his work at Leeds, but his later work, in both essays and drama, I found rather difficult"; he compared the difficulty of the essay with that of the young Nietzsche in *The Birth of Tragedy,* suggesting that "Soyinka, in assimilating its spirit has assimilated its manner" (Katrak 1986: 5, 57).[10] Soyinka did in fact try to solicit Knight's views on the piece, but as he was under arrest at the time, communication proved impossible (Katrak 1986: 40).[11]

It is certainly true that "The Fourth Stage" is densely written and at times rather opaque, but while Soyinka may indeed have assimilated the spirit and manner of Nietzsche, the essay is not about Western dramatic traditions.[12] What it does is to describe the role of the god Ogun in Yoruba culture in order to offer a distinctively African and ritualistic version of tragedy in response to the European assumption that the form was invented in Greece. As Soyinka was later to complain in an interview with Anthony Appiah: "I remember my shock as a student of literature and drama when I heard that drama originated in Greece... What are they talking about? I never heard my grandfather talk about Greeks invading Yorubaland" (Budelmann 2004: 6). The main direction of the essay is to argue that Yoruba tragedy is about the recovery of wholeness. Ogun is a god of war, Soyinka explains, but he also represents "the creative urge and instinct, the essence of creativity" (Soyinka 1976: 141). While there are parallels between Ogun and Dionysus, he is really "a totality of the Dionysian, Apollonian and Promethean virtues," and these give him a "revolutionary grandeur" (141, 142). The tragic myth itself depends upon an awareness of the separation

of human beings from the gods: "Man is grieved by a consciousness of the
loss of the eternal essence of his being and must indulge in symbolic
transactions to recover his totality of being. Tragedy, in Yoruba traditional
drama, is the anguish of this severance, the fragmentation of essence from
self" (144–5).

The role of Ogun, who is the embodiment of will, was to lead the
conquest of this separation by plunging into the gulf of transition. This
was a "redemptive action" through which Ogun "became the first symbol of
the alliance of disparities" (146). The gulf of transition itself is "the fourth
stage, the vortex of archetypes and home of the tragic spirit" (149). The role
of the human tragic protagonist then becomes complementary to that of
Ogun.[13] His own plunge into the fourth stage is an act of hubris, but also
one of ritual sacrifice, for it is through this act that cosmic harmony is
created. In the end, Soyinka writes, "Tragic fate is the repetitive cycle of the
taboo in nature, the karmic act of hubris witting or unwitting, into which
the demonic will within man constantly compels him" (156). This is the
origin of tragic drama and the term *hubris* takes us into what might seem
familiar European territory. But there is an essential difference between
African and European concepts of tragedy, Soyinka argues, which can be
expressed in moral terms: it is the difference between the African emphasis
on cosmic reparation – the repayment of a debt to nature – and the arbitrary
meting out of punishments to mankind by the gods in Greek and some later
European tragedy.[14]

"The Fourth Stage," then, documents an African (and specifically Yoruba)
mythology, but it does also have a European dimension. While it would be
absurd to suggest that Soyinka's account of Yoruba tragedy derives from the
rediscovery of ritual and archetype in European modernism, it seems likely
that the subject that he chose as his tribute to Wilson Knight was intended
to reflect the affinity between those aspects of modernism which helped to
shape Knight's Shakespearean interpretation and his own cultural traditions.
At the same time as "The Fourth Stage" stakes out its claim for the
distinctiveness, and indeed the priority, of the Yoruba tragic view of the
world, it also recognizes parallels between that worldview and certain
elements in Western culture – those elements, in fact, that were of particular
importance to Knight. Knight himself was shortly to express agreement with
Robert Graves's view that "Africa has powers which we have lost and need"
(Knight 1971: 81; Gibbs 1984: 264), but in his case the point is as likely to
have been prompted by Soyinka's essay as by *The White Goddess*. It is striking
that both Knight and Soyinka should be passionately committed to their

native traditions (in Knight's case, the English throne), while also being extraordinarily receptive to very different kinds of cultural experience. The Knight–Soyinka dynamic is very much about reciprocity.[15]

To point out the Western elements in "The Fourth Stage" is not to undermine its fundamental claims but to better understand that reciprocity. The bonding agent for Soyinka is Nietzsche, and he explains at the start of his essay that the "course to the heart of the Yoruba Mysteries leads by its own ironic truths through the light of Nietzsche and the Phrygian deity [i.e. Dionysus]" (140). The fourth stage itself is referred to by Nietzsche's phrase "the chthonic realm." Ogun's function as the embodiment of the will also allies him with the Nietzschean tragic hero, as does the role of *hubris* in the experience of the African ritual protagonist. Indeed, at the end of the essay Soyinka writes: "we approach, it seems, the ultimate pessimism of existence as pronounced by Nietzsche's sage Silenus: it is an act of hubris to be born" (158). This extensive reliance on Nietzsche almost certainly shows the influence of Wilson Knight, though perhaps the most striking point of similarity is in Knight's description of acting as "a plunging from Apollonian individuality into the Dionysian otherness," quoted above, which closely resembles parts of "The Fourth Stage."[16] From a different perspective, it is also worth noting that some Nigerian critics have questioned Soyinka's characterization of Ogun. Isidore Okpewho, for example, argues that Soyinka "has little support for setting up Ogun as such a creative essence when the myth tells us unequivocally that his business is to destroy what has been created." But to grant him those attributes clearly suits the Nietzschean framework. Okpewho goes on to say that there is a "rather thin line between Soyinka's portrait of the African transcendental outlook and European formulations of the nineteenth century" and that he uses "the same romantic language as nineteenth-century European poets and thinkers" (Okpewho 1983: 252, 254). Again, this last point, which is not unfair, would suggest a parallel with the romantic stylistic formulations of Knight's criticism.

"The Fourth Stage" was reprinted as an appendix to a series of lectures that Soyinka gave when he was a Fellow of Churchill College, Cambridge in 1973 and which appeared under the title *Myth, Literature and the African World*. These lectures, which I have drawn upon in my account of the earlier essay, also reveal significant points of contact with Knight's interests and views. A key theme in the lectures is the Western habit of compartmentalization, which Soyinka identifies as the enemy of ritual drama at the beginning of "Morality and Aesthetics in the Ritual Archetype." He returns to it in the second lecture, "Drama and the African World-View," where he argues that it is the compartmentalization of experience rather than the privileging of creative individualism over communal creativity that marks the crucial difference between Western and African views of tragic drama. This is a point that is entirely consonant with the driving principles of wholeness and synthesis that underpin Knight's Shakespearean interpretation. Knight's understanding of drama as space is an extension of the same principle, and this is something that Soyinka discusses at length in an African context in the lecture:

> Ritual theatre establishes the spatial medium not merely as a physical area for simulated events but as a manageable contraction of the cosmic envelope . . .
> Ritual theatre, viewed from the spatial perspective, aims to reflect through physical and symbolic means the archetypal struggle of the mortal being against exterior forces . . . Poetic drama especially may be regarded as a repository of this essential aspect of the theatre.
>
> (Soyinka 1976: 41, 43)

The main thrust of Soyinka's lecture is to argue that this sense of interconnected space is something that survives in African ritual drama, but was lost at an early stage in the development of Western theater as a result of the compartmentalizing mentality. The moralistic character of European culture goes hand in hand with this, as we see in medieval religious drama, where cosmic space is demarcated in rigidly punitive terms. Yet at the same time as he pursues this thesis, Soyinka goes to Shakespeare to illustrate what he means by interconnected space in tragedy. In the best poetic drama, he says, "powerful natural or cosmic influences are internalised within the protagonists," and "Shakespeare's *Lear* is the greatest exemplar of this" (143). Soyinka goes on to say that "a complete, hermetic universe of forces or being . . . is the most fundamental attribute of all true tragedy," and this is what we see in "the spatial architecture" of *Lear* (143). This is very much in the spirit of "The Lear Universe" in *The Wheel of Fire*. It is also the ground on which Knight and Soyinka, European and African theater, meet.

For Soyinka the period between "The Fourth Stage" and the Cambridge lectures was one of imprisonment and exile. From August, 1967 to October, 1969 he was held in jail, for some of the time in solitary confinement, for allegedly supporting secessionist Biafra against the Federal Government at the outset of the Nigerian civil war. Out of this harrowing experience came the prison memoir, *The Man Died* (1969), and a volume of poetry, *The Shuttle in the*

Crypt (1971). It was at this point that Knight tried unsuccessfully to respond to Soyinka's request for comment on "The Fourth Stage": "Not easy, but characteristic; he could probably simplify it if he returns to it at a later date. I wrote to thank him via the Nigerian London office, but did not hear from him" (Katrak 1986: 40).[17] Looked at from a very different vantage point, Soyinka's 27 months in jail span the period from the Summer of Love to Woodstock. To describe it in those terms might seem trivializing and irrelevant, but the climax of the 1960s in the hippy era does have some bearing on Soyinka's version of Euripides' *Bacchae* and on his relationship with Wilson Knight. One of the most characteristic events of that time was *Dionysus in 69*, a reworking of Euripides' play staged in New York by Richard Schechner's Performance Group. While it is difficult to imagine Knight giving whole-hearted support to this quintessential expression of the bacchanalian sixties, many of Schechner's ideas simply extend Knight's to their logical conclusion: the shock value of nakedness was essential to the *Dionysus in 69* spectacle, as were ritual, communality, and the understanding of drama as space (Zeitlin 2004: 49–75; Schechner 1994). Knight too might have been dubbed "Professor of Dionysiac Theater," as Schechner was in a newspaper article, though he would probably not have said: "There is a qualitative link between the Orokolo Fire Fight, the Greek chorus, and our own folk-rock discothèques. LSD is contemporary chemistry, but freaking out is ancient" (Zeitlin 2004: 58). As for Soyinka, this hedonistic interpretation of Euripides' play could hardly have been more remote from his own experience at the time. But by 1973, during his Cambridge year, when he was writing his own version of the *Bacchae* for the National Theatre in London, he was very much aware of the New York precursor and "its search for the tragic soul of twentieth-century white bourgeois-hippy culture" (Soyinka 1976: 7). It was clearly part of Soyinka's intention to make a careful distinction between his own *Bacchae* and contemporary Western youth culture, which is why he describes the music accompanying the Bacchic chorus as "extracting the emotional colour and temperature of a European pop scene without degenerating into that tawdry commercial manipulation of teenage mindlessness," adding that "The Slave Leader is not a gyrating pop drip" (Soyinka 1973: 248). Soyinka's play is aware of its contemporary Western resonances, but at the same time it aims to reshape Euripides in specifically African terms.

The main points of Soyinka's reworking of the *Bacchae* are well established: Dionysus is ruggedly masculine, not androgynous; a slave chorus is introduced whose spokesman has a significant part in the play; Tiresias has the role of surrogate scapegoat in the flogging ritual at the start and is a celebrant in the final communion rite; there are two inserted tableaux depicting bad and good wedding feasts; the play ends not on a note of retribution, with the destruction of the house of Cadmus, but regeneration, as Pentheus' blood is transformed into lifegiving wine.[18] Since Soyinka's version emphasizes communal regeneration through ritual sacrifice, both Dionysus and Pentheus are treated more positively than in Euripides: Dionysus because he is the vehicle of renewal and is associated with ripeness and natural fecundity, and Pentheus because he is given the dignity of the sacrificial victim whose death will save the community. All this is very much in line with "The Fourth Stage," where the cycle of destruction and creation through ritual sacrifice is embodied by Ogun, who is also, like Soyinka's Dionysus, an unambiguously masculine deity. But at the same time as Soyinka's *Bacchae* is shaped by ritual it is also grounded in a specific historical and political moment. The play is about the liberation of African states from British colonial rule in the 1960s, which is why the (male) slaves and their leader are assimilated into the (female) Bacchic chorus. And it is also why the sacrifice is transferred from the oppressed, in the form of the old slave who is to be flogged to death at the start, to the oppressor, Pentheus, who represents the colonial government. So we might say that Soyinka's *Bacchae* is doubly African, both in its use of Yoruba mythology and ritual to provide dramatic structure and in its location at a specific point in African history.

But like "The Fourth Stage" Soyinka's *Bacchae* is subject to other influences. The lesson that Wilson Knight drew from Euripides on "the dangers of ethic unrelated to deeper sources" is equally applicable to Soyinka's play, though in his version the recovery of wholeness is inseparable from political renewal. It also seems likely that the political deployment of Dionysiac myth and ritual to create a psychology of liberation owes something to Fanon, whose training in psychoanalysis underpinned much of his postcolonialist theory. For Fanon, colonization is not just a political but a psychological state, hence such statements as "After the conflict there is not only the disappearance of colonialism, but also the disappearance of the colonized man. This new humanity is bound to define a new humanism" (Fanon 1967: 198). That optimistic theme is close to the heart of Soyinka's interpretation of Euripides. But while Fanon may supply one context for Soyinka's *Bacchae* there is certainly no doubt that his reading of Euripides is again filtered through Nietzsche. This is true even of the postcolonial aspects of the play. Nietzsche, as we saw, associated the Apollonian principle of individuation with state formation and empire-building in what could have been a thumbnail sketch of Pentheus. Earlier in *The Birth of Tragedy* he had written about the ability of the

"Dionysiac magic" to bring about a reconciliation between man and man and between man and alienated nature, declaring "Now the slave is a free man, now all the rigid and hostile boundaries that distress, despotism or 'impudent fashion' have erected between man and man break down" (Nietzsche 1993: 17). The elision of boundaries is one of the elements of the Dionysiac magic that Pentheus, with his attachment to demarcation lines and border patrols, tries ineffectually to resist. His response to the Bacchic frenzy is to announce that "I have a duty to preserve/The territorial integrity of Thebes" (Soyinka 1973: 282). In Soyinka's *Bacchae* the Dionysiac alternative is expressed through oxymoron, the figure that dissolves boundaries by uniting opposites. This is how Dionysus describes himself at the outset: "I am the gentle, jealous joy. Vengeful and kind . . . Accept" (235); later, a slave says "A jealous joy, a ferocious, gentle joy/Is my Dionysos" and the Bacchante respond: "Consummate god, most terrible, most gentle/To mankind" (290). This echoes Nietzsche, but perhaps more immediately Wilson Knight writing about the acceptance of Dionysus in both Nietzsche and Euripides, and above all it echoes the themes of Knight's essay "The Avenging Mind."

That essay, first given as a lecture in 1947, is a companion piece to Knight's *Christ and Nietzsche*, published the following year, and it takes its title from a phrase in the section "Of Redemption" in *Thus Spake Zarathustra*. Nietzsche's work, Knight writes:

> is concerned throughout with the facing of instincts, the using of them . . . The book is a laboratory for the integration of those great principles, the Dionysian and the Apollonian, formulated in his early work, *The Birth of Tragedy. Thus Spake Zarathustra* is forward-looking and creative. There may be dangers in it, but, if there are, there are dangers in the New Testament.
>
> (Knight 1948: 193)[19]

Soyinka's *Bacchae* begins, like Euripides' play, with Dionysus swearing vengeance on those who deny his divinity and call his mother a "slut." Its ending, however, in which Pentheus' blood turns to wine, is completely unlike Euripides. Soyinka himself has denied that this "communion rite" – his subtitle for the play – is Christian: "you must realize I'm not talking about Christian communion . . . I'm talking about the universal communion which I could bring out with the symbolism of wine," he said in an interview with James Gibbs in Zimbabwe in 1981 (Gibbs 2001: 85–6). But this is not entirely convincing. Soyinka inherited strong Christian traditions from his family: both his parents were Christians and his great-grandfather had even preached at St. Paul's Cathedral (Hardwick 2004: 235). Whatever his intentions of translating the Greek original into an African context, the Christian elements in the play remain indelible, and they do not, of course, come from Euripides. This is why Biodun Jeyifo, at the same time as he claims the "communion rite" for Ogun, refers to the changing of the blood into wine as "transubstan-tiation" (Jeyifo 2004: 161). Furthermore, the sacramental conclusion is anticipated by the inserted tableau of Christ changing the water into wine at the wedding feast in Cana. The fact that Soyinka tells us that "his halo is an ambiguous thorn-ivy-crown of Dionysus" (Soyinka 1976: 286) hardly diminishes the specifically Christian context of the scene, since it is Christian symbolism that is being used to reinforce the message of the pagan myth.[20] Even the revolutionary figure of the slave leader is assimilated into the Christian tradition when he is presented as one of "the black hot gospellers" in the stage direction about pop music. All this is evidence of the play's syncretism: there is no doubt that Soyinka is deliberately mixing different cultural and religious traditions. While the basic trajectory of the play from vengeance to communion fits easily enough into the Yoruba rituals associated with Ogun, the combination of Christian symbolism with Nietzsche, who is directly acknowledged in "The Fourth Stage," is equally powerful and it would have reached Soyinka through Knight and the ideas that Knight elaborated in "The Avenging Mind," *Christ and Nietzsche*, and *The Golden Labyrinth*. An earlier observation of Knight's on the relationship between Shakespearean tragedy and ritual sacrifice is also directly relevant here: "What is the relationship of the Shakespearean play and the Christian Mass? The Mass or Communion service is at once a consummation and the transcending of pagan ritual . . . Paganism knew sacrifice to be essentially a creative and life-giving force: which led to various ceremonies, sometimes cruel and sadistic" (Knight 1936: 232–3).[21] The application of that to Soyinka's *Bacchae* is obvious; to translate his play back into Knightian terms one might describe it as a fusion of *The Wheel of Fire* and *The Crown of Life*.

To argue the case for the European dimension to Soyinka's work, and in particular for the influence of Wilson Knight, might seem to be offering fuel to those Nigerian critics who attacked Soyinka during the 1970s for being "anglo-modernist" and for betraying his native cultural roots (Gibbs and Lindfors 1993: 342). His response, ironically enough in view of the appellation given to Knight by his biographer, was to call them "Neo-Tarzanists" (Soyinka 1975). When asked again about these charges of Europhilia, in an interview with Biodun Jeyifo in 1985, the year before he was awarded the Nobel Prize, he replied, simply, that such critics were "missing out on a lot that can be enjoyed intellectually in the entire creativity of man. There's no way at all that I will ever preach the cutting off of any source of knowledge" (Jeyifo 2004: 123). In Soyinka's *Bacchae* the colonialist Pentheus tells Diony-sus "We have more sense than barbarians./Greece has a culture," to which Dionysus replies, "Just how much have you travelled, Pentheus?/I have seen even among your so-called/Barbarian slaves, natives of lands whose cul-tures/Beggar yours" (Soyinka 1973: 269). The meaning of this is clear enough in the context, but the recognition of cultural diversity cuts both ways, as Soyinka was well aware. And so too was Wilson Knight. The World Drama course that Soyinka took at Leeds may have been based on a narrower "world" than we might expect today, but it was certainly culturally adventurous for its time. In many ways the relationship between Knight and Soyinka presents a mirror image. In his role as the Tarzan of Athens (itself a fine oxymoron) Knight was constantly trying to understand Shakespeare in terms of underlying mythic origins and unifying mythic patterns, driving back drama into ritual, in a way that was consonant with the modernist project in general. Soyinka, on the other hand, while determined to create an African *Bacchae* and expound an African view of drama in his associated critical writings, actually produces something more syncretic through his assimilation of Nietzsche and Christian doctrine.

Paradoxically, however, Soyinka found himself fighting on two fronts at once: against those who accused him of betraying his native culture and against others, writing from a Marxist standpoint, who regarded his interest in myth as reactionary and, in Edward Said's terms, "nativist" (Said 1994: 275–8; Crow and Banfield 1996: 94–5). In fact, he had commented on these quite opposite positions himself in "Drama and the African World-View" in the context of "the viability of a tragic view in the contemporary world." Acknowledging the Marxist denunciation of "the insidious enervation of social will by tragic afflatus," he went on to describe the alternative view of a "decline in tragic understanding...and the related awareness that this represents a quite unnecessary loss of creative territory," pointing out that most major twentieth-century dramatists had been moved to rework Greek tragedy for new creative ends (Soyinka 1976: 47–8). He then cited George Steiner's argument that the death of tragedy was a result of a decline in the "organic world view and of its attendant context of mythological, symbolic and ritual reference" (48) in order to underline the persistence of such a view in African culture. This sounds remarkably like the Elizabethan World Picture. We should probably stop short of imagining a Tillyard of Africa to partner the Tarzan of Athens, but Soyinka's observations offer a salutary reminder that so many Western attempts to recuperate tragedy represent a search for what has never been lost, elsewhere.

Notes

1. Brotherton Library, University of Leeds, MS 20c Knight, (1) a), Mar. 6, 1939. I am grateful to the staff in Special Collections at the Brotherton for their help in my research for this chapter and also to the Carnegie Trust for a grant to support it.

2. The last remark alludes to Knight's epigraph from Pope which heads the chapter "The Golden Labyrinth" in *Christ and Nietzsche* (1948).

3. Brotherton MS 20c Knight, (1) a), Mar. 3, 1940.

4. Brotherton MS 20c Knight, (2) e), p. 189.

5. Brotherton MS 20c Knight, (1) a), Nov. 27, 1939.

6. *Sunday Independent*, Sept. 18, 1977.

7. Brotherton MS 20c Knight, (1) c), Mar. 25, 1981.

8. Personal communication to James Gibbs, Apr. 1, 1971; letter to Gibbs, July 18, 1982. I am most grateful to James Gibbs for his generous advice on this chapter and for permission to quote from these sources.

9. Letter to Gibbs, Sept. 18, 1982.

10. Personal communication to Gibbs, Apr. 1, 1971.

11. Letter to Gibbs, Oct. 27, 1970.

12. There is a good account of the essay in Maduakor 1993.

13. See also Soyinka 1976: 36.

14. See also Soyinka 1976: 14.

15. Knight continued to read Soyinka; see Knight 1971: 82–3 and Gibbs 1984: 259.

16. Cf. "Yoruba tragedy plunges straight into the 'chthonic realm' ... Into this universal womb once plunged and emerged Ogun, the first actor, disintegrating within the abyss" (142).

17. Letter to Gibbs, Oct. 27, 1970.

18. Some of these aspects are explored at greater length in Bishop 1993 and Okpewho 1999.

19. Pope's lines from the *Essay on Man* are also quoted at this point.

20. The merging of Christ with Dionysus originates in the Byzantine play *Christus Patiens* dating from the eleventh or twelfth centuries (see McDonald 1999).

21. On communion, the "primordial" sources of Shakespeare, and Soyinka see Brockbank 1983. This follows Soyinka's own discussion of *Antony and Cleopatra* in a paper given at the International Shakespeare Conference in Stratford-upon-Avon in August 1982.

Chapter 13

Postmodern Tragedy? Returning to John Ford

Mark Houlahan

The terms "postmodern" and "tragedy" lie uneasily beside each other, suggesting a generic hybrid that, in strict accordance with key assumptions of postmodernism, ought not to exist. This is so for two main reasons. First, a key trend in postmodern thought in the humanities and social sciences has been to question the stability of the human subject, presenting human beings as radically dispersed, decentered, unfathomable. Foucault famously and gleefully anticipated an epoch when "man would be erased, like a face drawn at the edge of the sea" (Foucault 1989: 422). In tragedy, Aristotle wrote, we can expect to see imitated the actions of people who "have some definite moral and intellectual qualities, since it is through a man's qualities that we characterize his actions" (Aristotle 1991: 58). Aristotle's theory, in other words, requires characters to be knowable and coherent. The incandescent tragic protagonists from the theater of the English Renaissance, such as Hamlet, are likewise presumed to project the fullness of an inner self. In the postmodern era, those characters ought to be read as analogous to the writing structures which contain them, where "everything is to be *disentangled*, nothing *deciphered* . . . there is nothing beneath" (Barthes 1988: 171).

Secondly, Aristotle calls for a single action, and prescribes its coherence. Tragic scenarios since ancient Athens thus typically revolve around the downfall of a single tormented character: Oedipus, Medea, Phaedra. Only rarely are two characters given equal weighting and stage time in the outcome. (Shakespeare's *Antony and Cleopatra* is a rare counter-example, and in any case is a hybrid historical tragedy.) But the paradigm of the tragic individual has become increasingly problematic. Events of the last two

centuries have inured us to catastrophe on a mass scale. From the famine in
the Soviet Union in the 1930s through the Holocaust to the bombing of
Hiroshima and Dresden, "tragic" events in "real life" habitually destroy
thousands, even millions of lives. In the wake of such catastrophes, how
could the tragic fall of one or two characters signify? And, even if we
were to switch the tragic focus to history's suffering masses, could any
representation evoke the full force of such horrors? In the early twenty-
first century, the attacks on the twin towers of the World Trade Center on
September 11, 2001 have become paradigmatic in this sense. Footage of the
collapsing towers quickly became repetitious and banal. It is not possible to
watch such sequences without understanding that the experience has been
Mediated, as Thomas de Zengotita (2005) puts it in his fine book on the
postmodern cultures of the West. So saturated in images and prior texts,
contemporary audiences ought to be so dulled as to be incapable of any
intense feeling, let alone those tragic emotions of pity and terror Aristotle
famously recommends in response to acts "involving destruction or pain"
arising from "deaths on stage and physical agonies and woundings"
(Aristotle 1989: 65).

Yet, as Terry Eagleton (2003) demonstrates, deep-seated incongruity has
always marked the space between tragic theory and tragic practice. People
continue to write and perform tragic fictions (as so many of the chapters in
this book show), and great actors continue to test themselves against the
power of the classics of the tragic tradition, from Olivier's famous turns as
Oedipus and Othello to Fiona Shaw's galvanizing incarnation of Medea as a
desperate, paparazzi-stalked film star. Irony, though, is the governing trope
of the postmodern era. In such an epoch, direct and voluble expressions of
intense emotion, the inevitable stock in trade of tragic characters, can be
embarrassing and difficult to endure. To be directly sincere is to risk seeming
false. Modern tragic scenarios thus risk emotional displays by embedding
them within various shadings of the tragic grotesque, using a bleak comic
wit to enliven situations where the human frame is made to suffer in
grotesquely severe ways. How can a tragedy be "cool" and "hip" enough
for a postmodern audience to approve while at the same time evoking the
white-hot rage and sorrow that would make an audience truly attend to the
power of the emotions it evokes?

Throughout his films, Quentin Tarantino has explored ways in which the
"postmodern" and the "tragic" might thus be reconciled. The clearest case
is his first film, *Reservoir Dogs* (1992). This presents perhaps the longest death
scene ever filmed. In an early sequence we see two Los Angeles crooks

fleeing a bank robbery that has gone awry. In the back seat Mr. Orange (played by Tim Roth) writhes in agony. A stomach wound bleeds profusely, as it will do until the end of the film. Speaking in the language of the street, Mr. Orange is stirred by the knowledge that all tragic characters come to: his death is near. "All this blood is scaring the shit outta me. I'm gonna die, I know it" (Tarantino 1994: 14). Mr. Orange is consoled by Mr. White, played by Harvey Keitel: as so often, the tragic protagonist needs an audience to attend his sufferings. The film loops back to narrate the events before the botched robbery, and then concludes with the death of Mr. Orange. The thieves have been given color codes, to prevent them knowing each other too well. In his death agony, in grotesque pain, Mr. Orange reaches for a heightened sense of intimacy. He needs to confess, both his real name, and his real role as an undercover cop. "I'm so sorry, I'm so sorry," he repeats, while Mr. White cradles him as a parent would a dying child, just before he "lifts his .45 and places the barrel between Mr. Orange's eyes" (Tarantino 1994: 109). The sequence is perverse, horrifying, and extraordinarily moving.

Tarantino is celebrated for the dazzling originality of his films. He does not invent new story lines, but rather recombines previous genres and character types to keep audiences entertained, and to elicit strong emotions with rapid juxtapositions of material. His supreme awareness of these genres, and his gleeful citation of film classics, is an essential part of his postmodern art. What Tarantino unfolds others have discovered as well. The way to create anew is to revisit the old. Perhaps this is especially the case with the construction of new tragic scenarios, where the great exemplars since Aeschylus and Sophocles are ever present, never more than in the early twenty-first century, when so much cultural production has become readily available in digitized form.

In the Anglophone world, of course, much of this process of reinvention is focused on Shakespeare. Yet the English Renaissance has more to offer than cyber-Hamlets, and recent practitioners in a variety of genres have found particularly eloquent ways of returning to the works of a later, lesser playwright, John Ford. Ford (1586–c.1639) is not now widely known outside academic circles. Yet his plays, with their preoccupation with the extremes of violence and sexuality, are in fact nicely calculated to hit the tastes of today's desensitized audiences. Several recent adaptations of Ford point up the ways in which his theater functions as a kind of meta-exemplar or avatar. Ford's greatest plays date from the 1630s, and self-consciously revisit the classics of Webster, Marlowe, and especially Shakespeare, which preceded them on the Renaissance stage. Ford seeks to do homage to those prior texts and at the same time to outgo them in physical sensation and wrenching pathos. These are paths that Ford's recent followers have attempted to emulate also, suggesting that Charles Lamb may have been right to claim as long ago as 1804 that "John Ford is the man after Shakespeare" (Lamb and Lamb 1976: 147).

Lamb was prescient, for it is only comparatively recently that Ford's output has been seriously reassessed. His position as a dubious, possibly unworthy Renaissance tragedian is nicely suggested in *Still Life*, the second of A. S. Byatt's quartet of novels depicting the life and psycho-cultural times of Frederica Potter, the abrasively intelligent daughter of a Yorkshire school-master. Early in this novel we find our heroine being interviewed for places at Oxford and Cambridge. In her adolescent phase, Frederica is never one to underestimate her intellectual prowess. Breathlessly she reports on her interviews, and, with graceless abandon, recounts trailing before the panels the arcana of her sixth-form reading list: "I got all sorts of things in, *Britannicus* and *Henry VIII* and *The Broken Heart*... and they didn't stop me, they said go on... I was in a place of my own – oh *glory*" (Byatt 1985: 20). She namedrops obscure plays by the famous (Racine and Shakespeare, respectively) and then, with Ford's *Broken Heart*, shows off her knowledge of the recondite. At Oxford, she sketches a future thesis: "They said they'd see me in three years to do my D.Phil. They asked me what it would be on. I said John Ford. It was the worst moment. They laughed so much, they couldn't go on with the interview" (Byatt 1985: 21). Fifty years on, it seems safe to suggest, they would not be laughing. For the 1950s English Faculty Frederica joins at Cambridge was heavily in thrall to F. R. Leavis, famously wedded to the moral elevation of the "great tradition" of heavyweight English novelists. Byatt freely admits the influence of "Dr. Leavis and the Cambridge-English school of moral seriousness and social responsibility" (Franken 2001: 2); in the last volume of the quartet Frederica herself confesses to Leavis's influence, mentally conflating her Yorkshire parent with her Cambridge teacher: "She felt about her father as most of her generation felt about Dr Leavis, that anything she could conceivably pro-duce must fall short of his high requirements" (Byatt 2002: 265). In such a climate, Ford's yoking of baroque violence with emotional extremes could only seem recherché and excessive.

After the closing of the theaters in 1642, Ford's works were "hardly ever acted, and hardly ever read" (Coleridge n.d.: xix), though Pepys saw *'Tis Pity She's a Whore* early in the Restoration (on September 9, 1661), and *Perkin Warbeck* was revived in 1715 and 1745. Ford's depiction of Warbeck as a usurper to the throne of Henry VII was ideal theater for the two crucial years when Jacobites seriously (yet of course unsuccessfully) threatened the English throne. Ford was taken up by Lamb and William Hazlitt, great defenders of the private reading of Renaissance drama against the noisy performance venues of the cavernous theaters of the Romantic era; and Ford's manipulation of blank verse was later famously defended by T. S. Eliot in 1932. However it was not until the 1960s that the critical climate, working in tandem with invigorating productions of Ford's major plays, would allow – a little late for Byatt's Frederica – for a full rehabilitation of Ford.

Both developments were anticipated by Artaud's famous inclusion of Ford in his manifesto "Theatre and the Plague," which calls for a post-Freudian liberation of the id. Artaud claims 'Tis Pity She's a Whore as a prime example of a "real stage play" which "upsets our sensual tranquility, releases our repressed subconscious, drives us to a kind of potential rebellion." More mystically, Artaud asserts that the play leads to a realm where "all true freedom is dark, infallibly identified with sexual freedom, also dark, without knowing exactly why" (Artaud 1985: 19, 21). These morbid exhilarations underpinned Peter Brook's legendary 1964 theater of cruelty season for the RSC and fueled the revival of Ford's critical fortunes, as evidenced by the two collections of essays produced around the time of the tercentenary of Ford's birth. Artaud's insights were given further impetus by the praise of Georg Lukács in his influential work The Historical Novel: "Ford not only has considerable dramatic talent, but a special ability for portraying extreme passions forcefully and realistically. Individual scenes...attain to an almost Shakespearean magnificence by the simplicity, directness and authenticity with which these total passions dominate the heroes' lives" (Lukács 1969: 130). Like Artaud's, Lukács's text was first published in English in the 1960s, at a time when the moral seriousness Leavis had so promoted among literary critics was being transformed by the influence of a wide range of European philosophers and critics.

Artaud evokes a Ford in command of the powers of darkness, orchestrator of solemn and compelling sexualized entertainments. That is the distinction also of the newly modeled Fords considered here. The recent performance history of Ford's plays themselves has been ably sketched by Roger Warren (Neill 1988); and the separate Revels editions of his plays usefully describe the all too brief performance tradition for individual plays. Creative adaptations by Tom Stoppard, Angela Carter, and Sarah Kane create different kinds of intertextual (and transhistorical) charge, citing the great sections of 'Tis Pity with particular force. You could point to the moments, for example, in

Stoppard's *The Real Thing* where two lovers rehearse Giovanni and Annabella as avatars for their own passion. Stoppard's conservative wit places Ford's tragic duets under comic restraint. Carter and Kane, however, perform Ford in wilder and more extravagant keys.

Stoppard's first assay at a Renaissance rewrite was his early hit *Rosencrantz and Guildenstern are Dead* (1966), an energetically comic piece of postmodern pastiche, where Stoppard imagines what life was like offstage for the minor characters in Shakespeare, subjected onstage to the violence and meditations of *Hamlet*, whose rhetorical urgency Stoppard mines for comic relief. *Rosencrantz* made popular a new sub-genre, the adaptation of an old play through the lens of modern preoccupations. Stoppard's return to Ford in *The Real Thing*, however is, in formal terms, much less radical, embedding Ford within an intricate romantic comedy of bad manners.

In the first scene we see an architect interrogate his wife, convinced that, rather than traveling on business, she has been having an affair, the stock conceit of a thousand West End farces. Stoppard has a character drolly dismiss the scenario: "Well, it wasn't about anything, except did she have it off or didn't she? What a crisis. Infidelity among the architect class. Again" (Stoppard 1999: 218). The play we see in the first scene of *The Real Thing* is called *House of Cards*, for it collapses so quickly. Stoppard's play then focuses on the playwright, Henry, who wrote *House of Cards*, and his wife, Charlotte, an actress. Henry leaves his first wife to live with their friend Annie, also an actress and with whom he has been having an affair. One adultery thus nestles within another, creating a series of receding frames. But which of these, the play wants to know, is *The Real Thing*?

This is as much a question for the writer as the sets of lovers he has invented. Even if you felt love as "real," how could you write about it in a way that was convincing and not embarrassing? Henry, Stoppard's playwright, seems to speak for Stoppard himself when he worries about how to write about love: "Perhaps I should write it completely artificial. Blank verse. Poetic imagery" (Stoppard 1999: 188). As *Rosencrantz* shows, Stoppard is keenly aware of Shakespeare's massive dominance over all subsequent English-language playwrights: "Shakespeare out in front by a mile, and the rest of the field strung out behind trying to close the gap" (Stoppard 1999: 201). Like the other contemporary writers discussed here, his recourse to Ford is partly a way of writing round Shakespeare's overwhelming presence.

Ironically the device Stoppard uses is one Shakespeare deployed brilliantly: the play within the play. Both of Henry's actress wives have played Ford's heroine Annabella. In Stoppard's play Annie travels to Glasgow to perform in a regional production of Ford's play. We see her rehearsing Ford's scenes, and watch her relationship develop with the actor playing her stage brother Giovanni. Together they use Ford's heartfelt, incantatory lines to explore realms of emotion the playwright Henry cannot access. Yet Annie's performance is not the "real thing," but rather a fine performance in a highly wrought play. Within the urbane dialogue Stoppard has written for his bourgeois philanderers Ford starts to sound exotic and bizarre. Ford is cited and performed at length, but is effectively dismissed for comic effect. In Glasgow, Stoppard imagines Ford played out for laughs: "We had a good finish – a woman in the audience was sick. Billy came on with my heart skewered on his dagger and – ugh – whoops!" (Stoppard 1999: 226). Ford's tragic form is then absorbed within the wit of Stoppard's social comedy. He returns to Ford in order to dismiss him, showing that, in comic forms, living well outflanks dying well.

Angela Carter's approach is different, reinventing and embracing the bravura of Ford's enactment of death, for readers assumed to be attuned both to the sensations of Ford's theater and the expansive pleasure of American movies. Ford's family is tragically fixed to their city-state, Parma. The couple at the centre of Carter's story (standing in for Ford's Annabella and her husband) dream of escaping their fate: "They talked, her husband and she; they would go, just go, out west, still further, west as far as the place where ocean starts again perhaps" (Carter 1995: 343). They are doomed to live out the twin premises both of Ford's drama and the psychodynamics of the classic Hollywood Western, as filmed so capaciously and poetically by Ford's namesake, the filmmaker John Ford. The playful significance of Carter's title "John Ford's 'Tis Pity She's a Whore" is thus gradually revealed. Carter transforms a found relationship into an inevitable yoking of the two genres of revenge tragedy and Western romance, folding Renaissance and twentieth-century fictions together. Carter uses Ford's tropes to inhabit a brooding, mythological American space: "the green breast of the continent, the earth, the beloved, cruel, unkind." The narrator does concede that what she describes as "the pure face of America" is the sight of the "North America looking at itself" (Carter 1995: 348, 338), a perspective shaped by the experiences of English-speaking United States. This excludes the very different context of the Latin American countries; but the tale is less concerned with "real" geopolitical boundaries than with delineating a mythical New World dreamscape. In this terrain desire is lethal. In a climax played out against the back drop scenery of the classic Western, Johnny (the American version of Giovanni) shoots both his brother-in-law and his pregnant sister on the sandy platform beside the waiting locomotive. And then he shoots himself.

"Brother, unkind, unkind" (Carter 1995: 348), Annie-Belle remarks, drawing for the first time in the story directly from her ancestor-figure Annabella. These are the same understated words Annabella uses at the comparable moment in 'Tis Pity when Giovanni sacrifices his sister, killing her with a dagger before cutting out her heart, in his despairing imitation of the traditional Catholic imagery of Christ holding his own bleeding heart to the world (5.5.94). Annabella's simple phrase is really the only one that would make sense in either version of the story, for the register of Renaissance tragedy jars against the idioms characters in Westerns would typically use.

In this respect perhaps the most arresting feature of Carter's treatment is the way she tessellates separate planes of storytelling modes to bring her two ages together. The first storyteller sounds like the fabulist readers know from Carter's celebrated fairytale book, The Bloody Chamber: ironic, mordant, detached. "There was a rancher had two children, a son and then a daughter" (Carter 1995: 333). This voice unfolds the key premises of the story: the death of the rancher's wife; the rancher as widower left with two handsome, blond children; their turning to each other for want of better company. As in 'Tis Pity, the drama of sexually aberrant children is heightened by them only having one parent to control their desires.

A more complex narrator figure, however (something like the "arranger" in Joyce's Ulysses) overlays this fatal story with two variants. Even as the story is told it morphs into a pastiche of a movie script telling the same story. Tactfully we are spared the consummation of the incest; rather it is merely implied by the following description:

EXTERIOR. PRAIRIE. DAY.
(Long shot) Farmhouse.
(Close up) Petticoat falling on to porch of farmhouse. (Carter 1995: 334)

Thus this narrator shows us how one Ford might have filmed the other Ford's work, the later John gifting the earlier the visual economy and taciturnity that have become key signifiers of the western. Yet if that feature film could thrive without Ford's rhetoric, the story is not prepared to do so, and, as so often, Carter's register is overdetermined, teetering on the brink of going too far. The patched-in screenplay syncopates with fragments from 'Tis Pity. Only the narratee, presumed then to be equally adept at reading screenplays, Caroline tragedy,[1] and American mythmaking, receives the complete variations of Carter's Ford medley.

Carter's Western myth deploys the overdetermined erotic structures which make Ford's initial scenario so arresting and yet so implausible. To restage the climax of the play, however, Carter keeps faith with the "realist" assumptions of the Western, eschewing Ford's Thyestean banquet in favor of a simple shootout and suicide beside a waiting train. Here again the narrator intrudes on behalf of the knowing narratee: "The Old World John Ford made Giovanni cut out Annabella's heart and carry it on stage . . . The New World John Ford would have no means of representing this scene on celluloid, although it is irresistibly reminiscent of the ritual tortures practiced by the Indians who lived here before" (Carter 1995: 348). Carter is aware of the violence practiced both by the First Nations of North America, as well as by greedy white settlers. Her focus here is on the horizon of possibility provided by the genres she is reworking. The first Ford was shockingly more extreme in his use of violence for tragic affect than Ford the filmmaker could have been. Film audiences have had to wait until the 1990s to encounter a cinematic match for the first John Ford: the films of Quentin Tarantino, which come laced with scenes of violence that are hysterically funny and exquisitely uncomfortable for audiences to endure.

The same Zeitgeist permeated the theater of the 1990s also, most strikingly (and shockingly) in the plays of Sarah Kane. Like Tarantino, Kane wrote for an audience which seemed jaded and all-knowing. Thus she sought to provoke them into response; the staggering plays from her too brief career call for the staging of obscene actions of violence, mutilation, cannibalism, and penetration to be staged.[2] On the page these seem impossible to realize; in performance they are gripping – you cannot bear to watch, nor can you avert your eyes.

Kane's theaterscape is designed to flesh out Artaud's imagery: "There is both something victorious and vengeful in theater just as in the plague, for we clearly feel that spontaneous fire the plague lights as it passes by is nothing but a gigantic liquidation" (Artaud 1985: 18). The climax of *Cleansed* revisits this pestilential purgation: "*The sun gets brighter and brighter, the squeaking of the rats louder and louder, until the light is blinding and the sound deafening*" (Kane 2001: 151). This is a sensual, surrealist overload. It emphasizes a kind of hyperrealism often found in contemporary theater, whereas photographic realism seems best left to the resources of film and television. The receivers of this poetic irradiation are Carl and Grace, survivors of the two love stories Kane intertwines. For the sake of his lover, Rod, Carl has his tongue cut out and his feet eaten by rats and then watches as Rod's throat is cut. Yet Carl himself survives, and the play holds out some kind of hope beyond its final apocalypse. Grace too remains alive. Her story line descends more directly from Ford. In the first scene we see her brother Graham's eyeballs injected with heroin. He does not survive this insult to his system, so Grace comes to claim his body. The body has disappeared, so instead Tinker, the presiding "Doctor" (in fact torturer) of the play, arranges a masquerade, persuading Grace to swap her dress for the shirt and jeans of Robin, a young man. Grace becomes Graham, who then returns in scene 6 as the embodied ghost of himself. Grace remembers her Ford: "Love me or kill me, Graham" (Kane 2001: 120); these are words Giovanni and Annabella exchange early in 'Tis Pity, when they profess their love for each other:

> ANNABELLA: Love me, or kill me brother...
> GIOVANNI: Love me, or kill me, sister...
> ANNABELLA: I'll swear't; and I.
> GIOVANNI: And I; and by this kiss-
>   *Kisses her*
>   (1.2.276–82)

This poses a false alternative, for loving and killing are intimately entwined in the paradoxes that both Renaissance and postmodern theater make so riveting. "No way but this," as Othello puts it, "Killing myself/ To die upon a kiss" (5.2.367–9).

Kane's literalizing of Ford's scenario is unflinching, exploiting a carnal directness available to contemporary writers as of course it was not to Ford: "*They begin to make love slowly at first, then hard, fast, urgent . . . They hold each other, him inside her, not moving. A sunflower bursts through the floor and grows above their heads*" (Kane 2001: 120). The surreal, impossible sunflower, erupting from this urgent consummation, evidently blesses the spectral, yet real, incestuous desire felt by Grace and Graham. By the end of the play Grace is not only dressed as a man but bears genitals stitched on her by Tinker, which, in turn, he has carved from Carl. The play calls this new "person" Grace/Graham. They are one, and yet not the same. Their fate is grotesque, ludicrous yet moving.

A fuller reading would trace the intricacies of the scenario of *Cleansed* and its links to Kane's other scenes of ultra-violence, such as her reworking of Seneca in *Phaedra's Love*. This too deals with the provocations of forbidden desire, so often the grounds of tragic theater. Further reflection would show also Ford's presence in Kane's work in greater detail. Clive James dismisses *'Tis Pity*: "I really think it is not much of a play" (James 1991: 456). The writers described here have found Ford more invigorating. For if it is true that Ford claims a complex allegiance with his literary forefathers then it is true also that Ford remains active as a paternal presence in our own times. The strange extremities of his theater compel us still. The reenactments of Ford sketched here – Stoppard's, Carter's, Kane's – are exemplary instances of a postmodern return to Ford. What follows the postmodern? It is too soon to tell; the epoch of postmodernism may already have ended. Whatever their wider ramifications, the examples here remind us why returning to Ford could no longer be considered a cause for laughter in the Senior Common Room. "Tragedy," Eagleton reminds us, "acts out the chaos of a socio-discursive order" (Eagleton 2003: 20). Likely world events will remain chaotic. Reworking tragic scenarios is one way for cultures to puzzle out the paradoxes of fate, desire, and freedom. Those questions have never easily been resolved but in skilled hands, they remain worth posing.

Notes

1   A footnote informs readers that John Ford was an "English dramatist of the Jacobean period"; perhaps for the sake of economy eliding the fact that *'Tis Pity*, like *The Broken Heart*, was published and likely performed instead early in the reign of Charles I.
2   Kane committed suicide in 1999, when she was only 28. She left five astonishing plays.

Chapter 14

Tragedy and the Future

Rowland Wymer

In Aldous Huxley's *Brave New World* (1932) the plays of Shakespeare are prohibited but, more significantly, the Controller Mustapha Mond claims that nobody would be able to understand a play like *Othello* anyway: "Because our world is not the same as Othello's world. You can't make flivvers without steel – and you can't make tragedies without social instability" (Huxley 1934: 259). Murderous jealousy would be incomprehensible to an audience conditioned to believe that "every one belongs to every one else" and strongly encouraged to change sexual partners as frequently as possible. What the Controller refers to as "high art" has been sacrificed in the name of compulsory "happiness." My main purpose in this chapter, however, is not to speculate about the future disappearance of tragedy as an art form but to make a number of connections between tragedy and science fiction, including some consideration of the ways in which they both engage with the future. These are two genres which are normally seen as carrying very different cultural and philosophical baggage, even though what is often thought of as the first science fiction novel, Mary Shelley's *Frankenstein*, was subtitled *The Modern Prometheus* and derives its theme of forbidden knowledge from Marlowe's *Doctor Faustus* as well as from Aeschylus. The potential for further fruitful interactions between the two genres has been most recently exemplified by Mary Doria Russell's magnificent novel *The Sparrow* (1996), which I shall conclude by looking at in some detail.

The critical efforts to construct a history and taxonomy of science fiction have associated it with many other literary forms. Brian Aldiss's most famous definition of science fiction is as a form of Gothic (Aldiss with Wingrove 1986: 25), and Patrick Parrinder has traced its connections with romance, fable, and epic while also pointing out its frequent resort to parody (Parrinder 1980). Neither writer chooses to foreground the relationship with tragedy, yet within a few lines of setting out his main definition of science fiction, Aldiss offers a more succinct and explicitly "tragic" one: "*Hubris clobbered by nemesis*" (Aldiss with Wingrove 1986: 26). Parrinder, likewise, when commenting on the frequent pattern of ironic reversal in Wells's "scientific romances," asks: "what are these but illustrations of hubris followed by nemesis, of a logic so neatly rounded that it speaks of poetic even more than of scientific or cognitive justice?" (Parrinder 1995: 11).

Parrinder's categorizations of science fiction in *Science Fiction: Its Criticism and Teaching* owe a great deal to the ambitious taxonomy of all literary forms in Northrop Frye's *Anatomy of Criticism* (1957), a book which foregrounds the *Iliad* and the *Odyssey* as the respective sources of some of the major oppositional groupings which structure subsequent literature – tragedy and comedy, realism and romance. Science fiction is normally situated within the traditions of romance and fantasy which begin with the *Odyssey* rather than within the stream of "tragic realism" which flows from the *Iliad*, yet Frye's own remarks about the *Iliad* make clear the close connection with the more rigorous forms of science fiction: "With the *Iliad*, once for all, an objective and disinterested element enters into the poet's vision of human life"; at this point in history, poetry acquires "an authority based, like the authority of science, on the vision of nature as an impersonal order" (Frye 1971: 319). But if tragedy and science fiction do indeed share a sense of nature as an unyielding, impersonal order, they normally continue to be strongly distinguished in the minds of most people by their employment of different "chronotopes" (Bakhtin's term for the spatio-temporal matrices in which all narratives are embedded)[1] which involve different ways of engaging with and representing past, present, and future.

Both dramatic performance and narration create an illusion of immediacy, an apparently direct access to the moment of choice, the deed of horror, the surge of feeling, in the very instant in which it occurs, *now*, in the present. This is true even when a past tense is used, as it usually is, to narrate events in a novel or short story. This illusion of immediacy is no more or less of an illusion than any other claim to be experiencing the present moment in all its fullness. By its very nature, the present moment, as St. Augustine realized, is ungraspable and is only apprehensible as part of a complex process of retrospection and anticipation.[2] All dramatic and literary forms engage the spectator or reader in a version of this process, but the emphasis falls very differently in different genres. The conventional view would be that tragedy is mostly concerned with the deterministic pressure which the past exerts upon the present, while science fiction extrapolates from the present to give us a range of future possibilities. This simple distinction, when explored further, is difficult to maintain, and I would choose instead to emphasize some of the continuities between the two genres.

In many tragedies, choices made and deeds performed before the start of the play initiate a chain of consequences whose inexorability can be conceptualized by both characters and spectators as "fate." The past is a continuing nightmare from which no one escapes. The curse which hangs over the House of Atreus predates the actions of any character in the *Oresteia*, yet condemns them all to a seemingly endless cycle of blood revenge. The word most commonly translated as "fate," *moira*, carries with it the implication of inevitable retribution for past bloodshed. Within such a framework the precise details of the future are hidden from most of the characters, but we know that it will be a future which has been determined by the past. When the chorus in the *Agamemnon* say "And we will know the future when it comes" (Aeschylus 1979: 111), they are uttering more than a platitude. They are implying that when we eventually see it we will recognize the logic of what comes to pass, the way it conforms to the principle of *ananke*, or "necessity," a principle which includes the inevitability of retribution. When the chorus quote the words of the prophet Calchas who "spoke the things to come" (Aeschylus 1979: 108) before the fleet sailed for Troy, they use a form of historic present which unites past, present, and future. Greek tragedy is filled with prophets, seers, and oracles, but the future which they see and predict is one which has been predetermined by the past and is therefore part of an "untensed" conception of time, in which all time is simultaneously present. Most of the characters, by contrast, struggle unknowingly toward their future with the quite different, and more fully human, consciousness of time as a developing and still uncompleted sequence of moments. Thus Greek tragedy enacts the paradoxical relationship between Being and Becoming which preoccupied many Greek philosophers.

The same paradox is also exploited in the many science fiction stories which involve time-travel loops. One of the most brilliantly extreme of these, Robert Heinlein's " '– All You Zombies –' " (1959), poses many of the same questions about identity, free will, and fate as *Oedipus the King*, despite the radically different tone adopted, which is one of jaunty black comedy. Like Oedipus, the protagonist is engaged in a futile and uncomprehending struggle within a closed time loop only to discover, at the end of the story, an incestuous nightmare from which there is no escape. Heinlein's protagonist, whose story is told by a barman working at "Pop's Place," finds out eventually that, through a combination of time travel and gender surgery, he is his own father and mother as well as the "I" who is narrating "his" story. Jocasta's advice to her husband and son ("Live, Oedipus,/as if there's no tomorrow" (Sophocles 2000: 215) would carry a similar irony if applied to Heinlein's hero or to the many other victims of time-travel paradoxes for whom tomorrow has already happened. The barman at "Pop's Place" wears a ring in the shape of "The Worm Ouroboros . . . the World Snake that eats its own tail, forever without end. A symbol of the Great Paradox" (Heinlein 1980: 127). This ancient Egyptian symbol is amenable to positive forms of psychological interpretation, but in Heinlein's story the final effect is of a desolating solipsism from which there can be no possible exit, since every "free" act of reaching out toward another exists only within the same endless time loop: "*You* aren't really there at all. There isn't anybody but me – Jane – here alone in the dark" (Heinlein 1980: 137).

The concept of an entirely closed time loop and hence of an inexorable fate is less important in Renaissance tragedy, where more significance is given to the moment of moral choice, though at times – in Marlowe, Webster, or Middleton – this choice is colored by a Calvinist Protestant sense of predestination. The pressure of the past is still felt strongly in many plays, most obviously perhaps in *Hamlet*, with its "classical" use of a ghost calling for blood revenge for a murder which took place before the play began. The diminished importance of fate is counterbalanced by the increased importance of death as the defining form of narrative closure. For the Renaissance, a tragedy was a play which ended in death rather than simply being, as it was for the Greeks, a form of "serious drama." The ending in death gives added force to the Aristotelian dictum that tragedy must consist of a "complete" action and seems to close off tragedy from any real engagement with the future. Within the confines of an Elizabethan or Jacobean play, however, the certainty of death stimulates the exploration of how individual characters might develop an existentially "authentic" and future-orientated form of consciousness, Heidegger's famous "being-to-wards-death." Again, *Hamlet* gives us perhaps the supreme example of a character struggling toward this "authentic" form of being, but all Webster's major characters go on a similar journey, though without necessarily arriving at the same destination. Hamlet himself reaches the desired Heideggerian state of "anticipatory resoluteness" in the augury speech ("The readiness is all"), where it is inflected by the Christian notion that there is a "special providence in the fall of a sparrow" (Shakespeare 1982: 5.2.215–16).

This hints (from the perspective of the character, at any rate) at something beyond the numerous deaths which will conclude the play, and most Renaissance tragedies gesture beyond their formal narrative closure toward some continuing future. This need not be a comforting gesture. In Marlowe's *Doctor Faustus* it is the fact that death does *not* end all which is the source of the protagonist's greatest psychological suffering, as he contemplates a future eternity of torment in hell. Sometimes the glimpse of the future which unfolds beyond the end of the play is deeply, if quietly, ironic, as when Oedipus commends his daughters, Antigone and Ismene, to the care of Creon at the end of *Oedipus the King*: "You're their only hope" (Sophocles 2000: 249). A less familiar example occurs in *Othello*. This does not seem like a play which would have struck its first audiences as being set in a remote historical past, which means that the fall of Cyprus to the Turks, which took place in 1571, must be inferred as imminent. The downfall of Othello will mean the fall of the island which he was sent to defend and Cassio, the new Governor installed in Othello's place, can look forward to being flayed alive in the near future.

Othello constructs a real historical background to frame its fictional plot but most Renaissance tragedies were grounded even more firmly in history, trapping the characters and their aspirations for the future in a past which was already known to have taken place. When Aristotle commented on the fact that tragedy used "real" names for its characters rather than the invented names used in comedy, he explained it, rather laboriously, on the grounds of increased plausibility. To be plausible something has to be possible and things which have already happened are, by definition, possible. This method of achieving plausibility locks tragedy into a close relation with history and allows it to speak only of futures which have already come to pass.

By contrast, science fiction has always presented itself, and been understood by its readers, as a "literature of the future." Although a setting in the future is not an absolute generic requirement, most science fiction stories do engage, implicitly or explicitly, with future scientific or social developments. According to Patrick Parrinder, H. G. Wells, the founder of modern science fiction, not only carried on the Hebraic role of the prophet as moral sage which had been adopted by some of his Victorian predecessors, he also combined this with the more classical role of the prophet as foreteller of the future, the image of the preacher being "overlaid with the classical images of the Delphic priestess, sphinx, and Sybil" (Parrinder 1995: 22). Wells is one of a number of science fiction writers who have also written important nonfictional futurological works. Others would include Arthur C. Clarke and Isaac Asimov, the latter of whom was a member of the seminal American group of SF writers, editors, and fans who called themselves "The Futurians." Publishers remain determined to market science fiction as a literature of the future, even when this involves an element of (faintly ridiculous) hyperbole. A series of critical anthologies published in the 1980s and dealing with such authors as Philip K. Dick, Ursula Le Guin, and Arthur C. Clarke was provocatively called "Writers of the 21st Century," a title which the passage of time has rendered either irritatingly misleading or banal, depending on whether the writer concerned survived into the new century.

Science fiction should not have to be judged by the literal accuracy of its speculations about the future. Indeed, despite such well-known successful predictions as the atom bomb (H. G. Wells and others) or the communications satellite (Arthur C. Clarke), it may be, as Fredric Jameson has argued, that any historical survey of science fiction gives us a better understanding not of the future but of "our incapacity to imagine the future" (Jameson 1982: 153). Nevertheless, science fiction knows, in a way which much of the traditional literary canon does not appear to do, that the future will be radically different from the past. "The future is a foreign country; they do things differently there," wrote Arthur C. Clarke (with apologies to L. P. Hartley) at the beginning of *Profiles of the Future*, a work of factual science prediction (Clarke 1982: 9). This way of thinking about the future developed originally in the context of an Enlightenment belief in progress. From the seventeenth century onward it became possible to think that as understanding of the physical world and its laws increased, existence could be transformed by the application of human reason. In contrast, the "tragic" perspective on the future is either that it has already happened and is therefore no longer a hopeful possibility, or that it will be much the same as the present, if not worse.[3]

Both the Enlightenment sense of the future as progress and the tragic sense of the future as simply the continuation of a wretched present existence are given eloquent expression in Chekhov's *Three Sisters*. Vershinin believes "that everything in this world must gradually change – is changing already, in front of your eyes. Two hundred years hence, three hundred years – a thousand, if you like – it's not a question of how long – but eventually a new and happy life will dawn" (Chekhov 2003: 34). In a manner which anticipates the "progressive" and "scientific" ideology of the future Soviet state, he thinks that the task of people in the present is to work hard to bring about the "new and happy life" which they will never live to see. For Tusenbach, however, even in a million years time, "life will still be just the same as it's always been. It doesn't change; it remains constant; it follows its own laws – laws which have nothing to do with you, or which at any rate you'll never discover" (Chekhov 2003: 35). Deciding which, if either, of these two voices is endorsed by the play in its entirety is central to the decision whether or not to read the *Three Sisters* as a tragedy.

Tusenbach's mention of "laws which have nothing to do with you" points to some of the darker, less Utopian, implications of the scientific revolution which began in the seventeenth century. The Enlightenment confidence in the power of human reason to understand the laws which governed the universe had, as its corollary, a chilling sense of the unimportance of individual human beings, or indeed the entire human race, in relation to those laws. A good deal of science fiction gains its intellectual and emotional force not from any Utopian speculations about the future but from a grim contemplation of how "the cold equations" of science, to use the title phrase of Tom Godwin's famous short story, impact upon human feelings and moral choices. As Chris Kelvin, the protagonist of Stanislaw Lem's *Solaris* (1961), says at the conclusion of the novel: "We all know that we are material creatures, subject to the laws of physiology and physics, and not even the power of all our feelings combined can defeat those laws. All we can do is detest them" (Lem 1981: 194). His own surname alludes to these laws, since a "kelvin" is a unit of thermodynamic temperature measurement. The apparent resurrection of Rheya, the woman who killed herself ten years before as a result of his indifference, seems at first to offer him a form of redemption, an answer to the yearning expressed by Frankford in Heywood's *A Woman Killed with Kindness* (1603) that the arrow of time could be reversed:

> O God, O God, that it were possible
> To undo things done, to call back yesterday;
> That Time could turn up his swift sandy glass,
> To untell the days, and to redeem these hours.
> (Heywood 1961: 8.54–5)

But the Greeks themselves, despite their elaborate mythologizing, understood that not even Zeus himself could bring back the dead without violating the fundamental laws of nature,[4] and Kelvin is forced to acknowledge that the being he has been conversing with is some*thing* (rather than some*one*) conjured up from his own brain by the mysterious planet which his space station is orbiting. Such knowledge does not bring psychological acceptance, however, and even after "she" has gone, he remains on the space station, vainly hoping that "the time of cruel miracles was not past" (Lem 1981: 195), unable to accept that we are "material creatures, subject to the laws of physiology and physics" and that death is final.

Godwin's short story "The Cold Equations" (1954) also shows human beings as apparently subject to scientific "necessity," but arguably the tragic effect is here more speciously contrived. The story concerns a female stowaway on a small spaceship carrying urgently needed medical supplies to a distant planet. She must be "tragically" sacrificed because the "cold equations" governing the relationship between mass and fuel mean that the ship cannot be landed safely with her extra weight on board. As John Huntington's penetrating analysis makes clear, this insistence on tragic inevitability is undermined by the story's frequent references to items like the pilot's chair, which could presumably have been thrown overboard instead of the woman: "behind the unchallengeable assertion of the 'neutrality' of the universe lies a fantasy about punishing a woman" (Huntington 1989: 84). Like the appeal to "necessity" and the will of the Gods in Greek tragedy, the "scientific" explanation permits a disavowal of full moral responsibility:

> [I]t allows all the men in the story and the fantasizing author himself (and perhaps the fantasizing reader) to assure themselves, even as they perform this rationally satisfying act of obeying the equations, that they do not want it this way, that they would change it if they possibly could. As a way of hiding the blame attached to the murder of such innocence, the scientific equation has all the brilliant efficiency of a dream.
>
> (Huntington 1989: 84–5)

A closely parallel analysis could be given of the sacrifice of Iphigenia at Aulis, a sacrifice which none of the male characters in Euripides' play claims to want, but which is made by the dramatist to seem "inevitable." Sometimes, however, the laws evoked in science fiction, laws "which not even the power of all our feelings combined can defeat," are less obviously a piece of narrative manipulation open to being deconstructed as a form of fantasy. They really are fundamental laws of existence whose implications for human life are grim.

One of the most important of these laws is the Second Law of Thermodynamics, which states that energy exchanges within a closed system will
always be inefficient, so that the stars will eventually burn themselves out,
leaving the universe without usable heat or light. This places an ultimate
limit on all human aspiration and is strongly intimated in the closing pages
of *The Time Machine*, where the speculations about social and biological
evolution which have dominated the story are superseded by the bleak vision
of a cooling sun, encroaching darkness, and the end of all life. In Pamela
Zoline's "The Heat Death of the Universe" (1967), one of the finest stories
to emerge from the British "New Wave" of experimental science fiction in
the 1960s, the mental disintegration of a Californian housewife is made both
more, and less, significant, by being juxtaposed with explanations of the
Second Law of Thermodynamics and the inevitable increase of entropy in
the universe which follows from it:

> The total ENTROPY of the Universe therefore is increasing, tending towards a
> maximum, corresponding to complete disorder of the particles in it. She is
> crying, her mouth is open. She throws a jar of grape jelly and it smashes the
> window over the sink. Her eyes are blue. She begins to open her mouth. It has
> been held that the Universe constitutes a thermodynamically closed system,
> and if this were true it would mean that a time must finally come when the
> Universe "unwinds" itself, no energy being available for use. This state is
> referred to as "the heat death of the Universe." Sarah Boyle begins to cry. She
> throws a jar of strawberry jam against the stove, enamel chips off and the
> stove begins to bleed. Bach had twenty children, how many children has Sarah
> Boyle? Her mouth is open. Her mouth is opening.
>
> (Zoline 1988: 64–5)

The use of a historic present and the constant renewal of actions which had
seemed to be completed ("She is crying, her mouth is open . . . She begins to
open her mouth . . . Sarah Boyle begins to cry . . . Her mouth is open. Her
mouth is opening") show her as caught up in an eternal process from which
there is no escape, even if there are a few small islands of order (such as the
music of Bach?) which briefly resist the encroaching sea of chaos.

The Second Law of Thermodynamics and the increase of entropy which it
posits preoccupied a number of SF writers in the 1960s, perhaps as a
pessimistic response to the unsettling speed of the social changes which
were taking place. In Philip K. Dick's *Do Androids Dream of Electric Sheep?*
(1968) the entropic process is reformulated with a certain amount of humor
in terms of Dick's neologism "kipple," a word which embraces all the

useless objects like chewing-gum wrappers and junk mail which multiply constantly until they overwhelm the individual, society, and the cosmos itself. "No one can win against kipple . . . It's a universal principle operating throughout the universe; the entire universe is moving toward a final state of total, absolute, kippleization" (Dick 1972: 53). The only serious opposition to kippleization comes either from the upward climb of the Christlike Wilbur Mercer, later revealed to be an actor with a drink problem, or the order and harmony of art, here represented by the music of Mozart rather than Bach, and which the bounty hunter Rick Deckard hears when pursuing the android Luba Luft, who has been working as an opera singer and is taking part in a rehearsal of *The Magic Flute*. However, Deckard reflects: "This rehearsal will end, the performance will end, the singers will die, eventually the last score of the music will be destroyed in one way or another; finally the name 'Mozart' will vanish, the dust will have won" (Dick 1972: 76). This insight is given an additional tragic twist when Deckard realizes that, as a bounty hunter paid to eliminate the android singer, he himself is "part of the form-destroying process of entropy" (Dick 1972: 77). The universal entropic principle is at work within his own soul.

The tendency to view things in a cosmic perspective, a characteristic of both science fiction and tragedy, operates usually as a form of irony, in which all human desires and achievements ultimately count for very little in the larger scheme of things. When Bloom parts from Stephen toward the end of Joyce's *Ulysses*, he feels "the cold of interstellar space, thousands of degrees below freezing point or the absolute zero of Fahrenheit, Centigrade or Réaumur" (Joyce 1968: 625), and the minutiae of the human drama of Bloom, Molly, and Stephen in which we have been immersed for 600 pages start to seem very minute indeed. In the fifth and last of the ever-increasing Time Scales which accompany Olaf Stapledon's vision of the next two thousand million years, *Last and First Men* (1930), there is no space left to record anything between "Planets formed" and "End of Man" (Stapledon 1963: 285).

A good deal of science fiction would consequently be categorized by Northrop Frye as "fifth-phase irony," a form of irony "corresponding to fatalistic or fifth-phase tragedy" and one "in which the main emphasis is on the natural cycle, the steady unbroken turning of the wheel of fate or fortune" (Frye 1971: 237). This sense of the movement of time as one of the components of an impersonal and unforgiving natural order is what Faustus expresses in his final soliloquy ("The stars move still; time runs; the clock will strike"). Neither he nor Giovanni in Ford's *'Tis Pity She's a*

Whore can "command the course/of time's eternal motion" (Ford 1975: 5.5.12–13), however much rhetorical energy they expend in trying to do so. The main reason for referring to most science fiction stories as ironic rather than tragic in tone is that their sense of human entrapment within an unyielding set of natural laws is not always counterbalanced by any strong emotional identification with a particular individual. When this does occur, as in the case of the tormented Jesuit priest in Mary Doria Russell's *The Sparrow* (1996), then we experience something close to the traditional tragic effect, in which pity is as important as terror in the face of cosmic indifference.

The Sparrow and its almost equally impressive sequel, *Children of God* (1998), have achieved "classic" status within the field of science fiction in a remarkably short space of time. Despite never having published any science fiction previously, Mary Doria Russell has gained numerous awards and a host of admiring reviews for her work,[5] which fulfills most of the generic expectations of SF readers by dealing with such topics as First Contact, space flight, relativity effects, artificial intelligence programs, and the intricacies of an alien society and language. *The Sparrow* – and it is an important part of one's immediate response to it as a "classic" – also happens to fulfill most of the generic expectations associated with tragedy, as its protagonist, acting from noble if misguided impulses, is brought to a state of physical ruin and psychological despair through a series of events which are shocking both for him and for us but which can be shown, though only after the event, to follow an inexorable logic: "It was totally predictable, in hindsight" (Russell 1997: 9).

The Sparrow concerns a Jesuit mission to the Alpha Centauri system, following the reception of extraterrestrial radio signals which take the form of hauntingly beautiful music. The mission to make contact with the singers is undertaken from the best of motives: "The Jesuit scientists went to Rakhat to learn, not to proselytize. They went so that they might come to know and love God's other children. They went for the reason Jesuits have always gone to the farthest frontiers of human exploration. They went *ad majorem Dei gloriam*: for the greater glory of God. They meant no harm" (Russell 1997: 10). Like their predecessors who voyaged to the New World in the sixteenth and seventeenth centuries, they set in motion consequences which they could not have possibly anticipated, and part of Russell's point was to reenact the disaster of those initial contacts with the New World without assigning any obvious individual or collective blame: "I thought that it would be almost inherently tragic. There is no way to do First Contact right – the language trouble alone would generate endless possibilities for disastrous errors and mistakes" (Gevers 2007).

The tragedy is inherent in the situation rather than being a consequence of deliberately malevolent behavior. Despite the fact that the personal life of one (alien) character was derived in part from biographies of the Marquis de Sade, this is a story in which "No-one was deliberately evil" (Russell 1999: 171). Skillful manipulation of the time scheme (the progress of the expedition is narrated alternately with the much later investigation into its failure) means that a sense of inevitable disaster is present from the first few pages, but the precise mechanisms of the disaster are occluded till very near the end, inducing in the reader that same compulsive desire to know the worst which possessed Oedipus and culminating in a series of revelations which are both deeply shocking and utterly logical. By page 18 we know that the sole survivor of the expedition, the Jesuit linguist, Emilio Sandoz, who has devoted his life to serving others, can be called, with some apparent justification, "a whore" and "a child killer," but we do not have the slightest understanding of how this could have come about, though we subsequently learn in *Children of God* that a misunderstanding about the connotations of "serve" was part of the problem (Russell 1999: 65, 170). One crucial *hamartia* which has the function of sabotaging, as effectively as anything in previous tragedy, any simple-minded attempt to equate moral guilt with suffering, was the decision to plant a garden on Rakhat. Emilio subsequently throws this innocently disastrous action back in the face of the ecclesiastical interrogator who is determined to find him guilty:

> He sat very still but looked steadily at Johannes Voelker. "It was the gardens."
> Knowing that he was being addressed directly for some reason but unable to see why, Voelker shook his head. "I'm sorry. I don't follow."
> "The mistake. What you've been waiting for. The fatal error."
>
> (Russell 1997: 466)

The title of the novel, it becomes clear in the closing pages, is taken from the same passage in St. Matthew which Hamlet recalled when about to fight the duel with Laertes: "Are not two sparrows sold for a farthing? And one of them shall not fall on the ground without your Father" (Matthew 10.29). Tragedy usually calls into question this notion of "special providence," and *The Sparrow* does so repeatedly in relation to the fate of Emilio Sandoz, who believed he had found God on Rakhat until his encounter with Hlavin Kitheri, the source of the songs which had inspired the whole mission, destroyed his faith: "I am in God's hands, I thought. I loved God and I trusted in His love. Amusing, isn't it? I laid down all my defenses.

I had nothing between me and what happened but the love of God. And I was raped. I was naked before God and I was raped" (Russell 1997: 490). It is left to another Jesuit to make explicit the obvious riposte to St. Matthew's assertion of an all-seeing God: "But the sparrow still falls" (Russell 1997: 499).

This is one of many passages in both of the Rakhat novels which touch, directly or indirectly, on the problem of post-Holocaust theology, a problem which Mary Doria Russell was forced to confront herself when, following the birth of a child, she took the decision to abandon the atheism into which she had lapsed following a Catholic upbringing and embrace Judaism. The juxtaposition in *The Sparrow* of the mass murder of children with attempts to see a divine purpose in everything takes us into an area equally difficult for Christian and Jew, the area from which there has been no escape since 1945. "The disproportion between suffering and every theodicy was shown at Auschwitz with a glaring, obvious clarity. Its possibility puts into question the multi-millennial traditional faith. Did not the word of Nietzsche on the death of God take on, in the extermination camps, the signification of a quasi-empirical fact?" (Levinas 1988: 162). Emilio Sandoz had made a garden and invited God to walk there but now "there is nothing left but ash and bone," and he asks repeatedly: "Where was our Protector? Where was God...Where is God now?" (Russell 1999: 48). For Emilio, "God is not innocent," and he will not accept the Pope's assurance that God is waiting for him, "in the ruins" (Russell 1999: 49, 50).

Not only did Auschwitz call traditional Judeo-Christian theodicy into question, it also challenged those attempts, frequently cited in discussions of tragedy, to give suffering a meaning by seeing it as a necessary path to wisdom. The *locus classicus* of such thinking is a passage in the *Agamemnon* (ll.177–84) which the Father General of the Jesuits points out, in the original Greek, to Emilio at the end of *The Sparrow*. Emilio translates it as: "In our sleep, pain which cannot forget falls drop by drop upon the heart, until, in our own despair, against our will, comes wisdom through the awful grace of God" (Russell 1997: 502). In view of the literal and spiritual rape Emilio has suffered, some of the phrasing of the Penguin translation by Robert Fagles ("from the gods...there comes a violent love") might have been more apt, but the point is that these Aeschylean lines, like the biblical ones about the sparrow, are there to be challenged as much as endorsed. In *Children of God* Emilio says dryly: "The redemptive power of suffering is, in my experience at least, vastly overrated" (Russell 1999: 75), and both novels explore the philosophical problem of "useless pain" which Emmanuel Levinas and many others think has been posed inescapably by the events of the twentieth century (Levinas 1988).

It is seems particularly offensive to speak of redemption through suffering in relation to the 1.5 million children who died in the Holocaust. The killing of the Runa children by a Jana'ata military patrol ("the martial arm of a sentient predatory species") is a "deed of horror" which drives the Jewish Sofia Mendes into active resistance and aligns *The Sparrow* with a number of particularly grim previous tragedies in which children are victims – *Medea*, *Thyestes*, *The Duchess of Malfi*. As in these plays, the deed provokes particularly searching questions about the nature of the God or gods who permit such things to happen. Could such a God or gods be "innocent"?

The centrality of children to both Rakhat novels is something that only becomes fully apparent by the end of *Children of God*. Hlavin Kitheri, the aristocratic Jana'ata who becomes Emilio's nemesis, is a third-born and so, by the rules of his society, forbidden to have children and thus "tragically" cut off from any future:

> Lacking a future, he became a connoisseur of the ephemeral ... And so he turned his aesthetic sensibilities to the experience of orgasm and found the courage to sing of that evanescent moment which, for the fertile, brings the weight of the past to bear upon the future, which holds all moments in its embrace, which links ancestry and posterity in the chain of being from which he was barred and exiled.
>
> (Russell 1997: 344–5)

The famous question posed mockingly by L. C. Knights – "How many children had Lady Macbeth?" – was in fact far from irrelevant, and the childlessness of the Macbeths is thematically central to Shakespeare's tragedy. Likewise, the most telling comment one could make on Kitheri in *The Sparrow* would be Macduff's highly charged line "He has no children" (Shakespeare 1990: 4.3.216). This simultaneously offers at least a partial explanation for his Sadeian tendencies, while allowing us to see him as in some sense a tragic double of Emilio who has remained true to his Jesuit vow of celibacy, to the extent of renouncing a genuine chance of happiness with Sofia Mendes. When he moves aside to allow Jimmy Quinn to court her, he is fully aware of the price he is paying: "What was dying, he recognized in those quiet hours, was the possibility of himself as a husband and a father" (Russell 1997: 381). The merchant Supaari, another Jana'ata third-born, whose apparent "gross betrayal of Sandoz's trust" (Russell 1999: 28) had remained unexplained at the end of *The Sparrow*, was driven in part by a need to escape his ordained childlessness and he did what he did "for the sake of a son and a future" (Russell 1999: 83). Supaari, Kitheri, Emilio, and Sofia Mendes all in fact do have children eventually and it is these children which enable the second of the two novels, despite the threatening shadows of religious despair and genocide, to move "beyond tragedy" in the manner of Shakespeare's last plays. The title of the second of the two Rakhat novels proves to be as significant as that of the first, and the ghosts of all the murdered Runa children, including that of Askama whom Emilio killed himself, are at least partly exorcised when, in the closing pages of *Children of God*, a grandson is placed in the arms of the once celibate priest.

The central intellectual tension in many classical and Renaissance tragedies arises from the hope, persistently entertained despite the apparent evidence to the contrary, that the natural order should also be a moral order, as it is in Stoic philosophy and Judeo-Christian thinking. One of the most impressive features of Russell's two Rakhat novels is her ability to keep in play both scientific and moral discourses, neither of which succeeds in being wholly foundational, though the former makes clear the kinds of "necessity" which always circumscribe any moral choice. On the one hand there is a neutral, scientific attitude toward events, one which draws on the disciplines of biology, anthropology, zoology, and sociology, and on the other a highly emotional moral and religious concern for justice and love. Even in the depths of his despair, Emilio, as someone with scientific training, can give a logical and nonjudgmental account of the events which brought him to despair, though the logic he uncovers only serves to increase his suffering.

The moral and theological debates never seem overly abstract because they take place in a fully rendered material environment, which presses in upon the characters the whole time. One such debate, about whether God was invented as a way of giving the universe meaning, ends like this: " 'The human condition.' Frans sighed dramatically. 'How we suffer in our anxiety and ignorance!' He brightened. 'Which is why food and sex are so nice. Have you eaten?' he asked" (Russell 1999: 248).

The real point, however, is not that the appetites for food and sex are an agreeable escape from the anxieties of the human condition; it is that they *are* the human condition, part of the *ananke* to which all life is tragically subject. The early part of *The Sparrow* is filled with lighthearted banter about food and sex which seems initially to do little more than round out the various characters for us. However, the importance of meat for both humans and Jana'ata becomes thematically very significant. It is one of the sources of shame and horror for Emilio that, when near death, he cannot bring himself to refuse the meat offered him by the Jana'ata, even when he knows its origin. The sexual drive is the source of as much pain as joy for all three species and the problem of overpopulation is central to the scientific "correction" of instinctive feelings of moral outrage at the Jana'ata's treatment of the Runa. It also leads, in the second novel, to a schism between the Jesuits and the less scientifically aware majority of the Catholic Church on the issue of birth control. Humans, Jana'ata, and Runa all make moral choices, but not in the conditions of their choosing. Rather, they make them in the context of a natural order which may, or may not, have any moral component but which certainly has its own logic of necessity.

Enthusiasts for science fiction have often emphasized its cognitive aspect, the fact that it is a form of literature which, in its more rigorous forms, does claim to offer some genuine understanding of the world as it really is, rather than the world as we would like it to be. This can be true even of the more Utopian forms of science fiction, since they commonly leave us uncomfortably aware of everything in the nature of things (including human nature), which prevents us achieving Utopia. Tragedy, too, is usually argued to have an important cognitive dimension, represented most obviously by *dianoia* in Aristotle's list of the six key components of every tragic play. However, whereas science fiction is capable of playing with ideas in a relatively abstract way, the cognitive dimension of tragedy is inextricably linked to the stirring up of emotions, something of which Brecht was famously critical but which forms the basis for tragedy's claim to provide the most fully integrated account of the human condition. Ursula Le Guin wrote: "The only valid reason for excluding science fiction from the literary canon has been its predominant lack of passion – human and intellectual – and therefore of beauty" (Le Guin 1989: 183). Mary Doria Russell writes with great moral passion while also, and paradoxically, writing with the *dispassion* of someone who respects the authority of science's "vision of nature as an impersonal order." Like the Greeks and like Shakespeare, she would wish the moral order and the natural order to coincide at some level, but leaves us painfully aware of the continuing gap between them. The sparrow still falls and, within a frequently despised form of modern popular culture, tragedy continues to have a future.

Notes

1   See "Forms of Time and of the Chronotope in the Novel," in Bakhtin 1981: 84–258.
2   See the discussion of time in St. Augustine's *Confessions* (Augustine 1961: XI, 261–80). I am grateful to Mark Currie for letting me see, prior to publication, the typescript of his *About Time: Narrative, Fiction and the Philosophy of Time*, which includes an interesting discussion of this section of the *Confessions* as well as other ideas which I have found useful.
3   One obvious exception is the *Oresteia*, which in its entirety seems to prefigure an optimistic "Enlightenment" attitude to the possibility of progress.
4   Zeus struck down with a thunderbolt the physician Asclepius, son of Apollo, because his resurrections of the dead broke the laws of nature. The obvious exception to death's finality in tragedy is the *Alcestis* of Euripides, where the many references to death as inescapable and final are a prelude to the miraculous restoration of Alcestis to her husband Admetus. The fact that *Alcestis* was performed as the fourth play in a tetralogy, occupying the place normally filled by a satyr play, goes a long way toward accounting for its untypicality.
5   The list of awards received and the texts of many of the reviews, together with a collection of interesting interviews with Mary Doria Russell, can be conveniently located on her own web site: www.marydoriarussell.info

Afterword: Ending Tragedy

Catherine Silverstone

Let the atrocious images haunt us.
(Sontag 2003: 102)

The terms "tragedy" and "tragic," which variously describe a genre, an aesthetic, an experience, and the horror of personal and public events are, of course, notoriously difficult to define. All definitions – the fall of a hero, suffering, death, pity, fear, etc. – are necessarily partial, all too easily punctured by compelling counter-examples. Tragedy, then, would seem to be more easily accounted for in terms of "family resemblance," to appropriate Ludwig Wittgenstein's definition of a game in his *Philosophical Investigations* (1953), as others have done. This chain of resemblance provides a way of linking *The Oresteia* (458 BCE), *Titus Andronicus* (*c*.1592), *Three Sisters* (1901), *Endgame* (1957), and *Cleansed* (1998), for example, without necessarily making claims for the precise tragic commensurability of these texts. But this "catch-all" position does little to articulate what Ewan Fernie suggestively calls "the messy affective intensity of this most stirring and upsetting of art forms" (34).

Many of the chapters collected here attempt to wrestle with this "messy affective intensity" of tragedy, ranging widely across genres, periods, and cultures. In their engagement with what Sarah Annes Brown, in her Introduction, calls tragedy's "capacity to be adapted and transformed" (1), the chapters tend to argue for transhistorical, and sometimes transcendent, understandings of tragedy, using concepts such as disgust, suffering, childhood, and the "real" to forge links between different cultures' tragic productions. Indeed, while tragic criticism following Raymond Williams in *Modern Tragedy* (1966) has tended to focus on the ways in which tragedy emerges out of particular historical, social, and cultural contingencies, several of the chapters here propose a simultaneity of tragic experience across cultures, such as Neil Rhodes's consideration of the affinities between the work of G. Wilson Knight and Wole Soyinka. My task here in "Ending Tragedy" is not, however, to attempt a synthesis of the preceding chapters, a move that would only serve to diminish the range of the chapters, both individually and collectively. Rather, as I set about ending *Tragedy in Transition* I am concerned to offer a series of reflections on aspects of these chapters, especially in relation to representation and tragic criticism, suffering and ethical relations, the limits of the human, the possibilities for contemporary tragedy in the aftermath of the Holocaust, and what it might mean to speak of "ending tragedy."

Tragedy, Representation, and Criticism

In its repeated scenes of horror – both physical and psychological – tragedy works at the limits of representation. That is, it attempts to give shape to that which, by its very nature, seeks to hollow out the structures of representational practices, such as language. Elaine Scarry's arguments about pain help to elucidate this point; she contends that "Physical pain does not simply resist language but actively destroys it, bringing about an immediate reversion to a state anterior to language, to the sounds and cries a human being makes before language is learned" (Scarry 1985: 4). Similarly, I would suggest that at its most affective, tragedy, like pain, resists and even works to destroy the capacity of language to order, structure, and represent the world. Lear's anguished "Howl, howl, howl, howl!" in response to the death of Cordelia (5.3.231),[1] along with many of the instances of ellipsis identified in Anne C. Henry's chapter for this collection, work in just such a way, exposing the inadequacy of words to represent fully the suffering which tragedy often seeks to lay bare.

Tragedy, then, might be said to share certain structural affinities with trauma with respect to the "impossibility" of representation, theorized in the field of trauma studies by critics such as Cathy Caruth, Shoshana Felman, and Dori Laub. As Judith Butler summarizes, "trauma is, by definition, not capturable through representation, or, indeed, recollection;

it is precisely that which renders all memory false... and which is known through the gap that dispels all efforts at narrative reconstruction" (Butler 2004b: 153). Similarly, the horror that tragedy frequently seeks to explore does not emerge from normative structures of representation, but from moments when those structures break down. While this proposition can be glossed in terms of "representing the unrepresentable," this formulation seems inadequate, not least because it rests on a paradox: that which is unrepresentable cannot be represented (unless, of course, it forces a whole-sale reconfiguration of the structures of representation). Rather, to quote Jean-François Lyotard in a different context: "What art can do is bear witness not to the sublime, but to this aporia of art and to its pain. It does not say the unsayable, but it says that it cannot say it" (Lyotard 1990: 47). And it is in this unsayability – this aporia that opens in much tragic art – that tragedy is perhaps at its most affective. It works to confound conventional structures of representation, exposing something of the Nietz-schean Dionysian underbelly of the world, driving toward "the fragmenta-tion of the individual and his unification with primal being" (Nietzsche 1993: 44).

If tragic art can be read as an effort to engage with something of the horror "beneath," or the inexpressibility of suffering, writing about tragedy might, in its boldest conception, be seen as a version of this activity. That is, it might be seen as an attempt to replay (but necessarily with a difference, if only in terms of form) the affect and dangerous potential that inheres within tragedy. Tragedy is, after all, a mode of artistic production, broadly con-ceived, which seems always already implicated in challenges to social struc-tures and subjectivity. In this sense the role of the critic, as Fernie puts it, "is in part to stand for – to *suffer for* – the shaken reading" (and, I would add, spectating) subject (35; original emphasis), albeit in a partial and provisional capacity. Thus tragic criticism can attempt, in a kind of double movement, to give expression to that which tarries with the inexpressible, the unbear-able. As such, tragic criticism might on occasions be seen to operate performatively, working to bring the "abyss" into view and offering what Fernie calls an "adventure into tragedy's suppurating heart" (34). This journey does, however, produce a tension between formal structures of representation (of criticism, of art) and the horrific, excessive content of tragedy. And these tensions are variously explored in several of the chapters collected here, such as Lyne's adroit literary taxonomy of neoclassicism and its intimate connection with the unsettling structure-rupturing effects of tragedy.

Suffering and Ethical Relations

As an art form, tragedy is commonly associated with narratives of suffering. Criticism of tragedy, from ancient Greece to the present, has been similarly transfixed by this phenomenon. Indeed, the history of tragic criticism might be read as a series of attempts to account for these appalling moments of psychological and physical pain. In this vein, Terry Eagleton opens *Sweet Violence: The Idea of the Tragic* with a consideration of tragedy's "shared essence" of "the fact of suffering" (Eagleton 2003: xvi). This is a claim which Edith Hall develops in her chapter for this volume, arguing that suffering and its philosophical investigation give tragedy "as a literary form and theatrical medium . . . its sense of generic continuity" (27). One of the dominant ways in which suffering in tragedy has been conceived is, as Alison Hennegan explores in her chapter on Oscar Wilde, as a process of "suffering into wisdom," a narrative that resonates in Judeo-Christian theology. In this model, suffering is the mechanism for the positive transformation of the subject, usually in terms of a greater self-knowledge and awareness. But this construction of suffering as a means of personal growth is problematic. As Rowland Wymer notes, the unparalleled loss of human life in the Holocaust challenges attempts "to give suffering a meaning by seeing it as a necessary path to wisdom" (272). If the conception of suffering as a precondition of wisdom disintegrates in the face of the horror of the Holocaust, simultaneously calling into question its function more broadly, how then might its *longue durée* in tragedy be (re)conceived?

Taking my cue from cultural critiques of events such as the Holocaust and 9/11, one way in which suffering in tragedy might be accounted for is as a means of modelling ethical relations between subjects. In his chapter for this volume, Robert Douglas-Fairhurst engages with this possibility when he asks: "How can we bear witness to events which are unbearable to the figure experiencing them? How can we be loyal to another person's pain, confronted by events which rupture the sufferer's capacity for rational and articulate thought, and at the same time make sense of it?" (60). For Hall, "To be a witness of tragic suffering means being shackled to the seat of a god, conscious and yet completely incapacitated, to watch the mortal passion" (32). In this configuration, the spectator is compelled to observe, but unable to stop the suffering of the other. Vanda Zajko also considers these possibilities in her chapter which draws on Martha Nussbaum's work on tragedy and compassion. In this work Zajko explores the ways in which the suffering endured by both Prometheus and Frankenstein's monster can be figured as soliciting compassion, both within and exterior to the narrative. As she concludes her chapter, Zajko draws out the implications of establishing compassion for the other, asking "how is it possible to conceptualize the influence of the other on the self without domesticating or annihilating its radical 'otherness'?" and "What does it mean to claim that subjectivity is strictly relational, that a subject must bear the traces of every encounter with the external world?" (173).

Tragic encounters with the suffering of the other can be thought of in relation to how the subject might act (or not act) upon the other. But, to develop Zajko's apposite questions, they might also be thought of in terms of their effects on the witnessing subject. To employ Butler's words, these encounters can be conceptualized as asking not "for recognition for what one already is" but as working "to solicit a becoming, to instigate a transformation, to petition the future always in relation to the Other" (Butler 2004a: 44). That is, to witness narratives of tragic suffering, which inevitably involve an encounter with the other – a term which carries the freight of individual others and that which is Other, as the term has been developed in psychoanalytic and poststructural theory and Levinasian ethics – is to be open to the way in which the encounter forces a transformation of the witnessing subject. To enter into a relation with the other, an other that is frequently subjected to suffering and death, is also to recognize both the "precarious life," to cite the title of Butler's book, of the other, and the self. One effect of this Levinasian recognition or "apprehension of the precariousness of life" (Butler 2004a: xvii) and the attendant corporeal and psychological vulnerability of the other, is the potential for an ethical relation of responsibility between the subject and the other, an other which is partly self-same, and just as easily annihilated.

For Jacques Derrida, an obligation of responsibility to the other simultaneously carries the failure of responsibility to all others, a problem that he explores via Abraham's sacrifice of Isaac to God:

> As soon as I enter into a relation with the absolute other, my absolute singularity enters into a relation with his on the level of obligation and duty...But of course, what binds me thus in my singularity to the absolute singularity of the other, immediately propels me into the space or risk of absolute sacrifice.
>
> (Derrida 1995: 68)

He continues, "I can respond only by sacrificing ethics, that is, by sacrificing whatever obliges me also to respond, in the same way, in the same instant, to all others" (Derrida 1995: 68). In this sense, the relation with the other, while invested with obligation, seems to entail a widespread failure of ethical relations, as such relations with all others must be sacrificed. However, tragedy, which provides multiple versions of the suffering other, carries the potential, at least, for an ethics of suffering that is in excess of a relation of singularity between the subject and the other. That is, it constantly shifts the object of responsibility, drawing the subject into a succession of relations with *others*, each of which works to reiterate the pervasiveness of suffering and the precariousness of life. As such, it forces a constant reassessment of the subject's ethical relations of responsibility and obligation to *many* others, notwithstanding the singularity of each encounter.

Borders of the Human

Jennifer Wallace begins her chapter on tragedy and exile with a description of the events that led to Walter Benjamin's suicide in a hotel room in Portbou on the border of France and Spain in 1940. Here tragedy occurs, literally, on the border, and Wallace goes on to explore a series of tragic border crossings – both "real" and creative – in relation to forced migration and exile. This association between tragedy and "the border" pervades, in more conceptual terms, many of the chapters in the volume, especially the discussions by Peter Hollindale, Anne C. Henry, Raphael Lyne, and Vanda Zajko. Tragedy pushes, then, variously at the boundaries of established conventions – of restraint, of form, of life stages, of behavior, and, most strikingly, of what it is to be human. Consider here the way in which Hollindale shows how the tragic feral child is caught between two modes of being, or the way in which Zakjo works through the ways in which Frankenstein's monster, an exemplary product of a humanist education, is unable to sustain recognition, within the narrative, as a human subject.

In examining the limits of the human, these narratives often concurrently probe the limits of what Butler, in one of her chapters in response to 9/11, calls a *"grievable life"* (Butler 2004a: 20; original emphasis). For instance, *Titus Andronicus* opens with Titus' efforts to claim the lives of his children as grievable, alongside his rejection of the same status to Tamora's sons.

Indeed, the sacrifice of Tamora's son Alarbus is used to affirm that Titus' sons have lived grievable lives; Titus asserts "and die he must,/T'appease their groaning shadows that are gone" (1.1.125–6). In Titus and Tamora's efforts to exact revenge for the deaths and mutilation of their children, *Titus Andronicus* might, then, be seen as tragedy that stems from competing efforts to establish what counts as a grievable life. This analysis is reinforced at the end of the play when Marcus announces the burial rites for his father, sister, and Saturninus, enabling them to be permanently memorialized. However, he refuses to extend the same rite to Tamora: she is figured as a carcass fit only to be thrown "forth to beasts and birds to prey" (5.3.197). Interestingly, Aaron is to be subjected to a vicious twist on Roman burial rites: he is to be set "breast-deep in earth and famish[ed]" (5.3.178), with death awaiting anyone who "relieves or pities him" (5.3.180). As such he is afforded neither an honorable death (in battle) nor a proper burial, and is hence denied the status of a grievable life.

One way to read these efforts to establish the boundaries of what counts as a "grievable life" is to see in these acts of mourning an attempt to demarcate the limits of what it is to be human. That is, explorations of what counts as a grievable life lead, in turn, to exclusions as to who, in Butler's words, is validated as "normatively human" (Butler 2004a: xv). To return to *Titus*, the designation of Tamora as carrion effectively denies her status as "human," whereas the mourning of Titus, Lavinia, and Saturninus ensures that they are invested and memorialized as human subjects. Consequently, the expulsion of those who no longer count (if they ever did) as human subjects allows the dominant forms of power to reassert themselves in these communities; the restitutions (or attempted restitutions) of order at the end of early modern tragedies, such as *Titus Andronicus*, lend themselves to being read in this way. However, those instances where tragedy pushes at the borders of definitions of the human and seeks to extend the range of what counts as a grievable life might be conceived as tragedy's potential to imagine, even if only briefly, alternative worlds which lay open the frailty of dominant systems of power and human behaviors.

Contemporary Tragedy?

Much critical writing on tragedy returns time and again to the searing dramatic outputs of Ancient Greece and early modern England, and this collection is no exception. But here these texts are often located in transhistorical narratives, such as Fiona Macintosh's excavation of the changing "fates" of Medea and Oedipus from Ancient Greece and Rome to Gilles Deleuze and Félix Guattari's *Anti-Oedipus* (1972) and beyond, frequently proposing diachronic rather than synchronic understandings of tragedy. In considering the repeated turn to ancient Greece and early modern England, Douglas-Fairhurst observes that some tragic "theorists, from Hegel onwards, have pointed out that tragedy often emerges particularly strongly at moments of historical transition" (76). It is thus perhaps surprising that, despite several sustained discussions, the chapters in this volume tend to give less weight to tragedies produced in the later twentieth and early twenty-first centuries, a period which has registered (and continues to register) massive political and cultural change and violence on an unprecedented global scale. For Susan Sontag in her 1964 article "Reflections on *The Deputy*":

> The supreme tragic event of modern times is the murder of the six million European Jews. In a time which has not lacked in tragedies, this event most merits that unenviable honor – by reason of its magnitude, unity of theme, historical meaningfulness, and sheer opaqueness. For no one understands this event.
>
> ...
>
> We live in a time in which tragedy is not an art form but a form of history. Dramatists no longer write tragedies. But we do possess works of art (not always recognized as such) which reflect or attempt to resolve the great historical tragedies of our time. Among the unacknowledged art forms which have been devised or perfected in the modern era for this purpose are the psychoanalytic session, the parliamentary debate, the political rally, and the political trial. And as the supreme tragic event of modern times is the murder of six million European Jews, one of the most interesting and moving work of art of the past ten years is the trial of Adolf Eichmann in Jerusalem in 1961.
>
> (Sontag 1966: 124, 125)

While tragic art is usually distinguished from tragic events, Sontag here redefines tragedy as a "form of history," rather than an art form, appropriating the conventional Aristotelian terminology of classical tragedy – magnitude, unity of theme – for the Holocaust. In a move which figures public acts as a mode of tragic performance, Sontag defines tragedy as a therapeutic process (which resonates with the classical notion of *catharsis*), which "reflect[s] or attempt[s] to resolve the great historical tragedies of our time."

Sontag's contention that modern drama has failed to engage with tragedy, as she conceives it, has been echoed, more generally, by commentators who have argued for the failure of art in the face of the cataclysmic event of the Holocaust. Perhaps the most arresting example of this position is Theodor W. Adorno's famous injunction that "To write poetry after Auschwitz is barbaric" (Adorno 1981: 34) in his postwar essay "Cultural Criticism and Society." While he later softened this claim, asserting that "Perennial suffering has as much right to expression as a tortured man has to scream; hence it may have been wrong to say that after Auschwitz you could no longer write poems" (Adorno 1973: 362), the force of his earlier sentiment continues in his claim that "All post-Auschwitz culture, including its urgent critique, is garbage" (Adorno 1973: 367). With brutalizing clarity Adorno points to the way in which all efforts to engage with the horror of Auschwitz are inadequate, detritus to be thrown away.

Standing as what Maurice Blanchot calls *"the* absolute *event of history – which is a date in history – that utter-burn where all history took fire, where the movement of Meaning was swallowed up"* (Blanchot 1986: 47; original emphasis), the Holocaust is a gaping tragic wound into which all attempts at representation seem to tumble. Indeed, Giorgio Agamben's *Remnants of Auschwitz* is a profound engagement with the notion of bearing witness "to something it is impossible to bear witness to" (Agamben 1999: 13). Yet efforts to engage with the Holocaust and also with post-holocaust atrocities, other histories of devastation, such as those wrought by colonization and slavery, and with suffering and the planes of human experience that seem to elude conventional forms of representation, persist in contemporary criticism such as Agamben's and also in forms of tragic production. Tragedy might, then, be seen as a response to Sontag's recent call – "Let the atrocious images haunt us" (Sontag 2003: 102) – standing as a kind of palimpsest of horror. This is evidenced most strikingly in this collection by Wymer's discussion of the long shadow of the Holocaust which is cast over Mary Doria Russell's vision of the future in her Rakhat novels, Mark Houlahan's engagement with the tragic afterlives of John Ford's *'Tis Pity She's a Whore*, especially with the sadistic nightmare world of Sarah Kane's *Cleansed*, and Fernie's journey through the excoriating psychological and physical terrain of Cormac McCarthy's *Blood Meridian*.

Ending Tragedy

At the end of his elegant chapter on the relationships between science fiction and tragedy, Wymer suggests that "within a frequently despised form of modern popular culture, tragedy continues to have a future" (275). Indeed, while many of the chapters collected here look backwards, they also look forward, such as John Henderson's riff on the remaking (or remixing) of the Roman "tragic brand" in early modern England, which, he argues, produces "a strategy for Tragedy with a prolific future" (122). Tragedy, then, stands Janus-like: it accretes past forms but also attempts to engage with what, in Hall's words, "lies beyond empirically, materially discernible human experience" (27). This is a phrase that at once describes the metaphysical concerns of much tragedy but also encapsulates "the future." To name this Afterword "Ending Tragedy" might, then, stand as a misplaced pun, especially in relation to the breadth of the chapters collected here, which, collectively, point to the ongoing possibilities for tragedy, possibilities exemplified by the collection's title, *Tragedy in Transition*. However, I would like to suggest that the phrase "Ending Tragedy" might contain similar possibilities. It draws attention to the way in which tragedy is marked by an obsessive and ongoing concern with endings. This repeated playing out of endings, of individuals, regimes, and epochs, which often recall other texts, times, and cultures – concerns which are cogently expressed by Adrian Poole in his recent study of tragedy (Poole 2005: 112–23) – does not yet seem to have been exhausted. This proliferation of endings thus stands as a testament to tragedy's ongoing status as one of the key sites from which to interrogate the messy affective business of what it means to be and to cease to be in a world which is frequently figured as hostile and disordered. Endings are, of course, intimately connected with beginnings, and this ending looks forward to new beginnings – both creative and critical – which engage with tragedy's past, present, and future.

Note

1 All references to Shakespeare are to *The Norton Shakespeare*, edited by Stephen Greenblatt *et al.* (1997).

Bibliography

Adorno, T. W. (1973 [1966]) *Negative Dialectics*, trans. E. B. Ashton. London: Routledge & Kegan Paul.

—— (1981 [1955]) *Prisms*, trans. S. Weber and S. Weber. Cambridge, MA: MIT Press.

Aeschylus (1953) *Agamemnon, The Libation Bearers, The Eumenides*, ed. D. Grene and R. Lattimore. Chicago: University of Chicago Press.

—— (1957) *Agamemnon, Libation-Bearers, Eumenides, Fragments*, trans. H. W. Smyth. Cambridge, MA: Harvard University Press.

—— (1963) *Works*, trans. H. W. Smyth. 2 vols., vol. 2. London: William Heinemann.

—— (1979) *The Oresteia*, trans. R. Fagles. Harmondsworth: Penguin.

—— (1983) *Aeschylus: Prometheus Bound*, ed. M. Griffith. Cambridge: Cambridge University Press.

—— (1985) *Septem Contra Thebas*, ed. with intro. and commentary by G. O. Hutchinson. Oxford: Clarendon Press.

—— (1996a) *Persians*, ed. and trans. E. Hall. Warminster: Aris & Phillips.

—— (1996b [1922]) *Prometheus Bound*, trans. H. Weir Smyth. Cambridge, MA and London: Harvard University Press.

—— (2005) *Prometheus Bound*, trans. J. Kerr. London: Oberon.

Agamben, G. (1999) *Remnants of Auschwitz: The Witness and the Archive*, trans. D. Heller-Roazen. New York: Zone Books.

Aldiss, B., with D. Wingrove (1986) *Trillion Year Spree: The History of Science Fiction*. London: Gollancz.

Allen, D. C. (1966) *The Star-Crossed Renaissance: The Quarrel about Astrology and its Influence in England*. New York: Octagon Books.

Anonymous (1606) *No-body, and some-body With the true chronicle historie of Elydure, who was fortunately three seuerall times crowned King of England*. London.

Aristophanes (1982) *Clouds*, ed. and trans. A. H. Sommerstein. Warminster: Aris & Phillips.

Aristotle (1974) *Poetics*, trans. L. Golden. In A. Preminger et al. (eds.), *Classical Literary Criticism: Translations and Interpretations*, pp. 97–139. New York: Fredrick Ungar.

—— (1991) *Poetics* in D. A. Russell and M. Winterbotham (eds.), *Classical Literary Criticism*. Oxford: World's Classics.

—— (1996) *The Politics and the Constitution of Athens*, ed. S. Everson. Cambridge: Cambridge University Press.

Arkins, B. (1995) Greek Themes in Donna Tartt's *The Secret History*. *Classical and Modern Literature*, 15: 281–7.

Armstrong, R. H. (2005) *A Compulsion for Antiquity: Freud and the Ancient World*. Ithaca, NY and London: Cornell University Press.

—— (forthcoming) Theory and Theatricality: Classical Drama and the Early Formation of Psychoanalysis. *Classical and Modern Literature*, 26.

Artaud, A. (1985) *The Theatre and its Double*, trans. V. Corti. London: John Calder.

Astley, N. (1991) *Tony Harrison*. Newcastle upon Tyne: Bloodaxe Books.

Augustine, St. (1961) *Confessions*, trans. R. S. Pine-Coffin. Harmondsworth: Penguin.

Bakhtin, M. (1968 [1965]) *Rabelais and his World*, trans. H. Iswolsky. Cambridge, MA: MIT Press.

—— (1981) *The Dialogic Imagination: Four Essays*, trans. C. Emerson and M. Holquist, ed. M. Holquist. Austin: University of Texas Press.

Barish, J. (1981) *The Antitheatrical Prejudice*. Berkeley, Los Angeles, and London: University of California Press.

Barrie, J. M. (1906) *Peter Pan in Kensington Gardens*. London: Hodder & Stoughton.

—— (1911) *Peter and Wendy*. London: Hodder & Stoughton.

—— (1924) *Mary Rose*. London: Hodder & Stoughton.

Barthes, R. (1988) The Death of the Author. In D. Lodge (ed.), *Modern Criticism and Theory: A Reader*. London: Longman.

Batstone, W. W. (1986) *Incerta pro certis*. An interpretation of Sallust *Bellum Catilinae* 48.4–49.4. *Ramus*, 15: 105–21.

—— (1988) The Antithesis of Virtue. Sallust's Synkrisis and the Crisis of the Late Republic. *Classical Antiquity*, 7: 1–29.

—— (1994) Cicero's Construction of Consular *ethos* in the *First Catilinarian*. *Transactions of the American Philological Association*, 124: 211–66.

Baudelaire, C. (1955 [1855]) On the Essence of Laughter. In J. Mayne (ed.), *The Mirror of Art*. London: Phaidon Press.

Beckett, S. (1964 [1957]) *Endgame*. London: Faber & Faber.

—— (1984) *Collected Shorter Plays*. London: Faber & Faber.

—— (1988) *Waiting for Godot*. London: Faber & Faber.

Benjamin, J. (1988) *The Bonds of Love: Psychoanalysis, Feminism, and the Problem of Domination*. New York: Pantheon.

Benjamin, W. (1973) *Illuminations*, ed. H. Arendt, trans. H. Zohn. London: Fontana.

—— (1978) *Reflections: Essays, Aphorisms, Autobiographical Writings*, ed. P. Demetz, trans. E. Jephcott. New York: Harcourt Brace Jovanovich.

—— (1979) *One-Way Street and Other Writings*. London: New Left Books.

—— (1980) *Gesammelte Schriften*, ed. R. Tiedemann and H. Schweppenhäuser. Frankfurt am Main: Suhrkamp.

Bertman, S. L. (1991) Children and Death: Insights, Hindsights and Illuminations. In D. Papadatou and C. Papadatos (eds.), *Children and Death*, pp. 311–29. New York: Hemisphere.

Bhabha, H. (1994) *The Location of Culture*. London and New York: Routledge.

Biet, C. (1994) *Oedipe en monarchie: tragédie et théorie juridique à l'âge classique*. Paris: Klincksieck.

Birkin, A. (1979) *J. M. Barrie and the Lost Boys*. London: Constable.

Bishop, N. (1993) A Nigerian Version of a Greek Classic: Soyinka's Transformation of *The Bacchae*. In Gibbs and Lindfors (eds.), pp. 115–126.

Blanchot, M. (1986 [1980]) *The Writing of the Disaster*, trans. A. Smock. Lincoln and London: University of Nebraska Press.

Blayney, Peter W. M. (1982) *The Texts of King Lear and their Origins. Volume I: Nicholas Okes and the First Quarto*. Cambridge: Cambridge University Press.

Bloom, H. (1998) *Shakespeare: The Invention of the Human*. New York: Riverhead Books.

Boehrer, B. T. (1992) *Monarchy and Incest in Renaissance England: Literature, Culture, Kinship and Kingship*. Philadelphia: University of Pennsylvania Press.

Booth, S. (1983) *King Lear, Macbeth, Indefinition and Tragedy*. New Haven, CT and London: Yale University Press.

Bosman, A. (2004) Renaissance Intertheater and the Staging of Nobody. *English Literary History*, 71: 559–85.

Boyd, B. W. (1987) *Virtus Effeminata* and Sallust's Sempronia. *Transactions of the American Philological Association*, 117: 183–211.

Boyle, A. J. (1997) *Tragic Seneca. An Essay in the Theatrical Tradition*. London: Routledge.

—— (2006) *An Introduction to Roman Tragedy*. London: Routledge.

Braden, G. (1985) *Renaissance Tragedy and the Senecan Tradition*. New Haven, CT: Yale University Press.

Bradley, A. C. (1904) *Shakespearean Tragedy*. London and New York: Macmillan.

Bradshaw, G. (1993) *Misrepresentations: Shakespeare and the Materialists*. Ithaca, NY and London: Cornell University Press.

Bratchell, D. F. (1990) *Shakespearean Tragedy*. London and New York: Routledge.

Brereton, G. (1968) *Principles of Tragedy*. London: Routledge & Kegan Paul.

Brockbank, P. (1983) Blood and Wine: Tragic Ritual from Aeschylus to Soyinka. *Shakespeare Survey*, 36: 11–19.

Brontë, Emily (1990 [1847]) *Wuthering Heights*. New York and London: W. W. Norton.

Brooks, P. (1993) *Body Work*. Harvard, MA: Harvard University Press.

Browning, R. (1971 [1868–9]) *The Ring and the Book*, ed. R. D. Altick. Harmondsworth: Penguin.

Buckley, G. T. (1962) "These Late Eclipses" Again. *Shakespeare Quarterly*, 13: 253–6.

Budelmann, F. (2004) Greek Tragedies in West African Adaptations. *Proceedings of the Cambridge Philological Society*, 50: 1–28.

Bullough, G. (ed.) (1957–75) *Narrative and Dramatic Sources of Shakespeare*, 8 vols. London: Routledge & Kegan Paul.

Burian, P. (1997) Myth into *Muthos*: The Shaping of Tragic Plot. In Easterling (ed.), pp. 178–208.

Burkhard, A. (1961) *Franz Grillparzer in England and America*. Vienna: Bergland.

Bushnell, R. W. (1988) *Prophesying Tragedy: Sign and Voice in Sophocles' Theban Plays*. Ithaca, NY and London: Cornell University Press.

Butler, C. (1633) *The English Grammar or the Institution of Letters, Syllables, and Words in the English Tongue*. London.

Butler, J. (2004a) *Precarious Life: The Powers of Mourning and Violence*. London and New York: Verso.

—— (2004b) *Undoing Gender*. London: Routledge.

Byatt, A. S. (1978) *The Virgin in the Garden*. Harmondsworth: Penguin.

—— (1985) *Still Life*. London: Chatto & Windus.

—— (1996) *Babel Tower*. London: Chatto & Windus.

—— (2002) *A Whistling Woman*. London: Chatto & Windus.

Camus, A. (1975) *The Myth of Sisyphus*, trans. J. O'Brien. Harmondsworth: Penguin.

—— (1983) *The Outsider*, trans. J. Laredo. Harmondsworth: Penguin.

Candland, D. K. (1993) *Feral Children and Clever Animals*. New York and Oxford: Oxford University Press.

Carpenter, E. (1895 [1889]) *Civilisation: Its Cause and Cure and Other Essays*. London: Swan Sonnenschein.

—— (1915 [1902]) *Iolaüs: Anthology of Friendship*. London: George Allen & Unwin.

—— (1920 [1896]) *Love's Coming of Age*. London: Methuen.

Carter, A. (1985) Peter and the Wolf. In *Black Venus*. London: Chatto & Windus.

—— (1995) *Burning Your Boats: Collected Short Stories*. London: Chatto & Windus.

Cartledge, P. (1993) *The Greeks: A Portrait of Self and Others*. Oxford: Oxford University Press.

Cavell, S. (1987) *Disowning Knowledge in Six Plays of Shakespeare*. Cambridge: Cambridge University Press.

Chekhov, A. (2003) *Three Sisters*, trans. M. Frayn. London: Methuen.

Chodorow, N. (1978) *The Reproduction of Mothering: Psychoanalysis and the Sociology of Gender*. Berkeley: University of California Press.

Cixous, H. (1978) *Le Nom d'Oedipe: Chant du corps interdit*. Paris: Éditions des Femmes.

Clarke, A. C. (1982) *Profiles of the Future: An Inquiry into the Limits of the Possible*. 2nd rev. ed. London: Gollancz.

—— (1990 [1953]) *Childhood's End*. London: Pan.

Classen, C., Howes, D., and Synnott, A. (1994) *Aroma: the Cultural History of Smell*. London: Routledge.

Clauss, H. J. and Johnston, S. I. (eds.) (1997) *Medea: Essays on Medea in Myth, Literature, Philosophy and Art*. Princeton, NJ: Princeton University Press.

Clifford, J. (1997) *Routes: Travel and Translation in the Late Twentieth Century.* Cambridge, MA: Harvard University Press.

Coetzee, J. M. (1998) *Disgrace*. London: Secker & Warburg.

Coleridge, H. (ed.) (n.d.) *The Dramatic Works of Massinger and Ford, with an Introduction by Hartley Coleridge. A New Edition*. London: George Routledge.

Corti, L. (1998) *The Myth of Medea and the Murder of Children*. Westport, CT and London: Greenwood Press.

Crahay, R. (1956) *La Littérature oraculaire chez Hérodote*. Paris: Les Belles Lettres.

Croally, N. (1994) *Euripidean Polemic: The Trojan Women and the Function of Tragedy.* Cambridge: Cambridge University Press.

Crow, B. with C. Banfield (1996) *An Introduction to Post-Colonial Theatre*. Cambridge: Cambridge University Press.

Cunningham, H. (1995) *Children and Childhood in Western Society since 1500*. London: Longman.

Currie, M. (2007) *About Time: Narrative, Fiction and the Philosophy of Time*. Edinburgh: Edinburgh University Press.

Dante (1971) *The Divine Comedy: Inferno*, trans. D. Sayers. Harmondsworth: Penguin.

Darwin, C. (1965 [1872]) *The Expression of the Emotions in Man and Animals*. Chicago: University of Chicago Press.

Dastur, F. (2000) Tragedy and Speculation. In de Beistegui and Sparks (eds.), pp. 78–87.

de Beistegui, S. and S. Sparks (eds.) (2000) *Philosophy and Tragedy.* London and New York: Routledge.

Deleuze, G. and F. Guattari (1983) *Anti-Oedipus: Capitalism and Schizophrenia*, trans. R. Hurley, M. Seem, and H. R. Lane. Minneapolis: University of Minnesota Press.

Delgado, M. M. and P. Heritage (1996) *In Contact with the Gods: Directors Talk Theatre*. Manchester: Manchester University Press.

Derrida, J. (1993) *Dissemination*, trans. B. Johnson. London: Athlone Press.

—— (1995 [1992]). *The Gift of Death*, trans. D. Wills. Chicago and London: University of Chicago Press.

—— (2002) *Acts of Religion*, ed. G. Andijar. London and New York: Routledge.

Dick, P. K. (1972) *Do Androids Dream of Electric Sheep?* London: Grafton.

Dickens, C. (1957) *Pictures from Italy.* Oxford: Oxford University Press.

—— (2001 [1848]) *Dombey and Son*. Oxford: Oxford University Press.

Dodds, E. R. (1973) *The Ancient Concept of Progress and other Essays on Greek Literature and Belief*. Oxford: Clarendon Press.

Dollimore, J. (1998) *Death, Desire and Loss in Western Culture*. London: Allen Lane, Penguin.

—— (2004 [1984]) *Radical Tragedy*. Brighton: Harvester.

Dougherty, C. (2006) *Prometheus*. London and New York: Routledge.

Douglas, M. (1966) *Purity and Danger: An Analysis of Concepts of Pollution and Taboo*. London: Routledge & Kegan Paul.

Dowling, L. (1996) *Hellenism and Homosexuality in Victorian Oxford*. Ithaca, NY and London: Cornell University Press.

Dryden, J. (1964) *Of Dramatick Poesie: An Essay*, ed. J. T. Boulton. Oxford: Oxford University Press.

—— (1984) *The Works of John Dryden: Plays* Vol. XIII: *All for Love, Oedipus, Troilus and Cressida*, ed. M. E. Novak. Berkeley and Los Angeles: University of California Press.

Eagleton, T. (2003) *Sweet Violence: the Idea of the Tragic*. Oxford: Blackwell.

Easterling, P. E. (ed.) (1997) *The Cambridge Companion to Greek Tragedy*. Cambridge: Cambridge University Press.

Eitner, L. (ed.) (1970) *Neoclassicism and Romanticism 1750–1850*. 2 vols. Englewood Cliffs, NJ: Prentice-Hall.

Eliot, G. (1986) *Daniel Deronda*. London: Penguin.

Eliot, T. S. (1950 [1920]) *The Sacred Wood: Essays on Poetry and Criticism*. London: Methuen.

—— (1971) *The Waste Land*, ed. V. Eliot. London: Faber & Faber.

Ellmann, M. (1994) Introduction. In *Psychoanalytic Literary Criticism*. London and New York: Longman.

Elton, W. R. (1966) *King Lear and the Gods*. San Marino, CA: The Huntington Library.

Epps, P. H. (1933) Fear in Spartan Character. *Classical Philology*, 18: 12–29.

Euripides (1865) *The Bacchanals*, trans. H. H. Milman. London.

—— (1959) *Electra, The Phoenician Women, The Bacchae*, eds. D. Grene and R. Lattimore. Chicago: University of Chicago Press.

—— (1963) *Hecuba, Andromache, The Trojan Women*, ed. D. Grene and R. Lattimore. Chicago: University of Chicago Press.

—— (1986) *Trojan Women*, with translation and commentary by S. A. Barlow. Warminster, England: Aris & Phillips.

—— (1988) *Electra*, with translation and commentary by M. J. Cropp. Warminster, England: Aris & Phillips.

—— (1998) *Medea*, trans. J. Morwood. Oxford: Oxford University Press.

—— (2000) Bacchae *and Other Plays*, ed. and trans. James Morwood. Oxford: Oxford University Press.

—— (2001 [1996]) *Bacchae*, with an introduction, translation and commentary by R. Sleaford. Warminster, England: Aris & Phillips.

Ewbank, I.-S. (2005) "Striking Too Short at Greeks": The Transmission of *Agamemnon* to the English Renaissance Stage. In Macintosh, Michelakis, Hall, and Taplin (eds.), pp. 37–52.

Fanon, F. (1967) *The Wretched of the Earth*, trans. C. Farrington. Harmondsworth: Penguin.

Fantham, E. (ed.) (1982) *Seneca's* Troades: *A Literary Introduction with Text, Translation, and Commentary.* Princeton, NJ: Princeton University Press.

Fernie, E. (2005) The Last Act: Presentism, Spirituality and the Politics of *Hamlet*. In E. Fernie (ed.), *Spiritual Shakespeares*, pp. 186–211. London and New York: Routledge.

Flashar, H. (1991) *Inszenierung der Antike: das griechische Drama auf der Bühne der Neuzeit*. Munich: C. H. Beck.

Foley, H. (2004) Bad Women: Gender Politics in Late Twentieth-Century Performance and Revision of Greek Tragedy. In Hall, Macintosh, and Wrigley (eds.), pp. 77–112.

Fontenrose, J. (1978) *The Delphic Oracle: Its Responses and Operations, with a Catalogue of Responses.* Berkeley and London: University of California Press.

Ford, J. (1975) *'Tis Pity She's a Whore*, ed. D. Roper. London: Methuen.

—— (1986) *The Selected Plays of John Ford*, ed. C. Gibson. Cambridge: Cambridge University Press.

Forsyth, A. (2002) *Gadamer, History, and the Classics: Fugard, Marowitz, Berkoff and Harrison Rewrite the Theatre.* New York: Peter Lang.

Foucault, M. (1977 [1975]) *Discipline and Punish*, trans. A. Sheridan. London: Allen Lane.

—— (1989) *The Order of Things.* London: Routledge.

Franken, C. (2001) *A. S. Byatt; Art, Authorship, Creativity.* London: Palgrave.

Fredericks, S. C. (1980) Greek Mythology in Modern Science Fiction. In W. Aycock and T. Klein (eds.), *Classical Mythology in Twentieth Century Thought and Literature*, pp. 89–106. Lubbock: Texas Tech Press.

Freud, S. (1985) *The Complete Letters of Sigmund Freud to Wilhelm Fliess, 1887–1904*, ed. and trans. J. M. Masson. Cambridge, MA: Harvard University Press.

—— (1991) *Case Histories: Rat Man, Schreber, Wolf Man, Case of Female Homosexuality.* London: Penguin.

Frye, N. (1971 [1957]) *Anatomy of Criticism: Four Essays.* Princeton, NJ: Princeton University Press.

Gellrich, M. (1988) *Tragedy and Theory: The Problem of Conflict since Aristotle.* Princeton, NJ: Princeton University Press.

Gevers, N. (2007) Of Prayers and Predators: An Interview with Mary Doria Russell, Jan. 5. http://www.iplus.zetnet.co.uk/nonfiction/intmdr.htm

Gibbs, J. M. (1984) Wole Soyinka: The Making of a Dramatist. PhD thesis, University of Leeds.

—— (2001) Soyinka in Zimbabwe: A Question and Answer Session [1981]. In B. Jeyifo (ed.), *Conversations with Wole Soyinka*. Jackson: University of Mississippi Press.

Gibbs, J. M. and Lindfors, B. (1993) *Research on Wole Soyinka*, Lawrenceville, NJ: Africa World Press.

Gildon, Charles (1698) *Phaeton, or the Fatal Divorce*. London.

Godwin, T. (1970) The Cold Equations. In R. Silverberg (ed.), *Science Fiction Hall of Fame*. New York: Avon.

Goffman, E. (1971) Territories of the Self. In *Relations in Public*. New York: Basic Books.

Goldhill, S. (1986) *Reading Greek Tragedy.* Cambridge: Cambridge University Press.

—— (1996) Collectivity and Otherness: The Authority of the Tragic Chorus: Response to Gould. In Silk (ed.), pp. 217–56.

Golding, W. (1954) *Lord of the Flies*. London: Faber & Faber.

Gomme, A. W. (1975) *A Historical Commentary on Thucydides*, vol. 1. Oxford: Clarendon Press.

Goodman, J. (1988) *The Oscar Wilde File*. London: Allison & Busby.

Gould, J. (1983) Homeric Epic and the Tragic Moment. In T. Winnifrith, P. Murray, and K. W. Gransden (eds.) (1983), *Aspects of the Epic*, pp. 32–45. London: Macmillan.

—— (1996) Tragedy and Collective Experience. In Silk (ed.), pp. 217–43.

Grady, H. (1991) *The Modernist Shakespeare: Critical Texts in a Material World*. Oxford: Clarendon Press.

Grafton, A. (2003) Some Uses of Eclipses in Early Modern Chronology. *Journal of the History of Ideas*, 64: 213–29.

Grene, D. and R. Lattimore (eds.) (1992) *The Complete Greek Tragedies*, 4 vols. Chicago and London: University of Chicago Press.

Hall, E. (2000a) Introduction to *Euripides:* The Trojan Women *and Other Plays*, trans. J. Morwood. Oxford: Oxford University Press.

Hall, E. (2000b) *Medea* on the Eighteenth-Century London Stage. In Hall, Macintosh, and Taplin (eds.), pp. 49–74.

—— (2002) The Ancient Actor's Presence since the Renaissance. In P. Easterling and E. Hall (eds.), *Greek and Roman Actors*, pp. 419–34. Cambridge: Cambridge University Press.

—— (2006) *The Theatrical Cast of Athens*. Oxford: Oxford University Press.

Hall, E. and F. Macintosh (2005) *Greek Tragedy and the British Theatre 1660–1914*. Oxford: Oxford University Press.

Hall, E., F. Macintosh, and O. Taplin (eds.) (2000) *Medea in Performance*. Oxford: European Humanities Research Centre.

Hall, E., F. Macintosh, and A. Wrigley (eds.) (2004) *Dionysus since 69: Greek Tragedy at the Dawn of the Third Millennium*. Oxford: Oxford University Press.

Hall, R. (1928) *The Well of Loneliness*. London: Jonathan Cape.

Hardwick, L. (2004) Greek Drama and Anti-Colonialism. In Hall, Macintosh, and Wrigley (eds.), pp. 219–42.

Hardy, T. (1978 [1891]) *Tess of the d'Urbervilles*. Harmondsworth: Penguin.

—— (2002 [1895]) *Jude the Obscure*. Oxford: Oxford University Press.

Hardyment, C. (1992) Looking at Children: The History of Childhood 1600 to the Present. In S. Holdsworth and J. Crossley (eds.), *Innocence and Experience: Images of Children in British Art from 1600 to the Present.* Manchester: Manchester City Art Galleries.

Harrison, T. (1990) *The Trackers of Oxyrhynchus.* London: Faber

—— (1992) *The Common Chorus.* London: Faber & Faber.

—— (1995) *Selected Poems.* Harmondsworth: Penguin.

Hattaway, M. (ed.) (2002) *The Cambridge Companion to Shakespeare's History Plays.* Cambridge: Cambridge University Press.

Heaney, S. (1990) *The Cure at Troy: A Version of Sophocles'* Philoctetes. London: Faber & Faber.

Hegel, G. W. F. (1975) *Hegel on Tragedy,* ed. A. and H. Paolucci. New York and London: Harper & Row.

Heidegger, M. (1962) *Being and Time,* trans. J. Macquarrie and E. Robinson. Oxford: Blackwell.

Heinlein, R. A. (1980) *"– All You Zombies –."* In *The Unpleasant Profession of Jonathan Hoag.* London: New English Library (Hodder & Stoughton).

Helms, L. (1992) "The High Roman Fashion": Sacrifice, Suicide, and the Shakespearean Stage. *Publications of the Modern Language Association,* 107: 554–65.

Henderson, J. (1998) *Fighting For Rome. Poets and Caesars, History and Civil War.* Cambridge: Cambridge University Press.

Henry, A. C. (2005) Quid ais Omnium? The emergence of suspension marks in Early Modern Drama. *Renaissance Drama,* 35: 47–67.

Herodotus (1908) *The Seventh, Eighth and Ninth Books with Introduction, Text, Apparatus, Commentary, Appendices, Indices, Maps,* ed. R. W. Macan. London: Macmillan.

—— (2003 [1954]) *The Histories,* trans. A. de Sélincourt, rev. with intro. and notes by J. Marincola. London: Penguin.

Hesse, H. (1973 [1905]) *The Prodigy,* trans. W. J. Strachan. Harmondsworth: Penguin.

Heywood, T. (1961) *A Woman Killed with Kindness,* ed. R. W. Van Fossen. London: Methuen.

Hill, S. (1970) *I'm the King of the Castle.* London: Hamish Hamilton.

Hölderlin, F. (1988) *Essays and Letters on Theory,* ed. T. Pfau. Albany: State University of New York Press.

Holland, M. (2003) *Irish Peacock and Scarlet Marquess: The Real Trial of Oscar Wilde.* London: Fourth Estate.

Holloway, J. (1961) *The Story of the Night: Studies in Shakespeare's Major Tragedies.* London: Routledge & Kegan Paul.

Homer (1924) *Iliad,* trans. A. T. Murray, 2 vols. London: William Heinemann.

Hornblower, S. (1991) *A Commentary on Thucydides.* Oxford: Clarendon Press.

Hughes, D. (1996) *English Drama 1660–1700.* Oxford: Clarendon Press.

Hughes, J. (1990) *Reshaping the Psychoanalytical Domain: The Work of Melanie Klein, W. R. D. Fairbairn, and D. W. Winnicott.* Berkeley, CA, and London: University of California Press.

Hughes, T. (1998) *Racine's* Phèdre *in a new version by Ted Hughes.* London: Faber & Faber.

Huk, R. (1993) Postmodern Classics: The Verse Drama of Tony Harrison. In J. Acheson (ed.), *British and Irish Drama since 1960.* Basingstoke: Palgrave Macmillan.

Huntington, J. (1989) *Rationalizing Genius: Ideological Strategies in the Classic American Science Fiction Story.* New Brunswick, NJ and London: Rutgers University Press.

Huxley, A. (1934 [1932]) *Brave New World.* London: Chatto & Windus.

—— (1961 [1923]) Tragedy and the Whole Truth. In H. Raymond (ed.), *Selected Essays.* London: Chatto & Windus.

Hyde, H. M. (1948) *The Trials of Oscar Wilde.* London, Edinburgh, and Glasgow: William Hodge.

Ibsen, H. (1971) *An Enemy of the People,* trans. J. W. McFarlane. Oxford: Oxford University Press.

—— (1986) *Plays: Five,* trans. M. Mayer. London: Methuen.

Inwood, B. (ed.) (2003) *The Cambridge Companion to the Stoics.* Cambridge: Cambridge University Press.

Irwin, D. (1997) *Neoclassicism.* London: Phaidon.

Jack, R. D. S. (1991) *The Road to the Never Land.* Aberdeen: Aberdeen University Press.

James, C. (1991) *Clive James on Television.* London: Picador.

Jameson, F. (1982) Progress versus Utopia: or, Can We Imagine the Future? *Science-Fiction Studies,* 27: 147–58.

Jefferson, D. W. (ed.) (1969) *The Morality of Art: Essays Presented to G. Wilson Knight by his Colleagues and Friends.* London: Routledge & Kegan Paul.

Jeyifo, B. (2004) *Wole Soyinka: Politics, Poetics and Postcolonialism.* Cambridge: Cambridge University Press.

Johnson, S. (1960) *Samuel Johnson on Shakespeare,* ed. W. K. Wimsatt, Jr. London: Macgibbon & Kee.

Jones, E. (1953), *Sigmund Freud: Life and Work. Vol. I: The Young Freud 1856–1900.* London: Hogarth Press.

Jones, J. (1962) *On Aristotle and Greek Tragedy.* London: Chatto & Windus.

Jonson, B. (1640) *Workes,* 2 vols. London.

—— (1925–53) *The Works of Ben Jonson,* ed. C. H. Herford, P. Simpson, and E. Simpson. Oxford: Oxford University Press.

—— (1973) *Catiline,* ed. W. F. Bolton and J. F. Gardner. London: Arnold.

—— (1990) *Sejanus. His Fall,* ed. P. J. Ayres. Manchester: Manchester University Press.

Joyce, J. (1960 [1916]) *Portrait of the Artist as a Young Man.* Harmondsworth: Penguin.

—— (1968 [1922]) *Ulysses.* Harmondsworth: Penguin.

Kakridis, J. T. (1975) Licht und Finsternis in dem Botenbericht der Perser des Aischylos. *Grazer Beiträge*, 4: 145–54.

Kane, S. (2001) *Complete Plays*. London: Methuen.

Katrak, K. H. (1986) *Wole Soyinka and Modern Tragedy: A Study of Dramatic Theory and Practice*. Westport, CT: Greenwood Press.

Kaufmann, W. (1968) *Tragedy and Philosophy*. New York: Doubleday.

Keats, J. (1970) *The Poems of John Keats*. London: Longman.

Kelleher, J. (1996) *Tony Harrison*. Plymouth: Northcote House.

Kierkegaard, S. (1944) *Either/Or*, trans. D. F. and L. M. Swenson. 2 vols., vol. 2. London: Oxford University Press.

—— (1983 [1843]) *Fear and Trembling; Repetition*, trans. and ed. H. V. Hong and E. H. Hong. Princeton, NJ: Princeton University Press.

Kipling, R. (1987 [1895]) *The Second Jungle Book*. Oxford: Oxford University Press.

Knight, G. W. (1936) *Principles of Shakespearian Production*. London: Faber & Faber.

—— (1948) *Christ and Nietzsche*. London: Staples Press.

—— (1949 [1930]) *The Wheel of Fire*. Rev. ed. London: Methuen.

—— (1951) *The Imperial Theme*. 3rd ed. London: Methuen.

—— (1958) *The Sovereign Flower*. London: Methuen.

—— (1962) *The Golden Labyrinth*. London: Phoenix House.

—— (1967) The Avenging Mind. In *Shakespeare and Religion*. London: Routledge & Kegan Paul.

—— (1971) *Neglected Powers*. London: Routledge & Kegan Paul.

Knox, B. (1979) *Word and Action: Essays on the Ancient Theater*. Baltimore, MD and London: Johns Hopkins University Press.

Konstan, D. (1993) Rhetoric and the Crisis of Legitimacy in Cicero's Catilinarian Orations. In T. Poulakos (ed.), *Rethinking the History of Rhetoric: Multidisciplinary Essays on the Rhetorical Tradition*, pp. 11–30. Boulder, CO: Westview.

Kott, J. (1974) *The Eating of the Gods: An Interpretation of Greek Tragedy*, trans. B. Taborski and E. J. Czerwinski. London: Eyre Methuen.

Kragelund, P. (2002) Historical Drama in Ancient Rome: Republican Flourishing and Imperial Decline? *Symbolae Osloenses*, 77: 5–105.

Kristeva, J. (1982) *Powers of Horror: An Essay on Abjection*, trans. L. S. Roudiez. New York: Columbia University Press.

—— (1989) *Black Sun: Depression and Melancholia*, trans. L. S. Roudiez. New York: Columbia University Press.

Krook, D. (1969) *Elements of Tragedy*. New Haven, CT and London: Yale University Press.

Krostenko, B. A. (2004) Text and Context in the Roman Forum: The Case of Cicero's *First Catilinarian*. In W. Joost and W. Olmsted (eds.), *A Companion to Rhetoric and Rhetorical Criticism*, pp. 28–57. Oxford: Blackwell.

Lacan, J. (1977) Desire and the Interpretation of Desire in *Hamlet*. *Yale French Studies*, 55–6: 11–52.

—— (1999) *The Ethics of Psychoanalysis 1959–60: The Seminar of Jacques Lacan*, ed. J.-A. Miller, trans. D. Porter. London: Routledge.

Lacroix, J. (1874) *Oeuvres de théâtre*, vol. III. Paris.

Laird, A. (ed.) (2006) *Ancient Literary Criticism*. Oxford: Oxford University Press.

Lamb, C. and M. A. Lamb (1976) *The Letters of Charles and Mary Anne Lamb*, ed. E. W. Marks, Jr. Ithaca, NY: Cornell University Press.

Legouvé, E. (1854) *Medée tragédie en trois actes et en vers*. Paris.

—— (1864) *La Femme en France au XIXe siècle*. Paris.

—— (1881) *La Question des femmes*. Paris.

—— (n.d) *Histoire morale des femmes*. Paris.

Le Guin, U. K. (1989) *The Language of the Night: Essays on Fantasy and Science Fiction*. 2nd rev. ed. London: The Women's Press.

Le Loyer, P. (1605) *A Treatise on Specters*. London.

Lem, S. (1981) *Solaris*, trans. J. Kilmartin and S. Cox. In *Solaris, The Chain of Chance, A Perfect Vacuum*. Harmondsworth: Penguin.

Leonard, Miriam (2005) *Athens in Paris: Ancient Greece and the Political in Post-War French Thought*. Oxford: Oxford University Press.

Levinas, E. (1988) Useless Suffering, trans. R. Cohen. In R. Bernasconi and D. Wood (eds.), *The Provocation of Levinas: Rethinking the Other*, pp. 158–67. London: Routledge.

Levine, G. (1979) The Ambiguous Heritage of *Frankenstein*. In G. Levine and U. C. Knoepflmacher (eds.), *The Endurance of Frankenstein: Essays on Mary Shelley's Novel*, pp. 3–30. Berkeley, Los Angeles, and London: University of California Press.

Lindfors, B. (1993) Beating the White Man at his Own Game: Nigerian Reactions to the 1986 Nobel Prize. In Gibbs and Lindfors, pp. 341–54.

Liveley, G. (2006) Science Fictions and Cyber Myths: or, Do Cyborgs Dream of Dolly the Sheep? In V. Zajko and M. Leonard (eds.), *Laughing With Medusa: Classical Myth and Feminist Thought*, pp. 275–94. Oxford: Oxford University Press.

Livy (1919) *Ab Urbe Condita*, trans. B. O. Foster. 14 vols. Cambridge, MA: Harvard University Press.

Lowe, N. J. (1996) Tragic and Homeric Ironies: Response to Rosenmeyer. In Silk (ed.), pp. 520–33.

Lucan (1969) *Pharsalia*, trans. J. D. Duff. London: W. H. Heinemann.

Lucas, F. L. (1957) *Tragedy: Serious Drama in Relation to Aristotle's Poetics*. 2nd ed. London: Hogarth Press.

—— (1965) *The Drama of Chekhov, Synge, Yeats and Pirandello*. 2nd ed. New York: Cassell.

Lukács, G. (1969) *The Historical Novel*, trans. H. and S. Mitchell. London: Peregrine.

—— (1973) *Soul and Form*. London: Merlin Press.

Lyly, J. (1584) *A moste excellent comedie of Alexander, Campaspe, and Diogenes*. London.

Lyotard, J.-F. (1990 [1988]) *Heidegger and "the Jews,"* trans. A. Michel and M. S. Roberts. Minneapolis: University of Minnesota Press.

MacDonald, Marianne (2000) Medea è Mobile: The Many Faces of Medea in Opera. In Hall, Macintosh, and Taplin (eds.), pp. 100–19.

Macintosh, F. (1994) *Dying Acts: Death in Ancient Greek and Modern Irish Tragic Drama.* Cork: Cork University Press.

—— (1995) Under the Blue Pencil: Greek Tragedy and the British Censor. *Dialogos,* 2: 54–70.

—— (1997) Tragedy in Performance: Nineteenth- and Twentieth-century Productions. In Easterling (ed.), pp. 284–323.

—— (2004) Oedipus in the East End: From Freud to Berkoff. In Hall, Macintosh, and Wrigley (eds.), pp. 313–28.

—— (2005) Medea between the Wars: The Politics of Race and Empire. In S. Wilmer and J. Dillon (eds.), *Rebel Women: Staging Ancient Greek Drama Today,* pp. 65–77. London: Methuen.

Macintosh, F., P. Michelakis, E. Hall, and O. Taplin (eds.), *Agamemnon in Performance 458 BC to AD 2004.* Oxford: Oxford University Press.

Mackinnon, K. (1986) *Greek Tragedy into Film.* London and Sydney: Croom Helm.

Maclean, C. (1977) *The Wolf Children.* London: Allen Lane.

Maduakor, O. (1993) Soyinka as a Literary Critic. In Gibbs and Lindfors (eds.), pp. 265–98.

Mandel, O. (1981) *Philoctetes and the Fall of Troy.* Lincoln: University of Nebraska Press.

Marcham, F. G. (1931) James I and the "Little Beagle" letters. In *Persecution and Liberty: Essays in Honor of George Lincoln Burr.* New York: Century.

Marlowe, C. (1993) *Doctor Faustus: A- and B-Texts,* ed. D. Bevington and E. Rasmussen. Manchester: Manchester University Press.

Martin, R. H. and Woodman, A. J. (eds.) (1989) *Tacitus* Annals *Book IV.* Cambridge: Cambridge University Press.

Marvell, A. (1972) *The Complete Poems,* ed. E. S. Donno. Harmondsworth: Penguin.

Maskell, D. (1991) *Racine: A Theatrical Reading.* Oxford: Oxford University Press.

Mason, P. (2002) *Henry V:* "the quick forge and working house of thought." In Hattaway (ed.), pp. 177–92.

Mastronarde, D. J. (1990) Actors on High: The Skene Roof, the Crane, and the Gods in Attic Drama. *Classical Antiquity,* 9: 247–94.

Maus, K. A. (1984) *Ben Jonson and the Roman Frame of Mind.* Princeton, NJ: Princeton University Press.

May, J. P. (1995) *Children's Literature & Critical Theory.* New York and Oxford: Oxford University Press.

McAlindon, T. (1991) *Shakespeare's Tragic Cosmos.* Cambridge: Cambridge University Press.

McCabe, R. A. (1993) *Incest, Drama and Nature's Law 1550–1700.* Cambridge: Cambridge University Press.

McCarthy, C. (1992) *Blood Meridian, or, The Evening Redness in the West.* New York: Vintage.

McDonald, M. (1992) *Ancient Sun, Modern Light: Greek Drama on the Modern Stage*. New York: Columbia University Press.

—— (1999) Black Dionysus: Greek Tragedy from Africa. http://www2.open.ac.uk/ClassicalStudies/GreekPlays/Conf99/mcDon.htm

Melvin, B. A. (1996) Failures in Classical and Modern Morality: Echoes of Euripides in *The Secret History. Journal of Evolutionary Psychology*, 17: 53–63.

Michelini, A. N. (1982) *Tradition and Dramatic Form in the Persians of Aeschylus*. Leiden: Brill.

Mikalson, J. D. (1991) *Honor thy Gods: Popular Religion in Greek Tragedy*. Chapel Hill and London: University of North Carolina Press.

Miles, G. (1996) *Shakespeare and the Constant Romans*. Oxford: Oxford University Press.

Millard, C. (1914 [1911]) *Oscar Wilde: Three Times Tried*. London: Frank & Cecil Palmer.

Miller, A. (1958) *Collected Plays*. New York and London: Cresset Press.

—— (1961 [1949]) *Death of a Salesman*. Harmondsworth: Penguin.

—— (1983) The Roman State in *Julius Caesar* and *Sejanus*. In I. Donaldson (ed.), *Jonson and Shakespeare*, pp. 179–201. Atlantic Highlands, NJ: Humanities Press.

Miller, W. I. (1997) *The Anatomy of Disgust*. Cambridge, MA and London: Harvard University Press.

Milton, J. (1962) *The Complete Prose Works of John Milton. Vol. III: 1648–9*, ed. M. Y. Hughes. New Haven, CT: Yale University Press.

Miola, R. S. (1985) *Julius Caesar* and the Tyrannicide Debate. *Renaissance Quarterly*, 38: 271–89.

—— (2002) Shakespeare's Ancient Rome: Difference and Identity. In Hattaway (ed.), pp. 193–213.

Mitchell, D. (2004) *Cloud Atlas*. London: Sceptre.

Monsarrat, G. D. (1984) *Light from the Porch: Stoicism and English Renaissance Literature*. Paris: Didier.

—— (1963) *Oscar Wilde: The Aftermath*. London: Methuen.

Montiglio, S. (2000) *Silence in the Land of Logos*. Princeton, NJ: Princeton University Press.

Moretti, F. (1988) The Great Eclipse: Tragic Form as the Deconsecration of Sovereignty. In *Signs Taken for Wonders: Essays in the Sociology of Literary Forms*, trans. S. Fischer, D. Forgacs, and D. Miller. London and New York: Verso.

Morrell, R. (1956) The Psychology of Tragic Pleasure. *Essays in Criticism*, 6: 22–37.

Mounet-Sully, J. (1914) *Souvenirs d'un tragédien*. Paris.

Mueller, M. (1980) *Childen of Oedipus and Other Essays on Greek Tragedy*. Toronto, Buffalo, NY and London: University of Toronto Press.

Mulryan, J. (2000) Jonson's Classicism. In *The Cambridge Companion to Ben Jonson*, ed. R. Harp and S. Stewart. Cambridge: Cambridge University Press.

Murray, G. (trans.) (1905) *The Trojan Women of Euripides*. London: G. Allen.

Neill, M. (1997) *Issues of Death: Mortality and Identity in English Renaissance Tragedy.* Oxford: Clarendon Press.

Neill, M. (ed.) (1988) *John Ford: Critical Re-visions*. Cambridge: Cambridge University Press.

Newton, M. (2002) *Savage Girls and Wild Boys: A History of Feral Children*. London: Faber & Faber.

Newton, R. M. (1980) Hippolytus and the Dating of the Oedipus Tyrannus. *Greek, Roman and Byzantine Studies*, 21: 5–22.

Newton, T. (ed.) (1581) *The Tenne Tragedies of Seneca*. London.

Nietzsche, F. (1956 [1887]) *The Genealogy of Morals*, Second Essay, III. In *The Birth of Tragedy and The Genealogy of Morals*, trans. F. Goffling. New York: Anchor Books.

—— (1972 [1872]) *Die Geburt der Tragödie*. In G. Colli and M. Montinari (eds.), *Nietzsche, Werke*, Part III, vol. i, pp. 5–152. Berlin and New York: de Gruyter.

—— (1993 [1872]) *The Birth of Tragedy: Out of the Spirit of Music*, trans. S. Whiteside. London: Penguin.

Nostrand, H. L. (1934) *Le Théâtre antique et à l'antiquité en France de 1840 à 1900*. Paris: Droz.

Nussbaum, M. (2001) *Upheavals of Thought: The Intelligence of the Emotions*. New York: Cambridge University Press.

Nuttall, A. (1996) *Why Does Tragedy Give Pleasure?* Oxford: Oxford University Press.

O'Donohoe, B. (2005) *Sartre's Theatre: Acts for Life* [*Modern French Identities*, 34]. Oxford: Peter Lang.

Okpewho, I. (1983) *Myth in Africa: A Study of its Aesthetic and Cultural Relevance*. Cambridge: Cambridge University Press.

—— (1999) Soyinka, Euripides and the Anxiety of Empire. *Research in African Literatures*, 30: 32–55.

Olorenshaw, R. (1994) From Mary Shelley to Bram Stoker. In S. Bann (ed.), *Frankenstein, Creation and Monstrosity*, pp. 158–76. London: Reaktion.

Ondaatje, M. (1993 [1992]) *The English Patient*. London: Picador.

—— (2000) *Anil's Ghost*. London: Bloomsbury.

Oost, S. I. (1975) Thucydides and the Irrational: Sundry Passages. *Classical Philology*, 70(3): 186–96.

Ormond, L. (1987) *J. M. Barrie*. Edinburgh: Scottish Academic Press.

Ovid (1984) *Metamorphoses*. 2 vols., vol. 1. Cambridge, MA: Harvard University Press.

Padel, R. (1992) *In and Out of the Mind: Greek Images of the Tragic Self*. Princeton, NJ: Princeton University Press.

Pagan, V. E. (2005) *Conspiracy Narratives in Roman History.* Austin: University of Texas Press.

Palmer, H. R. (1911) *List of English Editions and Translations of Greek and Latin Classics Printed before 1641*. London: Blades, East & Blades.

Parish, R. (1993) *Racine: The Limits of Tragedy.* Paris, Seattle, and Tübingen: PFSCL (Papers on French Seventeenth-Century Literature).

Parker, R. (1983) *Miasma: Pollution and Purification in Early Greek Religion.* Oxford: Clarendon Press.

Parrinder, P. (1980) *Science Fiction: Its Criticism and Teaching.* London: Methuen.

—— (1995) *Shadows of the Future: H.G. Wells, Science Fiction and Prophecy.* Liverpool: Liverpool University Press.

Pelling, C. (1997) Aeschylus' *Persae* and History. In *Greek Tragedy and the Historian.* Oxford: Clarendon Press.

Perry, C. (2006) *Literature and Favoritism in Early Modern England.* Cambridge: Cambridge University Press.

Phillippo, S. (2003) *Silent Witness: Racine's Non-Verbal Annotations of Euripides.* Oxford: European Humanities Research Centre.

Podlecki, A. (1966) *The Political Background of Aeschylean Tragedy.* Ann Arbor: University of Michigan Press.

Polybius (1814) *Anecdota Graeca,* ed. I. Bekkeri. Berolini: G. C. Nauckium.

Poole, A. (2005) *Tragedy: A Very Short Introduction.* Oxford: Oxford University Press.

Pope, A. (1963) *The Poems,* ed. J. Butt. London: Methuen.

Praz, M. (1933) *The Romantic Agony,* trans. Angus Davidson. Oxford: Oxford University Press.

Preminger, A. (ed.) (1974) *The Princeton Encyclopedia of Poetry and Poetics.* Princeton, NJ: Princeton University Press.

Pricket, R. (1606) *Times anotomie [sic]. Containing: the poore mans plaint, Brittons trouble, and hir triumph. The Popes pride, Romes treasone, and her destruction:* [. . .]. London.

Puttenham, G. (1589) *The arte of English poesie.* London.

Quintilian (1969) *Institutio Oratoria,* trans. H. C. Butler. London: William Heinemann.

Racine, J. (1950) *Œuvres complètes,* ed. Raymond Picard. Paris: Gallimard.

—— (1963) *Iphigenia, Phaedra, Athaliah,* trans. J. Cairncross. Harmondsworth: Penguin.

—— (1967) *Andromache, Britannicus, Berenice,* trans. J. Cairncross. Harmondsworth: Penguin.

Rank, O. (1924) *The Trauma of Birth.* London: Kegan Paul.

Reichardt, J. (1994) Artificial Life and the Myth of Frankenstein. In S. Bann (ed.), *Frankenstein, Creation and Monstrosity,* pp. 136–57. London: Reaktion.

Reynolds, M. (2005) Agamemnon: Speaking the Unspeakable. In Macintosh, Michelakis, Hall, and Taplin (eds.), pp. 119–38.

Richards, I. A. (1924) *Principles of Literary Criticism.* London: Routledge.

Ricks, C. (1974) *Keats and Embarrassment.* Oxford: Clarendon Press.

Riess, E. (1896) Superstitions and Popular Beliefs in Greek Tragedy. *American Journal of Philology,* 18(2): 189–205.

Rocco, C. (1997) *Tragedy and Enlightenment*. Berkeley, Los Angeles, and London: University of California Press.

Ronan, C. (1995) *Antike Roman: Power Symbology and the Roman Play in Early Modern England, 1585–1635*. Athens: University of Georgia Press.

Roper, L. (1994) *Oedipus and the Devil: Witchcraft, Sexuality and Religion in Early Modern Europe*. London: Routledge.

Rose, J. (1984) *The Case of Peter Pan, or The Impossiblity of Children's Fiction*. London: Macmillan.

Rossiter, A. P. (1961) *Angel with Horns*. London: Longman.

Roth, P. (1998) *American Pastoral*. London: Vintage.

Rozin, P. and A. E. Fallon (1987) A Perspective on Disgust. *Psychological Review*, 94: 23–41.

Rozin, P., L. Hammer, H. Oster, T. Horowitz, and V. Marmora (1986) The Child's Conception of Food: Differentiation of Categories of Rejected Substances in the 1.4 to 5 Year Age Range. *Appetite*, 7: 141–51.

Rudnytsky, P. L. (1987) *Freud and Oedipus*. New York: Columbia University Press.

Russell, D. A. and M. Winterbottom (1972) *Ancient Literary Criticism: The Principal Texts in New Translation*. Oxford: Oxford University Press.

Russell, M. D. (1997) *The Sparrow*. London: Black Swan.

—— (1999) *Children of God*. London: Black Swan.

Rutherford, R. B. (1982) Tragic Form and Feeling in the *Iliad*. *Journal of Hellenic Studies*, 102: 145–60.

Said, E. (1994) *Culture and Imperialism*. London: Vintage.

Santoro L'hoir, F. (2006) *Tragedy, Rhetoric, and the Historiography of Tacitus' Annales*. Ann Arbor: University of Michigan Press.

Sartre, J.-P. (1965) *Euripide, Les Troyennes, adaptation de J.-P. Sartre*. Paris: Gallimard.

—— (1969) *Three Plays: Kean, Nekrassov, The Trojan Women*. Harmondsworth: Penguin.

Scarry, E. (1985) *The Body in Pain: The Making and Unmaking of the World*. New York and Oxford: Oxford University Press.

Schechner, R. (1994 [1973]) Nakedness. In *Environmental Theater*, pp. 87–124. New York: Applause Books.

Scheer, E. (ed.) (2004) *Antonin Artaud: A Critical Reader*. London: Routledge.

Schelling, F. W. (1989) *The Philosophy of Art*, trans. D. W. Stott. Minneapolis: University of Minnesota Press.

Schiesaro, A. (2003) *The Passions in Play. Thyestes and the Dynamics of Senecan Drama*. Cambridge: Cambridge University Press.

Schlegel, A. W. (1815) *Lectures on Dramatic Art and Literature*, trans. J. Black. London.

Schleiner, L. (1990) Latinized Greek Drama in Shakespeare's Writing of *Hamlet*. *Shakespeare Quarterly*, 41: 29–48.

Scot, R. (1584) *The Discoverie of Witchcraft*. London.

Scott, W. (ed.) (1808), *The Works of John Dryden, Vol. VI*. London.

Sebald, W. G. (1997 [1996]) *The Emigrants*, trans. M. Hulse. London: Panther.

Segal, C. (1996) Catharsis, Audience, and Closure in Greek Tragedy. In Silk (ed.), pp. 149–72. Oxford: Clarendon Press.

Seneca (2002) *Eight Tragedies*, trans. J. G. Fitch. Cambridge, MA: Harvard University Press.

Shakespeare, W. (1982) *Hamlet*, ed. H. Jenkins. London: Methuen.

—— (1985) *Hamlet, Prince of Demark*, ed. P. Edwards. Cambridge: Cambridge University Press.

—— (1986) *The Complete Works*, ed. S. Wells and G. Taylor. Oxford: Clarendon Press.

—— (2005) *The Complete Works: the Oxford Shakespeare*, ed. S. Wells, G. Taylor, J. Jowett, and W. Montgomery. Oxford: Oxford University Press.

—— (1990) *Macbeth*, ed. N. Brooke. Oxford: Oxford University Press.

—— (1997) *The Norton Shakespeare*, ed. S. Greenblatt, W. Cohen, J. E. Howard, and K. E. Maus. New York and London: W. W. Norton.

—— (1997) *Riverside Shakespeare*, ed. G. Blakemore Evans et al. 2nd ed. Boston: Houghton Mifflin.

—— (1997) *Othello*, ed. E. A. J. Honigmann. Walton-on-Thames: Thomas Nelson.

—— 2004) *Julius Caesar*, ed. M. Spevack. Cambridge: Cambridge University Press.

—— (2005) *The Tragedy of King Lear*, ed. J. L. Halio. Cambridge: Cambridge University Press.

Shelley, M. (1831) *Frankenstein*. Oxford: Oxford World's Classics.

Shelley, P. B. (1959) *Prometheus Unbound: A Variorum Edition*, ed. L. J. Zillman. Seattle: University of Washington Press.

Shifflett, A. (2004) *Stoicism, Politics and Literature in the Age of Milton*. Cambridge: Cambridge University Press.

Sidney, Sir P. (1973) *Miscellaneous Prose of Sir Philip Sidney*, ed. K. Duncan-Jones and J. van Dorsten. Oxford: Clarendon Press.

Silk, M. (2004) Shakespeare and Greek Tragedy: Strange Relationship. In C. Martindale and A. B. Taylor (eds.), *Shakespeare and the Classics*, pp. 241–60. Cambridge: Cambridge University Press.

Silk, M. S. (ed.) (1996) *Tragedy and the Tragic: Greek Theatre and Beyond*. Oxford: Clarendon Press.

Simmons, D. (1991) *Hyperion*. London: Headline.

Smith, A. (2006) Immigrants' Last Resort. *Sunday Times Magazine*, March 19.

Smith, J. A. (2003) Flavian Drama: Looking Back with *Octavia*. In A. J. Boyle and W. J. Dominik (eds.), *Flavian Rome: Culture, Image, Text*, pp. 391–40. Leiden: Brill.

Smith II, P. E, and Helfand, M. S. (1989) *Oscar Wilde's Oxford Notebooks: A Portrait of a Mind in the Making*. New York and Oxford: Oxford University Press.

Smith, W. D. (1958) The Elizabethan Rejection of Judicial Astrology and Shakespeare's Practice. *Shakespeare Quarterly*, 9(2): 159–76.

Sontag, S. (1966) *Against Interpretation and Other Essays*. New York: Noonday Press, Farrar, Straus & Giroux.

—— (2003) *Regarding the Pain of Others*. London: Penguin.

Sophocles (1969) *Ajax, The Women of Trachis, Electra*, ed. D. Grene and R. Lattimore. Chicago: University of Chicago Press.

—— (2000 [1984]) *The Three Theban Plays*, trans. R. Fagles. Harmondsworth: Penguin.

—— (1994) *Antigone, Oedipus the King, Electra*, trans. H. D. F. Kitto, ed. E. Hall. Oxford: Oxford University Press.

Soyinka, W. (1973) *Collected Plays*: vol. 1. Oxford: Oxford University Press.

—— (1975) Neo-Tarzanism: The Poetics of Pseudo-Tradition. *Transition*, 48: 38–44.

—— (1976) *Myth, Literature and the African World*. Cambridge: Cambridge University Press.

—— (1983) Shakespeare and the Living Dramatist. *Shakespeare Survey*, 36: 1–10.

Spark, M. (1951) *Child of Light. A Reassessment of Mary Wollstonecraft Shelley*. Hadleigh, Essex, UK: Tower Bridge.

"Speranza" (Jane, Lady Wilde) (1871) *Poems by "Speranza."* Glasgow and London: Cameron & Ferguson.

Spillius, E. B. (1983) Some Developments from the Work of Melanie Klein. *International Journal of Psychology*, 64: 321–32.

Stapledon, O. (1963) *Last and First Men: A Story of the Near and Far Future*. Harmondsworth: Penguin.

Steel, D. (1999) *Eclipse: The Celestial Phenomenon Which Has Changed the Course of History*. London: Headline.

Steele, M. (1995) *Christianity, Tragedy, and Holocaust Literature*. Westport, CT and London: Greenwood Press.

Steiner, G. (1984) *Antigones*. Oxford: Clarendon Press.

—— (1996) Tragedy, Pure and Simple. In Silk (ed.), pp. 534–46.

Stoppard, T. (1997) *The Invention of Love*. London: Faber & Faber.

—— (1999) *Plays 5*. London: Faber & Faber.

Strabo (1968) *The Geography*, trans. H. L. Jones. London: William Heinemann.

Styan, J. L. (1968) *The Dark Comedy*. Rev. ed. Cambridge: Cambridge University Press.

Sweeney, J. (1985) *Jonson and the Psychology of Public Theatre*. Princeton, NJ: Princeton University Press.

Swinburne, A. C. (1914 [1866]) *Poems and Ballads* (First Series) London: Chatto & Windus.

Symonds, J. A. (1984) *The Memoirs of John Addington Symonds*, ed. P. Grosskurth. London: Hutchinson.

Tacitus (1999) *Annals XIII–XVI*, trans. J. Jackson. Cambridge, MA: Harvard University Press.

Taplin, O. (1972) Aeschylan Silences and Silences in Aeschylus. *Harvard Studies in Classical Philology*, 76: 57–97.

Tarantino, Q. (1994) *Reservoir Dogs*. London: Faber & Faber.

Tartt, D. (1992) *The Secret History*. New York: Knopf.

Taylor, G. (1983) Monopolies, Show Trials, Disaster, and Invasion: *King Lear* and Censorship. In G. Taylor and M. Warren (eds.), *The Division of the Kingdoms: Shakespeare's Two Versions of* King Lear. Oxford: Clarendon Press.

Tennyson, A. (1971) *Tennyson's Poetry,* ed. R. W. Hill. London: W. W. Norton.

Thomas, K. (1989) Children in Early Modern England. In G. Avery and J. Briggs (eds.), *Children and their Books.* Oxford: Clarendon Press.

Thucydides (1881) *History of the Peloponnesian War,* trans. B. Jowett. Oxford: Clarendon Press.

Trendall, A. D. and T. B. L. Webster (1971) *Illustrations of Greek Drama.* London and New York: Phaidon.

Trilse, C. (1975) *Antike und Theater heute.* Berlin: Academie-Verlag.

Van Domelen, J. E. (1987) *The Tarzan of Athens: A Biographical Study of G. Wilson Knight.* Bristol: Redcliffe.

Vernant, J.-P. (1988) Ambiguity and Reversal: On the Enigmatic Structure of *Oedipus Rex.* In Vernant and Vidal-Naquet, pp. 87–119.

—— (1991) Speech and Mute Signs. In F. I. Zeitlin and J.-P. Vernant (eds.), *Mortals and Immortals: Collected Essays.* Princeton, NJ: Princeton University Press.

Vernant, J.-P. and P. Vidal-Naquet (1988 [1981, 1972]) *Tragedy and Myth in Ancient Greece,* trans. J. Lloyd. Brighton: Harvester.

Vernay (1888) Chez Mounet-Sully. À propos d'*Oedipe Roi. Revue d'Art Dramatique,* XI (juillet–septembre): 136–40.

Virgil (1999) *Works,* trans. H. R. Fairclough. 2 vols., vol. 1. Cambridge, MA: Harvard University Press.

Voltaire, M. A. de (1719) Oedipe, *Tragédie (avec Lettres écrites par l'auteur).* London.

Wallace, J. (1996) *Shelley and Greece: Rethinking Romantic Hellenism.* Basingstoke: Palgrave Macmillan.

Waters, D. D. (1994) *Christian Settings in Shakespeare's Tragedies.* London and Toronto: Toronto University Press.

Webster, J. (1996) *The Duchess of Malfi,* ed. R. Weis. Oxford: Oxford University Press.

Wellek, R. (1986) *A History of Modern Criticism 1750–1950,* vol 5. New Haven, CT and London: Yale University Press.

Wilamowitz-Moellendorff, U. von (1919) *Griechische Tragödie.* Berlin.

Wilde, O. (1945 [1891]) The Decay of Lying. In *Intentions.* London: Unicorn Press.

—— (1980) *The Happy Prince and Other Stories.* In *Complete Shorter Fiction,* ed. I. Murray. Oxford: Oxford University Press.

—— (1990) De Profundis. In *The Soul of Man and Prison Writings,* ed. I. Murray. Oxford: Oxford University Press.

—— (1997a) *Complete Poetry,* ed. I. Murray. Oxford: Oxford University Press.

—— (1997b) *Tragedy in Athens.* Cambridge: Cambridge University Press.

Wiles, D. (1997) *Tragedy in Athens: Performance Space and Theatrical Meaning.* Cambridge: Cambridge University Press.

Williams, B. (1990) Reading Tacitus' Tiberian Annals. In A. J. Boyle (ed.), *The Imperial Muse, Volume II: Flavian Epicist to Claudian*, pp. 140–66. Bendigo, VA, Australia: Aureal.

Williams, R. (1966) *Modern Tragedy*. London: Chatto & Windus.

—— (1992 [1966]) *Modern Tragedy*. London: Hogarth Press.

Williams, T. (1958) *The Rose Tattoo and Camino Real*. Harmondsworth: Penguin.

Willis, A. (2005) Euripides' *Trojan Women*: A 20th-Century War Play in Performance. D.Phil. dissertation, University of Oxford.

Wilson, L. (2000) *Theaters of Intention: Drama and the Law in Early Modern England*. Stanford, CA: Stanford University Press.

Wilson, R. (1595) *The Pedler's Prophecie*. London.

Woodman, A. J. (1988) *Rhetoric in Classical Historiography. Four Studies*. Beckenham: Croom Helm.

Worden, B. (1994) Ben Jonson among the Historians. In K. Sharpe and P. Lake (eds.), *Culture and Politics in Early Stuart England*, pp. 67–90. Basingstoke: Palgrave Macmillan.

—— (1999) Politics in *Catiline*: Jonson and his sources. In M. Butler (ed.), *Re-Presenting Ben Jonson: Text, History and Performance*, pp. 152–73. Basingstoke: Palgrave Macmillan.

Wyndham, G. (ed.) (1895) *Plutarch's Lives of the Noble Grecians and Romans Englished by Sir Thomas North anno 1579*, vol. 2. London: David Nutt.

Youngquist, P. (2003) *Monstrosities: Bodies and British Romanticism*. Minneapolis and London: University of Minnesota Press.

Zeitlin, F. I. (2004) Dionysus in 69. In Hall, Macintosh, and Wrigley (eds.), pp. 49–75.

Zengotita, T. de (2005) *Mediated: How the Media Shapes Your World and the Way You Live in It*. London: Bloomsbury.

Zitner, S. P. (1974) *King Lear* and its Language. In R. L. Colie and F. T. Flahiff (eds.), *Some Facets of* King Lear: *Essays in Prismatic Criticism*. Toronto and Buffalo, NY: University of Toronto Press.

Žižek, S. (1999) *The Ticklish Subject: The Absent Centre of Political Ontology*. London: Verso.

—— (2000) *Enjoy Your Symptom! Jacques Lacan in Hollywood and Out*. London and New York: Routledge.

—— (2001) *Did Somebody Say Totalitarianism?* London: Verso.

—— (2002) *Welcome to the Desert of the Real!* London: Verso.

—— (2003) *The Puppet and the Dwarf: The Perverse Core of Christianity*. Cambridge, MA: MIT Press.

Zoline, P. (1988) The Heat Death of the Universe. In *Busy About the Tree of Life*, pp. 50–65. London: The Women's Press.

Index